Performance Autoethno~

This book is a manifesto. It is about rethinking performance autoethnography, about the formation of a critical performative cultural politics, about what happens when everything is already performative, when the dividing line between performativity and performance disappears. This is a book about the writing called autoethnography. It is also about what this form of writing means for writers who want to perform work that leads to social justice. Denzin's goal is to take the reader through the history, major terms, forms, criticisms and issues confronting performance autoethnography and critical interpretive. To that end many of the chapters are written as performance texts, as ethnodramas.

A single thesis organizes this book: the performance turn has been taken in the human disciplines and it must be taken seriously. Multiple informative performance models are discussed: Goffman's dramaturgy; Turner's performance anthropology; performance ethnographies by A. D. Smith, Conquergood and Madison; Saldana's ethnodramas; Schechter's social theatre; Norris's playacting; Boal's theatre of the oppressed; and Freire's pedagogies of the oppressed. They represent different ways of staging and hence performing ethnography, resistance and critical pedagogy. They represent different ways of "imagining, and inventing and hence performing alternative imaginaries, alternative counter-performances to war, violence, and the globalized corporate empire" (Schechner 2015).

This book provides a systematic treatment of the origins, goals, concepts, genres, methods, aesthetics, ethics and truth conditions of critical performance autoethnography. Denzin uses the performance text as a vehicle for taking up the hard questions about reading, writing, performing and doing critical work that makes a difference.

Norman K. Denzin is Distinguished Emeritus Research Professor of Communications at the University of Illinois, Urbana-Champaign, USA. He is the author, co-author or co-editor of over 50 books and 200 professional articles and chapters. He is the past President of The Midwest Sociological Society, and the Society for the Study of Symbolic Interaction. He is founding President of the International Association of Qualitative Inquiry (2005–) and Director of the International Center of Qualitative Inquiry (2005–). He is past editor of *The Sociological Quarterly*, founding co-editor of *Qualitative Inquiry* and founding editor of *Cultural Studies – Critical Methodologies, International Review of Qualitative Research* and *Studies in Symbolic Interaction: A Research Annual.*

Performance Autoethnography
Critical Pedagogy and the Politics of Culture

Second Edition

Norman K. Denzin

Routledge
Taylor & Francis Group

LONDON AND NEW YORK

Second edition published 2018
by Routledge
2 Park Square, Milton Park, Abingdon, Oxon OX14 4RN

and by Routledge
711 Third Avenue, New York, NY 10017

Routledge is an imprint of the Taylor & Francis Group, an informa business

© 2018 Norman K. Denzin

First edition published by SAGE 2003

British Library Cataloguing in Publication Data
A catalogue record for this book is available from the British Library

Library of Congress Cataloging in Publication Data
Names: Denzin, Norman K., author.
Title: Performance autoethnography : critical pedagogy and the politics of culture / Norman K. Denzin.
Description: Abingdon, Oxon ; New York, NY : Routledge, 2018. | Includes bibliographical references and index.
Identifiers: LCCN 2017052825| ISBN 9781138066281 (hbk) | ISBN 9781138066298 (pbk.) | ISBN 9781315159270 (ebk)
Subjects: LCSH: Ethnology--Biographical methods. | Social interaction. | Critical pedagogy.
Classification: LCC GN346.6 .D47 2018 | DDC 305.8--dc23
LC record available at https://lccn.loc.gov/2017052825

ISBN: 978-1-138-06628-1 (hbk)
ISBN: 978-1-138-06629-8 (pbk)
ISBN: 978-1-315-15927-0 (ebk)

Typeset in Sabon
by Taylor & Francis Books

Contents

Preface

This book is a manifesto, it is about rethinking performance autoethnography, about the formation of a critical performative cultural politics, about what happens when everything, as Du Bois (1926, p. 134) observes, is already performative, when the dividing line between performativity and performance disappears. This is a book, to quote James Salvo (2019), about the writing called autoethnography. It is also about what this form of writing means for writers who want to perform work that leads to social justice. This book reflects my desire to contribute to a critical discourse that addresses central issues confronting democracy and racism in post-postmodern America, life, narrative and melodrama under the auspices of late neo-liberal capitalism.[1]

My goal is to take the reader through the history, major terms, forms, criticisms and issues confronting performance autoethnography and critical interpretive inquiry (see Appendix A).[2] To that end many of the chapters are written as performance texts, as ethnodramas, to use Saldana's (2005, 2011) term. I disappear into the plays, occasionally appearing as narrator. The chapters tell by showing; that is they enact the very form of inquiry that is being interrogated.

A single thesis organizes this book: the performance turn has been taken in the human disciplines and it must be taken seriously. There are multiple performance models that we can learn from: Goffman's (1959) dramaturgy, Turner's (1982) performance anthropology, A. D. Smith's (2003/2004), Conquergood's (2013) and Madison's (2012) performance ethnography, Saldana's (2011) ethnodramas, Schechner's (2015) social theatre, Norris's (2009) playacting, Boal's (1985) theatre of the oppressed, Freire's pedagogies of the oppressed (1970/2000). These models will be discussed in the chapters that follow. They represent different ways of staging and hence performing ethnography, resistance and critical pedagogy. They represent different ways of "imagining, and inventing and hence performing alternative imaginaries, alternative counter-performances to war, violence, and the globalized corporate empire" (Schechner 2015, p. 15, paraphrase).

Stealing from Bochner and Ellis (2016a, p. 10; also 2016b), the intent is to "provide a systematic treatment of the origins, goals, concepts, genres, methods, aesthetics, ethics and truth conditions" of critical performance autoethnography. I use the performance text as a vehicle for taking up the hard questions about reading, writing, performing and doing critical work that makes a difference.

***

Performance autoethnography is a blurred genre. It is many things at the same time. It bends and twists the meanings of ethnography, ethnographer and performance. There is no separation between the writer, the ethnographer, the performer and the world. Performance autoethnography makes the writer's self visible through performance, through performance writing, through the writer's presence in the world. Performance autoethnograhers are committed to changing the world one word, one performance at a time. The community is global.

Autoethnography is easily confused with other terms. It is not: ethnography, autobiography, biography, personal narrative, personal history, life history, life story or personal experience story. It is not deeply theoretical. It is more than personal writing or cultural critique. It is more than performance. But it is performative. It is transgressive. It is resistance. It is dialogical. It is ethical. It is political, personal, embodied, collaborative, imaginative, artistic, creative, a form of intervention, a plea for social justice. Clearly this discourse is not standing still. Writing selves are performing new writing practices, blurring fact and fiction, challenging the dividing line between performer and performed, observer and observed.

Performance autoethnography is at a cross-roads (Bagley 2008; Sughrua 2016). While the performance turn in ethnography is well established in communication studies, this is less the case in educational research (see Madison and Hamera 2006; Gannon 2017). Bagley (2008), Rinehart, Barbour and Pope (2014, p. 3) despite the fact that anthropologists of education make the case for treating ethnography, on a global stage, as performance. This turn understands performance to be a way of knowing, a way of creating and fostering understanding, a method that persons use to create and give meaning to everyday life (Pelias 2008, pp. 185–186).

But moving into a thorough-going performance space remains a challenge for mainstream anthropological, communication, educational, healthcare and sociological ethnographers. And the method has not been without its critics (Atkinson 2017, p. 66). Many remain committed to traditional, post positivist values of objectivity, evidence and truth. They find little of value in the performance approach. The criticisms, as Ellis (2009, p. 31; Bochner and Ellis 2016a, pp. 35–38) observe, fall into three overlapping categories. Authoethnography is (1) too aesthetic and not sufficiently realistic; that is it does not provide hard data; (2) too realistic and not mindful of poststructural criticisms concerning the "real" self and its place in the text; (3) insufficiently aesthetic, or literary, that is autoethnographers are second-rate writers and poets.

Hammersley (2008, pp. 134–136, 144) extends the traditional critique, finding little value in the work of ethnographic postmodernists and literary ethnographers.[3] This new tradition, he asserts, legitimates speculative theorizing, celebrates obscurity and abandons the primary task of inquiry, which is to produce truthful knowledge about the world (p. 144). Whose truth, though? There seems to be no space for the literary performance turn in this school of ethno-graphy, a school which seems to stand outside time, in a strange timeless space.

Ignored in the criticisms of Hammersley and others is the basic point that all forms of knowledge involve a politics of representation, that is nothing stands outside representation. Further, as Madison and Hamera (2006, p. xx) argue, performance and globality are intertwined; that is performances have become the enactment of stories that literally bleed across national borders. Being a U.S. citizen is to be "enmeshed in the facts of U.S. foreign policy, world trade, civil society and war" (p. xx).

More deeply, in a globalized, post-postmodern world, race and the staging and performance of racialized and gendered identities remains, as W. E. B. Du Bois (1978) would remind us, "the problem of the twenty-first century" (Du Bois 1978 [1901], pp. 281, 288). (Witness the crises surrounding the Trump Administration's immigration ban against persons from Muslim countries.) Modern democracies cannot succeed "unless peoples of different races and religions are also integrated into the democratic whole" (Du Bois 1978 [1901], pp. 281, 288). Multi-racial democracy cannot succeed unless critical qualitative scholars are able to adopt methodologies that transcend the limitations and constraints of a lingering, politically and racially conservative postpositivism. This frame-work attaches itself to state organized auditing systems. These links and these historical educational connections must be broken. Never before has there been a greater need for a militant utopianism which will help us imagine a world free of conflict, terror and death, a world that is caring, loving, truly compassionate, a world that honours healing and difference.

To these ends, I locate performance ethnography within a racialized, spectacle pedagogy. Drawing on Garoian and Gaudelius (2008), I contend that the most important events in the United States in the last two decades include the wars in Iraq and Afghanistan, the global war on terror, the global spread of a radial right-wing racist, neo-fascist political ideology, the great recession of 2007–2008, the election of Donald Trump as president of the United States, new immigration bans, the institutionalization of a new surveillance regime that affects every traveling body entering or leaving the United States (Bratich 2017). A critical performance (auto) ethnography must locate itself in these historical spaces, which now include surveillance regimes in virtually every institutional setting in the United States (and the world) today.

This book

In the chapters that follow I read, write and perform performance [auto] eth-nography. Performance "writing is never innocent" (Richardson 2001, p. 879). Writing creates the worlds we inhabit. I hope to create the spaces for a radical cultural politics that imagines a more humane, pluralistic and just racial order.

The Introduction situates this project within a family of terms: border crossing, critical indigenous pedagogy, decolonizing processes, rhetorical reflexivity, forum theatre, spectactors, embodied epistemology. Chapter 1 takes an immediate autoethnographic turn, troubling key terms, from research, to acts of activism, theatre, performance, race and ethnography. Chapter 2 reviews basic interpretive assumptions and terms – epiphany, mystory, experience, performance – and locates them within a critical framework. Chapter 3 brings performance, pedagogy, politics and rhetoric together. I lay the foundations for a critical performative cultural politics which is informed by the new materialisms, theories of affect, theatre and the politics of resistance. The concept of performance is paired with six terms: pedagogy, culture, praxis, hermeneutics, writing as performance and performance after the affective turn. The chapter ends with reflections from the Laramie Project, ten years after Matthew Shepard's tragic death (Kaufman 2014).

The four chapters in Part II examine the relationship between ethnography, performance and theatre. Chapter 4 revisits the origins of the alliance between ethnography, ethnodrama and reality theatre by reviewing the arguments of Turner, Schechner, Butler and Saldana. Saldana' concepts of autoethnodrama, ethnodrama and ethnotheatre are incorporated into a theory of theatre as resistance after Freire, Boal, Garoian, Smith, Madison and Finley. Chapter 4 includes excerpts from a short play, "Custer's Last Rally," part of a larger project on Native Americans, cultural memory, identity, performance and violence in the new west (Denzin 2008, 2011, 2003a, 2015a).

Chapter 5 offers a reading of Augusto Boal's theatre of the oppressed, which is an extension of Paulo Freire's pedagogy of the oppressed. Because of their politics and critical pedagogies, Freire and Boal were imprisoned, exiled from Brazil and forced to work abroad. They literally put their theory and method on the line. Chapter 6 performs acts of resistance by reading Paulo Freire and the ghosts in his life through Pedagogy of the Oppressed. For Freire and Boal there is no separation between critical pedagogy, theatres of the oppressed, resistance as performance and acts of activism. The weapons are dialogue, love, hope, respect. Chapter 7 begins with Gloria Anzaluda's borderlands project, then moves from writing decolonizing autoethnographies, to the many pedagogies and children of Paulo Freire.

The three chapters in Part III – Toward a Critical Performative Inquiry– move this project into the cinematic, new social media, post-surveillance society. Chapter 8 reads the reflexive interview as a key feature of the post-televisual society. Chapter 9 moves toward a critical performative discourse drawing again on the work of Anna Deavere Smith. Chapter 10 examines criteria for reading and writing the performance texts.

Part IV – Bone Deep in Landscapes[4] – contains two short chapters, "Grandma's Story," and "A Family Tradition."[5] These chapters are part memoir, part essay, part short story, part literary autoethnography. They travel back and forth between personal history biography and family life in the Midwest.

The three chapters in Part V – Pedagogy, Politics and Ethics– return to the themes in Chapter 1 concerning the ethics and practical politics of performance autoethnography and critical pedagogy. I anchor these chapters in the post-September 11, 2001 terrorist discourse in the United States, as well as the aftermath of the 2016 election of Donald Trump as President of the United States. Chapter 13 encourages the importance of critical historical memories which can inspire persons to become critical inquirers and critically engaged citizens. I outline an indigenous performance ethic in Chapter 14. Chapter 15, a brief Coda, looks to the future.

Need

This project reflects two concerns. For five decades I have been working with undergraduate and graduate students at the University of Illinois, experimenting with new ways of reading, writing and performing culture. We learned how to write and co-perform texts based on epiphanies surrounding race, gender and the politics of identity. I owe these students a great debt; together we worked through many of the themes and issues in this book. This book is partial payment on this debt.

Secondly, I continue to believe that the current generation of college students, not just those in North America, have the opportunity and the responsibility to make a difference in the global race relations arena. It is possible to imagine and perform a multi-racial society, a society where differences are honored. If this generation is to make a difference, that difference will be defined, in part, in terms of opposition, resistance to and acceptance of the representations and interpretations of the racial order and the color line that circulate in the media and in social science writings. This resistance, in turn, is shaped by how we read, write, perform and critique culture.

I advance a critical performative pedagogy which turns the ethnographic into the performative, and the performative into the political. This pedagogy hopefully allows us to dream our way into a militant democratic utopian space, a space where the color line disappears and justice for all is more than a dream.

I believe the performance-based human disciplines can contribute to radical social change, to economic justice, to a cultural politics which extends critical race theory and "the principles of a radical democracy to all aspects of society" (Giroux 2000a, pp. x, 25; 2014b, p. 217) and to change which "envisions a democracy founded in a social justice that is 'not yet'" (Weems 2002 p. 3). This book reflects my desire to contribute to a critical discourse on democracy and racism in postmodern, but *not* **post-racial societies** (Donnor and Ladson-Billings 2017). I believe that interpretive, performance autoethnographers should be part of this project.

Norman K. Denzin

Notes

1 By my reading, the field of [performance] autoethnography started to come of age just as the first edition of this book was being published (see Ellis and Bochner 2000; Schechner 2002; Madison and Hamera 2006; and Appendix A). This second edition,

newly titled, builds on this literature, while continuing to forge a link between performance, [auto] ethnography, pedagogy, social justice and theatre.
2 Gannon (2017) offers an inclusive history of the uses, meanings, definitions and criticisms of autoethnography, from 1975 to the present. See also Jones, Adams and Ellis (2013, pp. 25–32).
3 His blanket term for auto, performance, post-structural ethnography.
4 From Blew (1999).
5 These two chapters re-work material in Denzin (2016) and (2015b).

Acknowledgments

I would like to thank Mitch Allen, Arthur Bochner, Carolyn Ellis, Helen Salmon and Hannah Shakespeare for their quick and early support of this project which started out as a book on performance narrative and somewhere along the way turned into a book on critical pedagogy, performance and [auto] ethnography. Helen secured valuable reviews of the first edition which shaped my revisions. I thank Hannah and Matt Bickerton for moving my transformed project to conclusion, including Matt's wonderful assistance with the cover design. Presentations in sessions at the Annual International Congress of Qualitative Inquiry organized by Stacey Holman Jones and Gaile Cannella helped to clarify my arguments. Exchanges on earlier versions of Chapters 1, 2, 3, 4, 5 and 14 with Tony Adams, Lydia Turner, Nigel Short, Paul Atkinson, Cliff Christians, Sara Delamont, Dennis Beach, Carl Bagley, Magdalena Kazubowski-Houston, Virginie Magnat and Pat Sikes forced revisions. I greatly benefited from on-going conversations on performance, ethnography and politics with Katherine Ryan, Consuelo Chapela, Tami Spry, Johnny Saldana, James Salvo, Nick Trujillo, Bud Goodall, Chris Poulos, Henry Giroux, Soyini Madison, Robert Rinehart, Peter McLaren, Bryant Alexander, Laurel Richardson, Jack Bratich, Michael Giardina, Mary Weems and Patricia Clough. I wish to thank Helen Strain who saw my book through production to publication, Sarah Fish for copy editing, James Salvo for his meticulous reading of the page proofs and all other matters, and S. Jane Henderson for the production of the index. I also thank the students at the University of Illinois who patiently sat through formal and informal seminars, listening to earlier versions of my arguments about performance, autoethnography, critical qualitative inquiry, politics, ethics and pedagogy. Finally, I acknowledge the long-term moral, intellectual and financial support provided this project and the International Congress of Qualitative Inquiry by the College of Media at the University of Illinois, Urbana-Champaign.

Introduction

In 1963 I was a beginning graduate student in the Sociology Department at the University of Iowa. I was profoundly influenced by two books, C. Wright Mill's *The Sociological Imagination* (1959) and Erving Goffman's *The Presentation of Self in Everyday Life* (1959). Mills was bold, compassionate, challenging me to develop a critical sociological imagination that would allow me to connect biography, history and culture, to understand larger historical scenes. He challenged me to link my biography to my historical moment (Mills 1959, p. 5).[1]

Goffman was coldly analytic, aloof, cynical.

> The perspective offered in this report is that of theatrical performance;
> The principles derived are dramaturgical ones. I shall consider the way in which the individual presents him/herself and his activity to others, the ways in which he guides and controls the impression they form of him, and the kinds of things he/she may or may not do while sustaining his/her performance before them
>
> (Goffman 1959, p. xi)

Impression management, masks, hidden intentions, no sociological imagination here, no concern for men and women feeling their private lives as a series of traps (Mills 1959, p. 3). In 1963 I was not prepared to accept Goffman's model. I followed Mills instead. Today a half century later I return to Mills and Goffman, for performance studies today is not what it was in 1959 when Goffman launched his dramaturgical theory.

Indeed, the projects of performance studies and performance autoethnography must always start

> with a person, a body, a place, and a historical moment. I offer my performing body and my experiences as the raw material for cultural critique. My body carries the traces of my historical moment. I am the universal other. I am the performative I struggling to disrupt the status quo, resisting hegemonic systems of control and injustice
>
> (Spry 2011, p. 20, paraphrase).

Understanding that

> Performance studies – as a practice, a theory, an academic discipline – is dynamic, unfinishable. Whatever it is, it wasn't exactly that before and it won't be exactly that again
>
> (Schechner 2013, p. ix; 2015, pp. 163–164)

For at least two decades rhetoric and performance studies scholars, ethnodramatists, critical interpretive ethnographers, community theatre activists and autoethnographers have been staging performance events. These performances create spaces for a merger of praxis, ethnography, rhetoric and activism in public (and private) life (Saldana 2011; Madison 2012; Gencarella and Pezzullo 2010). We are in the ninth or tenth moment, a post-experimental, post-humanist, post-neoliberal open-ended phase, critiquing culture as we write and perform it.[2] We need to recommit to a reflexive performance [auto] ethnography[3] that will engage a postcolonial, post-civil-rights, post-cold war, postfeminist, post-racial and postmodern world (Madison 2006, pp. 347–348, paraphrase).

***

In the beginning there was *ethnography*, an inscriptive practice captured in the phrase writing culture (Clifford & Marcus 1986). Then there was *performance*, the understanding that people perform culture, through their interpretive practices (Conquergood 1985). This implied that we could study persons as performers and cultures as performative or ethnodramatic accomplishments (Saldana 2011). *Performance autoethnography* inserted itself in the picture when it was understood that all ethnographers reflexively (or unreflexively) write/perform themselves into their ethnographies. The ethnographer's writing self cannot not be present, there is no objective space outside the text. *Duoethography* and *collaborative writing* move the project into a dialogical space, two or more autoethnographers merge their writing selves into a multi-voiced performance autoethnographic texts, including those that disrupt the status quo.

There has been an explosion of literatures, theories, frameworks and turns, from the affective turn (Gregg and Seigworth 2010; Clough and Halley 2007), to the new[feminist] materialisms and ontologies (Coole and Frost 2010), to calls for post-methodological, post-humanist, post-empirical and post-qualitative frameworks (Taylor and Hughes 2016; Lather 2007; St. Pierre 2011, p. 613; MacLure 2011; Jackson and Mazzie 2012), to transnational queer indigenous studies (Driskill et al. 2011), performative critical race theories (Alexander 2012; Johnson 2006), to new alignments between rhetoric and performance studies (Gencarella and Pezzullo 2010; Fenske and Goltz 2014), to a resurgence in the global community performance and applied theatre movements (Cohen-Cruz 2005 2006; Kuppers and Robertson 2007; Prentki and Preston 2009; Madison 2010).

We are in a transdisciplinary, global space, performance studies has "evolved into a grand mix of intellectuals, activists, artists, scholars, and all combinations of in between, that employs the theory and practice of performance" (Madison 2013, p. 207). We are well beyond taking the performance turn, we are in an uncertain future which confronts the methodological backlash associated with refurbished postpositivism and the evidence-based social movements. It is concerned with moral discourse, with the development of sacred textualities.

The ninth moment asks that the social sciences and the humanities become sites for critical conversations about democracy, race, gender, class, nation-states globalization, freedom and community.[4] The postmodern and post-experimental moments were defined in part by a concern for literary and rhetorical tropes and the narrative turn, a concern for storytelling, for composing ethnographies in new ways. Richardson (2000a) observes that this moment was shaped by a new sensibility, by doubt, by a refusal to privilege any method, or theory. But now, in the second decade of this new century we struggle to connect performative qualitative research to the hopes, needs, goals and promises of a free democratic society (Denzin and Lincoln 2017, p. 2; Jones and Olomo 2007, p. 379; Koro-Ljungberg 2016, p. 2).

All of these turns and writing forms place traditional concepts of performance, the other, the self, ethnography, narrative, meaning, voice, presence and representation under erasure. Together they politicize the "interpretive, affective turn." They open spaces for a focus on the body, trauma, memory, the emotions, the tyrannies of language, the economies of space, the post-technological body cut loose, in free-fall in a post-cyber universe (Clough and Halley 2007; Hoffman-Davis and Lawrence-Lightfoot 2002).

In this space theory turns back on itself, re-reading itself through the biographical, the historical and the ideological. A re-born critical theory is imagined. Strategies and tactics of resistance against a global geopolitical system of control are called for. The affective turn resists the war machine, untangling and re-doing nested relations of power, bodies, life, death and desire (Brady 2012; Garoian and Gaudelius 2008). In this new political economy any person is at risk of arrest, of becoming a victim, a prisoner, at best collateral damage in a global space where performance principles, pretense, illusion, deception and technological rationality regulate daily life (McKenzie 2006, p. 35).

Critical indigenous pedagogy

I seek a critical autoethnographic discourse. This requires a productive dialogue between indigenous and critical [race] scholars. It involves a re-visioning of critical pedagogy, a re- grounding of Paulo Freire's pedagogy of the oppressed (2007, 2005, 2000, 1999, 1998) in local, indigenous contexts (see Smith 2012; Bishop 2008; Kovach 2009; Diversi and Moreira 2009; Grande 2008a). I call this merger of indigenous and critical methodologies, critical indigenous pedagogy

(Denzin and Lincoln 2008, p. 2). It understands that all inquiry is political and moral. It confronts the tension between the Western critical theory paradigm and indigenous knowledge, theory and praxis (Grande 2008a, p. 238).[5] It uses methods critically, for explicit social justice purposes. It values the transformative power of indigenous, subjugated knowledges. It values the local pedagogical practices that produce these knowledges. At the same time it studies the political, ethical and aesthetic technologies that transform the practices of indigenety into marketable commodities and performances.[6] It seeks forms of praxis and inquiry that are emancipatory, collaborative and empowering. The critical scholar is an allied other (Kaomea 2004, p. 32). Building on this framework, in the chapters that follow I attempt to chart a performance-based critical discourse modeled in part after the arguments of Madison (2012, 2010), Saldana (2011) Giroux (2014a, 2014b) and Conquergood (2013).[7] A single, yet complex thesis organizes my argument.

We inhabit a performance-based, dramaturgical culture. Performance autoethnography enters a racialized and gendered culture with nearly invisible boundaries separating everyday from theatrical, staged performances (Schechner 2013, p. 2). Performance is always situated in complex systems of discourse, where traditional, everyday and avant-garde meanings of theatre, film, video, ethnography, cinema, performance, text and audience circulate and inform one another (Bial 2004, p. 2). Digital technologies, the new social media and the endlessly multiplying forms of screen culture further erode the division between real and virtual realities (Giroux 2014a, p. 195; 2014b, p. 222).

From selfies and Instagram to Facebook we perform ourselves to ourselves and our fellows (Farago 2017, p. C6). Camouflage, canvas, mirror or mask, whose self are we looking at? Of course, as artist Cindy Sherman reminds us (quoted in Farago 2017, p. 6), "we are almost never the selves in our selfies, our most hazardous disguises are the frozen smiles we now whiten with our index fingers" (Farago 2017, p. C6).

Henry Giroux (2010) observes that these technologies have the potential of turning persons into zombie-like consumers of postmodern culture. It works both ways. With desire, money, technology and minimal skills persons can have an on-line presence, transforming themselves into objects of consumption and desire. Pick your site: YouTube, Facebook, Twitter, Linked In, My Space, Flickr, Word Press, Second Life, the list changes daily, it seems.[8] The meanings of lived experience are inscribed and made visible ("selfies") in these performance sites where video and performance writing prevails. Virtual selves with their life stories and video performances are everywhere present.[9] These cultural apparatuses constitute powerful forms of public pedagogy (Giroux 2014a, p. 195; 2014b, p. 222).[10]

Critical performance autoethnography is anchored in these performance technologies. It begins with an ethical responsibility "to address processes of unfairness within a particular *lived* domain" (Madison 2012, p. 5, italics in original). There is a desire to simultaneously create and enact moral texts that move from the personal to the political, the local to the historical and the cultural.

Following Conquergood (1985), these dialogical works create spaces for give and take, doing more than turning the other into the object of a voyeuristic, fetishistic, custodial or paternalistic gaze.

A performance based discourse is based on minimalist principles. It shows. It does not tell. Less is more. It is not infatuated with theory. It uses few concepts. It is performative. It stays close to how people perform everyday life. Phrased differently, it is concerned with "doing and being, with what people do in the activity of being present in the moment" (Schechner 2013, pp. 1–2, paraphrase). A performative discourse simultaneously writes and criticizes performances. The writer is both an insider and an outsider, commenting on her own performances, as she performs (and writes) them. In showing how people enact cultural meanings in their daily lives, the focus is on how these meanings and performances shape experiences of injustice, prejudice and stereotype.

Shaped by the critical sociological imagination (Mills 1959), this version of doing critical inquiry attempts to do more than just show how terms like biography, history, gender, race, ethnicity, family and history interact and shape one another in concrete social situations. The desire is to show how the histories and the performances that persons live are shaped by forces that go on behind their backs (Marx 1888/1983). The goal, as Marx wrote, is to change not just interpret history.

A critical sociological imagination responds in three ways to the successive crises of democracy and capitalism that shape daily life on the global electronic stage. It criticizes those formations, by showing how they repressively enter into and shape the stories and performances persons share with one another. At the same time, it shows how people bring dignity and meaning to their lives through these self-same performances. In so doing, it also offers kernels of utopian hope, suggestions for how things might be different, and better. Such moves are healing, educative and transformative (Boal 1995; Freire 1998).

The performance turn

The poststructural, materialist, narrative and performance turns in the human disciplines pose three closely interrelated problems for my project: namely how to construct, perform and critically analyze performance and performance texts for morally ethical purposes. How can I situate my work so that it makes the greatest contribution to social justice and social equity? (Madison 2012, pp. 4–5, 15).

In taking up these questions I borrow from Spry (2016) and Boal (1985, 1995). I privilege utopian performatives, **forum theatre**[11] techniques (the participating audience, spec-actors, simultaneous dramaturgy, improvised scenes, historical re-enactments, co-performance texts).[12] Spec-actors (co-performing audience members) bring audiences back into the text, creating a field of shared emotional experience. A resistance model of textual performance and interpretation is foregrounded. A good performance text must be more than cathartic; it must be political, moving people to action and reflection.

At the same time it exposes the dramaturgical scaffolding, from scripts, to costumes, rehearsals, staging and impression management that permeate everyday life (Goffman 1959, p. 254). It is simultaneously an intervention, an interpretation, an artistic performance that erases the distinction between theory, praxis and practice (Conquergood in Johnson 2013, p. 41).[13]

A performance vocabulary

Tables 1.1 and 1.2 summarize the concepts and terms that have historically defined the performance, ethnography, autoethnography writing culture

Table 1.1 Terms/forms and varieties of the autoethnographic performance method

Term/method	Key features	Forms/variations
1. Method	A way of knowing	Subjective/objective
2. Life	Period of existence; lived experiences	Partial/complete/edited/public/private
3. Self	Ideas, images and thoughts of self	Self-stories, auto-biographies
4. Experience	Confronting and passing through events; meanings are constructed	Problematic, routine, ritual
5. Epiphany	Moment of revelation in a life	Major, minor, relived, illuminative
6. Autobiography	Personal history of one's life	Complete, edited, topical
7. Ethnography	Written account of a culture or group	Realist, interpretive, descriptive
8. Auto-ethnography	Account of one's life as an ethnographer	Complete, edited, partial, betweener
9. Biography	History of a life	Autobiography
10. Story	A fiction, narrative	First or third person
11. Fiction	An account, something made up, fashioned	Story (life, self)
12. History	Account of how something happened	Personal, oral, case
13. Discourse	Telling a story, talk about a text, a text	First or third person
14. Narrator	Teller of a story	First or third person
15. Narrative	A story, having a plot and existence separate from life of teller	Fiction, epic, science, folklore, myth

Term/method	Key features	Forms/variations
16. Writing	Inscribing, creating a written text	Logocentric, deconstructive
17. Difference	Every word carries traces of another word	Writing, speech
18. Personal history	Reconstruction of life based on interviews and conversations	Life history, life story
20. Oral history	Personal recollections of events, their causes and effects	Work, ethnic, religious, personal, musical, etc.
21. Case history	History of an event or social process, not of a person	Single, multiple, medical, legal
22. Life history	Account of a life based on interviews and conversations	Personal, edited, topical, complete
23. Life story	A person's story of his or her life, or a part thereof	Edited, complete, topical, fictional
24. Self story	Story of self in relation to an event	Personal experience, fictional, true
25. Personal experience story	Story about personal experience	Single, multiple, episode, private or communal folklore
26. Performance	Verb, form of being, action	Mimesis, kinesis, poiesis, dialogic, ritual, liminal, minstrelsy, way of knowing, way of being, theatrical forms (realistic, oppositional, spec-actor, ritualized), embodied pedagogy, repetition, act of activism, twice-behaved behavior, utopic, form of resistance, an event, form of story-telling, actions, ritual, play, everyday life, performing arts, enactment of social identities/ roles

framework. They provide a road map for the chapters that follow. Appendix A provides a historical timeline for our project.

***

Coda

To repeat, we are in uncharted, global spaces. We struggle to find new ways of being on this violent world, new ways of performing pedagogies of hope and forgiveness, new ways of being in solidarity with one another, new pedagogies of freedom.

Table 1.2 A glossary of terms/forms and varieties of the autoethnographic method

1	*Performance:* to enact: mimesis (imitation), poesis (construction), kinesis (resistance) as transgressive accomplishment; an act of intervention or resistance; dialogic, as experience, as performance of possibilities, as deconstruction, as ethical mandate.
2	*Performance:* to study persons as if they were performers, or to study performers; an interpretive event; dialogical performance as ethical imperative; performance ethnography as the doing of critical theory.
3	*Performance (performative) writing:* writing that shows, does not tell, hesitates, stutters, enacts what it describes, is evocative, reflexive; writing to embrace, enact, embody, effect.
4	*Performativity/performative "I":* the speaking subject is constituted for, by and in language.
5	*Ethnography* inscribing culture, writing culture vs. performing culture; **types:** realist, confessional, dramatic, critical, auto.
6	*Critical autoethnography:* critical cultural analysis using personal narrative and an intersectional approach. Some parallels to *heightened performance auto-ethnography* in which the author-researcher is a protagonist, or a witness-narrator in the narrative (Sughrua 2016).
7	*Autoethnography:* reflexively writing the self into and through the ethnographic text; isolating that space where memory, history, performance and meaning intersect; types (**form**): social scientific, interpretive, critical, artistic, poetic, critical reflexive, analytic, evocative, dramaturgical, narrative, heightened performative, collaborative, political, postcolonial, transnational, relational; (**content**): family, place, other, trauma (loss, illness, abuse, sexuality, race, death, divorce), embodied, queer (see Manning and Adams 2015; Spry 2016; Bochner and Ellis 2016).
8	*Autoethnography as disruptive practice:* inclusive, political, utopian.
9	*Autocritography:* critical autoethnography, reflective storytelling; storytelling as performance (Chawla 2007a, p. 376).
10	*Ethnodrama:* monologues, monologues with dialogue and ethnodramatic extensions, often involving the audience in post-performance feedback.
11	*Ethnotheatre:* Joins ethnography and theatre to create a performance event of research participants experiences.
12	*Duoethnography:* a collaborative research methodology in which two or more researchers juxtapose their life histories in order to provide multiple understandings of a social phenomenon. Duoethnographers use their own biographies as sites of inquiry and engage in dialogic narrative, often realized in collaborative writing and collaborative autoethnography.
13	*Collaborative writing,* collaborative autoethnography; the co-production of an autoethnographic (duoethnography) text by two or more writers, often separated by time and distance;
14	*Collective biography:* a co-produced, intertwined, reflexive biography, working with memory and storytelling. It begins with storytellers in a group listening and questioning each other concerning their earliest memories in relation to the chosen topic. A cycle of talking, listening, writing and rewriting continues until everyone is satisfied with the way the stories. Collective biography is done as collaborative writing.
15	*Deconstructive [auto]ethnography:* shifts attention from the narrative I to the performative I, contesting the meanings given to voice, presence, experience and subjectivity; decolonizing.

16 *Critical performance [auto] ethnography*: Conquergood's triad of triads: (1) the I's: imagination, inquiry, intervention; (2) the A's: artistry, analysis, activism; (3) the C's: creativity; citizenship, civic struggles for social justice (Madison 2005, p. 171; 2012, pp. 189–190).

17 *Performance [auto]ethnography*: the merger of critical pedagogy, performance ethnography and cultural politics; the creation of texts that move from epiphanies to the sting of memory, the personal to the political, the autobiographical to the cultural, the local to the historical. A "dramatized reenactmenet of ethnographic fieldotes" (Chawla 2007a, pp. 375–376)

18 *Pedagogy*: theory and practice of cultural education: forms: border, critical, disruptive, emancipatory, collaborative, dialogic, feminist, postmodern, prosthetic, theatrical, ritual, spectacle.

19 *Script*: an assemblage of emotional experiences that are carefully crafted, memorized and staged in performance autoethnographies. They can be solo or group-based (Spry 2016, p. 132).

20 *Social drama*: application of the theatrical model to the study of social interaction. elements: story/plot/narrative, actor, scene, crisis, temporal order, moral: stages: breech, crisis, redress, reintegration.

21 *Utopian performative* (Spry 2016, p. 97): a performance that knits together performance and performativity, creating those moments when persons feel a sense of utopia, community, solidarity, potential, warmth, joy, desire, caring, a flash of mutual understanding, sharing (V. Turner 1982).

Notes

1 Historical Dates; Fall 1961, U.S. involvement in Vietnam War escalates; Cuban missile crisis: October 1962. The anti-war, women's and civil rights movements helped define the decade. The emotional tenor and energy of the decade was captured in its popular music (folk, rock, blues, R and B), from the Beatles, to the Rolling Stones, Bob Dylan, Jimi Hendrix, Simon and Garfunkel, Janis Joplin, B. B, King, Phil Ochs, Donovan, Johnny Cash, Buffalo Springfield, Jefferson Airplane, Joni Mitchell, Nina Simone, Pete Seeger.

2 Denzin and Lincoln (2017, p. xix; also 2011, p. 7) define the these moments as: the traditional (1900–1950), the modernist or golden age (1950–1970), blurred genres (1970–1980), the paradigm wars (1980–1985), the crisis of representation (1986–1990), the postmodern (1990–1995), postexperimental inquiry (1995–2000), the methodologically contested present (2000–2004), paradigm proliferation (2005–2010) and the fractured, post-humanist present which battles managerialism in the audit-driven academy (2010–2015), an uncertain, utopian future, where critical inquiry finds its voice in the public arena (2016 –) These moments overlap in the present (see Clarke, Friese & Washburn, 2015, pp. 21–43 for an expanded treatment of this history).

3 Throughout I will connect reflexive ethnography with autoethnography using both terms to reference the most recent developments in performance, I will locate those arguments in first person, multi-layered texts that work outward from the writer's life. Thus understood the researcher becomes the research subject. This is the topic of reflexive performance autoethnography. Researchers stage and perform ethnographies of their own experience.

4 See Denzin and Lincoln (2005, pp. 13–21; 2017, pp. 9–10) for an extended discussion of each of these phases. This model has been termed a progress narrative by Alasuuutari (2004, pp. 599–600), Seale et al. (2004, p. 2), and Atkinson, Delamont and Coffey (2004). The critics assert that we believe that the most recent moment is the most up-to-date, the avant-garde, the cutting edge (Alasuuutari (2004, p. 601).

Naturally we dispute this reading. Tashakkori and Teddlie (2010, pp. 5–8) have modifed our historical periods to fit their historical analysis of the major moments in the emergence of mix methods in the last century.

5   These tensions turn on differing models of the individual, subjectivity, spirituality, property, the land and sovereignty (Grande, 2008a, p. 238).

6   See www.indigeneity.net/– *Indigeneity in the Contemporary World: Performance, Politics, Belonging* is a five-year research initiative funded by the European Research Council and based at Royal Holloway, University of London.

7   Several chapters draw from an on-going study of Native Americans, minstrelsy, Western Art, museums and 19th century wild west shows (Denzin, 2008, 2011, 2013, 2015a).

8   The technologies also include video and audio recordings made on smartphones, SKYPE encounters, discussions in online recovery groups, internet forums, weblogs, social blogs, wikis, podcasts and LinkedIn exchanges. These technologies allow persons in virtual communities to share information about themselves, their biographies and their intimate experiences. Virtual selves have material presences in these electronic spaces.

9   By-passing contemporary critics who challenge terms like voice and presence, indigenous persons in colonized spaces turn to oral history, myth, and performance narratives to make sense of their lives, themselves and their collective histories (see Smith, 2012; Kovach, 2009).

10 Consider in this space the pervasive, omnipresent, largely negative influence of Donald Trump's tweets on American civic culture.

11 Boal defines *forum theatre*: it consists of proposing to a group of spectators, after a first improvisation of a scene, that they replace the protagonist and try to improvise variations on his actions. The real protagonist should, ultimately, improvise that variation that has motivated him the most (1985, p. 184; also 2000, 1998, 1995).

12 I discuss each of these techniques in Chapter 5.

13 No scholar has done more than Dwight Conquergcood to advance our understandings of the intersections between performance, ethnography, politics and praxis (P. Johnson, 2013). Conquergood's framework consists of a series of triads which locate performance within a larger framework. Unlike Goffman, his model moves from textual ethnography to performance autoethnography. Performance in Conquergood's model is an object of study, a pragmatics of inquiry, and a tactic of intervention

Part I
Performance autoethnography

1 Autoethnography as ~~research~~ redux[1]

Part One

Memory

Begin in the autobiographical present, a moment frozen in the past. My brother and I in our cowboy outfits sitting on sway-backed Sonny, our deaf and partially blind pony. We are 5 and 9 at the time, Grandpa and Grandma are watching us from behind the corral fence. We have toy pistols. We are wearing little leather vests, chaps, cowboy boots, cowboy hats. We are smiling. We think we are cowboys in the corral, just like Roy Rogers and Gene Autry.

Willie Nelson cautions:

Mammas, don't let your babies grow up to be cowboys.[2]

Mark and I thought we had it both ways. An Indian one day, a cowboy the next day. Maybe we did. As little white boys in our grandparents' Iowa farm playground we had the power to be white or red, cowboy or Indian. Our grandparents gave us the costumes, and showed us how to enact a minstrel show, how to play the cowboy-Indian game, how to do the masquerade. White face, Red face. Little white boys thoughtlessly playing the race game, all in the name of fun. Or was it? All innocence?

Mark and I always seemed alone. A lonely white boy playing cowboy to his brother's Indian. We knew it was all pretend, make-believe. But underneath we were running away from the fear of loneliness, would our divorced parents ever get back together again? Were we destined to hide our fears behind these imaginary wild west identities? Once you retreat into the cowboy or Indian identity there is nowhere else to go. We were trapped in an imaginary world.

***

My heroes are no longer cowboys.

***

I seek ethnographic texts turned into performance events, into ethnodramas, into ethnotheatre, into narrative poems, scripts, short stories, texts with narrators, action, shifting points of view; dramaturgical productions co-performed with audiences; life, narrative and melodrama under the auspices of late neoliberal capitalism. I seek stories of love, loss, pain, resistance, stories of hope, stories that dig deep beneath ideology, stories that contest how history goes on behind our backs.

***

> **auto**: self-reflection
> **ethno**: to explore people's experiences
> **graph**: to write, to make an image,
> to perform a script that I (or you) create;
> **autoethnography**: bending the past to the present;
> I write my way into and through my experiences;
> I treat myself as an universal singular;
> I devise a script and play myself.

***

Willie's cowboy, my nemesis – always alone, never stays home, don't let your baby grow up to be cowboys.

Cowboy songs, country western swing, Bob Wills is still the King.

My mind drifts, July 1981, country-Western bar, Macomb, Illinois, Willie is on the juke box. I look into the mirror over the bar. My haggard face stares back at me, Willie is singing:

> "Mammas, don't let your babies grow up to be cowboys."
> Merle Haggard. Where are you now?

***

I seek a new genealogy. A new language. A new beginning. But where to begin? Who am I? What is performance? What is theatre? What is research? What is autoethnography? How did I get lost?

> No home on the range?
> You lost your faith in a meaningful world
> It's a journey, stuck in a nightmare.
> Betrayed by yourself,
> Madness, torture chambers
> More madness, no way home.

***

The essence of theatre, Boal reminds us, is the human being observing itself. *The human being not only "makes" theatre: it is theatre* (Boal 1995, p. 13, italics in original) What does performing mean? Is all of social life a performance? Are we all performers presenting and performing selves to one another in everyday life, putting on first one mask and then another, engaging in endless rounds of impression management (Goffman 1959)? Are we only the characters we play? Are we actors following a script devised by others? Are we performers following our own script, playing ourselves (Schechner 2017, p. 8)?

> actor/performer/actor/performer/performer/actor/
> are actors performers
> are performers actors
> do we create ourselves through performance?
> Is Donald Trump an actor or a performer?
> Was Ronald Reagan a performer or an actor
> (Schechner 2017, p. 8).
> Autoethnographers are performers
> Ethnography is a performance

We became human when we invented theatre (Boal 1995, p. 14).

> Is there only fiction?
> Fake News?
> Fake people
> Can facts trump fiction?
> Trump's performances
> an actor playing himself
> trumps reality fiction

***

Today an Indian, tomorrow a lonely cowboy. Is everything an illusion, pretense. Are we confined to studying the metaphysics, the fundamental nature of performance itself. But performance is a contested concept, no single definition can contain it.

Still, Madison reminds us,

> if we accept the notion of human beings as *homo performans* and therefore as a performing species, performance becomes necessary for our survival. That is we recognize and create ourselves as Others through performance ... in this process culture and performance become inextricably interconnected and performance is a constant presence in our daily lives.
>
> (Madison 2012, p. 166, paraphrase)

***

There is only performance.
There is only performance.
There is only performance.
There is only performance.
What is performance?
Performance matters.

***

Boal says we became human when we invented theatre (1995, p; 14).

I became human when I became a cowboy.
Then I invented theatre.
I called it the wild west show.

As homo performan I engage the world as a performative-I, as an embodied, moving reflective being. I establish my presence as a universal singular, an embodied self interacting with culture/history/society in the lived present (Spry 2011, p. 53).

Sway-backed blind Sonny,
Horses, toy guns, vests, western hats,
pretend Indian warriors, Gay Bucks,
Red Skin squaws
Gene Autry, Roy Rogers, cowboy songs,
Hi Ho Silver
Ghost Rider in the Sky
Yippee-Ki-Yay Cowboy
Gay Cowboy Bregade
LGBT Chorus

Dodging, moving, hiding, on the run,
whose history? I've lost my hold on the past.

Whiskey River, let me be.
Whiskey River, don't ever leave.
You're all I've got.[3]

Who am I running from? What am I running from? Does it even matter?
I look in the mirror. The looking-glass
I see Sartre's universal singular
A broken down Vladimir,
waiting for Beckett's
Godot who never shows.
A sometimes sad pathetic figure, universal by the
singular universality of human history.

Performer, moral agent, actor, everybody is an universal singular, known only through her performances. The autoethnographer is a dramatist. I'm a dramatist! I'm a performer.

I'm drowning in whiskey river.

> Mammas, don't let your babies grow up to be cowboys.
> Don't let 'em pick guitars or drive them old trucks.
> Let 'em be doctors and lawyers and such.
> Whiskey River, take my mind.
> Whiskey River, don't run dry.
> You're all I've got, take care of me.[4]

Who is the autoethnographer running from?

> No home on the range
> be careful desperato, mr
> Boy Named Sue
> Country Road, Take Me Home
> No way

Autoethnographer as performer

Performance matters for ethnography. Conquergood (2006):

> with renewed appreciation for boundaries, border-crossings, process, improvisation, contingency, multiple identities, and the embodied nature of fieldwork practice, many ethnographers have turned to a performance-inflected vocabulary.
>
> (p. 358)

Ethnographers become methodological actors who creatively play, improvise, interpret, re-present roles and enact scripts in concrete field settings. The [auto] ethnographer is a co-performer in a social drama, a participant in rhetorically framed cultural performances, enacting rituals, writing fieldnotes, recording interviews, videotaping, observing, talking, doing the things ethhnographers do, turning research into performative inquiry (Conquergood 2006, p. 360).

> Ride that horse cowgirl, lasso that steer
>
> Performance matters. You can be my Indian, if I can be your cowboy.
> You can be in my dream,
> if I can be in your dream.[5]
> After all, performance matters.

***

Schechner clarifies. The "relationship between studying performance and doing performance is integral. One performs fieldwork, which is subject to the 'rehearsal process' of improvising, testing and revising and no position is neutral. The performance scholar is actively involved in advocacy" (Schechner 2013, p. 4, paraphrase).

Ride that horse cowgirl, lasso that steer***

Cowboys ain't easy to love and they're harder to hold.
They'd rather give you a song than diamonds or gold.
Lonestar belt buckles and old faded levis.
Blue Eyes Crying in the Rain
Faded Love
Cry Baby

***

Interpretive aside: fieldwork as performance

Conquergood again, describing a moment in his fieldwork in Big Red, a dilapidated polyethnic tenement in Chicago where he lived for 20 months, starting in December 1987. Here Dwight gets caught up between being Dwight and being Dwight the ethnographer:

> At 10:00 A.M. on August 16, 1988, Bao Xiang, a Hmong woman from Laos, stepped out the back door of her top-floor Big Red apartment and the rotting porch collapsed beneath her feet. All summer long I had swept away slivers of wood that had fallen from the Xiong's decrepit porch onto mine, one floor below. Six families were intimately affected by Bao Xiong's calamity. We shared the same front entrance and stairwell. Our back porches were structurally interlocked within a shaky wooden framework of open landings and sagging staircases that cling precariously to the red-brick exterior of the Chicago tenement. Within minutes of arriving home on that day, I heard multiple versions of the story.
> (Conquergood 1992b, in Johnson 2013, pp. 170–171)

Rubbing shoulders with his neighbors, participating in their lives on a daily basis, Conquergood became known as "Mr. Dwight" the white man who lived in Big Red, and his neighbors shared stories about their lives with him, and he with them. Mr. Dwight was also known as the white man who read books, helped people, took pictures, let persons use his camera, worked on a research project.

Where is the dividing line?
Performer, ethnographer,

performance as fieldwork,
fieldwork as performance
research as performance

A performance-centered ethnographic approach is participatory, intimate, precarious, embodied, grounded in circumstance, situational identities and historical process. The [auto] ethnographer' body is anchored in time and place. The ethnographer engages in face-work that is "part of the intricate and nuanced dramaturgy of everyday life" (Conquergood 2006, p. 359; Goffman 1959). The power dynamic of inquiry moves from the gaze of the detached observer, to the interactions, the give-and-take between situated actors. Performance-sensitive ethnography strains to produce situated understandings, ethnodramas, performance events that make the injustices in the world socially visible. Through cultural performances persons participate in public life, in vital discussions central to their communities (Conquergood 2006, p. 360). The performance autoethnographer works in those dialogic spaces where bodies, selves and emotions interact.

Ride that horse cowgirl, lasso that steer

The performance autoethnographer is not studying the other. She is reflexively writing herself into her performance text, into those spaces where she intersects with the other. Her primary interests are showing, not telling, social justice, critical reflexivity, interpretation and ethically responsible inquiry (Madison 2012, p. x). She makes this world visible through her performative acts. Little boys playing cowboys and Indians.

You can be in my dreams if I can be in our dreams

The world as performance

Performance is many things at the same time. It is a contested term. It is a verb, a noun, a form of being, an action, a form of doing, a form of mimicry, of minstrelsy, showing, a way of knowing, a way of making the world visible, an incitement to action, an entanglement (Madison and Hamera 2006, pp. xi–xii, Schechner 2013, p. 28; Spry 2016). There are multiple forms of acting which frame performances: realistic (Stanislavsky), oppositional-alienation (Brechtian), spec-actor (Boal), highly codified (ballet, opera) (Schechner 2013, pp. 174–185).

***

GODOT: Words Words Words.

***

Performance operates at three levels and in three different discourses at the same time: *human being as homo performan, ethnographer* as *homo performan,* and *ethnographer as homo politican.*[6]

Performance is dramaturgical, theatrical. It is about "putting the body on the page, lifting it to the stage, understanding that body and paper and stage are one another" (Spry 2011, p. 26). Performance is always embodied, involving feeling, thinking, acting bodies moving through time and space. The stage actor pretends to have the emotions of the character she is playing. She may even become the emotion, like the singer who acts out the sad lyrics in the song she is singing (see Bob Dylan 2015 in Love 2015).

The singer is the song,
the song is the performance,
the performance is the singer

Every performance is unique, even when it is a form of repetition (Phelan 1993, p. 148). Phelan reminds us that there are no original performances, or identities, no "preexisting identity by which an act or attribute might be measured" (p. 141).

Ride'em Cowboy

Every performance is an imitation, a before and an after, a form of mimesis, "if heterosexuality is an impossible imitation of itself, an imitation that performatively constitutes itself as the original, then the imitative parody of 'heterosexuality' ... is always and only an imitation, a copy of a copy, for which there is no original" (Butler 1993, p. 644). Every performance is an original and an imitation. But, as Boal argues (1985, p. xiv) moved to the aesthetic space, the goal of performance is to change the world, not to imitate it; "change starts in the theatre itself. Theatre is action" (p. 155; 1995, xviii).

Ghost Riders in the Sky

Performance's temporality is utopic, always in the future, not the past or the present, rather the future that unfolds in the present, as a succession of what has just been (Munoz 2005, p. 10). Utopian performatives help us re-write the past, uncover structures of oppression and imagine hopeful futures (Spry 2016, p. 97). Performance is always a form of restored behavior, or twice-behaved behavior, "performed actions people train for and rehearse and then perform" (Schechner 2013, p. 28). Still each twice-behaved performance is an unique event. Disappearance is the hallmark of performance, a representation without representation (Phelan 1993, p. 148–49; but see Munoz 2005, p. 10).

Ride'em Cowboy

Pollock provides an example. She describes seeing Carol Channing performing in Hello Dolly at the Auditorium Theatre in Chicago:

> There she was, at the top of the winding staircase, one long gloved hand laid along the white balustrade: she was every dame, mame, belle who had ever descended ... a long winding staircase to a waiting chorus of high-kicking men. She and we relished every wigged, lip-sticked, and sequined step, each timed so perfectly that she arrived on the stage apron with the final crescendo of the music, which seemed to rise on our cue, as we rose to clap and clap and clap, performing a standing ovation literally to beat the band. And yet, this was still Dolly – or was it Carol? ... When a stunned hush finally reigned Carol/Dolly – Dolly/Carol took one more carefully balanced step toward us, bent slightly at the hip, as if to share a secret ... she spoke with glowing, exaggerated precision in an absolutely delicious stage whisper – "Shall we do that again?" ... Now the performance launches onto ... a new plane of repetition ... that exceeds both the thing done and the doing of it.
>
> (Pollock 2007, pp. 243–44; see also Denzin 2014, pp. 11–12)

This is an instance of the utopian performative expressed in performance writing, an attempt to enact "the affective force of the performance event again, as it plays itself out in an ongoing temporality" (Phelan 1997, pp. 11–12). Here the theatre and performance intersect, but that is not always the case. Persons do not need the machinery of the theatre and the stage to be performers.

Ride'em Cowboy
Mommas, don't let your babies grow up to be cowboys.

Performance can be a form of resistance, as when one refuses to comply with an order, or Dolly speaks directly to the audience and says, shall we do this again? Performance can be a form of imitation or pretense or make-believe. A child wears the costume of a witch on Halloween. Performance can be a form of story-telling, an event, a ritual. Performance stands between persons, their embodied presence in a situation and their presentation of self.

Cowboys ain't easy to love and they're harder to hold.

The triadic relationship between performance, performance ethnography and doing performance studies is crucial (Schechner 2013, p. 2). Ethnography is always a performance, and always grounded in the self-identity of the ethnographer. What people do is made visible in performance.

Dwight, the fieldworker,
exchanges news and recipes with Bao Xiang,
his Hmong neighbor in Big Red

The author as performer or as autoethnographer performs the very inquiry that produces the text that is performed. The performing material, corporeal body is read as a text, it is assigned words that give it meaning.

As Spry (2011, pp. 27–28) observes, performance autoethnography becomes an engaged, critical, embodied pedagogy. The writer-as-performer draws on personal experience and history, and embraces vulnerability, hoping to create a critical relationship with the audience that moves persons to action (Jones, Adams and Ellis 2013, paraphrase).

Mills (1959) reminds us

> that our project is to read
> each person into their
> historical moment,
> to grasp the relationship
> between history, biography,
> personal troubles and public issues,
> to see each human being as a universal singular.

Critical autoethnography focuses on those moments, epiphanies in a person's life that define a crisis, a turning point that connects a personal trouble, a personal biography, with larger social, public issues. The sting of memory locates the moment, the beginning. Once located this moment is dramatically described, fashioned into a text, or mystory to be performed (Ulmer 1989, p. 209). A "mystory" begins with those moments, those epiphanies that define a crisis in the person's life. This moment is then surrounded by those cultural representations and voices that define the experience in question. These representations are then contested, and challenged.

The writer-as-ethnographer-as-performer is self-consciously present, morally and politically self-aware. She uses her own experiences in a culture to "reflexively to bend back on herself and look more deeply at self-other interactions" (Ellis and Bochner 2000, p. 740). A key task of performance autoethnography is now apparent, it helps the writer "make sense of the autobiographic past" (Alexander 1999, p. 309). Autoethnography becomes a way of "recreating and re-writing the biographic past, a way of making the past a part of the bio-graphic present" (Pinar 1994, p. 22; also cited in Alexander 1999, p. 309).

Here is an extended example from a larger study, *Searching for Yellowstone* (Denzin 2008, pp. 57, 71). Whose present am I bending to the past?

***

Scene One: memories, blankets and myths narrator re-remembers the past: 1955

> This is a short story within a larger story. I want to go back to the Spring and Summer of 1955. That spring my father sold me a $5000 life insurance policy from the Farm Bureau Life Insurance Company. I was 16 years old, and a life

insurance policy at that age seemed a stretch. But Dad was desperate. He said this sale would put him over his quota for the month and qualify him for a fishing trip to Ontario, Canada. On July 5, 1955 my father returned to our little house on Third Street in Indianola, Iowa from his company-sponsored fishing trip in Ontario, Canada. Mother greeted him at the door. Slightly drunk, Dad handed her a Hudson's Bay wool blanket as a present, and promptly left for the office. I still have that blanket. In this family we value these blankets and exchange them as gifts. This exchange system gives me a somewhat indirect history with Canada, Hudson's Bay Company blankets, the fur trade, nineteenth century British and French traders and Native Americans. This history takes me right into the myths about Yellowstone Park, Lewis and Clark, the Corps of Discovery, and Sacagawea. Lewis and Clark, it appears, also traded blankets and other gifts for good will on their expedition. But this was a tainted exchange, for many of these blankets were carriers of the small pox disease. Likewise, the blanket father gave to mother was embedded within a disease exchange system, in this case alcoholism. While father's alcoholism was not full-blown in 1955, it would be within two years of his return from this fishing trip.

Today that blanket is in the blanket chest at the foot of our bed.

Scene Two: narrator remembers another version of the past: 1994:

The Hudson's Bay blanket that my father bought for me and my wife at a farm auction in Kalona, Iowa in the winter of 1994 was expensive. He and his best friend bid against one another, driving the price up over $300.00. The price was fitting, for the blanket is marked with four black pelt or point lines, which defined the blanket's worth in that nineteenth century economy where pelts were traded for blankets. A four-pelt blanket is indeed pricey. Today that four-pelt blanket is in the guest room in our cabin outside Red Lodge, Montana.

As I said earlier, in this family we value these blankets and exchange them as gifts.

***

It's all here, memories, biographies, family histories, the salesman as an iconic American figure, crises, alcoholism, ritual, family performances, pretense, impression management, gift-exchange systems, fathers and sons, larger historical, cultural and economic structures and systems: life insurance companies, Lewis and Clark, Native Americans, nineteenth century U.S. colonialism, Yellowstone Park, blankets, nature, wildlife, tourism. Buying that insurance policy from my father implicated me (and my family) in his dreams, connecting us to a global exchange system that is still in place today, making us complicit with Lewis and Clark's and Hudson's Bay's mistreatment of Native Americans.

When I reflect on the day my father sold me that life insurance policy and I signed that check I feel flashes of anger, guilt, shame and pride. How

could he have done this to me? Whose version of a father was he performing that day, and whose version of a son was I performing? What choices
did we have?

***

Mammas, don't let your babies grow up to be cowboys
Tainted Hudson's Bay blankets, Native Americans,
U.S. Colonialism, family alcoholism,
Shame, guilt
No exit

Race and the call to performance

As the dividing line between performativity (doing) and performance (done)
disappears, matters of gender and racial injustice remain. On this W. E. B. Du
Bois reminds us that "modern democracy cannot succeed unless peoples of different races and religions are also integrated into the democratic whole" (Du
Bois 1978 [1901], pp. 281, 288). Du Bois addressed race from a performance
standpoint. He understood that "from the arrival of the first African slaves on
American soil .... the definitions and meanings of blackness, have been intri-
cately linked to issues of theatre and performance" (Elam and Kraesner 2001, p.
4).[7] Being black meant wearing and performing the masks of blackness. It
meant wearing black skin. It meant hiding inside and behind blackness. Bryant
Alexander (2012, pp. 154–55) elaborates:

> I am interested in skin as performance;
> I am interested in skin on "colored" bodies.
> I am interested in Skin as in a box checked.
> I am interested in skin – performing it, seeing it, dark, light skin,
> Skin as a marketing tool.
>
> (paraphrase)

Race as performance, as skin, as mask, blackface, white face, a minstrel
show. "Black, white, red, yellow, is it about color, or something else?" (Diversi
and Moreira 2009, pp. 90–91, paraphrase).

bell hooks elaborates the need for a black political performance aesthetic. In
another time, as a child, she and her sisters learned about race in America by
watching,

> the Ed Sullivan show on Sunday nights ... seeing on that show the great
> Louis Armstrong, Daddy who was usually silent, would talk about the
> music, the way Armstrong was being treated, and the political implications
> of his appearance ... responding to televised cultural production, black

people could express rage about racism ... unfortunately ... black folks were not engaged in writing a body of critical cultural analysis.

(hooks 1990, pp. 3–4)

But in America today unarmed black male teenagers with their hands in the air can be shot by the police and a twelve-year-old black boy can be shot and killed by police in Cleveland because the officer mistook a toy gun for a real gun (Kelley 2014). It is no longer safe for black teenage males to even walk alongside, let alone cross over Du Bois' color line.

I fold my project into Du Bois's, Alexander's and bell hooks's by asking how a radical performative discourse can confront and transcend the problems surrounding the color line in the second decade of the twenty-first century. Such a project will write and perform culture in new ways. It will connect reflexive autoethnography with critical pedagogy, and critical race theory (see Donnor and Ladson-Billings 2017). It will call for acts of activism that insist on justice for all. Unarmed young black males can no longer just be shot down by police without recrimination.

Robin Kelley (2014) reminds:

we know their names and how they died. The police killed at least 258 black people in 2016. We hold their names like recurring nightmares, accumulating the dead like ghoulish baseball cards. Except that there is no trading. No forgetting. Just a stack of dead bodies: Trayvon, Michael, Eleanor Bumpurs, Michael Stewart, Eula Love, Amadu Diallo, Oscar Grant, Patrick Dorismond, Malice Green, Tyisha Miller, Sean Bell, Aiyana Stanley-Jones, Margaret LaVerne Mitchell. Names attached to dead black bodies. Symbols of police violence and this does not even begin to count the harassed, the beaten, the humiliated, the stopped-and-frisked, the raped.

(Kelley 2014, paraphrase)

A never-ending list of names.

There is no longer,
but there never was,
an age of innocence for
persons of color in America.[8]

Turn the page to the recent present.

***

White on White: of race and statues

WASHINGTON POST: Heather Heyer, 32, died on Saturday August 12, 2017 after a car plowed into a crowd of anti-racist protesters following a white

nationalist rally in Charlottesville, Va. At the center of the chaos is a statue
memorializing Robert E. Lee. It depicts the Confederacy's top general,
larger than life, astride a horse. The white nationalists were in Charlottesville
to protest the city's plan to remove that statue, and counterdemonstrators
were there to oppose them.[9]

(On the violence in Charlottesville, Virginia August 15, 2017):

DONALD TRUMP: Oh, those beautiful statues! Beautiful statues, magnificent
statues. Both sides including the "alt-left" were to blame for the violence.
Very fine people on both sides. Some of them were there to protest the
removal of a statue of Robert E. Lee. So, this week, it's Robert E. Lee. I
noticed that Stonewall Jackson is coming down. I wonder: Is it George
Washington next week? And is it Thomas Jefferson the week after? You really
do have to ask yourself, "Where does it stop?" Washington and Jefferson were
slave owners.

What about the alt-left that came charging, do they have any sem-
blance of guilt? They came charging with clubs in their hands, swinging
clubs? Do they have any problem? I think they do. You had a group on
one side that was bad, and you had a group on the other side that was
also very violent, and nobody wants to say that, but I'll say it right
now. You had a group – you had a group on the other side that came
charging in without a permit, and they were very, very violent. There's
blame on both sides.[10]

SUSAN BRO (MOTHER OF HEATHER HEYER): The White House tried to reach me
with "frantic" messages, presumably to set up a call with Trump: I'm
not talking to the president now. I'm sorry. After what he said about
my child. I saw an actual clip of him at a press conference equating the
protesters, like Ms. Heyer, with the KKK and the white supremacists. ...
You can't wash this one away by shaking my hand and saying, "I'm
sorry."[11]

NARRATOR: Yippee! A mother calls out the President.

ANDREW ANGLIN, THE DAILY STORMER (NEO-NAZI WEBSITE): These "protests"
are happening across the country, and I guarantee you, they are going to go
to Washington, and they are going to demand that the Washington
Monument be torn down. They might even try to pull it down. Because
George Washington owned slaves. More importantly, he was a white man
who built something.[12]

DAVID LANE: We must secure the existence of our people and a future for white
children.

SUSAN BRO: No over my daughter's dead body.

REPORTER TO DONALD TRUMP: How concerned are you about race relations in
America? And do you think things have gotten worse or better since you
took office?

TRUMP: I think they've gotten better or the same – look, they've been frayed for a long time. And you can ask President Obama about that, because he'd make speeches about it. You know I own the country's largest winery and it is in Charlottesville.[13]

***

White on white,
where do we go next?
Racial violence as performance,
White nationalists clashing with protesters,
racial epithets, tear gas, tiki torches,
Nazi slogans, World War II helmets,
Black Lives Matter posters,
Confederate flags
Black Lives Matter Black Lives Matter Black Lives
Matter Black Lives Matter.

The goal is to contest and undo official racial history, to push back, to create a space for marginalized voices, to speak truth to power, create alternative histories, new ways of writing and performing the past so new futures can be imagined, non-violent futures, war is not the answer.

NARRATOR: When NO is not enough
a mother refuses
to be silenced.

(Klein 2017)

We seek a new politics of resistance, a new politics of possibility, new ways of re-imagining the future and the past. Madison, after Dolan (2005), calls these re-imaginings utopian performatives They are akin to Freire's pedagogies of hope (Madison 2012, p. 182; 2010, p. 26; Freire 1999/1992; Dolan 2005, p. 5).
Freire reminds us:

Without hope there is
only tragic despair,
hopelessness.
(Freire 1999/1992, pp.
8–9)

***

We have no choice. We must contest the KKK, White Nationalist, racist, fascist discourse where ever it appears.

***

Without hope the Donald Trumps
of the world prevail.

Part Two

Hope and acts of activism[14]

Performances of possibility create spaces "where unjust systems ... can be identified and interrogated" (Madison 2010 p. 159). Persons can become radicalized when confronted with such performances. As Madison notes. "One performance may or may not change someone's world... but one performance can be revolutionary in enlightening citizens as to the possibilities that grate against injustice" (Madison 2010, p. 159). Utopian performatives offer a reflexive "what if," an utopian imagining of how a situation could be performed differently (Conquergood 2002/2013, p. 29). It is a retooling, a re-doing, a renewing (Spry 2016, p. 96).

The utopic stages itself. It pushes and pulls us forward. It incites the imagination. It offers blueprints for hope, bare "outlines of a world not quite here, a horizon of possibility, not a fixed scheme" (Munoz 2005, p. 9). Utopia is flux, change, stasis, chaos, and disorganization all jumbled together, a fluid "moment when the here and now is transcended by a then, and a there that could be and indeed should be" (Munoz 2005, p. 9). Utopia is always a critique of the here and now. It involves a politics of emotion, an insistence that something is missing from the present, hope, a dream, freedom. It involves the belief that things can be different, better, there can be social justice in a place called utopia where hope dwells.

A performative, pedagogical politics of hope imagines a radically free democratic society, a society where ideals of the ableist, ageist, indigenist, feminist, queer, environmental, green, civil rights and labor movements are realized. In their utopian forms these movements offer "alternative models of radical democratic culture rooted in social relations that take seriously the democratic ideals of freedom, liberty, and the pursuit of happiness" (Giroux 2001, p. 9).

Madison is quite explicit: critical, performative autoethography begins:

> With a duty and ethical responsibility to address suffering, unfairness and injustice within a particular historical moment. There is a commitment to perform acts of activism that advance the causes of human rights.
> (Madison 2012, p. 5; 2010, p, 1, paraphrase)

Accordingly, a radical performative discourse revolves around specific acts of resistance and activism, performances were persons put their bodies on the line, staged reenactments which incite resistance. These acts are public interventions. That is performance is used subversively, as a strategy for awakening critical consciousness and moving persons to take human, democratic actions in the face of injustice, efforts that serve social justice, and that are expected to bring net gains in the lives of people (Madison 2010, p. 1; Cohen-Cruz 2005, p. 4). These explicit acts of activism imply an embodied epistemology, a poetic reflexive performing body moving through space, an ethical body taking responsibility for its action.

Corey (2015) observes that the use of performance

> "to initiate social change predates the theatres of Greece, where, by way of example, in Lysistrata, Aristophanes created a lead character who corals her friends to withhold sex from their husbands in order to stop the wars." Contemporary examples include Brecht's Epic Theatre, Boal's Theatre of the Oppressed, agit prop, and guerilla theatre.
>
> (p. 1, paraphrase)[15]

Gloria Anzaldua's (1987, pp. 2–3) writing performs its own acts of resistance. She speaks of border crossing, crossing the borders:

> I walk through the hole in the fence
> To the other side
> Beneath the iron sky
> Mexican children kick the soccer ball across,
> run after it, entering the U.S.
> 1,950-mile-long open wound …
> staking fence rods in my flesh …
> This is my home
> this thin edge of barbwire.
> This land was Indian always and is
> And will be again.
> And Donald Trump
> wants to build a wall!

The work of advocacy

In moving from fieldwork and inquiry to page and then to stage autoethnographers as advocates resist speaking for the other (Spry 2011). Rather they assist in the struggles of others, staging performance events, screening and re-presenting history, offering new versions of official history, performing counter-memories, exposing contradictions in official ideology, reflexively interrogating their own place in the performance thereby taking ethical responsibility for the consequences of their own acts and performances (Madison 2010, p. 11).

> The performance is not a mirror,
> it is, the hammer that breaks the mirror,
> shatters the glass, builds a new realities,
> incites transformations, causes trouble,
> The performer self-consciously
> becomes part of the performance,

an instrument of change engaged
in ethical acts of advocacy,
radical acts addressing underlying
root causes embedded in the machinations
of neoconservatism and a corrupt corporate global
political economy.

      (see Madison 2010, pp. 12, 19)Augusto Boal:

Performance is the method for making
a slice of contested reality visible.
The performance brings the audience
and/or Spec-Actors into a state of critical reflexivity.
The act of witnessing (and performing)
utopian performatives is itself a performative,
interpretive act, somehow the world **can**
be a better place.

      (Dolan 2005, p. 5)

Maggie Kovach struggles to find this place:

> I am taking Cree, it is my first class today. Walking into the First Nations University there are Indians everywhere with shiny hair flying as both instructors and students race down the hall to class. The instructor is Plains Cree, he was raised with the language. He asks who is Cree. We put up our hands. He asks why we do not know our language. He points to me. I say adopted. He nods.
>
>   (Kovach 2009, p. 113)

Kovach's performance text brings a painful memory alive. She is a product of Canada's "Baby Scoop Era" (1945–1990) when Native babies and young children were taken from their Native mothers and placed for adoption in non-Native homes. Their native heritage was often denied by their adoption parents and their birth mothers were denied access to them (Johnson 1983). This is why Kovach did not learn how to speak Cree.

Can the healing ever even begin? How?

Part Three

Coda (back to Willie)

I look in the mirror, another Willie song comes on the jukebox, "Angel Flying Too Close To The Ground."[16]

If you had not have fallen
Then I would not have found you

Angel flying too close to the ground
I knew someday that you would fly away.

Whiskey River and flying too close to the ground got me in front of that mirror in that Macomb tavern. Eventually that mirror lead me to Hudson's Bay blankets. I'm wrapped inside a Hudson's Bay blanket, trapped inside a sad Willie Nelson song.

Let's get serious.
Back to Cowboys and Indians.
Willie Nelson's Wild West Imaginary
is about lonely white men running
from themselves, using wild west imagery:
Lonestar belt buckles, faded jeans,
guitars, old trucks, clear mountain mornings,
girls of the night, redskins, Indians.

We now understand how, over the course of five centuries, state-sponsored killing machines – the American military, the U.S. Government, the media, the schools, state legislatures and the Catholic Church – systematically engaged in genocide against Native Americans. Benjamin Madley calls it American geno-cide (Madley 2016). There was an intentional attempt to destroy communities, cultures and persons through the willful "spreading of diseases, dislocation, starvation, mass death in enforced confinement on reservations, homicides, battles and massacres" (Madley 2016, p. 3). For example, between 1846 and 1870 California's Indian population was reduced from 150,000 to 30,000, the victim of disease, famine, war, massacre (Madley 2016, p. 3).

Deep down inside this killing machine was the belief that the darkskinned unassimilated native other needed to be relocated to reservations, concentration camps, or destroyed. (Beebe and Senkewicz 2015, p. 30; Madley 2016, pp. 26–27).[17]

Willie Nelson's lonely cowboys are part of that killing machine. I grew up not knowing I was inside this killing machine. My father and my grandfather were part of that killing machine. With their guidance I grew thinking I could be a cowboy

But Mammas, don't let your babies grow up to be cowboys

No more.

Notes

1 The line through research is meant to suspend the usual meaning(s) of research, indeed to suggest that autoethnography IS NOT research per se, it is performance, performative interpretive inquiry.
2 Ed Bruce and Patsy Bryce, writers, released 1975, United Artists. Chosen as one of the top 100 Western songs of all time. Waylon Jennings and Willie Nelson covered the song in their 1978 duet album, "Waylon and Willie."

3 Co-written and recorded by Johnny Bush 1972, RCA Victor. One of Willie Nelson' signature concert songs.

4 Co-written and recorded by Johnny Bush 1972, RCA Victor. One of Willie Nelson' signature concert songs.

5 From Bob Dylan. 1963. "Talkin; World War III Blues." The Freewheelin' Bob Dylan. Warner Brothers, Inc. Special Rider Music.

6 Performance, the word, the noun, performs differently in performance studies (Schechner 2013), in the theatre (Dolan 2001), and in [auto] ethnography and communication studies.

7 Race and racism for Du Bois, were social constructions, performances, minstrelsy, blackface, powerful devices that produce and reproduce the color line. Du Bois believed that African Americans needed performance spaces where they could control how race was constructed. Consequently, as Elam observes, African American theatre and performance have been central sites for the interrogation of race and the color line (Elam and Krasner 2001, pp. 5–6). The inherent "constructedness of performance and the malleability of the devices of the theatre serve to reinforce the theory that blackness ... and race ... are hybrid, fluid concepts" (Elam and Krasner 2001, pp. 4–5).

8 Buckley (2017) reviews new documentaries which explore racism and the racial-divide in pre-and post-Ferguson America.

9 The statue had stood in the city since 1924. Most recently residents and city officials, along with organizations like the N.A.A.C.P., had called for it to come down (see www.nytimes.com/2017/08/13/us/charlottesville-rally-protest-statue.html).

10 See   www.charlotteobserver.com/news/politics-government/article167364607.html# storylink=cpy

11 See   www.washingtonpost.com/blogs/plum-line/wp/2017/08/18/heather-heyers-mother-just-brutally-unmasked-trumps-racism-and-cruelty/?utm_term=.b55b8df35598

12 Anglin's site takes its name from Der Stürmer, a newspaper that published Nazi propaganda. The site includes sections called "Jewish Problem" and "Race War." See http://www.charlotteobserver.com/entertainment/tv/article167401592.html#story link=cpy

13 See http://www.charlotteobserver.com/news/politics-government/article167364607. html#storylink=cp

14 I steal the phrase acts of activism from Madison (2010, 2012).

15 Cohen-Cruz (2005, p. 1) expands Corey's examples to include such community-based performances as public protests, skits at union halls, rallies, ritual, dance, music making and public theatre.

16 Written by Willie Nelson, 1981, Columbia.

17 Consider the racist Indian insults Jeff Bridges directs to his half-Comanche, half-Mexican deputy (Gil Birmingham) in the recently released neo-western, Come Hell or High Water (2016).

    Bridges: "Who invented soccer, them Aztecs? Kickin' around skulls, must be a Comanche sport. Your gonna miss me Alberto when I'm gone."

    Albert: "God I hope its tomorrow."

2   The call to performance[1]

Apples and oranges, are these different tasks, or different sides of the same coin? C. Wright Mills and Holman Jones want to re-write history. Anderson wants to improve autoethnography by using analytic reflexivity. Ellis wants to embed the personal in the social. Spry's (2011) self-narratives critique the social situatedness of identity (see also Adams 2011). Neumann (1996) wants to "democratize the representational sphere of culture" by writing outward from the self to the social (p. 186). So do I.

I want to turn the autoethnographic project into a critical, performative practice, a practice that begins with the biography of the writer and moves outward to culture, discourse, history and ideology. Interpretive auto-ethnography allows the researcher to take up each person's life in its immediate particularity and to ground the life in its historical moment. We move back and forth in time, using a critical interpretive method, a version of Sartre's (1963, pp. 85–166) progressive-regressive method. Interpretation works forward to the conclusion of a set of acts taken up by the subject, while working back in time, interrogating the historical, cultural and biographical conditions that moved the person to experience the events being studied (Denzin 2001 p. 41).

With Sartre, there is a political component to interpretive autoethnography, a commitment to a social justice agenda – to inquiry that explicitly addresses issues of inequity and injustice in particular social moments and places.

In this chapter I want to connect the dots between lives, performance, representation, epiphany and interpretation. I weave my narrative through family stories. I conclude with thoughts concerning a performance-centered pedagogy, and the directions, concerns and challenges for autoethnography.

Epiphanies and the sting of memory

The subject matter of interpretive autoethnographic research is meaningful bio-graphical experience (Pelias 2011; Tamas 2011). Interpretive studies are organized in terms of a biographically meaningful event or moment in a subject's life (Poulos 2008; Ulmer 1989). This event, the epiphany, how it is experienced, how it is defined, and how it is woven through the multiple strands of a person's life, constitutes the focus of critical interpretive inquiry (Denzin 2001).

The biographical project begins with personal history, with the sting of childhood memory, with an event that lingers and remains in the person's life story (Ulmer 1989, p. 209). Autoethnography re-tells and re-performs these life experiences. The life story becomes an invention, a re-presentation, an historical object often ripped or torn out of its contexts and recontextualized in the spaces and understandings of the story.

In writing an autoethnographic life story, I create the conditions for rediscovering the meanings of a past sequence of events (Ulmer 1989, p. 211). In so doing, I create new ways of performing and experiencing the past. To represent the past this way does not mean to "recognize it 'the way it really was.' It means to seize hold of a memory as it flashes up at a moment of danger" (Benjamin 1969a, p. 257), to see and re-discover the past not as a succession of events, but as a series of scenes, inventions, emotions, images and stories (Ulmer 1989, p. 112).

In bringing the past into the autobiographical present, I insert myself into the past and create the conditions for rewriting and hence re-experiencing it. History becomes a montage, moments quoted out of context, "juxtaposed fragments from widely dispersed places and times" (Ulmer 1989, p. 112). Thus are revealed hidden features of the present as well of the past. I want to invent a new version of the past, a new history. This is what interpretive autoethnography does. Here is an example, an excerpt from an on-going project (Denzin 2005, 2008, 2011, 2013a, 2013b, 2015a, 2015b).

Scene One: The past: docile Indians

VOICE 1: NARRATOR-AS-YOUNG-BOY: When I was little, in the 1940s, living in south central Iowa, my grandmother would tell stories about Indians. She loved to tell the story about the day a tall Indian brave with braided hair came to her mother's kitchen door and asked for some bread to eat. This happened when Grandma was a little girl, probably around 1915.

VOICE 2: GRANDMOTHER: This Indian was so polite and handsome. Mother said his wife and children stood right behind him in a straight row. The Indian said his name was Mr. Thomas. He was a member of the Fox Indian Nation. He said that he and his wife and his children were traveling to the Mesquaki Reservation near Tama, Iowa, to visit relatives. Mother believed him. He said that they had run out of money and did not like to ask for hand-outs, but this looked like a friendly farm house. Mother said it is a crime in this country to be hungry! I believe that, too!

VOICE 3: GRANDMOTHER-AS-YOUNG-DAUGHTER: Mother made lunch for Mr. Thomas and his family. They sat under the big oak tree in the front yard and had a picnic. Later, when they were leaving, Mr. Thomas came back to the kitchen and thanked Mother again. He gave her a small hand-woven wicker basket as a gift. I treasure to this day this basket. It has become a family heirloom.

Scene Two: Real Indians

VOICE 4: NARRATOR-AS-YOUNG-BOY: When I was not yet ten one Sunday Mother and Dad took my brother and me to Tama, to the Mesquaki Fox Indian Reservation, to see a Pow Wow. I wondered if we'd see Mr. Thomas, if I would even recognize him if he was there. We walked through the mud, past teepees to the center of a big field. Indians in ceremonial dress with paint on their faces and long braids of hair were singing and dancing. Some were drumming and singing. At the edge of the field tables under canvas tents were set up. Dad bought some Indian fry bread for all of us, and bottles of cold root beer. We took the fry bread and pop back to the dance area and watched the dancers. Then it rained and the dancing stopped, and we got in the car and drove home.

Scene Three: Made-for-movie Indians

VOICE 5: NARRATOR-AS-YOUNG-BOY: The next time I saw an Indian was the following Saturday night when grandpa took me to a movie at the Strand Theater in Iowa City. We watched *Broken Arrow* with Jay Silverheels, Jimmy Stewart, Debra Paget, Will Geer and Jeff Chandler, who played Chief Cochise. Those Indians did not look like the Indians on the Tama Reservation. The Tama Indians were less real. They kind of looked like everybody else, except for the dancers in their ceremonial dress.

The sting of memory

By revisiting the past through remembered experiences I insert myself in my family's history with Native Americans. This history is part of a deeper set of mid-century memories about Indians, reservations, life on the Midwest plains and American culture. As I narrate these experiences, I begin to understand that I, along with my family, am a participant in this discourse. I am a player in a larger drama, performing the parts culture gives to young white males. From the vantage of the present I can look back with a critical eye on those family performances, but the fact of my participation in them remains. We turned Native Americans into exotic cultural objects. We helped them perform non-threatening versions of Indian-ness, versions that conformed to those tame Indians I watched on the silver screen.

A "mystory" text begins with those moments that define a crisis, a turning point in the person's life. Ulmer (1989) suggests the following starting point:

> Write a mystory bringing into relation your experience with three levels of discourse – personal (autobiography), popular (community stories, oral history or popular culture), [and] expert (disciplines of knowledge). In each case use the punctum or sting of memory to locate items significant to you.
>
> (p. 209)

The sting of memory locates the moment, the beginning. Once located this moment is dramatically described, fashioned into a text to be performed. This moment is then surrounded by those cultural representations and voices that define the experience in question. These representations are contested, challenged.

The sting of the past. A string of childhood and young adulthood memories: My brother and I are watching *The Lone Ranger*. We are playing cowboys and Indians – I'm Tonto. Thanksgiving, fourth grade, Coralville, Iowa: I'm dressed up as Squanto in the Thanksgiving play; my grandparents are in the audience. Summer 1960: I'm older now, drinking and driving fast down country roads, playing loud country music. I'm a cowboy now, not an Indian. I fall in love with June Carter singing "Ring of Fire." Wedding, Winter 1963: I close my eyes and remember Sunday fish fries along the Iowa River, hayrides and football on Friday night, homecoming dances in the University High School gym, pretty girls in blue sweaters and white bobby socks, tall young men with blue suede shoes, flat top haircuts, Elvis singing "Heart Break Hotel."

I wish I could reach back and hold on to all of this, things I loved then. James Lee Burke (2009) reminds me that the secret is "to hold on to the things you loved, and never give them up for any reason" (p. 274). But did I really love them or was I just afraid to act like I didn't love them? Which self was I performing? Have I really talked myself into giving them up?[2]

I've always been performing, even in front of the black and white TV. The dividing line between person and character, performer and actor, stage and setting, script and text, performance and reality has disappeared, if it ever existed. For a moment I was Tonto, and then I was Squanto. Illusion and make-believe prevail, we are who we are through our performative acts. Nothing more, nothing less.

Process and performance

The emphasis on self, biography, history and experience must always work back and forth between three concerns: the concerns of performance, of process, and/or of analysis. A focus on performance produces performance texts, the tale and the telling, like the narrative above. A focus on process examines a social form, or event, for example epiphanies. The focus on analysis looks at the specific lives of individuals who live the process that is being studied in order to locate their lives in their historical moment.

Building on Pollock (2006), Madison (2006, 2012), and Thompson (1978), interpretive, biographical materials may be presented in four different ways. First, complex, multi-leveled performance texts may be written, staged and performed, for example the performance narratives assembled by Pelias (1998, 2004, 2011).

Second, following Spry (2006, 2011) single personal experience narratives may be presented and connected to the life-story of a given individual. Spry (2006) writes that after she lost her son in childbirth,

> Things fell apart. The shadowlands of grief became my unwanted field of study. ... After losing our son in childbirth, writing felt like the identification

of body parts, as if each described piece of the experience were a cumbersome limb that I could snap off my body and lay upon the ground.

(pp. 340–341)

Third, a collection of self and personal experience stories may be collected and grouped around a common theme. Stewart (2005) does this in her essay on cultural poeisis. She records and performs episodes from mundane, everyday life, including making trips to daycare, the grocery store and picking the sick dog up at the vet.

My story, then, is not an exercise in representation ...
Rather it is a cabinet of curiosities designed to excite curiosity.

(p. 1040)

Fourth, the researcher can offer a cross-case analysis of the materials that have been collected, paying more attention to the process being studied than to the persons whose lives are embedded in those processes. Glaser and Strauss (1964) did this in their famous analysis of the awareness contexts (open, closed, suspicion, pretense) that surround death and dying in the modern hospital.

It is recommended that interpretive autoethnographic studies be sensitive to each of the above modes of presentation. Because any individual can tell multiple stories about his or her life, it must be understood that a life will consist of multiple narratives. No self, or personal experience story will encompass all of the stories that can – or could – be told about a single life, nor will any personal history contain all of the self-stories that could be told about that life's story. Multiple narratives, drawn from the self-stories of many individuals located in different points in the process being interpreted, can be secured. This triangulation, or combination of biographical methods, insures that performance, process, analysis, history and structure receive fair and thorough consideration in any inquiry. The interpreter always works outward from the epiphany to those sites where memory, history, structure and performance intersect, the spaces of Tami Spry's "performative-I" (2006, p. 340; see also Madison 2012). These are performances that interrupt and critique hegemonic structures of meaning (Spry 2011, p. 35).

Interpretive assumptions

A life refers to the biographical experiences of a named person. A person is a cultural creation. Every culture, for example, has names for different types of persons: male, female, husband, wife, daughter, son, professor, student and so forth. These names are attached to persons. Persons build biographies and identities around the experiences associated with these names, (that is, old man, young man, divorced woman, only daughter, only son and so on).

These experiences have effects at two levels in a person's life. On the *surface level*, effects are unremarkable, barely felt. They are taken-for-granted and are non-problematic, as when a person buys a newspaper at the corner grocery.

Effects at the *deep level* cut to the inner core of the person's life and leave indelible marks on him or her. These are the *epiphanies* of a life. Interpretive researchers attempt to secure self and personal experience stories that deal with events – mundane and remarkable – that have effects at the deep level of a person's life.

Experience can only be studied through performance (Bruner 1986, p. 6). However, what counts as experience or performance is shaped by a politics of representation, and hence is "neither self-evident nor straight-forward: it is always contested and always therefore political" (Scott 1993, p. 412), shaped by matters of race, class, gender, sexuality and age. Representations of experience are performative, symbolic and material. Anchored in performance events, they include drama, ritual, and storytelling.

This view of experience and the performative makes it difficult to sustain any distinction between "appearances and actualities" (Schechner 1998, p. 362). Further, if, as Butler (1993, p. 141) reminds us, there are no original performances, then every performance establishes itself performatively as an original, a personal, and locally situated production.

An extended quote from Goffman (1959) summarizes my position.

> The legitimate performances of everyday life
> are not "acted" or "put on" in the sense that the
> performer knows in advance just what he [she]
> is going to do, and does this solely because of the effect
> it is likely to have. The expressions it is felt he [she] is
> giving off will be especially "inaccessible" to him [her] …
> but the incapacity of the ordinary individual to formulate
> in advance the movements of his [her] eyes and body does not mean that he
> [she] will not express him [her] self
> through these devices in a way that is dramatized and
> pre-formed in his [her] repertoire of actions. In short,
> we all act better than we know how.
>
> (pp. 73–74)

Liminality, ritual and the structure of the epiphany

Within and through their performances, persons are moral beings, already present in the world, ahead of themselves, occupied and preoccupied with everyday doings and emotional practices (see Denzin 1984, p. 91). However, the postmodern world stages existential crises. Following Turner (1986a) the autoethnographer gravitates to these narratively structured, liminal, existential spaces in the culture. In these dramaturgical sites people take sides, forcing, threatening, inducing, seducing, cajoling, nudging, loving, living, abusing and killing one another (p. 34). In these sites on-going social dramas occur. These dramas have complex temporal rhythms. They are storied events, narratives that rearrange chronology into multiple and differing forms and layers of meaningful experience (p. 35). They are epiphanies.

The critical autoethnographer enters those strange and familiar situations that connect critical biographical experiences (epiphanies) with culture, history and social structure. He or she seeks out those narratives and stories people tell one another as they attempt to make sense of the epiphanies, or existential turning point moments, in their lives. In such moments persons attempt to take history into their own hands, moving into and through, following Turner (1986a), liminal stages of experience.

Here is an example. Yvonna Lincoln writes about grieving immediately after the attacks on the World Trade Center Towers and the Pentagon on September 11, 2001, "Grief in an Appalachian Register":

> For two weeks now, we have watched the staggering outpouring of grief, shock and horror as a nation struggles to come to terms with the attacks.... And I, too, have sat numb with shock, glued to the television screen, struggling with the incomprehensibility of these acts, overwhelmed by the bewildering world view which could have led people to commit such atrocities. But I have been numb for another reason, and it will be important to see my reasons as another part of the phenomenon which has struck so deeply at the heart and soul of the United States. I sat numb because my reactions to grief are always usually private. They are always delayed. ...
>
> My people – my family (of English and Dutch and Scottish stock) were born and raised, as were their parents before them, in the southern Appalachian mountains. ... Mountain people ... keep their emotions to themselves, especially those of a most private nature.... The end result, I have come to realize, is a human being who lives with his or her grief for all their days. The future, like tears, never comes.
>
> (Lincoln and Denzin 2003, p. 147)

Epiphanies, like reactions to September 11, are experienced as social dramas, as dramatic events with beginnings, middles and endings. Epiphanies represent ruptures in the structure of daily life.[3] Turner (1986a) reminds us that the theatre of social life is often structured around a four-fold processual ritual model involving *breach, crisis, redress, reintegration* or *schism* (p. 41). Each of these phases is organized as a ritual; thus there are rituals of breach, crisis, redress, reintegration and schism. Americans sought rituals of reintegration after 9/11, ways of overcoming the shocks of breach, crisis and disintegration.

Many rituals and epiphanies are associated with life-crisis ceremonies, "particularly those of puberty, marriage, and death" (Turner 1986b, p. 41). Turner contends that redressive and life-crisis rituals "contain within themselves a liminal phase, which provides a stage ... for unique structures of experience" (p. 41). The liminal phase of experience is a kind of no-person's land, on the edge of what is possible (Broadhurst 1999), "betwixt and between the structural past and the structural future" (Turner 1986a, p. 41).[4]

Epiphanies are ritually structured liminal experiences connected to moments of breach, crisis, redress, reintegration and schism, crossing from one space to another.

The storied nature of epiphanic experiences continually raises the following questions: Whose story is being told (and made) here? Who is doing the telling? Who has the authority to make their telling stick (Smith 1990)? As soon as a chronological event is told in the form of a story it enters a text-mediated system of discourse where larger issues of power and control come into play (Smith 1990). In this text-mediated system new tellings occur. The interpretations of original experience are now fitted to this larger interpretive structure (Smith 1990).

The reflexive performance text contests the pull of traditional "realist" theatre and modernist ethnography wherein performers, and ethnographers, re-enact and recreate a "recognizable verisimilitude of setting, character and dialogue" (Cohn 1988, p. 815), where dramatic action reproduces a linear sequence, a "mimetic representation of cause and effect" (Birringer 1993, p. 196). An evocative epistemology demands a postmodern performance aesthetic that goes beyond "the already-seen and already-heard" (p. 186). This aesthetic criticizes the ideological and technological requirements of late-capitalist social realism and hyperrealism (p. 175).

Performances must always return to the lived body (Garoian 1999). The body's dramaturgical presence is "a site and pretext for ... debates about representation and gender, about history and postmodern culture" (Birringer 1993, p. 203). At this level, performance autoethnography answers to Trinh's (1991) call for works that seek the truth of life's fictions, where experiences are evoked, not explained (p. 162). The performer seeks a presentation that, like good fiction, is true in experience, but not necessarily true to experience (Lockford 1998, p. 216).

The body in performance is blood, bone, muscle, movement. "The performing body constitutes its own interpretive presence. It is the raw material of a critical cultural story. The performed body is a cultural text embedded in discourses of power" (Spry 2011, pp. 18–19). The performing body disrupts the status quo, uncovers "the understory of hegemonic systems" (p. 20).

Whether the events performed actually occurred is tangential to the larger project (Lockford 1998, p. 216). As dramatic theatre, with connections to Brecht (Epic Theatre) and Artaud (Theatre of Cruelty), these performance texts turn tales of suffering, loss, pain and victory into evocative performances that have the ability to move audiences to reflective, critical action, not only emotional catharsis (on Brecht's theatre, see Benjamin 1969b).[5]

The performed text is lived experience, and lived experiences in two senses (Pelias 1998). The performance doubles back on the experiences previously represented in the writer's text. It then re-presents those experiences as an embodied performance. It thus privileges immediate experience, the evocative moment when another's experiences come alive for performers and audiences alike. One way the performed text is given narrative meaning in interpretive autoethnography is through the mystory.

Mystory as montage

The mystory – for example, the excerpts from my family story earlier in this chapter – is simultaneously a personal mythology, a public story, a personal narrative and a performance that critiques. It is an interactive, dramatic performance. It is participatory theatre, a performance, not a text-centered interpretive event; that is, the emphasis is on performance, and improvisation, and not on the reading of a text.

The mystory is a montage text, cinematic and multi-media in shape, filled with sounds, music, poetry and images taken from the writer's personal history. This personal narrative is grafted into discourses from popular culture. It locates itself against the specialized knowledges that circulate in the larger society. The audience co-performs the text, and the writer, as narrator, functions as a guide, a commentator, a co-performer.

Focusing on epiphanies and liminal moments of experience, the writer imposes a narrative framework on the text. This framework shapes how experience will be represented. It uses the devices of plot, setting, characters, characterization, temporality, dialogue, protagonists, antagonists – showing, not telling. The narration may move through Turner's four-stage dramatic cycle, emphasizing breach, crisis, redress, reintegration or schism.

Jameson (1990) reminds us that works of popular culture are always already ideological and utopian. Shaped by a dialectic of anxiety and hope, such works revive and manipulate fears and anxieties about the social order. Beginning with a fear, problem or crisis, these works move characters and audiences through the familiar three-stage dramatic model of conflict, crisis and resolution. In this way they offer kernels of utopian hope. They show how these anxieties and fears can be satisfactorily addressed by the existing social order. Hence, the audience is lulled into believing that the problems of the social have in fact been successfully resolved.

The mystory occupies a similar ideological space, except it functions as critique. The mystory is also ideological and utopian, it begins from a progressive political position stressing the politics of hope. The mystory uses the methods of performance and personal narrative to present its critique and utopian vision. It presumes that the social order has to change if problems are to be successfully resolved in the long run. If the status quo is maintained, if only actors, and not the social order, change, then the systemic processes producing the problem remain in place. We are left then with just our stories.

Staging lives

In the summer of 1953 I was twelve and my brother Mark was eight. This was the summer my parents divorced for the first time. This was also the summer my father joined Alcoholics Anonymous. Mark and I were spending the summer on the farm with Grandpa and Grandma.

This was the summer
of the Joseph McCarthy Hearings
on television, black and white screens.
Eisenhower was president,
Nixon was his vice-president.

This was the summer Grandpa bought the first family TV.
In the afternoons
we watched the McCarthy Hearings,
and each evening
we had a special show to watch:
Ed Sullivan on Sundays,
Milton Berle and Cardinal Sheen on Mondays,
Norman Vincent Peale and Pat Boone on Tuesday.
This was the summer my parents
divorced for the first time.
This was the summer my father's life started to fall apart.
I look today at the face of Joseph McCarthy
in George Clooney's movie, *Good Night and Good Luck*,
a scared lonely man,
Clooney's movie tells me McCarthy died from alcoholism.

***

I thought of that summer of 1953, and Clooney's movie as I was going through Dad's scrapbook. The pictures are all from the late 1940s and early 1950s. Mark and I were little and living with Grandpa and Grandma. Mother and Dad lived in Coralville, just outside Iowa City. Dad was a county agent for the Farm Bureau, and Mother kept house and was ill a lot.

I think this is when Dad's drinking
started to get out of hand.
He'd work late, come home drunk.
Some nights friends from work drove him home.
Mother and Dad had put knotty pine siding
on the walls of the family rec room,
which was in the basement of our new house.
Dad built a bar,
And mother got cocktail glasses, a blender,
shot glasses, glass coasters –
really fancy stuff.
On the weekends men from the insurance agency
brought their wives over,
and the house was filled with smoke, laughter,
and Benny Goodman and Harry James
on a little Philco phonograph.

Fats Domino was on the jukeboxes
Singing "Ain't That a Shame" and "Blueberry Hill."
Mother was drinking pretty heavily.
She liked manhattans and maraschino cherries.
Dad drank Pabst Blue Ribbon (a "Blue"),
and straight shots of Jim Beam whiskey.

***

Around this time the Communist scare had gotten all the way to Iowa City. World War III was on the horizon. The John Birch Society was gaining strength. *This Is Your FBI, The Lone Ranger, The Shadow* and *Inner Sanctum* were popular radio and TV shows. We were all learning how to be imaginary consumers in this new culture: Gillette Blue Blades, Bulova Time, Lava Soap. Life Savers (Dylan 2004).

Citizen Civil Defense Groups were forming.
People were worried about Communists,
and air attacks at night,
atomic bombs going off in big cities.
People started building bomb shelters.
Dad built a shelter in the back yard.
Every town had a Civilian Civil Defense team.
Dad was a team leader,
gone from midnight
until 6:00 in the morning two times a week.
He stood guard with a three other men,
scanning the skies with binoculars and telescopes
looking for low-flying Russian planes.
He would come home drunk.

***

Bob Dylan wrote a song about this post-WWII paranoia: He called it "Talkin' John Birch Paranoid Blues." In it, Eisenhower is a Russian spy.

***

We became an A.A. Family in 1953. The drinking had gone too far. About one year later, Mom and Dad had some A.A. friends out for a cookout on the farm. There was a new couple, Shirley and George. Shirley had black hair like Mom, and she was small and petite. She was wearing an orange dress that flowed all around her knees. Dad set up the archery set behind the lilacs in the side-yard. The men gathered with bows and you could hear the twang of the arrows all the way back in the house. But nobody was very good.

Mom had Pete Fountain and his clarinet playing on the portable record player. Everybody came back in the house, and before you knew it the dining room was filled with dancing couples. Men and women in 1950s dress-up clothes, wide collar shirts, pleated slacks and greased back hair. Women with Mamie Eisenhower bangs, hose, garter belts and high heels.

All of sudden Dad was dancing with Shirley, and Mom was in the kitchen fixing snacks. I thought Dad and Shirley were dancing a little close to just be friends.

***

About a month later our little world changed forever. I came home from high school and found a note from Dad. It was short and read, "I have to leave you. You and Mark are on your own now." I was 18 and Mark was 14.

> Civilian Civil Defense teams,
> Bomb shelters,
> Talking John Birch Society paranoia,
> The CIA, the Cold War, Communists, the Axis of Evil,
> another war, global terror, an out of control right wing government.

***

My father's life segues into this question, "What went wrong with our generation's and our parent's generation's version of the American Dream?" And like in George Clooney's movie, good luck was no longer enough, even if Mamie Eisenhower did wear bangs, just like my grandmother, and even if my father kept the United States safe from the Communists.

Back to the beginning

Today I want to write my way out of this history, and this is why I write my version of autoethnography. I want to push back, intervene, be vulnerable, tell another story; I want to contest what happened (Pelias 2011, p. 12).

I want to return to the memories of my childhood, fish fries along the Iowa River, that Sunday morning when my family visited the Mesquaki Reservation. We were happy that day. Alcoholism had yet not yet hit our little house, but A.A. was not far off. As a family we were slipping. A day on the reservation brought escape from what was coming. Could things have happened differently if my father had stopped drinking on that day? I know my brother and I fought, and we were not grateful. Could my father and mother have recovered a love that day that would have withstood infidelities and drunkenness? Did Indians have anything at all to do with this? Maybe an alternative ending is fruitless, why even try?

***

I think I'm like the narrator in Guy Maddin's 2007 film, *My Winnipeg*.[6] In the film Maddin returns to his family home and rents the house for a month so he can re-do some things that happened in that house when he was twelve years old.[7] He hires actors to play his mother, father, brother and sister. He rents a pet dog. When the month is up, there are still issues that have not been resolved.

***

I could be like Guy Maddin. I'd rent the Iowa farm house for one week, the house where Dad and Shirley danced too close, and I'd have Mom tell Shirley to take her hands off of her husband. Or maybe I'd go back the little house on Coralville and have Dad and Mom pretend that they didn't have to be drinking in order to act as if they loved each other.

Performing the text: writing to change history

The goal is to produce an interruption, a performance text that challenges conventional taken-for granted assumptions about the racialized past. Let's return to Indians, Squanto, Tonto and to my opening scenes with Mr. Thomas and the Fox Reservation. For example, in my current research (Denzin 2008, 2011, 2013) I criticize the representations of Native Americans by such nineteenth century artists as George Catlin and Charles Bird King. I also critically read William Cody's (aka Buffalo Bill) Wild West Shows, which staged performances by Native Americans in Europe and America from 1882 to 1910.

Recurring figures in my narrative include the voices of marginalized Native Americans, including: Ms. Birdie Berdashe,[8] a two-spirit person, an aboriginal dandy, a man who assumes a female gender identity painted by George Catlin; Miss Chief, the drag-queen alter ego of Cree artist Kent Monkman (2007, 2008a, 2008b, 2009, 2010); Lonesome Rider, a gay cowboy; Virile Dandy, a Mandan warrior, close friend of Birdie Berdashe; the LGBT Chorus. These figures literally and figuratively "queer" my text (Adams and Holman Jones 2008, p. 383). These transgressive figures challenge the stereotype of the masculine heterosexual Indian warrior. They refuse to be submissive. Miss Chief and Ms. Birdie bring agency and power to queer Indians who were mocked and ridiculed by Catlin, King and Cody. Imagine these queer Indians dancing on the Fox Reservation.

Here is a sample text. It appears at the end of a four-act play titled "The Traveling Indian Gallery, Part Two." In the play, thirty-five Fox, Iowa and Ojibwe tribe members, along with the LGBT Chorus, Birdie, Miss Chief and Lonesome Rider, contest their place in Catlin's Traveling European Indian Gallery (1843–1846). The play culminates in a play-within-the-play on stage outside the Boudoir Berdashe. Fox Indians, perhaps related to the Fox Indians my brother and I saw dance in the Reservation Pow Wow in 1950, perform in Catlin's play. The excerpt begins with Birdie.

BIRDIE: Before we walk off this stupid stage I want to do a "Dance for the Berdashe." George called it an "unaccountable and ludicrous custom amongst the Sacs and Foxes which admits not of an entire explanation."

(Catlin, 1848, p. 286)

VIRILE DANDY: The dance honors the power of the Berdashe. In his painting, George demeans the Berdashe, contrasting his/her passive femininity with the raw, virile masculinity of the bare-chested male dancers who are wearing loincloths and holding weapons.

NARRATOR: At this point I try to remember back to the Pow Wow. I wonder if we only saw bare-chested warriors waving weapons. What if a young two-spirited Fox was also one of the dancers? Would we have been able to identify him/her and understand his/her place in the tribe's hierarchy of male/female identities?

(Off-stage: "The Hot Club of Cow Town," a Cowboy swing band from Austin, Texas, breaks into a slow dance waltz, "Darling You and I Are Through."[9] At the opposite end of the hall, the "All-Star Sac and Fox Drummer and Dance Band" (from IndigeNow)[10] begins playing a soft blues ballad led by Clyde Roulette (Ojibway), aka Slidin Clyde Roulette, blues guitarist.)[11]

(Stage Directions: The stage is transformed into a dance floor, the lights dim. The members of the LGBT and Indian Show Choruses pair off as couples, men waltz with men, women with women, men with women, children with children. Off come Berdashe masks. Bodies swirl around the dance floor. Virile Dandy dares to take the Queen by her hand and put his arm around her waist, leading her in a two-step waltz across the stage.)

***

In this excerpt the Native American players mock and queer the concept of the straight Indian performing as an Indian for a white Anglo-European audience. They turn the performance event upside down; in so doing they expose and criticize a racist heterosexualist politics buried deep inside the nineteenth century colonizing imaginary. This performance bleeds into the earlier Native American narratives. Surely there were queer or two-spirited Indians on the reservation, but they were not visible to a young white boy on that Sunday in 1950.

Like Guy Maddin I'd try to go back and re-do that Pow Wow. I'd bring in Birdie, Virile Dandy and the LGBT Show Chorus. I'd have Indian vendors sell cheap copies of George Catlin's paintings of Fox Indians. I'd write myself into the storyline and tell my parents that I think we should not go to these kinds of performances.

Working to transgress

The goal with this interpretive work is to create a safe space where writers, teachers and students are willing to take risks, to move back and forth between the personal and the political, the biographical and the historical. In these spaces they perform painful personal experiences. Under this framework we teach one another. We push against racial, sexual and class boundaries in order to achieve the gift of freedom; the gift of love, self-caring; the gift of empowerment, teaching and learning to transgress. We talk about painful experiences, those moments where race, class gender, sexuality intersect. We take these risks because we have created safe space for such performances – from classrooms, to conference sessions, to the pages of journals, and in our books – and the pay-off is so great. We are free in these spaces to explore painful experiences, to move forward into new spaces, into new identities, new relationships, new, radical forms of scholarship, new epiphanies.

This is performance-centered pedagogy that uses performance as a method of investigation, as a way of doing autoethnography, and as a method of understanding. Mystory, performance, ethnodrama and reality theatre are ways of making visible the oppressive structures of the culture – racism, homophobia, sexism (Saldana 2005, 2011). The performance of these autoethnographic dramas becomes a tool for documenting oppression, a method for understanding the meanings of the oppression, and a way of enacting a politics of possibility.

The pedagogical model I offer is collaborative. It is located in a moral community created out of the interactions and experiences that occur inside and outside the walls of the seminar room. In this safe space scholars come together on the terrain of social justice. While this is done in the sacred safe spaces of collaborative discourse, the fear of criticism and misunderstanding is always present. When they occur, we seek pedagogies of forgiveness.

Notes

1 I thank Stacy Holman Jones and Tony Adams who commented on earlier versions of this chapter which draws in materials in Denzin (2013b).
2 This paragraph steals from Burke (2009, p. 274).
3 The next three paragraphs draw from Denzin (2001, pp. 38–39).
4 Clearly Turner offers a traditional Judeo-Christian model of selfhood and change. Non-Western models of self-hood turn this framework upside down.
5 Benjamin (1969b) contends that Brecht's Epic Theater is diadatic and participatory because it "facilitates ... interchange between audience and actors ... and every spectator is enabled to become a participant" (p. 154).
6 Maddin is a well-known Canadian filmmaker. *My Winnipeg* was awarded the prize for Best Canadian Feature Film in 2007.
7 His pet dog died. His sister had a big fight with his mother. His father may have died.
8 My name. An American or First Nation Indian who assumes the dress, social status, and role of the opposite sex (see Califia 1997).

9 From the first album (*Swingin' Stampade*) by the Hot Club of Cowtown, the Texas Jazz/Western Swing Trio from Austin, Texas
10 Compliments of IndigeNOW with Gordon Bronitsky and Associates.
11 Clyde sounds a little like Stevie Ray Vaughan. He recently played with the Neville Brothers in Sioux City, Iowa.

3 Performance pedagogy, culture, politics[1]

A MANIFESTO in the form of an abstract

What you are about to read is not your traditional encyclopedia entry. It is intended to be a subversive, genre busting, manifesto, a call to arms. The structure and content are not conventional. The topic demands nothing less.

I seek ethnographic texts turned into performance events, into ethnodramas, into ethnotheatre, into narrative poems, scripts, short stories, texts with narrators, action, shifting points of view; dramaturgical productions co-performed with audiences; life, narrative and melodrama under the auspices of late neo-liberal capitalism.

I seek a new genealogy. Autoethnography is easily confused with other terms. It is not: ethnography, autobiography, biography, personal narrative, personal history, life history, life story or personal experience story. It is not analytic, nor is it deeply theoretical. It is more then personal writing or cultural critique. It is more than performance. But it is performative. It is transgressive. It is resistance. It is dialogical. It is ethical. It is political, personal, embodied, collaborative, imaginative, artistic, creative, a form of intervention, a plea for social justice.

It is clear that performance autoethnography is a blurred genre. It is many things at the same time. It bends and twists the meanings of ethnography, ethnographer and performance. There is no separation between the writer, the ethnographer, the performer and the world. Performance autoethnography makes the writer's self visible through performance, through performance writing, through the writer's presence in the world. Performance autoethnographers are committed to changing the world one word, one performance at a time. The community is global.

In the beginning

But where to begin? There are at least six models of performance in the ethnography- theatrical paradigm (see Conquergood in Johnson 2013, pp. 56–57): (1) Conquergood's notion of fieldwork as performance, as poiesis, as a dialogic relationship based on co-witnessing between researcher and researched; (2)

Goffman's mimetic all the world's a stage model. All social interaction is staged and a performance. Backstage, people prepare for their performances, which are shaped by ritual rules. They confront others by wearing masks (Turner 1986b, p. 74). (3) In contrast, Turner's performance as kinesis, as "making, not faking" (1982, p. 93), performances as dramas that occur in very specific situations defined by conflict, performance as moral events that move through the four phases (breach, crisis, redress, reintegration) outlined above. (4) Schechner's notion of performance as restored, or twice-behaved behaviors (2013, p. 28); (5) Madison's critical ethnography which is based on a dialogical performance model where the performative I is vehicle for enacting a radial politics of resistance; (6) Saldana's ethnotheatre performances are very narrowly defined, embodied, artistic works presented to an audience.

These performance models rest on distinctly different [auto] ethnographic materials and lead to distinctly different forms of performance, ethnography and theatre.

But what is performance? What is theatre? What is ethnography? The essence of theatre, Boal reminds us, is the human being observing itself. *The human being not only "makes" theatre: it is theatre* (1995, p. 13, italics in original) What does performing mean? Is all of social life a performance? Are we all performers presenting and performing selves to one another in everyday life, putting on first one mask and then another, engaging in endless rounds of impression management (Goffman 1959)? Are we only the characters we play?

Madison reminds us,

> if we accept the notion of human beings as *homo performans* and therefore as a performing species, performance becomes necessary for our survival. That is we recognize and create ourselves as Others through performance ... in this process culture and performance become inextricably interconnected and performance is a constant presence in our daily lives.
>
> (Madison 2012, p. 166, quote is paraphrase)

Boal says we became human when we invented theatre (1995, p; 14). As homo performan I engage the world as a performative-I, as an embodied, moving reflective being. I establish my presence as a universal singular, an embodied self interacting with culture/history/society in the lived present (Spry 2011, p. 53).

Autoethnographer as performer

Performance matters for [auto] ethnography. Conquergood states:

> with renewed appreciation for boundaries, border-crossings, process, improvisation, contingency, multiple identities, and the embodied nature of fieldwork practice, many ethnographers have turned to a performance-inflected vocabulary
>
> (2006, p. 358)

As if anticipating Madison and Conquergood, Turner (1986b, p. 81), like Goffman, appropriates the language of drama and performance. Ethnographers become methodological actors who creatively play, improvise, interpret, re-present roles and enact scripts in concrete field settings. The [auto]ethnographer is a co-performer in a social drama, a participant in rhetorically framed cultural performances, enacting rituals, writing fieldnotes, recording interviews, video-taping, observing, talking, doing the things ethhnographers do (Conquergood 2006, p. 360; Atkinson 2015).

Schechner clarifies. The "relationship between studying performance and doing performance is integral. One performs fieldwork, which is subject to the 'rehearsal process' of improvising, testing and revising and no position is neutral. The performance scholar is actively involved in advocacy:" (Schechner 2013, p. 4, paraphrase).

Conquergood again, describing a moment in his fieldwork in Big Red, a dilapidated nonwhite tenement in Chicago where he lived for 20 months, starting in December 1987. Here Dwight gets caught up between being Dwight and being Dwight the ethnographer:

> At 10:00 A.M. on August 16, 1988, Bao Xiang, a Hmong woman From Laos, stepped out the back door of her top-floor Big Red apartment and the rotting porch collapsed beneath her feet. All summer long I had swept away slivers of wood that had fallen from the Xiong's decrepit porch onto mine, one floor below. Six families were intimately affected by Bao Xiong's calamity. We shared the same front entrance and stairwell. Our back porches were structurally interlocked within a shaky wooden framework of open landings and sagging staircases that cling precariously to the red-brick exterior of the Chicago tenement. Within minutes of arriving home on that day, I heard multiple versions of the story.
>
> (Conquergood 1992b, pp. 170–171)

A young Mexican mother told him how her wash had been ruined by the dust and falling debris. A Puerto Rican grandmother worried about the safety of her grandchildren. Seeking to understand why the porch collapsed at that precise moment when she stepped out her back door, Bai Xiong consulted with a Hmong shaman who lived in another wing of Big Red – "Oh-h-h, very, very scared. Why me?"– (p. 171).

A performance-centered ethnographic approach is participatory, intimate, precarious, embodied, grounded in circumstance, situational identities and historical process. The [auto]ethnographer's body is anchored in time and place. The ethnographer engages in face-work that is "part of the intricate and nuanced dramaturgy of everyday life" (Conquergood 2006, p. 359; Goffman 1959). The power dynamic of inquiry moves from the gaze of the detached observer, to the interactions, the give-and-take between situated actors. Performance-sensitive ethnography strains to produce situated understandings, ethnodramas, performance events that make the injustices in the world socially visible. Through cultural performances persons participate in public life, in vital discussions central to their communities (Conquergood 2006, p. 360). The performance autoethnographer works in those dialogic space where bodies selves, and emotions interact.

The performance autoethnographer is not studying the other, per se. She is reflexively writing herself into her performance text, into those spaces where she intersects with the other. Her primary interests are showing, not telling, social justice, critical reflexivity, interpretation and ethically responsible inquiry (Madison 2012, p. x). She makes this world visible through her performative acts.

Defining terms

Performance autoethnography is defined by a commitment to a politics of resistance, to a commitment to change, not just interpret the world. Performance autoethnography addresses the structures and beliefs of neoliberalism as a public pedagogy, understanding that the cultural is always political (Giroux 2014b, p. 222). The political is always performative. The performative is always pedagogical. To perform, to write is to resist. Moral witnessing, civic courage, and moral outrage are sustained forms of resistance (Giroux 2014b, p. 223).

Here is Anzaldua on the politics of performance along the US Mexico border. These words could have been written yesterday:

> The border Patrol hides behind the local McDonalds on the outskirts of Brownsville, Texas ... They set traps along the river beneath the bridge. Hunters in army-green uniforms stalk and track these economic refugees using the powerful nightvision of electronic sensing devices. Cornered by headlights, frisked, their arms stretched over their heads, *los mojados* are handcuffed, locked in jeeps, and then kicked back across the border, no home, just the thin edge of barbwire.
>
> (Anzaldua 1987, p. 12–13 paraphrase)

"Refugees in a homeland that does not want them, " wetbacks, no welcoming hand, only pain, suffering, humiliation, degradation, death (Turner 1986b, p. 12). South of the Border, down Mexico way, North America's rubbish dump, no direction home (p. 11).

Toward a performative ethnography

Thinking the world as performance raises questions that can be clustered around six intersecting planes analysis.[2] Each plane is predicated on the proposition that if we are all performers, and the world is a performance, not a text, then we need a model of inquiry which is simultaneously political, reflexive, rhetorical and performative. This means it is necessary to rethink the relationship between politics, the performative I and:

** performance, pedagogy and rhetorical reflexivity;
** performance and cultural process;
** performance and ethnographic praxis;
** performance and hermeneutics;
** performance and the act of scholarly representation;
** performance after the affective (new materialism) turn.

Performance, pedagogy and rhetoric

The rhetorical/pedagogical turn in performance studies interrogates the ways in which the performance text functions as an ideological document. Key terms include:

> Pedagogy: To teach, to instruct, the pedagogical is ideological. Spectacle: A performative relationship between people, images and events (Garoian and Gaudelius 2008, p. 24). Spectacle Pedagogy: The staging of media events using the visual codes of corporate, global capitalism (Garoian and Gaudelius 2008, p. 24). Critical Spectacle Pedagogy: A pedagogical practice that reflexively critiques the apparatuses of global capital (Garoian and Gaudelius 2008, pp. 24, 75; also Debord 1967/1994; Evans and Giroux 2015).

This performance paradigm travels from theories of critical pedagogy to views of performance as intervention, interruption and resistance. Critical indigenous performance theatre contributes to utopian discourses by staging doubly inverted minstrel performances. Using ventriloquized discourse, and the apparatuses of minstrel theatre, white-and-black face performers force spectators to confront themselves

Native Canadian whiteface performers in Daniel David Moses's play, *Almighty Voice and His Wife* (1992)[3] use these devices to turn the tables on whites. Just before the play's finale, the Interlocutor, dressed in top hat and tails, along with white gloves and studded white boots turns and taunts the audience.

INTERLOCUTOR: You're the redskin! You're the wagon burner! That feather
    Head, Chief Bullshit. No Chief Shitting Bull! Oh, no, no.
    Bloodthirsty savage. Yes, you're the primitive. Uncivilized
    A cantankerous cannibal …You are the alcoholic, diseased,
    dirty … degenerate.

(quoted in Gilbert 2003, p. 693)

Here critical spectacle pedagogy confronts the racist discourse defining First Nation and Native American persons. The language itself makes a spectacle of phrases like No Chief Shitting Bull. It brings the racism directly in front of the reader, it stages the racism in the here and now of the present.

Critical pedagogy understands performance as a form of inquiry. It views performance as a form of activism, as critique, as critical citizenship. It seeks a form of performative praxis that inspires and empowers persons to act on their utopian impulses. These moments are etched in history and popular memory. They are often addressed in testimonial and fact-based (and verbatim) theatre, theatre which bears witness to social injustice and encourages active ethical spectatorship.

Moises Kaufman, and his oral history play, The Laramie Project (2001),[4] is illustrative. He observes:

> There are moments in history when a particular event brings the various ideologies and beliefs prevailing in a culture into deep focus. At these junctures the event becomes a lightning rod of sorts, attracting and distilling the essence of these philosophies and convictions. By paying careful attention in moments like this to people's words, one is able to hear the way these prevailing ideas affect not only individual lives but also the culture at large.
>
> The trial of Oscar Wilde was such an event ... The Brutal murder of Matthew Shephard (1976–1998) was another event of this kind.
>
> (Kaufman 2014, p. ix)[5]

Spectacle pedagogy addresses these moments, those lightening rod occasions when power, ideology and politics come crushing down on ordinary people and their lives. It does so by staging and re-staging performances which interrogate the cultural logics of the spectacle itself. Staged performances of culture are always appraisal of culture (Madison 2010, p. 13) These re-stagings raise a series of questions asking always, "How did this happen? What does it mean? How could it have been prevented? What are its consequences for the lives of ordinary people?" (Madison 2010, pp. 12–13).

To answer these questions Kaufman's Laramie Project enlisted the help of Laramie citizens in the production of the play's script:

KAUFMAN: We devoted two years of our lives to this Project. We returned to Laramie many times over the course of a year and a half and conducted more than two hundred interviews (Kaufman 2001, p. vii).

When the project was completed, a member of the community reflected on the Shepard death and the play:

JONAS SLONAKER: Change is not an easy thing, and I don't think people were up to it here. They got what they wanted. Those two boys got what they deserve and we look good now. Justice has been served ... You know it has been a year since Matthew Shepard died, and they haven't passed shit in Wyoming ... at a state level, any town, nobody anywhere, has passed any kind of laws or hate crime legislation. ...What's come out of it? (p. 99).

A community member replies:

DOC O'CONNOR: I been up to that site (where he was killed). I remembered to myself the night he and I drove around together, he said to me, "Laramie sparkles, it?" ... I can just picture what he was seeing. The last thing he saw in this earth was the sparkling lights (p. 99).

And as Kaufman's little theatre group left Laramie, for the last time, a member commented:

ANDY PARIS: And in the distance I could see the sparkling lights of Laramie, Wyoming (p. 101).

Matthew's legacy, the pure, sparkling lights of Laramie, what a town could be.
Critics have argued that Kaufman's play smooths over the raw edges of homophobia in Laramie. Taken out of context, the play, as Pollock notes, reads a bit like a version of Our Town,[6] but this impression may be due, in part to the effect "of repeated productions in communities across the United States in which the original actors/interviewers are re/displaced by actors playing inter-viewer/actors" (Pollock 2005, p. 6). This puts the representations of the Laramie and the murder "at one further remove from the reality of the audience members who might otherwise identify with the members of the Tectonic Theater as people-like-themselves" (p. 6).
Being further removed speaks directly to the relationship between repre-sentation, performance and reality, that is "actual" events. Paraphrasing Pollock (2005 pp. 2–3), too many representations of living history try to collapse reality and representation. The goal is to give the impression that "you were there." But that is only an ideological construction, a modernist realist myth which ignores the politics of representation.
The goal is to use critical pedagogy as the means to disrupt, expose and critique these structures of injustice. The stage becomes the site of resistance, the place where performative-I's confront and engage one another.
Paraphrasing Conquergood:

The aim of performance is to bring self and other, the performative-I and the audience together so they can question, debate, and challenge one another. The performance resists conclusions. It is open-ended. It is com-mitted to creating and keeping a dialogue ongoing. It is more like a hyphen, than a period.

(2013, p. 75, paraphrase)

Madison elaborates:

Performance involves seeing ourselves and showing ourselves to ourselves in a way that allows you to understand something new about who you are, it is a doubling, a kind of meta-narrative, performing performances of our inner and outer lives. For fieldwork performance there is another kind of performance going on as a result of invoking the nonfiction of other people's stories and vulnerabilities.

(2005, p. 146, paraphrase)

A goal is to bring the audience into this space so they can co-experience this doubling, this meta-narrative and apply it to their own lives.

Critical spectacle pedagogy in action

Picture the following scene. Bourbon Street, New Orleans, November 1985. A funeral and eulogy for the Free Southern Theatre.[7]

> A black man, fringed, red, white and blue umbrella held high overhead leads Free Southern Theatre members down Bourbon Street. They are carrying a casket and they are on their way to a funeral and an eulogy. African American musicians play brass and percussion. Theatre members place old costumes, props, and scripts into the coffin which also contains a broken mirror. They are mourning the demise of the theatre. The funeral party moves to Armstrong Park in front of Perseverance Hall II in Congo Square. The band plays "Just a Closer Walk with Thee." The casket is lowered into the grave.
>
> (Cohen-Cruz 2005, p. 60, paraphrase)

Caron Atlas, who was present at the funeral, describes the event's impact:

> The funeral told me there was another way that art and politics connected with activism that went beyond artists as constituents. Here was theatre tied to a social movement. Community-based theatre companies[8] inspired by the Free Southern were challenged to ask, how do you do this with your own people, within your own context and culture.
>
> (quoted in Cohen-Cruz 2005, p. 61)

Performers, audiences, a stage, death, mourning, music, community, critical pedagogy, bodies acting together in the service of social change. Civil rights on the move.

Rhetorical reflexivity, as Conquergood notes, troubles the assumption that the world out there can be easily moved into a written text. There is always a gap between studying others where they are and representing them where they aren't (2006, p. 364). The flesh-and-blood subject cannot just be plunked down in a text through the use of quotations from fieldnotes. We cannot speak for the other, and they have only a complicated, compromised presence outside our text. A critical performative reflexivity turns back on itself.

Ellis provides an example:

> As I reconstruct and revise a portion of my life-story, I seek to provide a framework that marks and holds the scenes in place, one that moves from beginning to end, and circles back to the beginning again. My goal is to model a way to reflectively make sense of experience... As an auto-ethnographer I am both the author and focus of the story, the one who tells and the one who experiences, the observer and the observed ... an ethno-grapher and ... a storyteller.
>
> (2009, p. 13)

Multiple identities circulate in Ellis's text: ethnographer, autoethnographer, observer, subject, storyteller, narrator, the composer of a life story worth telling a life worth living (p. 13).

Spry (2011, p. 35) extends the discussion, explicitly focusing on critical performances that interrupt, and challenge exiting structures of power:

> In performative autoethnography the heart, body, mind, spirit et al are openly and critically reflective; as such, epistemologies of pain and of hope often emerge.

Autoethnography is not an innocent practice.

Performance, cultural process, politics

All pragmatists and performance ethnographers who have read Dewey would agree with the second pair, culture is a verb, a process, an on-going performance, not a noun, or a product or a static thing. We cannot study cultural experience directly. We study experience in its performative representations, staged performances of culture. Experience has no existence apart from the storied acts of the performative-I (Pollock 2007, p 240). Performance becomes a tactic, a form of advocacy, of resistance, a cry for human rights and social justice. Madison (2010, p. 9) provides an example, an imaginary scene in a death camp?[9]

> A death camp in Treblinka. A dancer stands naked in line waiting for her turn to enter the gas chamber. We see a human being with a natural power to command space reduced to a body taking up space, passively submitting to the prospect of death. A guard tells her to step in line and dance. She does, and carried away by her *authoritative action* and by her *repossession of self and a world* she dances up to the guard and – now within the compass of her space – takes his gun and shoots him. What a surprise, a zombie-like creature can spring back to like by means of a performance.

The dancer is moved, carried away by the forces of performance and justice to enact the unimaginable (Madison 2010, p. 10).

Performance and ethnographic praxis

The third cluster brings the performative-I, performance and ethnographic praxis into play, highlighting the methodological implications of thinking about fieldwork as a collaborative process, or a co-performance (Conquergood 1991, p. 190). The observer and the observed, the writer and the subject are co-performers or dueoethnographers in a performance event (Norris and Sawyer 2012) Dueoethnographers enter a collaborative relationship with the other in order to learn about themselves. The writer and the other co-construct inquiry as a site of resistance (Norris and Sawyer 2012, p. 10). This allows collaborative narratives of resistance to be constructed. Ethnographic praxis is a performance fashioned between "mutually engaged collaborators in a fragile fiction" (Conquergood 1986/2013, p 21). Acts of activism are forged in such moments.

Performance autoethnographers struggle with the moral tensions and ethical ambiguities that surround this fiction. Geertz cautions, in doing fieldwork "There is something very complicated and not altogether clear about the nature of sincerity and insincerity, genuineness and hypocrisy and self-deception" (Geertz 1968, p. 155; also in Conquergood 2013, p. 22). Autoethnographers-as-performers insert their experiences into the cultural process, as when Conquergood came to the assistance of his neighbors in Big Red.

In the following scene Madison is caught in a dilemma involving praxis, politics and ethics. She is teaching in the English department at the University of Ghana at Legon in August 1999. A student strike protesting an increase in fees and tuition is going on. She supports the strike, but instructors have been encouraged to not cancel classes. In the midst of a class young men wearing red bandanas and red T-shirts burst into the room, shouting:

YOUNG PROTESTERS: You know there is a strike. Why are you holding class? Do you know we are striking?
MADISON: Yes, I know. I support you. Please look what is on the chalk board: read the words: Hegemony, alienation, neocolonialism, postcolonial theory. The students have listed your demands. See the lines they drew between empire and citizenship.
YOUNG PROTESTER: Why are you teaching at Legon?
MADISON: So I can teach what is on the board to students here.

(pointing to the blackboard):

YOUNG PROTESTER: This is what you are teaching?
SECOND PROTESTER: Okay, let's go. But Prof. no more classes today.
MADISON: No more classes today.

(with great bravado):

YOUNG PROTESTERS: Onward!

(Madison 2010, p. 22)

MADISON: Days after the rally, the campus was closed and students were required to leave the university grounds. Several weeks after the closing Queen Elizabeth II visited the campus. Students were allowed back. The streets and gutters were swept clean, Ghanaian and British flags adorned the streets, and the government reduced fees by 30 percent. There were celebrations.

(Madison 2010 p. 23, paraphrase)

In this complex performance, it is impossible to separate Ghanaian culture from the local acts of activism, and the politics of neoliberal political economy. The Ghanaian activists – student protesters – staged radical performances. These performances brought Madison, as a performance ethnographer, directly into the protesters' story, a story which also included the Queen of England. Stories or scenes of activism cannot be told without invoking politics, economy and culture.

Performance, hermeneutics, interpretation

The fourth pair connects performances to hermeneutics, and privileges performed experience as a way of knowing, as a method of critical inquiry, and as a mode of understanding. Hermeneutics is the work of interpretation and understanding. Knowing refers to those embodied, sensuous experiences which create the conditions for understanding (Denzin 1984, p. 282). Through performance I experience another's feelings which are present in a performance text. Thus performed experiences are the sites where felt emotion, memory, desire and understanding come together.

I structure the interpretive process by using Conquergood's triad of triads. I seek performative interpretations that are poetic, dramatic, critical and imaginative, interpretations that are interventions.

Listening to the different voices in Kauffman's play or reading Madison's performance texts out loud allows me to hear my voice doing her voice, or the voices of the townspeople in Laramie. Through my version of their voice I connect to these performances. In these sounds and feelings I enter a co-constructed interpretive space. I become a storyteller, a performer.

The self-as-subject-as-performer of another's text enters onto an ethical relationship with the other. I honor their presence. The other is no longer the other, there is no other, only a multitude of voices, movements, gestures, intersecting selves, performing for one another (Pollock 2005, p. 6, paraphrase). I bring my body, my flesh, my voice to your text. I circle around the hidden meanings in your narrative, I make these meanings visible with my voice and my body. This *archeology of unearthing*, Madison's phrase, is a continuous process of resurfacing, of digging, looking, feeling, moving, inspecting, tracing and re-tracing memories, new memories (Madison 2005, p. 150).

As an autoethnographer I embed myself in my own history, in my memories, in my stories from my past.

Performance and the politics of scholarly representation

The fifth pair questions the unbreakable link between hermeneutics, politics, pedagogy, ethics and scholarly representation. Writing in 1991 Conquergood (1991, p. 190) remains firm on this point. We should treat performances as a complementary form of research publication, an alternative method, or way of interpreting and presenting one's ethnographic work. The performance text – a text meant to be performed – can take many forms, from ethnodrama, to ethnotheatre, poetry, to a short story. It involves a movement from body (experiences) to paper (text) to stage (performance) (Spry 2011, p. 26).

Contemporary performance studies projects move in several directions at the same time, back and forth between written scholarly texts, to literary, poetic creative representations, to dramatic performances. Many supplement performances with traditional written research. Performance texts, like an ethnodrama (Saldana 2005, p. 2), are not intended "to replace scholarly reports and articles … it is just one of several forms that is available for representing ethnographic inquiry " (Saldana 2005, p. 2, paraphrase). Some work entirely within the field of performance – solo and collaborative performances, ethnodramas, ethnotheatre, arts-based interventions. Some perform theory, where theory, writing and performing intersect (Madison 1999, p. 107).

SOYINI MADISON: This essay performatively expresses specific theoretical ruminations on class, language, and race. This writing is a performance, while it is or is not necessarily for the "stage." The performance seeks a felt-sensing meeting between theory, writing, and performing. The performer claims an uneasy possession of performance as a means of both subjectivity and freedom. Theory becomes another way to know performance better; and performance becomes the desired illuminator of theory. From the burlesque to the sublime, the performer conjures four different encounters with her theoretical fathers: Karl Marx, Ferdinand de Saussure, Jacques Derrida, and Frantz Fanon. Needing useful theory-from the "high" ground of scholarship to the "low" ground of ancient re/tellings-for useful purposes, the performer must first remember where theories begin.

Prologue

Embodied writing

> (*The performer sits under a spotlight surrounded by books on performance. She touches, smells and tastes some of the books. She holds one up to her ear. She notices you are there. She looks up to speak.*)

SOYINI MADISON: Performance has become too popular. Performance is everywhere. Today I want to perform a conversation with Karl Marx, Ferdinand de Saussure, Jacques Derrida, and Frantz Fanon, the only way I can make them meaningful is to talk with them. Bear with me

(Madison 1999, p. 107, paraphrase)

***

Stage Right: Spotlight shines on a diorama of Karl Marx, Ferdinand de Saussure, Jacques Derrida and Frantz Fanon.

***

SOYINI MADISON: These fathers are long on insight, but they have troubled me. They have come to occupy too much space, the inside, the outside and the in-between. This performance will help relocate them. I meet them as "not-not-me." I beg here for a space of imagination, for joy, purpose.(Madison

1999, p. 110, paraphrase)

Madison's performance of theory undoes the classic article format. She turns canonical sources (references) into speaking voices in a performance text where everybody is on the same level, the same stage.

Now listen to Tami Spry. Picture her in your mind. She is seated in a wooden chair, on a small stage. A spotlight shines on her.

TAMI SPRY: For some time now my work has focused upon an ethnography of loss and healing. The body is tantamount as it is the presence and absence of bodies that constitute the experiential evidence of loss. Here is a passage from a work on the loss of our child: "Paper and Skin: Bodies of Loss and life:"

The words are enmeshed
in the blood and bones of
the mother and child.
Arms ache and disarm themselves
with the visceral absence
of the other.
Writing doesn't help me
put my arms back on,
but it does help me
to remember that I had arms,
and then, to show me
that the arms are
still usable in a way
I can't yet understand

(2011, p. 21)

Loss, mourning, grief, pain. Performative autoethnography in motion. Words fail us and we fall back on our bodies, lurching, flailing, stumbling over shards of language (Spry 2011, p. 27). Body as text. Karl Marx on stage with Soyini and Tami.

Performances deconstruct, or at least challenge the scholarly article as the preferred form of presentation (and representation). A performance authorizes itself, not through the citation of scholarly texts, but through its ability to critique, arouse, evoke and invoke emotional experience and understanding between performer and audience.

Performances become a critical site of power, and politics, in the fifth pair. A radical pedagogy underlies this notion of performative cultural politics. The performative becomes an act of doing, an act of resistance, a way of connecting the biographical, the pedagogical and the political (Conquergood 2013, p. 41 in Johnson).

Performance, affect and the new materialisms

A rupture: The traditional concepts of narrative, meaning, voice, presence and representation are put under erasure by the new material feminists (Jackson and Mazzei 2012, p. vii; Koro-Ljungbeerg 2016, p. 2). New (and familiar) names: Barad, Massumi, Braidotti, Pickering, Latour, Clough, Haraway, Lather.

Coole and Frost describe three themes that frame this discourse:

> First, is an ontological reorientation that is posthumanist in the sense that it conceives of matter itself as exhibiting agency. Second are biopolitical, and bioethical issues concerning the status of life and of the human. Third, the new scholarship reengages political economy emphasizing the relationship between the material details of everyday life and broader geopolitical and socioeconomic structure.
>
> (2010, pp. 6–7, paraphrase)

New terms: mobile assemblages, infra-assemblage, intra-action, inter-assemblage, defraction, entangled, transversal, entangled agencies, eventful, immanent, transmutational, blockage, event, doings, plugging in, rhizomatic activity, BWOs, entanglement, agential realism.

For the new materialists, and for many performance studies scholars (Spry 2011; Madison 2012), terms as agency, voice, subject, experience, presence, self, narrative, subjectivity, meaning, mind, consciousness, data, analysis, interpretation and science are to be used carefully, if at all. They privilege discourse, mind and culture over matter, body and nature. They are the remnants of an outdated humanism, their continued use reproduces a postpositivist interpretive discourse (see MacLure 2015).

The materialist critique opens up multiple spaces, including a focus on cyborgs, and post-technological and post-human bodies, new ontologies of being and inquiry, a move away from epistemology, new views of voice, presence and performance. A concept of post-humanist performativity emerges. It embraces the mangle of post-human bodies, new body-machine-material entanglements (Jackson and Mazzei 2012, p. 123).[10] One more time: **the mangle of body, paper, stage.**

Butler's concept of performativity is as central to the new discourse as it is for performance studies. Jackson and Mazzei (2012, pp. 117, 126, 127) elaborate on what they term posthumanist performativity

> We re-think voice ... and the subject, not as a separation of the theoretical from the material, but as an enactment, as a performative practice, as posthumanist performativity, as performative practice, as the entanglement of material practices/doings/actions/understandings.
>
> (paraphrase)

BUTLER: Performativity is both an agent of and a product of the social and the political. Gender and sexuality are performatives made visible through a process of making, doing and repetition. The performative "I" is to a certain extent unknowable, threatened with becoming undone altogether.

(2004, p. 4, paraphrase)

Susan Hekman clarifies, using the language of the new materialism:

> The "I" is a mangle composed of multiple elements, The social scripts defining subjecthood are a key aspect of that mangle. But the mangle also encompasses a body that is sexed and raced, a body that is located at a particular place in the social hierarchy, and a body/subject that has had a range of experiences. The result may be a subject that fits neatly into the definition of subject the social script circumscribe. Or, the results may be an "I" that cannot find a script that fits, that resists scripts available to her/him.
>
> (2010, pp. 100–101, paraphrase)

This is Spry's performative-I, her textualized body:

> The performative-I is the
> positionality of the researcher
> in performative autoethnography,
> the feeling, thinking moving
> performing writer
> wanting to write in a way
> that seeps into the skin
> of the reader, melt into her bones.
> Move through her blood,
> Until the words become transformed
> through her own body,
> Her own life and recognition of self
> where she then looks into her
> own/other-made mirror

looking back and forth,
and then, passionately crafts something.
Some scholarship, some episteme,
some epiphany that seeps
into my skin, into my bones, into my blood
where borders bleed,
differences are connective tissues
and the lines between our bodies become traversable.
I want to be personally and politically
entangled by scholarship
Otherwise
what
is the point?

(Spry 2011, pp. 211–212, paraphrase)

Borrowing from the new materialist discourse, Spry's argument is framed by Barad's concept of agential realism which:

situates knowledge claims in local experience where objectivity is literally embodied, privileging neither the material or the cultural, while interrogating the boundaries of reflexivity, and underlining the necessity of a ethic of knowing that has real, material consequences.

(Barad 2007, 23, paraphrase)

Back to square one, body, paper stage, the flesh and blood body intersects with the performative I in a historical moment, writing its way forward, doing what's done, performatively seeking a discourse that moves the world (Spry 2011, p. 23).

Consider Jackson and Mazzei's discussion of fashion and women's dress and the legacies of the 1980s:

Suits with big shoulder pads, wide lapels, and "ties" that said the more you can look like a man while still presenting a feminine image, the greater chance you will have for advancement. We could feel the affect, what it produced in us as women trying to assert ourselves and to be taken seriously ... we were brought back to our own need to conform and fit in.

(2012, p. 133).

The suit, the tie, shoulder pads, wide lapels, the entire material ensemble, being feminine, while looking like a man, Butler's "I," performative acts, wearing the suit, the suit as a site of power (2012, p. 133)

A materialist feminist discourse opens a space for dialogue between critical performance studies, the performative I, critical pedagogy, and the concept of posthumanist performativity. Recall Della Pollock's materialist reading of Carol Channing descending the stairs in the Auditorium Theatre in Chicago. Here the material, the discursive and the performative I intertwine, bringing a stunned audience (a material presence) to its feet.

A *reapprochment?*

Feminist materialisms move in at least three directions at the same time. They interrogate the practices and politics of evidence that produce empirical material. They support the call for new ways of making the mundane, taken for granted everyday world visible through disruptive post-empirical methodologies. These unruly methodologies read and interrupt traces of presence, whether from film, recordings or transcriptions. They do not privilege presence, voice, meaning or intentionality. Rather they seek performative interventions and representations that heighten critical reflective awareness leading to concrete forms of praxis.

Underneath it all it is assumed that we still make the world visible through our interpretive practices. All texts have a material presence in the world. Nothing stands outside the text, even as it makes the material present. Neither the material nor the discursive are privileged. They fold into one another, get tangled up in one another. How a thing gets inside the text is shaped by a politics of representation. Language and speech do not mirror experience. They create experience and in the process transform and defer that which is being described. Meanings are always in motion, incomplete, partial contradictory. There can never be a final, accurate, complete representation of a thing, an utterance or an action. There are only different representations of different representations. There is no longer any pure presence, description becomes inscription becomes performance.

A new paradigm is on the horizon, one which doubles back on its self and wanders in spaces that have not yet been named. It celebrates the implications for qualitative methodology of the recent (re)turn to materiality across the social sciences and humanities (MacLure 2015, pp. 94–95). The "new materialisms" promise to go beyond the old antagonisms of nature and culture, science and the social, discourse and matter. Performance studies scholars would agree. There is a reapprochment, threaded through the eye of the needle that passes from Conquergood to Butler to Barad to Madison to MacLure, to Spry to Alexander.

Theatre and a politics of resistance

The emphasis on the politics of resistance connects performance auto-ethnography to the global community-based performance movement, to Third World popular Theatre, to applied theatre, the International Popular Theatre Alliance, to performance art, performance studies and to critical participatory action theories (Schechner 2013, pp. 158–59; Cohen-Cruz 2005; Kuppers and Robertson 2007; Prentki and Preston 2009; McLaren 2001; Kemmis and McTaggart 2000, p. 568). Participatory action theories have roots in liberation theology, neo-Marxist approaches to community development, and human rights activism in Asia and elsewhere (Kemmis and McTaggart 2000, p. 568). These theories enable social criticism through performance, and sanction nonviolent forms of civil disobedience (Christians 2000, p. 148).

In this formation, performance autoethnography becomes a civic, participatory, collaborative project, an arts-based approach with parallels to Boal's Theatre of the Oppressed (1985, and below; also Dennis 2009, pp. 72–74).[11] For the dramatic, participatory model to be effective, the following elements need to be present. Scholars must have the energy, imagination, courage and commitment to create these texts (see Conquergood 1985, p. 10). Audiences must be drawn to the sites where these performances take place, and they must be willing to suspend normal aesthetic frameworks, so that coparticipatory performances can be produced.

Boal is clear on this, "In the Theatre of the Oppressed we try to ... make the dialogue between stage and audience totally transitive" (1995, p. 42; 1985, 2006). In these sites a shared field of emotional experience is created, and in these moments of sharing, critical cultural awareness is awakened. Performers enact scenes of oppression, and acknowledge the presence of the audience. Acting as a catalyst, the actor, or Joker, as Boal calls the person, introduces the scene and guides the audience in providing different endings, or solutions to a problem (Madison 2012, p. 236; Boal 1985, p. 186; 1995, p. 42; Schutzman and Cohen-Cruz 2006b, p. 237).

This is a project centered around an on-going moral dialogue, struggles for justice involving the shared ownership of the performance-project itself. Spectator-actors enact the cop in their head, improvised scenes become reality, spec-actors are transformed into protagonists, resistance to oppression is enacted, turning fiction into real life (Boal 1995, p. 42).

These interpretations, which are central to Boal's Theatre of the Oppressed, represent an emancipatory commitment to community action which performs social change. It is grounded in the moral spaces of the community, based on shared place, ethnicity, class, race, sexual preference, circumstance or politics (Cohen-Cruz 2005, p. 2;). Like Du Bois' all-black theatre, art of, by and for Blacks, community-based theatre performances are "of the people, by the people, and for the people" (Cohen-Cruz 2005, p. 2).[12] Paraphrasing Kemmis and McTaggart (2000, p. 598), this form of performance inquiry helps people collectively recover, and release themselves from the repressive constraints embedded in the racist structures of global techno-capitalism.

In these performances the personal becomes political. This happens precisely at that moment when the conditions of identity construction are made problematic, and located in concrete history. As when Mary Weems, the poet-performer, says this "Evolution will not be televised." In this moment, performers claim a positive utopian space where a politics of hope is imagined. At its best autoethnography is about the practice of freedom, the use of dramatic performance for social justice, for the development of an activist mindset (Weems 2015, p. xiii)

This performance ethic asks that interpretive work provide the foundations for social criticism by subjecting specific programs and polices to concrete analysis. Performers show how specific policies and practices affect and effect their lives.

The autoethnographer invites members of the community to become co-performers in a drama of social resistance and social critique. Acting from an informed ethical position, offering emotional support to one another, co-performers bear witness to the need for social change (Langellier 1998, pp. 210–211). As members of an involved social citizenship, they enact a politics of possibility, a politics that mobilizes people's memories, fantasies, and desires (Madison 1998, pp. 277, 282). These are pedagogical performances that matter. They give a voice to the subaltern. They do something in the world. They move people to action.

Baraka (1998, p. 1502) said,

we want poems that wrestle cops into
alleys
and take their weapons ...

Pedagogical performances have artistic, moral, political and material con-sequences (Madison 1998, pp. 283–284). In a performance of possibilities moral responsibility and artistic excellence combine to produce an "active intervention to ... *break through* unfair closures and remake the possibility for new openings" (Madison 1998, p. 284, italics in original). A performance of possi-bilities gives a voice to those on the margin, moving them for the moment to the political center (Madison 1998, p. 284).

Local acts: community based [theatre][13] performances

This kind of political theatre is organized by four principles – communal context, reciprocity, hyphenation and active culture. Community based artists and perfor-mers use their craft and the communal context to fashion a moral community of persons committed to action. Community-based performances are frequently staged in natural gathering places – parks, churches, schools or community centers (Cohen-Cruz 2005, p. 93).

Community-based performance is opposed to hierarchy, it implements community-building, reciprocity, dialogue and mutual exchange between the community and the performers. These performances are defined by a hyphen that fosters a shared culture, and connects the person to the community, to the performance, to the theatre and its goals, the performance event.

Cohen-Cruz offers an example, his experience at a Broadway production of *Falsettoland* in the early 1990s (2005, p. 97):

As the play's protagonist mourned the loss of his friend (lover?) to AIDS, I wept at the loss of my dear friend David and inadvertently leaned to the stranger to my left. He, weeping with an abandon that also seemed to transcend the death of the character, leaned in to me too, communicating great empathy. Everywhere I saw weeping spectators and felt that the theatrical event was a mass public funeral for our beloved friends lost to AIDS.

Community based-performance is a process, moving through phases, from training to workshop, rehearsal, warm-up, performance, cool-down, to aftermath (Cohen-Cruz 2005, pp. 101–103). In each phase members interact with one another, with persons in the community, collecting stories, interviewing people, forming relationships, connecting to the media and the community, involving spectators as active participants rehearsing. A mantra says the production should leave something behind for the community. In the cool-down, aftermath and post-performance phases community and performers work to leave something behind, a legacy of action: money for a theatre, or a community center, or housing for the homeless or commitment to perform a new play and train a new group of performers. The goal is to give back. It views performance as a form of activism, as critique, as critical citizenship. It seeks a form of performative praxis that inspires and empowers persons to act on their utopian impulses. These moments are etched in history and popular memory.

Back to Laramie, Wyoming, ten years later

Kaufman and the members of the Tectonic Theater Project returned to Laramie, Wyoming on the 10th anniversary of Mr. Shepard's death (Healy 2008, p. A19). They re-interviewed town members, intending to use the new interviews in an epilogue to the play. They were disappointed to learn that nothing had been done to commemorate the anniversary of Matthew's death. Mr. Kaufman was angry that there were as yet no hate-crimes law in Wyoming. But the city had changed.

LOCAL CITIZEN: Laramie has changed in some ways. The city council passed a bias crimes ordinance that tracks such crimes, but it does not include penalties for them. There is an AIDS Walk now. Several residents have came out publicly as gay, in their churches or on campus, in part to honor Mr. Shepard's memory. The university hosts a four-day Shepard Symposium for Social Justice each spring, and there is talk of creating a degree minor in gay and lesbian studies. But there is no memorial to Mr. Shepard here in town. The long fence has been torn down where he lay dying for 18 hours on Oct. 7, 1998. There is no marker. Wild grass blows in the wind. You can see the lights of Laramie from the spot where he died.Performance ethnography disguised as spectacle theatre in the service of memory, social change and social justice.

***

Effects like these in Laramie represent, at some deep level, an emancipatory commitment to community action which performs social change, even if change is only an idea, whose time has yet to come. This form of performance inquiry helps people recover, and release themselves from the repressive constraints embedded in repressive racist and homophobic pedagogies.

A dramatic production like Laramie moves in three directions at the same time: it shapes subjects, audiences and performers. In honoring subjects who have been mistreated, such performances contribute to a more "Enlightened and involved citizenship" (Madison 1998, p. 281). These performances interrogate and evaluate specific social, educational, economic and political processes. This form of praxis can shape a cultural politics of change. It can help create a progressive and involved citizenship. The performance becomes the vehicle for moving persons, subjects, performers and audience members, into new, critical, political spaces. The performance gives the audience, and the performers, "equipment for [this] journey: empathy and intellect, passion and critique" (Madison 1998, p. 282).

Such performances enact a performance-centered evaluation pedagogy. This fusion of critical pedagogy and performance praxis uses performance as a mode of inquiry, as a method of doing evaluation ethnography, as a path to understanding, as a tool for engaging collaboratively the meanings of experience, as a means to mobilize persons to take action in the world. This form of critical, collaborative, performance pedagogy privileges experience, the concept of voice and the impor- tance of turning evaluation sites into democratic public spheres (see Worley 1998). Critical performance pedagogy informs practice, which in turn supports the peda- gogical conditions for an emancipatory politics (Worley 1998, p. 139).

Extending Toni Morrison, the best art, the best performance auto- ethnographies are "unquestionably political and irrevocably beautiful at the same time" (Morrison 1994, p. 497; also quoted in Madison 1998, p. 281).

Conclusions

Coming full-circle. I have outlined a performance-based approach to [auto] ethnography, culture, politics and pedagogy. My [auto] ethnographer is a per- former, a poet, a playwright, ethnodramatist, a storyteller, a critic, a social justice advocate. My [auto] ethnographer refuses to be hemmed in. Refuses to be confined to a narrow set of terms or procedures. My autoethnographer is wild, unruly, passionate, a wily coyote, a circus clown, a disrupter committed to the belief that we change reality by making social injustice visible. Close your eyes, listen to the music, imagine a circus, a carnival, animation, laughter, clowns, people in costume wearing masks, think avant garde theatre, dadism, surrealism, the situationalists, political theatre, welcome to my autoethnographic theatre of the oppressed (Boal 1985).

Notes

1 I thank Paul Atkinson and Sara Delamont for their comments on an earlier version of this chapter.

2 Conquergood has five intersecting planes. I add rhetoric and the new materialisms.
3 Almighty Voice was a 19th century Saskatchewan Cree, whose poaching of a settler's cow resulted in his incarceration and escape from jail, and his shooting of a Mountie. He was finally tracked down by a large group of police and civilians, and shot.
4 On October 7, 1998 a young gay man, Matthew Shepard, was discovered bound to a fence outside Laramie, Wyoming, savagely beaten, left to die. Matthew's death became a national symbol of intolerance. In the aftermath Kaufman and the members of the Tectonic Theatre Project went to Laramie and conducted more than 200 interviews. From these transcripts the playwrights constructed the Laramie Project. Ten years later they returned to Laramie, producing a second play based on the ways the community was grappling with Matthew's legacy. The play has been performed over 2000 times. The Tectonic Theater Project collaborated with Home Box Office (HBO) to make a film based on the play. It starred Peter Fonda, Laura Linney, Christina Ricci and Steve Buscomi. It opened the 2002 Sundance Film Festival, and was nominated for four Emmys.
5 Similar events include the murders of Michael Brown and Trayvon Martin, and the June 17, 2015, mass *shooting* of nine people, including a pastor, in the Emanuel African Methodist Episcopal Church in downtown *Charleston*, South Carolina.
6 Our Town is a 1938 three-act play by American playwright Thornton Wilder. It tells the story of the fictional American small town of Grover's Corners between 1901 and 1913 through the everyday lives of its citizens.
7 On the history of the theatre see Cohen-Cruz (2005, p. 37).
8 Cohen-Cruz (2005, pp. 7–8) distinguishes the amateur productions of community theatre groups from the community-based performances of politically activist groups, from the Harlem Renaissance to working class theatre, the Little Theatre Movement, the Federal Theatre Project, the Free Southern Theatre, El Treatro Campesino and recently ActUp Theatre.
9 From Hallie (1969, p. 46).
10 See Maggie MacLure's Museum of Qualitative Data. http://museumofqualitativeda ta.info
11 For histories of these movements in People's Theatre, Epic Theatre, Theatre of the Oppressed, participatory action research education, and critical ethnography see Conrad (2004) and Dennis (2009).
12 1868–1963: Sociologist, historian and civil rights activist, W.E.B. Du Bois helped found the National Association for the Advancement of Colored People (NAACP).
13 By inserting [theatrical] into this section heading I subvert the title to Cohen-Cruz's (2005) book.

Part II

An uneasy alliance: ethnography, performance, theatre

4 Performance ethnography[1]

A MANIFESTO in the form of an abstract

Dear Reader: Allow me to disrupt our conversation, even as I continue our interrogation of the ethical and political implications of the interdisciplinary turn to performance and theatre in critical ethnography. What you are about to read is intended to be a non-history, a story of an arranged marriage, a marriage of convenience and necessity. I offer a performance about performance, theatre and ethnography. I propose an alignment of Paulo Freire (1970/2000) and Augusto Boal's Pedagogy and Theatre of the Oppressed (1985), with Erving Goffman's dramaturgy (1959). Victor Turner's performance anthropology (1982), Dwight Conquergood's model of performance as resistance (2013), Richard Schechner's theory of performance as twice behaved behavior (2015) and Johnny Saldana's ethnodrama (2011). It is time to bring these theorists back together on the same stage.

This is a messy and complicated marriage. There are multiple models of performance in the ethnography-theatrical paradigm. The models turn back on one another. Turner uses performance as a way of representing fieldwork, envisioning the work of the fieldworker as a performance; Schechner wants to move performance out of the theatre, into a new field called performance studies; Saldana holds to a very specific meaning of drama, theatre and performance; all the world is a stage for Goffman, Boal and Freire; and Conquergood uses theatre as a weapon for confronting social injustice. We can not privilege one model over another.

My [auto] ethnographer is a performer, a poet, a playwright, a ethno-dramatist, a fieldworker, a storyteller, a critic, a social justice advocate. She borrows from everyone. My [auto] ethnographer refuses to be hemmed in or confined to a narrow set of terms or procedures. My autoethnographer is wild, unruly, passionate, a wily coyote, a circus clown, a disrupter committed to the belief that through performance we can change reality by making social injustice visible. Globally and locally democratic public life is under siege. We have fallen prey to a politics of extremism, racism, misogyny and ultra-nationalism. Welcome back to Donald Trump's world.

***

Act One: Scene One: Exiles and evil worlds

NARRATOR: Close your eyes, listen to the music, imagine a circus, a carnival, laughter, clowns, people in costume wearing masks, social media meets avant garde theatre, dadaism, surrealism, the situationists and political theatre, welcome to my autoethnographic theatre of the oppressed (Boal 1985).

Let the play begin. Together we will expose and dismantle Donald Trump's evil world. Listen to D. Soyini Madison.

D. SOYINI MADISON: I have witnessed courageous interventions by men and women who have faced great risks in the defense of human rights and social justice. I have also witnessed how they employ performance as a subversive tactic to win hearts and minds in their efforts toward a more humane and democratic society (Madison 2010, p. 1, quote is paraphrase).

NARRATOR (TO SELF): We are called to answer the call to resist:
to celebrate community
c. wright mills challenged me to
look at how private troubles became public issues
troubles, issues
connect your biography to history
connect history to identity, to injustice
push back, resist,
write words that change the world
one word at a time.
This was back then, before there was autoethnography,
and flesh and blood bodies and performances,
body, paper, stage
a response to the call ...
Life, art, ethnography, politics, turned upside down.

PAULO FREIRE AND AUGUSTO BOAL: Hold in wright,
You need a theatre to change the world.
Words alone won't do it
Theatre is your weapon, people freely singing in the open air
Voices cry out, demanding a free open society
Radical performances enacting pedagogies of the oppressed
Rehearsals for a revolution that you can sink your teeth into
Go to prison if you have to, dress in black, be an exile,
A wife rehearses leaving her violent husband,
A wife leaves her violent husband

AUGUSTO BOAL: Ah, life in exile: Prisoners in freedom. Dead Man Walking.
Take your pick: the cost is high
Solitary suicides,
disintegrated families,
nightmares at mid-day,
fingernails dig into the memory of

clawing out
chunks of the future,
daggers in the chest,
neighbors who drowned
themselves in confusion, relatives,
surrounded by the present,
looking into the future,
seeing nothing
kill themselves by
jumping out of very high windows
We can stand no more death
we seek a radical pedagogy of the heart,
a pedagogy of hope and love, forgiveness
COYOTE: So this is why you wanted us to make Paulo
and Augusto part of his play.
They believe in putting lives on the line.
They have lived the call. They have lived
lives of resistance. It is not idle talk for them.
In their hands theatre becomes the means to revolution.

Act One: Scene Two: For a Theatre of the Oppressed

COYOTE: **History lesson.**
Never mind the beginning. As we said earlier, in the mid-1980s Turner
(1982, 1986b), Conquergood (1985), and Schechner (1985, 1988) outlined a
theory of culture, ritual, drama, theatre and spectacle.
The ethnographer studies and records
the rituals performed in a cultural setting.
These rituals are incorporated into ethnographic texts.
The "processed ethnoscript is transformed
into a workable preliminary playscript"
Playscripts are then rehearsed and
performed by drama students (Turner 1982, pp. 98–99).
This is all fine. Where's the politics?
VICTOR TURNER: The politics came later.
With the ethnoscript text
the know-how of theatre people –
their sense of dialogue, understanding
of setting and props, ear for a telling, revelatory phrase –
could combine with the anthropologist's
understanding of cultural meanings,
Indigenous theory, and material culture.
JOHNNY SALDANA: The playscript would be subject to continuous modification
during the rehearsal process, which would lead up to the actual performance before an audience.

VICTOR: The theatre people needed us. Ethnographers could help drama students during rehearsal, if not by direct participation, at least in the role of *dramaturg*, that is as advisers to the performers and director.

This is how theatre, performance and anthropology come together.

DWIGHT: We needed a performance paradigm
   that privileged struggle, agency, praxis,
   resistance, the spaces where
   doing and the done collide.
   There was not enough of this in Victor for me.

COYOTE: Hold on. Back up in your history.
   Paulo Freire's *Pedagogy of the Oppressed* appears in 1970.
   Augusto Boal's 1974 *Theatre of the Oppressed*
   moves Paulo' framework into the spaces of radical social theatre.
   The links between theatre,
   pedagogy and critical inquiry
   are in place by 1974,
   but nobody was ready to take it up.
   Boal had his own radical theory of theatre
   which implemented Freire's critical pedagogy.

AUGUSTO BOAL: In simultaneous dramaturgy, a participant describes a problem.
   When a husband drinks he becomes violent
   He beats his wife.
   A spectator is invited to address this situation
   She proposes an intervention – make him feel guilty,
   refuse to prepare his meals, no sex,
   change the locks on the doors,
   leave him.

COYOTE: This short scene is performed for an audience
   Actors improvise with the script, and
   develop the scene to the point of a crisis.
   They stop the performance.
   The audience is asked for solutions.
   The audience writes a new script
   which the actors simultaneously perform.
   This is simultaneously dramaturgy
   (Boal 1974/1985, pp. 132, 134).

PAULO FREIRE: Augusto Boal's theatre is a rehearsal for revolution,
   for resistance, for empowerment.
   The spectator rehearses a real act.
   A wife leaves her violent husband.
   This performance makes the experience concrete.
   It creates the desire to seek
   fulfillment through real action (Boal 1974/1985, p. 142).

AUGUSTO BOAL: We wanted a new form of theatre,
   a theatre for the oppressed.

We called this use of crisis
our anti-model. It stops action.
It is meant to instill intervention,
to invite spect-actors to act
out alternative actions.

Act One: Scene Two: Uneasy alliance: [auto] ethnodrama, ethnotheatre and reality theatre

NARRATOR: In two books Johnny Saldana (2005, 2011), while citing Boal's project, moved Turner's ethnoscripts into an arts-based framework, what he labeled ethnodrama, ethnotheatre and autoethnodrama. *Ethnotheatre,* a word joining ethnography and theatre, merges ethnography and theatre in a live or mediated performance event (Saldana 2005, p. 1). *Ethnodrama,* a word joining ethnography and drama, is a play script that dramatizes ethnographic narrative collected from interview transcripts, participant observation field notes, journal entries, personal memories/experiences, print and media artifacts, and ... historical documents (Saldana 2011, p. 13; 2005, pp. 1–2).

JOHNNY: Ethnodramas are solidly rooted
in nonfictional, or researched reality –
"not realism, but reality" (Saldana 2011, pp. 14, 47).

NARRATOR: Consider the following excerpt from Susan Finley's "Dream Child: The Role of Poetic Dialogue in Homeless Research" (Finley 2000).

DREAM CHILD: Hey, que pasa? I just got out of jail here in Austin.
Wrote a poem while I was in jail and decided to mail you a copy.

A young girl writes a sad poem.
Is This My Life?

Once in a while I awaken, asking myself "what am I doing?"
Am I going to live on the streets forever? ...

She sleeps in a too large sweater,
a cold, lonely night.
She dreams.
Morning sun awakens
She hears her father leave the house for work
Dreams of poetry.
And a young girl writes a sad poem
in a squat in New Orleans,
her home

(Finley 2000, pp. 433–434, paraphrase).

COYOTE: A poetic monologue woven
out of snippets of audiotaped conversations,

lines of poetry written by Dream Child,
arts-based participatory action research
ethnodrama on the road to being homeless,
but not hopeless in New Orleans.

NARRATOR: Ethnodramas examine moments of crisis in the culture, liminal moments, suspended in time. They open up institutions and their practices for critical inspection. Depending on the goals of the ethnodramatist, the artistic project is not only aesthetic, it possesses "emancipatory potential" for motivating social change within participants and audiences.

COYOTE: Ethnotheatre can be a manifesto
that exposes oppression and challenges
the existing social order through
moral and political discourse (Saldana 2005, p. 3, paraphrase; see also Mienczakowski and Morgan 2001).

NARRATOR: A performer speaks from the pages
of Mary Weems 2013 book:

What It Means to Be Young, White, and Lesbian

(Young lesbian [20s–early 30s] enters stage left, wearing a rainbow tie-dyed t-shirt, a short jean skirt, red high-topped tennis shoes, and white socks)

YOUNG LESBIAN: The itsy bitsy spider crawls up the water spout,
down came the rain and washed the spider out.

[PAUSE]

YL: I tried to kill the spider once.
I kind of felt like that spider most of the time,
caught in my own web.

[PAUSE]

YL: I decided you can't kill a spider with rainwater
and maybe being caught in your own web wasn't so bad

[PAUSE]

YL: I'm gay ... Yep, I'm a lesbian.
I'm a spider. Rainwater is cleansing.
I can't drown in it. I only start drowning
when I'm not being myself

[PAUSE].

YL: One day, when I was nine,
   my parents left me with Uncle Herman.
   I was in the garden watching a spider
   when I heard a strange gurgling sound,
   turned, and there he was standing behind
   me with his pants around his ankles

[PAUSE].

YL: I started to back up.
   I felt the thorns in my back.

[PAUSE].

YL: Hey, little girl, come to Uncle Hermie.
   I started to cry. He held me there.
   When he finished he wiped my face
   with his handkerchief.
   Practicing to kill myself used to be a game

(Weems 2013, p. 8, paraphrase).

NARRATOR: Her monologue stands on its own two feet as critique of patriarchy and incest, a cry of pain, abuse, betrayal, no help from the itsy-bitsy spider.

Act One: Scene Five [aside]: historical [auto] ethnodrama: Custer's Last Stand

NARRATOR: Historical [auto] ethnodrama is a cousin to Boal's Theatre of the Oppressed. Here is an example from a short play based on ethnographic fieldwork in museums, and galleries, and imaginative re-workings of original print and media materials (Denzin 2011, pp. 185–187). As the ethnodramatist, I have multiple identities: narrator, Tonto, Ms Coyote, and Coyote. My Coyote, like Boal's joker (1974/1985, p.182), creates scenes, directs action, disrupts, function as a master of ceremonies.

Speakers are designated as Speaker One, or Speaker Two. Each speaker names the character – for example Ms. Coyote – before reading the character's lines. Who reads which character is assigned arbitrarily. I was guided by Walter Benjamin's argument (1969a) that a critical text consists of a series of quotations, documents, excerpts and texts, placed side by side. Quotations attributed to a speaker, are paraphrases from an original text which is cited. Following Boal (1985), these are improvised, invented texts, fictions that become reality, blueprints for acting that are realized in performance (1995, p. 185).

***

This caveat operates at all times: This play is a product of my ethnographic imagination. Names, characters, places, events and incidents are used fictitiously. Any resemblance to actual events, or locales or persons, living or dead is at least partially coincidental.

***

NARRATOR: (again): Carol Rambo says the point of the play is this:
There is no Custer's Last Stand.
There is no stand.
There is no last.
There is no where to stand.
And dear reader my dramatic format leaves you with nowhere to stand
(except to know that what you knew
before was certainly not the whole picture).
The story was the "Real" Last Stand, this play is an ambush
that that story walked right into.

"Custer's Last Stand"

Act One: Scene One: Meet Buffalo Bill Cody

>   (Stage right: spotlight shines on 1886 Advertisement for "Custer's Last Rally")
>   "Buy your tickets for Custer's Last Rally"
>   (Stage right: spotlight shines on Cody in stage outfit)

SPEAKER ONE (NARRATOR): Allow me to introduce the famous
William F. Cody, performer
extraordinaire. He still rides today,
along with the cowboy angel (Dylan 1965) across our imagined
horizon ... huckster, entertainer,
celebrity, myth-maker.

(Stage right: spotlight shines on photo of William Cody and Sitting Bull, p. 86 in Reddin 1999)

SPEAKER TWO (WILLIAM FREDERICK CODY, 1858): I killed my first Indian when I
was 12.
SPEAKER ONE (MS. COYOTE): As you can see, the Custer epic is ritual drama.
Custer
is eternal youth. The ritual of re-enactment holds
out the promise that there really is no Last Stand, for its
self-sacrificing heroism assures that the Last Stand will
flourish forever in memory, enjoying perpetual life.

Scene Two: Cody, Custer and The Western Minstrel Show

SPEAKER ONE (TONTO): What's the point of this play?

SPEAKER TWO (COYOTE): You keep asking this question.
  Nobody wants to die.
  Cody keeps Custer alive.

SPEAKER ONE (SAM SHEPARD, PLAYWRIGHT, ACTOR): Cody's Wild West fantasy
  helps the American male
  address a deep-seated anxiety
  concerning his manhood.
  Engaging in violent acts, including
  killing Indians, wipes out some of this guilt.

SPEAKER TWO (COWBOY ANGEL): Who said no sound ever
  comes from the Gates of Eden?
  I just heard Bruce Willis yell "Yippee Ki Yay"
  and a white man dressed
  as an Indian said "Custer Died for your Sins."

NARRATOR: When I was little, when my brother and I
  were not playing cowboy and Indian,
  he was Buffalo Bill and I was Wild Bill Hickok,
  then he was Roy Rogers and I was Gene Autry.

SPEAKER ONE (COYOTE): Let's hear it for the Cowboy Angel.
  You know Roy Rogers played Buffalo Bill
  in a 1940 movie.

SPEAKER TWO (MS COYOTE): Just like Hollywood, to use famous actors to play
  famous people. Western minstrel shows are all
  about the ability of Americans to be racist and
  seemingly non-racist at the same time; a talent
  Cody cultivated. He created racialized
  spectacles and sold them to audiences around the
  world as authentic history, history as entertainment.
  This is what his Wild West Show was all about.

SPEAKER ONE (COYOTE): Sam Shepard got it right.
  There is no true west. It is all a myth.
  Buffalo Bill gave us that truth.

Act Two: Scene One: Writing ethnodrama

NARRATOR: Devising, or crafting an ethnodramatic script
  involves moving from epiphanic experiences
  to a fully crafted performance text.
  A goal is to create and perform a story
  that is credible, vivid, persuasive and
  captures verisimilitude and universality

through vignettes, scenes, characters,
evocative scripts, monologue, dialogue
and performance (Saldana 2005, p. 2, paraphrase;
Norris 2009, pp. 22–23).

JOHNNY: The purpose is to give the reader
the sense of being there,
the production, the narration, monologue,
dialogue, staging must "ring true to life"
and evoke the world of its participants,
giving the audience member
not a sense of "being there,"
but, during performance
of "being here" (Saldana 2005, p. 141).
I see ethnodrama as a tool for
Drawing attention
to specific issues,
with one side critical and emancipatory,
the other side evocative,
dialogical, self-expressing, and intentionally creative.

D. SOYINI MADISON: I agree with Johnny.
Based on acts of intimate habituation
I endeavor to share with the reader,
as intimately and directly as possible,
the actual worlds of Ghanians themselves (2010, p. 24).
This means I show how I inhabited my fieldwork,
and connected, through my fieldwork to small stories
about and with the lives of others.
I became a performer, a co-performative witness
in these small stories, these acts of activism (p. 25).
I use performance "as a method in the defense of
human rights in the actualization of social justice" (p. 26).

COYOTE (DISGUISED AS JOKER): How does this work now?

D. SOYINI MADISON: We've said this before.
Performance is the vehicle for making injustice visible.
It is the agent of change, the site where resistance
is staged and performed.
Performance and activism are mutually constitutive:
together public space is transformed, heightened,
and made more communal. The ethics of radical performance
demand that we pay attention to the deep layers of
political economy of poverty and injustice
that are inseparable from human rights and social justice (2010, p. 224).

JOHNNY: Ethnotheatre, like critical ethnography,
troubles the boundaries and barriers between stakeholders,
professionals, policy-makers and the general public (p. 469).

Grounded in local understandings and experiences,
these texts provide the basis for the critical evaluation
of existing programs. They return the ownership
of programs to immediate stakeholders.
(Mienczakowski 2001, p. 470).

Act Two: Scene Two: Anna Deavere Smith

NARRATOR: Over the last three decades Anna Deavere Smith (1993, 1994, 2004)
 has created a series of one-woman performance pieces about race and
 racism in America (1993, p. xvii; 2004). She titles her series On the Road: A
 Search for American Character. Her ethnodramas advance the causes of
 social justice.[2]

ANNA: I've tried to deploy a documentary theatre style,
 speaking in the voice and manner of historical figures
 (living and dead) who are present in my plays
 (President Clinton, Thomas Jefferson, Sally Hemings,
 Monica Lewinsky, Anita Hill).
 In my plays gender and race do not need to
 match those of the characters (2004, p. 7).
 This does not mean race and gender are insignificant.
 Rather an actor's race and gender
 is on one side of the bridge,
 and the other they pursue is across the bridge.
 The effort to cross the bridge is the drama (2004, p. xviii).

NARRATOR: In Piano (2004) Smith was looking for a time in American history
 in which people of all different races could be in one living room.

ANNA: In Piano we see the turning of a servant class into
 a powerful class. We see those who are the subjects strive
 to become the authors of their history ...
 These plays, based on facts, take dramatic
 license and are not offered as truths,
 but as fictions that attempt to tell other truths,
 the kinds of truths that live
 in fiction and in imaginary worlds (2004, p. xix).

PAULO FREIRE: By interrogating and performing the facts of history
 Anna's plays enact a politics of possibility.
 She deals with truths that matter
 using fictionalized histories as a way to expose
 the truths of past injustices.
 She worries about those who write the facts.
 She quotes James Baldwin on facts and history.
 Baldwin is speaking to Margaret Mead:

JAMES BALDWIN: I do not care what the facts are.
 I cannot afford to care.

You, historically write the facts which

I

Am expected to believe.

The difference is that you

Historically,

Generically,

Have betrayed me so often

And lied to me so long

That no

Number of facts

According to you

Would ever convince! (James Baldwin quoted in Smith 2004, p. xv).

ANNA: When the facts have been exhausted,

"we must imagine a future and work

to make it real, to go beyond the evidence,

to make history present,

to make the not yet now real" (p. xvi, paraphrase).

COYOTE (DISGUISED AS JOKER): Right on, for Baldwin and Anna history

belongs to those who record the true facts,

the fictions that are truths.

AUGUSTO BOAL: The actor's job, the autoethnographer's job,

is double-sided, to make the past and the future

present at the same time.

The task is to embrace the murky truth as tragic,

as absurd, and if we are lucky, as inspiring.

When the past and the future collide in the present,

the possibilities of change and hope are created.

Performed dramatic works become catalysts for social change.

ANNA: The value of politicized theory, of activist art,

like critical performance ethnography,

lies in the ability to initiate a continuing process of

social criticism in the public sphere.

This form of theatre and art engages defined publics

on issues from the pipeline that moves black males

from schools to prison, homelessness to the survival of the rain forests,

and domestic violence.

It transgresses the confines of public and domestic domains.

It shows how public laws and policies influence

personal decisions. It shows how the limits of the

public sphere shape changes in the private sphere.

Act Two: Scene Three: Mr. Trump's wall

NARRATOR: Here is Gloria Anzaldua, on the politics of performance along the
U.S. Mexico border. These words could have been written yesterday:

I press my hand to the steel curtain –
chainlink fence crowded with rolled barbed wire –
rippling from the sea where Tijuana touches San Diego
unrolling over mountains
and plains
and deserts,
this "Tortilla curtain" turning into el *río Grande*
A 1,950 mile-long open wound
dividing a *pueblo*, a culture
running down the length of my body,
staking fence rods in my flesh,
splits me splits me
me raja me raja
This is my home
this thin edge of
barbwire.[3]

GLORIA: I seek a queer-free zone.
    Colored, poor, white,
    latent queer passing for white, seething with
    hatred, anger, rage, crazed with not
    not knowing who you are,
    let me pick at the masks
    Thank you Mr. Trump for your wall
    (1987, p. 171, paraphrase).
AISHA DURHAM: We write our way
    back home again.
    Lost and found.
GLORIA: I may be mad, but I choose this madness.
    Read the signs
    145 acres for sale
    the Indians safely locked up in reservations
    or urban ghettos.
    There's a forest fire in the Cuyamaca Peaks,
    a sign: 4 parcels For Sale,
    the Indians safely locked up in reservations
    and Til'pu behind glass in museum
    (Anzaldua 1987, p. 183 paraphrase)
COYOTE: How do you read
    a sign that says
    "4 parcels for sale and
    Indians behind glass in museums"?
AISHA DURHAM: Meanwhile, in another time and another place in the USA
    on the block
    home girls huddle

to talk crap and take shots of cheap wine to chase
the Uncle Willie boogiemen and the 40 oz. spirits that haunt us.
we drink for an excuse to cut a fool
to be the 13-year-girls we really are.
We sit around retelling the 'remember when' stories so many times they
turn into project folklore
(Durham 2014, pp. 57–58, paraphrase).
TAMI SPRY: I write autobiography to place myself in history.
ANNA: There is no other place to go.

In conclusion

Boal and Freire's theatre's (and pedagogies) of the oppressed, like Smith's
monologues, Saldana's ethnodramas, and Madison's critical ethnography, use
performance, ethnography, theatre and dramatic theory to criticize neoliberal
discourse, to inspire acts of activism. Here the theatrical, the performative and
the ethnographic come together. Not exactly a marriage, but surely a con-
vergence of views. The dramatist, with the assistance of spect-actors, uses the
facts and experiences of oppression to change history. This is critical pedagogy
in action, a politics of liberation, inquiry and theatre for justice. There is no
going back.

Notes

1 I thank Magdalena Kazubowski-Houston and Virginie Magnat for their comments on
   earlier versions of this chapter. I write the opening words for this chapter the morning
   (August 15, 2017) after Donald Trump refused to explicitly condemn white supremacy
   groups or use the term domestic terrorism after a woman was killed when a car
   smashed into anti-racism protesters at a August 11, 2017 rally in Charlottesville,
   Virginia marking the removal of a statue honoring Confederate General Robert E.
   Lee. The white nationalists were in Charlottesville to protest the city's plan to remove
   that statue, and counterdemonstrators were there to oppose them.
2 Her current project is *The Pipeline Project*, a work in progress about the "school-to-
   prison pipeline"; www.philly.com/philly/entertainment/arts/20150503_Probing_the_p
   ipeline_with_Anna_Deavere_Smith.html#QTRF4Ds5CW8rc9es.99
3 Excerpts from *Borderlands/La Frontera: The New Mestiza*, 1987, pp. 12–13,
   paraphrase.

5 Staging resistance as performance

Act One: Scene One: History: starting out negative?

ANNOUNCER: Welcome to center stage at Lyceum Theatre on the campus of
 Arizona State University, Tempe, Arizona. Tonight the Forum Theatre
 Performers[1] with the Joker,[2] will perform a three-act play based on
 Augusto Boal's Theatre of the Oppressed. The curtains are drawn back
 slowly. The lighting is Arizona intense (Badley 2015, p. 764).
JOKER: This play is all about
   history, power, freedom,
   progressive pedagogies,
   using the *facticities*[3] of experience
   to change history,
   resisting neoliberal discourse,
   imagining new futures,
AUGUSTO: Bodies in motion,
   everybody a playwright.
SKEPTIC AKA DAVID S. GEORGE: Dear audience. Don't get too carried away here.
   What Boal invented is a term, theatre of the oppressed which
   he borrowed from Paulo Freire's "pedagogy of the oppressed."
   It has spawned a critical industry that puts out an
   assembly-line repetition of clichés
   about 'liberating' the oppressed (George 1995, p. 40).
JOKER: Ouch. This is pretty harsh.
SOYINI MADISON: Many of his techniques
   can be used by critical performance
   ethnographers (see Dennis 2009; Conrad 2004; Madison 2012, pp. 235–236).

***

Curtain lowers. Lights dim, stage right: spot light shines on photo of the
Lyceum Theatre.[4] YouTube videos showing scenes from Boal workshops
are projected on the giant drop down screen in the center of the stage.[5]

***

JOKER: Hold these images
    in your mind. Imagine you
    are in a TO workshop.
SKEPTIC: Hog wash. Touchy-Feely Mumpo Jumpo.

Act One: Scene Two: A new language

    Curtain rises, lights dim

AUGUSTO: It begins with Paulo.
    He broke the hierarchal divide
    between teacher and pupil.
    I broke the divide between actor,
    spectator and stage.
    I moved the spectator out of the audience
    and onto the stage
JOKER: Augusto gave us
    a new language, new terms:
    simultaneous dramaturgy, spectators as actors (spect-actors),
    metaxi, osmosis, aesthetic space,
    Chinese crisis, the four catharses,
    stages of the image, cops in the head,
    He redefined and contested old
    terms: mimesis, catharsis, tragedy.
    Even theatre (Schutzman and Cohen-Cruz 2006b).
AUGUSTO: Brecht taught me
    I have an obligation
    to shed light on reality
    and to try to change it.
    To do this I drew on
    street theatre, political vaudeville
    and the Brazilian circus,
    (see Boal interview in Driskell 1975, p. 72).
PAULO: The person who has reached conscientization
    is able to connect facts and problems,
    for example to see the connections
    between hunger and agrarian reform
    hunger as violence,
    hunger and politics.
SKEPTIC: How do you hold on to utopian dreams when you are starving and
    out of work?
DWIGHT CONQUERGOOD: Oppressed people are able to
    enter the historical process as
    responsible subjects, as agents
    capable of taking action

against their oppressors (Freire 2000, p. 67; Schutzman and Cohen-Cruz 2006a, pp. 2–3).

JOKER: How do you get them to this space?

AUGUSTO: The basis of our theatre
is not to give solutions,
not to incite people, per se.
We try to create the space
where they express
their own solutions.
This involved taking a play
up to a crisis point and then
letting the spectators take over?
The real beginning of TO and Forum
Theatre began when I was doing
simultaneous playwriting using people's
real experiences. In one of these a woman
told us what the protagonist should do.
We knew what had happened,
but we did not know what *should* happen.[6]
We reached a crisis point.
We tried her suggestions over and over again
but she was never satisfied.
So I said "Come to the stage to show us
what we should do because
we cannot interpret your thoughts."
She came on stage and showed us
what to say and what to do. By doing what
she demonstrated we understood immediately the enormous
differences between our interpretations and her own words and actions
(Boal in Taussig and Schechner 1994, pp. 22–23, paraphrase).

MICHAEL TAUSSIG: So you learned to perform up to a crisis and then stop and
ask spectators, "What do you believe should happen?" Then you asked
them to "make up their own lines, to write their own script" (Boal in
Taussig and Schechner 1994, p. 23, paraphrase).

AUGUSTO: Let me tell you a story about this (see Boal in Taussig and Schechner
1994, p. 23, paraphrase).

Curtain lowers, lights dim

Act One: Scene Three: In the beginning: real guns?

Curtain rises, lights dim

AUGUSTO: We wanted a new form of theatre,
a theatre for the oppressed.

We called this use of crisis
our anti-model. It stops action.
It is meant to instill intervention,
to invite spect-actors to act
out alternative actions.
This model came from a
experience in north-east Brazil
when we did a play that ends
with our telling people to
fight for their freedom,
to give their blood for the cause.
Someone came up to us and asked:

SPECTATOR AKA VIRGILLO: OK, if you think like that,
   come with us and let's
   fight the government. We have guns.

AUGUSTO: Virgillo, our guns are not real,
   they are fake. They are for doing plays,
   they can't actually be fired. We are just artists.

SPECTATOR AKA VIRGILLO: Yes, we know your rifles are false,
   but you are true. Come with us.
   We will give you real rifles.

AUGUSTO: Yes, we are true. We are serious artists.
   We believe in what we preach. We are not peasants.
   I am ashamed to say this, but I cannot
   take a rifle and kill someone.
   I must apologize. Never again will
   I incite an audience to
   do something I will not do myself.

SPECTATOR, AKA VIRGILLO: So when you true artists talk
   of blood that must be spilt, this blood
   you sing about spilling – it's our blood,
   not yours, isn't that so?

AUGUSTO: I'm embarrassed to say yes.
   But we are true to the cause.
   Absolutely, we are true artists.
   Please come back, let's talk about it.
   Come back. Virgillo walked away
   and I never saw him again (Boal 1995, pp. 2–3).

JOKER: So no Agit-prop for you.

BOAL: Exactly. Che Guevara wrote a beautiful phrase:
   solidarity means running the same risks.
   This helped me understand my error:
   agit-prop is fine, but not for me.
   We white men from the big city,
   there is very little we can

teach a black woman from the country.
Everyone should make their
own suggestions.
That is not our job (1995, p. 3).
We took this model back to the field.
We worked with peasants, poor people with
police, money and boss problems,
ordinary oppressed people with
free time to preoccupy themselves
with things like incommunicability, emptiness, loneliness.

Curtain lowers, lights dim

Act One: Scene Four: The dramaturgical model

Curtain rises, lights dim

JOKER: So how did you go forward? Who did you work with?[7]

AUGUSTO: We took this model back to the field. We worked with peasants, poor people with police, money and boss problems, battered wives, factory workers, teachers, anti-drug, anti-racist groups, ordinary oppressed people with free time to preoccupy themselves with things like incommunicability, emptiness, loneliness.

JOKER: The initial contact with a potential performance group (workers, students or villagers) can be difficult if they are confronted with a proposal to put on a theatrical performance.

AUGUSTO: They may have never heard of theatre, or they have misconceptions based on the media, or movies, or television, or they are self-conscious and are too embarrassed to perform. For these reasons it can help, in some situations at least, if the contact begins with an educator or leader who belongs to the same community. The experience should not begin with theatrical techniques that are just imposed. Beginning with the body is key. It should begin with Stage One – *Knowing the body* – then Stage Two, *making the body expressive* (see below). In *Stage Three* the spectator is encouraged to intervene in an action, to perform a short scene, to improvise with the aid of a script. The audience helps write the script which spect-actors then perform.

JOKER: We begin with a basic model which has these elements:

1   Script detailing oppression and a crisis;
2   An oppressor, the Antagonist;
3   An oppressed person, the Protagonist who has been defeated by the Antagonist;
4   The play is conducted by a facilitator who becomes the 'joker', the enabler, the mediator;

5   The Protagonist is replaced by spect-actors who offer alternatives to the actions of the Protagonist. together they rehearse change;
6   The joker guides, supports, decides nothing, but consults with the audience.[8]

AUGUSTO: I use theatre and performance to focus on crises in people's lives. In some versions of reality theatre actors pretend to be who they are not. "I am me and I am an actor, and I am a character, and I am pretending to be that character, but that is not who I am" (2006, pp. 67–68, paraphrase). In my Theatre of the Oppressed (TO) the spect-actors are performing scenes from their own, or other's lives. *The image of the real is as real as the image* (2006, p. 66, italics in original, paraphrase). Classical theatre established a division between actors (protagonists, chorus) and passive audiences, spectators. My intent, like Brecht, has to been to create a theatre which breaks down these walls.

JOKER: In classic theatre the stage belongs to the actors. The actor knows she is an actor and consciously tries to be unaware of the audience. In a Brechtian production the actor is completely aware of the presence of the audience, which she transforms into *silent interlocutors*. She of course is still an actor playing a character.

TAMI: Brecht's actor does not hide behind the character being played. By means of song, music, video, commentary and distance, she engages in some role distance. He separates herself from her character. She exposes her thinking to the audience, but the stage remains her property (Boal 2006, p. 73). Only in Forum Theatre do the spect-actors acquire a presence of their own, defined by voice, desire, movement, by sound and color. That is why the Theatre of the Oppressed was invented and continues to be reinvented (Boal 1995, p. 23).

AUGUSTO: In the Theatre of the Oppressed people are invited to come on stage to recount an episode of oppression in their lives. In so doing they are simultaneously narrator and narrated. For this reason they are able to imagine themselves in the future (2006, p. 62). The spectator becomes an actor who liberates a critical consciousness, her body invades the stage and transforms the images shown there. The act of acting, the act of narrating is potentially transformative and liberating.

JOKER: Who are you kidding? This is all pretend, the stage is not a real space. You need the illusion that pretense is real.

AUGUSTO: No, no, you are wrong. Here is an example: In one of our theatre workshops a woman in a barrio in Lima as both *oppressed, and protagonist* proposed a controversial theme.

Some years earlier her husband (*oppressor*) had given her some documents and asked her to keep them. He said that were important. She could not read them because she was illiterate. One day she and husband had a fight and she re-discovered the documents. She took them to a friend and asked her friend to read them for her. Her friend told her they were love letters from her husband's mistress. The woman was furious. She wanted revenge. What should she do? The *spect-actors* improvised alternative scenes. Each of these solutions was performed with spect-actors as the scripts were being written (simultaneous dramaturgy):

1 Cry a lot and make him feel guilty;
2 Leave her husband;
3 Lock him out of the house;
4 Let him come in, get a big stick and hit him as hard as you can until he repents. Put the stick away, serve him dinner and forgive him (Boal 1985, pp. 133–134).

The last solution was accepted unanimously by the entire audience, men and women.

SKEPTIC: The women were all pretending. Nothing changed. The wife hit her husband and cooked him a big meal, and forgave him. She changed, the husband did not change.

AUGUSTO: I can't accept this argument. Reality was enacted on that stage. Our performances often re-work and fit classic and contemporary theatre, from Shakespeare's Hamlet to Brecht's Three Penny Opera and the Jewish Wife, to the forum model itself. In The Jewish Wife,[9] for example, we did it exactly as Brecht wrote it, except when the Wife makes her phone calls. Then every person she calls does the work Brecht says they do, but they do not speak. The Doctor doctors, the Reporter writes, the friend acts like a friend, and so on. When the play was over I asked the audience:

'*Would you do the same thing as the wife in her situation?' As you were leaving would you ask someone to take care of your husband? (paraphrase)*

Then, using Forum Theatre we performed the play again. Spect-actors replaced the Wife and started discussions with the other actors (doctor, reporter wife, friend) who answered back. It was fascinating because spect-actors brought their own analogous problems into the play. It was not Hitler's Germany any longer, not Nazism, but it was struggles for freedom in France, Lebanon and elsewhere.

So this play, written to show how horrible reality was under Hitler, was used for another purpose, not to repeat Brecht's play but to show how totalitarian realities in other national settings can be changed (Boal in Taussig and Schechner 1994, p. 29).

SKEPTIC: Nobody disputes the horror of Hitler. But what does this little revision of Brecht do **to that horror?**

JOKER: The entire apparatus places a lot of weight on people pretending to be solving problems. There must be *huge willing suspension of disbelief*, to use Samuel Taylor Coleridge' term.

Curtain lowers, lights dim

Act One: Scene Five: Into action: schools, slums

> Curtain rises, lights

JOKER: In 1986 you went into public schools in the slums and worked with thirty-five social-cultural workers (cultural animators), who had never done theatre before. There was a network of public schools where students from the slums had breakfast, classes, lunch, afternoon arts or sports, a bath, dinner and some would take food home (Boal in Taussig and Schechner 1994, p. 17).

AUGUSTO: People started writing about racial and sexual aggressions, about oppressions and violence. They prepared five short plays complete with sets and music and costumes.

JOKER: You went from school to school. You transformed school cafeterias into small theatres. You performed the plays for students, teachers, neighbors.

AUGUSTO: We asked spectators which play they wanted to make into a forum. Spect-actors came forward and wrote their own endings for the plays. Then the plays were performed. People were beginning to experience freedom.

SKEPTIC: Says who? What does freedom mean here? A full stomach?

STUDENT AND HER MOTHER: Augusto and his actors helped us see how we could take part in our own education. We felt like we belonged, for the first time.

SKEPTIC: Did this really happen? Did they take the next step and act on this newly felt freedom by demanding change in the schools?

JOKER: No, that did not happen. Then there was a new election. The program was cancelled. Once more schools became places where sometimes classes happened sometimes not. No more forum theatre (Boal in Taussig and Schechner 1994, p. 23, paraphrase pp. 17–18).

AUGUSTO: Forum Theatre transforms spect-actors into agents who get out in front of history. They may have read Marx. Their goal is to change, not just understand history. The goal is to no longer allow history go on uncontested behind their backs (2002, pp. 25, 28; 2006, p. 7).

SKEPTIC: Do we really need Marx here?

JOKER: Do workers and peasants really need middle-class heroes to lead the revolution?

FORUM CLOWN: Of course not.

SKEPTIC: Here is the paradox. Is TO a form of populism that speaks to the oppressed, or does it make popular theatre deficient in the hands of the people; that is can the oppressed on their own make TO work? If they cannot, who should be the leader? Can a white male lead a workshop around issues of violence with aboriginal community members (George 1995, p. 41; Diamond 1994, p. 52; Schutzman and Cohen-Cruz 1994 p. 8).

RURAL TEACHER: I keep it simple. I taught a peasant how to write the word 'plough'; and he taught me how to use it (Boal 1998, p. 128).

GREEK CHORUS: Three cheers for rural teachers!

Lights dim, curtains lower.

Act Two: Scene One: Forms of the Theatre of the Oppressed

Curtain rises, lights dim

JOKER: So this is the background to Augusto's project, how he moved away from agit-prop to more participatory and therapeutic models of TO. The project divides into two parts, pre-1976 (Latin America), and post-1976 (Europe, U.S.).

AUGUSTO: The Theatre of the Oppressed evolved through several stages, moving away from early efforts at *agit-prop* preaching revolution (1964–1968) to: *Forum Theatre* (1970-);[10] *Image Theatre* (1973-); *Invisible Theatre* (1976-); *Legislative Theatre* (1992-); the Cop in the Head/ *Rainbow of Desire* (1995-). Any given workshop might involve elements of each of these formations, culminating in scenes on a street (Invisible Theatre) and then presentation to an audience in Forum Theatre, then performance events using exercises from the Rainbow of Desire.[11]

***

Stage Right: spotlight shines on the **Tree of the Theatre of the Oppressed** by Augusto Boal (2006, p. 3):

	Legislative Theatre[12]	
Direct Actions[13]	Forum Theatre	Invisible Theatre[14]
Newspaper Theatre[15]	Image Theatre[16]	Rainbow of Desire[17]
Ethics	Games	Politics
Solidarity		History
Sound	Image	Words

***

SKEPTIC: Let it be recorded that Augusto did not invent these theatre forms out of whole clothes. *Invisible theatre* belongs to a "category of 1960s U. S. experiments known as '*street theatre*' and 'guerrilla theatre'." *Newspaper theatre* can be traced to grass-roots community activist theatre from the 1920s forward in the U.S., as well as the global Popular Theatre Alliance (George 1995, p. 43). In the early 1990s Jim Mienczakowski's public-voice ethnography put issues surrounding community health care back in the hands of the community (Dennis 2009, p. 72; Mienczakowski 2001).

JOKER: Augusto never claimed he invented invisible theatre. He credits the term to an actor who had the idea of playing a scene as 'invisible theatre' inside a restaurant. This removed the need for a stage set (Boal 2001, p. 304).

AUGUSTO: Since 1970 the tree of the Theatre of the Oppressed has never stopped growing, starting in Brazil it has spread across five continents. Each of its parts has the same origin, the same interconnection between ethics, politics, history and philosophy. Each part has remained true to the original proposition, which is the unwavering support of the theatre in the struggles of the oppressed, ways of using TO to address the effects of the cop in the head (2002, p. 206; 2006, p. 4).

PAULO: The oppressions suffered by persons in authoritarian regimes can be profoundly damaging, penetrating into their unconscious. The cop steps out of the barracks moves into one's head. We carry the cops with us, they are our 'cops in the head' (2002, p. 206).

AUGUSTO: When we started working in Europe we discovered great depths of loneliness and alienation. These are also caused by cops-in-our heads. We have new Image Theatre techniques, the Rainbow of Desire, that help us get these cops out of our heads. We've given these techniques names: dissociation, analytical image, mirror image, somatization, circuit of rituals, screen image. They are actions we can take to make the cop more visible, to recognize, to know, and to transform, to become free of the cop's presence (1992/2002, p. 207).

SKEPTIC: This is psychotherapy gibberish.

JOKER: Clearly there is some confusion here. For some TO is psychotherapy with parallels to J. L. Moreno's sociodrama for individuals. For others it is a tool for radical social change (Schutzman and Cohen-Cruz 1994, p, 10). I believe Augusto believes it is both, therapy and tool.

Lights dim, curtains lower.

Act Two: Scene Three: A new poetic, a new theatre

Curtain rises, lights dim
   Stage Right: spotlight shines on the cover to *The Aesthetics of the Oppressed* by Augusto Boal, translated by Adrian Jackson.

AUGUSTO: Joker, hold off a minute. For now we are agreed. The main goal is to help human beings who are suffering. We teach a new language, a new poetic. Aristotle's spectator delegates power to characters on the stage who act and think for her. In Brecht's theatre a spectator also delegates power to the character, but she reserves the right to think for herself, often in opposition to the character. In the case of Aristotle a *catharsis* occurs, in Brecht's case it is the creation of a *critical consciousness*.

TAMI: But how does TO differ from Brecht? You encourage the development of a critical consciousness.

AUGUSTO: Here is where we differ, the *poetics of the oppressed* of TO focuses on action itself. The spect-ator delegates no power to the character, either to think, or act in her place. On the contrary, she assumes the protagonist role. She changes the dramatic action, tries out solutions, discusses plans for change, rehearses action, trains herself for real action. This is a poetic for revolution (1985, p. 122).

JOKER: Isn't there some pretending going on here. We're back to Coleridge's suspension of disbelief.

TAMI: Hold that thought. What happens to Aristotle's catharsis?

RICHARD SCHECHNER: Remember, Aristotle's catharsis is produced by actors on the stage for passive audience members who vicariously experience the actor's catharsis. As I understand it Augusto avoids this entirely.

AUGUSTO: Richard is right. Spect-actors create their own catharsis through the actions they take on and off the stage. For too long we have been seduced by plays in which actors make the revolution on stage and spectators sit in their seats and feel themselves to be triumphant revolutionaries.

JOKER: Augusto locates his model of catharsis in the ability of the spect-actor to make the action happen. She intervenes, she acts on her own behalf and with others. This produces a different kind of catharsis, a dialogical, self reflective catharsis (1995, pp. 70–72; 1985, p. 122). It also produces critical consciousness, the sine qua non of revolution.

TAMI: Got it! Amazing. This is my poetic too, a transformational catharsis grounded in the actions and dialogical relationships of the performative I.

SKEPTIC: Is this really transformative? Is she really experiencing catharsis?

NORMAN: Not so quick here. Aristotle, Brecht, Boal, I'm an ethnographer, not a playwright! Why all this fuss about catharsis? I want a text that tells a story, and moves people to action. They do not have to have an experience of catharsis. How will TO help me do this? You give me very few models.

AUGUSTO: What can I say. It is hard work,

JOKER: Transforming the spectator into an actor who becomes a performer in TO involves at least four steps, or stages (Boal 1985, p. 126).

SKEPTIC: Four steps? Says who? Munbo Jumpo again.

JOKER: Nothing happens all at once.

Lights dim, curtains lower.

Act Two: Scene Four: The stages of the Theatre of the Oppressed

Curtain rises, lights dim

AUGUSTO: I must note, without steps, stages, rules and procedures, we get no where. Permit me to lay out the stages:

First Stage: *Knowing the body*: A series of exercises to get to know the body.

Second Stage: *Making the body expressive* through a series of games. At the trunk of the tree of the Theatre of the Oppressed are the games, and games have rules (Boal 2006, p. 4; 1985, p. 126).

Third stage: *The theatre as language*: practicing the theatre as a living language

First degree: Simultaneous dramaturgy: Spectators write simultaneously with the actors with protagonists, antagonists, spect-actors, joker.

Second degree: Image theatre: Spectators intervene directly, speaking through images made with the actor's bodies.

Third degree: Forum Theatre: Spectators intervene directly in dramatic action (1985, p, 126).

Fourth Stage: *The theatre as discourse*: spectator-actors create scripts according to need and occasion, using techniques from newspaper, image and invisible theatre, as well as focusing on other forms of oppression from daily life (myth, ritual, popular culture) (1985, p. 126; 2006, pp. 4–5).

SKEPTIC: Augusto and I argue all the time over how people progress through these stages, but clearly his workshops and performance events are designed to help people transition from stage one to stage four.

JOKER: In a sense the four stages are *the* Theatre of the Oppressed.[18] These essential elements have been in place since 1974 when the book *Theatre of the Oppressed* first appeared in Spanish.

AUGUSTO: I like to think in terms of stages, or phases of development of critical awareness. I like to use games, and rules, and categories, and exercises that reflexively bring the actor's mind and the body together. We experiment with many different exercises:

** ways of walking (crab, crossed leg, camel, elephant, kangaroo);
** ways of hearing, breathing, seeing, looking;
** ways of using and moving in space;
** games using masks and rituals, games that create characters;
** ways of reconnecting sensations, memory, emotion, imagination and the body
** ways of experimenting with multiple identities based on
gender, sexuality, race, class, nation, language, disability.[19]

JOKER: These activities are very important. They are ways of moving people into the right mental space.

AUGUSTO: Many of my workshops last up to six days (Boal 2002, pp. 18–19):[20]
Days One and Two: Knowing the body, making the body expressive;
Days Three and Four: Prepare and rehearse scenes and scripts;
Day Five: Perform Invisible Theatre on the streets;
Day Six: Forum Theatre presented to an audience.[21]

SOYINI MADISON: This is an elegant scheme, everyday actors creating and confronting scenes of social injustice.

RICHARD SCHECHNER: I call this doing social theatre, using theatre to bring about social change (Schechner 2015, pp. 11–12; Thompson and Schechner 2004, p. 11).

TAMI: There is a lot of heavy lifting going on here. Augusto makes this look easy. It is not easy. I suspect it can go south at a moment's notice. There has to be trust and a willingness to work together within a set of rules.

NARRATOR: I've had a few experiments that blew up! There were mis-understandings, emotions heated up, lines were crossed, trust was broken, students walked away, never to come back.

JOKER: What does it mean for TO to work? What does it mean?

Lights dim, curtains lower.

Act Two: Scene Five: Theatre of the Oppressed as critical ethnography[22]

    Curtain rises, lights dim

NARRATOR: Time is of the essence. We must move on to the topic of pedagogy, and working with our students. Many of them want to do critical perfor-mance ethnographies and combine it with TO. They ask how have critical performance ethnographers used TO on the past? What techniques from TO have they employed?

JOKER: From our discussion thus far it would appear that there would be perfect fit with performance ethnography. Augusto is all about perfor-mance, intervention, and social justice. Critical performance ethnography is framed by the same concerns.

TAMI: Yes but, Augusto is not an ethnographer, he is a director.

BARBARA DENNIS: I combined these two activities – ethnographer and director– in my school ethnography. I worked with a team of graduate students. I used a modified version of TO's forum theatre with the joker system in a long-term critical ethnography which examined the integration of English language learners (and their teachers) in a Midwestern U.S. high school. I used TO with teachers to explore their role in the bullying activities of stu-dents. The use of TO led me to blur the line between critical ethnographic inquiry (gathering empirical materials), interpretation and performance.

JOKER: What did you do?

BARBARA: We used warm-up activities from image theatre, asking participants to act as sculptors on static images formed with bodies, in this case to assume a position they felt personally empowering. We then asked them to dramatize a bullying scene from our data. The bullying scene takes place in the hallway during the change of classes:

    A teacher is standing in the hallway. Two Latino kids are walking together down the hall and three Euro-American kids are calling the Latinos names, like "Speak English or go home." "Get out of here, you dirty Mexican." The teacher is witness to the activities (Dennis 2009, p. 75, paraphrase). In the afternoon session the teacher stops the white students and challenges them for what they said to the Latino students. At that point I stopped the action and asked the teacher, "Why did you say that?" And then started the action up again, asking the students how they felt and how they were affected by the experience. A succession of re-enacted iterations followed the first set, with spectators and actors swapping roles, new characters were introduced and new possibilities imagined. Each iteration was followed by dialogue (p. 77).

JOKER: You used TO to blur the lines between traditional, performance and critical ethnography. You dramatized your empirical materials through dialogue and performance. The participants created scene reenactments and dialogue through the interpretive process. You and your co-researchers committed yourselves to authentic dialogue with the teachers. Like Boal, you maximized your involvement on the project. Your participants were also researchers, they were like Boal's spect-actors.

SKEPTIC: What do you mean by authentic dialogue? By scene reenactments? Did the students and teachers as spect-actors take this seriously? Or where they just pretending?

BARBARA: We developed a long-term relationship with the school, the teachers and the students. It was clear the teachers had difficulty seeing themselves as oppressors. They proposed that students should be the ones making changes not themselves, only later did they turn a critical eye on their part in the oppressive relationships. However, teachers came to understand how newcomers were being victimized in the bullying process. This understanding happened as a result of the ethnographic process itself, and the techniques we borrowed from TO.

JOKER: You used Boal to frame your critical school ethnography. Your use of his techniques turned your ethnography into a dialogical, collaborative project. You went beyond critique to offering suggestions for transforming the process itself. Inquiry was turned into moral discourse.

SKEPTIC: For whom was it a moral discourse?

TAMI: Listen to Soyini. She is doing the same thing. She is talking about a fieldworker and a local activist in West Africa named Joan who also used Boal's methods (Madison 2012).

SOYINI: Joan wanted to stage a performance that brought her fieldnotes and fieldwork alive. She wanted to serve as a translator for people who would not have access to the materials she had witnessed, She wanted to communicate to a larger pubic, to appeal to the emotions, to be a force for advocacy.

JOKER: How did she use TO?

SOYINI: Joan used Boal's image theatre to form representations of freedom, justice, dream and a politics of possibility. Her researcher-actors transformed their bodies into three-dimensional conceptual pictures (Madison 2012, p. 235). During rehearsals Joan used the 'joker' to help enact a scene, or image. She used the anti-method of stopping a scene and inviting performers (spect-actors) to provide different endings for the scene. Her critical ethnography was doubly performative. It combined elements of Boal's dramaturgy with a commitment to script and perform acts of radial activism.

DIANE CONRAD: I did some of this in my Popular Theatre project with at-risk, Aboriginal high school drama students in a rural Alberta Community. In this project my use of Popular theatre drew on autoethnography, Theatre of the Oppressed, participatory action research, performance ethnography and arts-based research. Following Johnny Saldana I wrote a series of scripted descriptions, or 'ethnographic vignettes' that students then enacted (Conrad 2004, p. 18). I played the part of 'joker.' In the midst of a re-enactment, like Dennis, and Joan, I would stop action temporally to question the performer-actors, to delve more deeply into the moment of action.

The script involved a group of students illicitly drinking alcohol on the bus ride home from a class trip. The students improvised a scene which involved buying alcohol. In the midst of the re-enactment Diane, in the role of joker (teacher), stopped the action to question the actors to delve more deeply into their decision making.

SHADZZ: (to Daryl): So give me some money man, to buy the stuff.

DARYL: Na, forget it.

SHADZZ: Come on man you said you wanted to.

DARYL: Naw, Okay, what the hell, here

(gives Shadzz some money.)

TEACHER (DIANE): (Interrupting the improvisation): Stop it there a minute Daryl. I want to ask your character a question. You hesitated to give him the money. Why?

DARYL: I wasn't sure if I wanted to risk it.

TEACHER: Go on.

DARYL: You might get caught,

TEACHER: So why do you do it?

SHADZZ: I don't know, the rush I guess. Just the rush,

TEACHER: For the rush. Something risky gives you a rush?

(Echoes of agreement around the room.)

Diane's intervention explored the meanings behind the student's actions, revealing they sometimes engaged in risky behavior for the rush (Conrad 2004, p. 20).

JOKER: So she used a script, or vignette, and a joker, but who was the Protagonist and who was the Antagonist? Where was the forum participation?

SKEPTIC: Irrelevant. She broke out of a mold and experimented, pure Boal, pushing the envelope. This is critical pedagogy in action.

Lights dim, curtains lower

Act Three: Scene One: Whose performance poetic?

Curtain rises, lights dim

TAMI SPRY: Lets go back to the title. Theatre of the Oppressed. It's all here: Body, Paper, Stage, the three words in the title of my book. These are the three key elements of Augusto's theatre, and the key elements of TO, theatre's core materiality: a expressive performing body, with a script and a stage. Here are rules to make the body expressively available to the other, a talking moving body, my body implicated with your body, my body as a site of and an agent of resistance.

SOYINI: Augusto is very participatory. His exercises are not unlike the studio exercises used by Joe Norris, and Johnny Saldana, and they have similarities to Victor Turner's fieldwork workshops which turned classrooms into rehearsal spaces (see Saldana 2011, pp. 47, 58). I've even used some of them in my studio classes,

JOHNNY: Soyini is right. I use a lot of Augusto in my ethnodramas. Some of my ethnodramatic studio exercises involve improvisational activities, for example embodying characters in as 'if dialogues' or mimicking their physical movements and gestures. Other exercises involve writing scripts dramatizing a current event reported in the media. Conversational dramatism is another technique, it involves performing verbatim talk from everyday life on the stage.

JOE NORRIS: I suppose we all steal from Augusto (Norris 2009, p. 33; Saldana 2011, p. 58). I use many of his techniques, from storytelling, to the use of guided imagery, photographs, slide shows, cards and posters, props, costumes, music, lighting, darkness, sound, narration anything to get the spect-actor into the right interpretive frame (Norris 2009, pp. 4–53).

JOKER: Of course these are all performances, rehearsing for a performance is a performance.

VICTOR TURNER AND RICHARD SCHECHNER: Correct. Performance is making, not faking, not pretending, performance is real, it has a material presence in the world, performance is a way of creating reality, making, re-making, interrupting.

AUGUSTO: My view exactly. Forum Theatre is all about harnessing performance, using performance to create critical awareness. I'm delighted to discover all of these connections between TO, ethnotheatre, and performance ethnography

DWIGHT: We all agree. Performance is always performative, always political. Tami's performative I is constantly re-making the world. Augusto turns the performative I into an active political agent. Performing is an embodied way of knowing. Augusto's strategies, stages and games are all ways of implementing this embodied performative way of knowing.

JOKER: We got way off track here. Of course it is good to see these overlaps.

ANNA DEAVERE SMITH: Augusto's theatre is a living language. It is the actor's and director's task to make history present, to make the future present, to make the unreal present, to confront history in the rearview mirror, to confront, not just react to history (2003, p. xvi).

AUGUSTO: This is what spect-actors do in Stage Three. They write, they intervene, they speak through images, through others, through texts, objects, and history. This is why I have the joker, the character who helps make all of this happen.

TAMI: In Stage Four theatre turns into spectacle, the performative I takes over, using any and every available material object to enact a politics of hope.

DWIGHT CONQUERGOOD: Let me jump in. Here is where my three major triads come together: the I's (intervention), the A's (activism, artistry), the C's (critique, citizenship). Performance ethnography uses performance (theatre) to make structures of oppression visible.

JOHNNY SALDANA: This is what ethnodrama can do. We are all on the same page or on different pages in the same book.

SOYINI: I've experimented with Forum Theatre performances. They create great excitement. They give spect-actors the feeling that they can intervene in their own and others' fate, that they can challenge situations of injustice. More importantly, as Augusto points out, actors interpret for the group, not just for themselves. This becomes a collaborative project. The actor-as-writer-as-performer creates a text for the community, not just for herself (Boal 1985, p. 134). These are the kinds of scripts I included in Acts of Activism: Human Rights as Radical Performance. They were staged ethnographies, moral discourses based on an embodied performative epistemology.

JOKER: What do you mean by embodied epistemology?

SOYINI: Exactly what Augusto means, performing as a way of knowing. I privileged witnessing over observation, and performance over participation. I called this, after Dwight, co-performative witnessing. It involves a radical interactive engagement with the other, a politics of the body actively grounded in a shared space where speaking subjects produce lived history, radical acts of activism (Madison 2007, p. 826; 2012, pp. 13, 24–25).

AUGUSTO: Maybe the theatre itself is not revolutionary, but these theatrical forms are without a doubt a *rehearsal for revolution*. The spectator-as-actor produces a real act, even though she does it in a fictional manner, she is rehearsing a real act, whether it is throwing a bomb on stage, or leaving a spouse, it is a concrete act. The rehearsal simulates the practice of the act in reality, in the world outside the stage (1985, pp. 141–142, paraphrase).

TAMI: Remember what James Arthur Baldwin said (paraphrase):
We write and perform in order to change the world. The world changes according to the way people perform it. If you alter, even by a millimeter, the way people look at reality, then you can change it, and you have been a success.[23]
This is what performance does, it changes the way people look at reality.

JOKER: All forms of TO are poetics for the oppressed, blueprints for freedom. The spect-actor imagines a new beginning, confronts pain in her life, she imagines alternative ways to address her situation, the thinks, talks with others, tries out different solutions. She frees herself, she feels, thinks, casts off her sorrow, and acts for herself. Her improvised scenes, don't call them fictions, penetrate reality, and become reality (1995, p. 185; 1985, p. 155).

Lights dim, curtains lower

Act Three: Scene Two: Situating the Theatre of the Oppressed

> Curtain rises, lights dim

NARRATOR: Let's step back for a moment. We've talked about Turner's performance anthropology, Conquergood's performance ethnography, Madison's critical ethnography, Spry's performance autoethnography, Saldana's ethnodramas, Norris' playacting, Mienczakowski's public voice ethnography. Each of these forms, in one way or another, focus on crises and moments of epiphany in the lives of persons. Suspended in time, the crisis is a liminal moment. Isn't this what TO does?

SOYINI: I would agree, I want to use performance ethnography as a way of making instances of social injustice visible. These instances occur as crises, or epiphanies in daily life.

I think Jim and Tami would agree, Johnny too.

JOHNNY: My ethnodramas move the ethnographic study of epiphanies into the performance spaces defined by traditional theatre. I use all the standard terms: persons, actors, performers, characters, protagonists, scripts, stages, props, costumes, audiences.

JIM MIENCZAKOWSKI: In traditional, but not participatory ethnotheatre, the stage belongs to the characters and the actors, not the audience. The wall between stage and audience does not come down (Boal 2006, p. 73).[24] In our work with at risk groups we take up matters of life, death, health, illness. The wall comes down. Actors and audience share the same space, the same stage. This is especially so in post-performance debriefing interactions between audience and performers.

MADY SCHUTZMAN AND JAN COHEN-CRUZ: Augusto Boal's Theatre of the Oppressed (TO) does nothing less than re-invent the language of classic theatre. His is a poetics of liberation, the spectator no longer delegates power to the characters, or the actors, either to think or act in her place. The spectator frees herself; she thinks and acts for herself!

JOKER: This sounds pretty laudatory, really, he re-invented the language of classic theatre? Come on! Do you really want to go that far? I mean he wasn't the only person to take theatre in new directions. Brecht, Sophocles, Shakespeare, Marlow?!

SKEPTIC: Augusto puts a lot of weight on the shoulders of spectators and actors. Remember his spect-actor is not a trained stage actor. He or she is a spectator, an audience member brought onto a performance. How does she embrace her part? Is she improvising, pretending? Does she believe in what she is doing? What does it mean to say she is acting for herself? After all she is playing the part of a person who is enacting an instance of oppression, she is not necessarily that person, in fact she seldom is. So in terms of claims and in terms of arguments about what happens to spect-actors let's back-off a little here.

> Curtain lowers, lights dim

Act Three: Scene Two: a new social theatre

Curtain rises, lights dim

JAMES THOMPSON AND RICHARD SCHECHNER: We want to throw our hats into the ring. Augusto's project helped open the space for a new performative theatre, a social theatre that stands alongside, sometimes in place of 'aesthetic theatre' (including experimental, art, and commercial theatre) (Schechner 2015, p. 11; Thompson and Schechner 2004, p. 11).

JOKER: What is social theatre?

JAMES AND RICHARD: Social theatre is a theatre practiced in times and places of crisis (Thompson and Schechner 2004, p. 14). It is theatre with a social agenda. It is not theatre where aesthetics or making money are the ruling objective. It is theatre outside the realm of commerce, and the cult of the new which drives the avant-garde (p. 12).

JOKER: Sounds a lot like Theatre of the Oppressed.

JAMES AND RICHARD: Agreed. Social theatre takes place in the places where people are struggling, where they feel oppression, in slums, shelters for the homeless, prisons, refugee camps, hospitals, schools, classrooms, orphanages, homes for the elderly, in places where persons are displaced, vulnerable, marginalized. Social theatre occurs in nontheatrical spaces where theatre and community intersect. We turn everyday nonperformers into performers.

JOKER: I thought you said every person is a performer, even in everyday life, so what does it mean to turn a nonperformer into a performer?

JAMES AND RICHARD: We train them to be social theatre practitioners, to be activists, facilitators. They are like Boal's joker and his spect-actors. They help persons perform acts of resistance (Thompson and Schechner 2004, p. 15).

SKEPTIC: This feels like applied theatre. Applied theatre is also responsive to ordinary people and their stories and their needs. Like social theatre it happens in informal, non-theatre spaces: schools, day centers, the street, prisons, village halls. Often there is no audience, only participants. It goes by all sorts of names: prison theatre, popular theatre, interventionist theatre, theatre for development.

JOKER: Remember, what is called theatre is itself problematic. Theatre is always responsive to the circumstances in which it is used. However the purpose of staging applied theatre, like social theatre, is to produce changes in the world (Prentki and Preston 2009, pp. 9–10).

SKEPTIC: You could say this is theatre for, produced with and performed by a local moral community (Prentki and Preston 2009, p. 10). It is W. E. B Du Bois's theatre by, for and with oppressed peoples.

RICHARD: I agree completely. We also bring social theory into the picture, that is theory that pertains to the site where performances happen. Theatre in schools uses critical pedagogy from Friere to Giroux, Kincheloe and

McLaren. Theatre in prison uses different models of criminology, from conflict to radical criminology. Of course we are also informed by theories of performance, the avant-garde, postmodernism, poststructuralism, psychoanalysis, feminism, queer and critical race theory.

SKEPTIC: But why theory? Denzin says theory has to pass through the eye of a needle before it is useful. Too much theory is filled with big words. Often it is disconnected from the real world. It just amounts to theorists talking back and forth to one another.

RICHARD: For me performance is a category of theory, it is sui generis, a fact of experience. Ed Bruner and Victor Turner reminded me that we do not study experience, we study performance events that represent experience. This means it becomes increasingly difficult to sustain distinctions between appearances and illusions, between facts, surfaces, depths, the underneath, the hidden, the real (Schechner 2015, p. 7).

JOKER: What's real?

RICHARD: Performances are real. Appearances are actualities that drive action, they are real. For those of us who are postmodernists, the performance, the simulation is the real, the distinctions between surface and deep disappear. It is all fluid, interactive, constantly moving (2015, p. 8).

JAMES: I'm not going to defend high level theory. Applying theory to a situation means the dramatist enters an existing context, or discursive space already filled with constraints and understandings connected to gender, race, class, language and community. These understandings must be honored and understood.

SKEPTIC: Fair enough!

RICHARD: These constraints raise the issue of gaining permission to perform from those who control the setting, which can include prison officers, school administrators, social workers, as well as local community leaders.

JAMES: Remember, these are sites where theatrical performances are already occurring in the dress, demeanor, speech, and actions of the participants. The act of bringing theatre into these contexts represents a process, a rubbing up against of existing performative understandings. There can be no predictable outcome (Thompson and Schechner 2004, p. 13).

RICHARD: It ought to be a performance that transforms practitioners, the participants and the public's understandings of the situation at hand. It should create new forms of critical awareness and critical consciousness.

JOKER: Of course social theatre has to sell or market itself: claiming it supports self-esteem, builds character and self-confidence, helps with anger management, heals psychological wounds, brings communities together, creates new approaches for reducing crime and violence.

JAMES: Showing the value of our work is one thing, but we must never sell out. We must never mistake performances intended to persuade for critical analysis (2004, p. 12).

RICHARD: At the same time, there must be a dynamic interaction between the intentions of social theatre and the needs of a community. This interaction should produce change in both directions (2004, p 13).

JAMES: For example, before placing theatre inside a disability community, the artist must discover the needs of young disabled people in the setting. Creating a theatre project in a prison means working with people who are forced to wear costumes and live according to managed scripts which are rehearsals for life in the real world out-side the four-walls of the prison (Thompson and Schechner 2004, p. 13; also Forber-Pratt 2015).

RICHARD: Creating a theatre project in a war zone means working with persons characterized as victims, perpetrators, combatants, civilians, persons traumatized by witnessing actions of violence (2004, p. 14).

JOKER: In each of these examples social theatre celebrates the human spirit and inspires utopian dreams of possibility.

JAMES: There are several different types of performance, or forms of performing involving memory and forgetting that can emerge from sites of crisis, oppression and pain, including (2004, p. 15):

Performing/staging acts of testimony of whose who have experienced violence and oppression, for example testimony before South Africa's Truth and Reconciliation Commission;

Performing/staging symbolic acts which accuse oppressors of violence, for example the group of Argentinian mothers dressed in black who marched in a silent circle every Thursday afternoon around Buenos Aires Plaza de Mayo protesting the torture and murders that occurred during Argentina's "dirty war" (1976–1983) (2004, p. 14);

Performing/staging acts of resistance as in Boal's Theatre of the Oppressed;

Performing/staging acts of alleviation which help people in crisis to meet personal and community needs, for example providing food, water, medicine, shelter, jobs, schooling;

Performing/staging acts of entertainment and art which can help people remember, forget and heal (Thompson and Schechner 2004, pp. 14–15).

JAMES AND RICHARD: Remembering, forgetting, and performing are necessary for the resumption of everyday life and for long-term health and healing (p. 15). We can say there are four types or forms of social theatre:

1 Theatre for healing.
2 Theatre for action
3 Theatre for community
4 Theatre for transforming experience into art (2004, p. 15).

These four forms can happen simultaneously, they can logically unfold as a sequence from misery, to action, to community building, to art. Without alleviating misery and taking action there can be no community, and without community there can be no art.

C. WRIGHT MILLS: Through performance applied social theatre helps persons translate private troubles into public issues; that is into representations that can be used to mobilize social action and critical analysis. This form of theatre can be used to influence public policy. It can contribute to social justice in the following ways (Denzin 2010, pp. 24–25):

1   It can help identify different definitions of a problem where there may or may not be agreement that change is required.
2   In such situations the assumptions, often belied by facts, that are held by various interested parties – policy makers, clients, welfare workers, on-line professionals – can be represented through performance and dialogue, and shown to be correct, or incorrect (Becker 1967, p. 23).
3   Strategic points of intervention into social situations can then be identified.
4   It is possible to suggest "alternative moral points of view from which the problem," the policy, and the situation can be interpreted and assessed (see Becker 1967, pp. 23–24). The Social theatre model suggests that problem situations must always be judged by and from the point of view of the persons most directly affected.
5.   The limits of neo-liberal audit procedures can be exposed. The emphasis on the uniqueness of each life holds up the individual case as the measure of the effectiveness of any proposed change.

Applied, social theatre performance offers a method of understanding what goes in in a site. Performance becomes a way of intervening, participating in and collaborating with a moral community, helping, hopefully, to change the world in positive ways (Thompson and Schechner 2004, p. 16).

Curtain lowers, lights dim

Act Three: Scene Three: Lessons learned

Curtain rises, lights dim

NARRATOR: What do we take-away from all of this?
JOKER: Simple: One long word: ethnographer-as-director-as-inquirer-as facilitator-as critic, performance-as moral-inquiry.
AUGUSTO: It gives me great delight to see the many ways my friends in critical performance ethnography use my ideas and words including. Let the words move across the page:

forum theatre,
image theatre,
the joker social justice,
critical pedagogy workshops
dramaturgy dramatic theory

performance, the media,
simultaneous playwriting,

acts activism,
taking a scene up to a crisis and then stopping,
staging re-enactments,

dialogue,
turning persons into co-performers,
turning participants into actors,
taking the side of the oppressed,
inspiring utopian dreams,
creating moral
communities

Invisible theatre masks, oppression, cops in the head
healing hope, forgiving, new poetic,
self-reflection,
body, paper, stage,
stories, scenes of injustice,
doing social theatre
as intervention

performative I
rehearsals for revolution
epiphanies

brecht, Aristotle,
schechner, conquergood, Thompson
turner, saldana, goffman,

madison, boal, freire,
spry, smith, mienczakowski,
cohen-cruz, taussig,
schutzman, dennis, conrad,
joker, clowns, coyote
AMEN

Lights dim, curtains lower

Act Three: Scene Four: Ethical injunctions

Curtain rises, lights dim

PAULO: In the end Augusto is quite clear. And I agree with him. Theatre of the
Oppressed, (and social theatre) creates dialogical performances that show how

1   Every oppressed person is a subjugated subversive.
2   The Cop in our Head represents our submission to this oppression.

3   Each person possesses the ability to be subversive
4   The Theatre of the Oppressed, as a form of Critical Pedagogical Theatre, can empower persons to be subversive, and to be active agents in resisting oppression.

SKEPTIC: Mere words.
TAMI SPRY: Skeptic, be quiet! There are ethical injunctions that follow. Does this performance event, this workshop, this instance of social theatre:

1   Expose and neutralize the cop in the head?
2   Bear witness to an injustice?
3   Nurture critical race, class, and gender consciousness?
4   Use historical re-stagings to subvert official oppressive neoliberal ideologies?
5   Heal, empower, respect, create community solidarity?
6   Recover, enhance and preserve the integrity, stability and beauty of a moral community? (Leopold 1949).
7   Enact dialogue and a feminist communitarian ethic of hope?
8   Give persons a language for confronting oppression in the future.
9   Speaks to acts of activism, acts of resistance, acts of rebellion, of resiliency, acts of indignation, the just anger of those who have been deceived and betrayed by the powerful (Freire 1998, p, 93).

JOKER: Aren't you asking a lot of any performance event? Is this list even realistic? What do these words mean?
TAMI AND AUGUSTO, JAMES AND RICHARD: There is more, and it is complicated. While doing social theatre involves taking the side of the oppressed, there will always be multiple points of view. It is never simple. We have a duty to hear everyone, to see and understand contradictions, to understand that ethical choices arise in moments of crisis and conflict, these are the times of intervention. In these moments, those spaces, people will be hurt, oppressors may be shamed, embarrassed, challenged, or feel they are misunderstood, or mis-represented.
PAULO: Every oppressed person has the right to rebel against the ethical and moral transgressions committed by the oppressor. The oppressed must be encouraged to speak out (1998, p. 93).
AUGUSTO: When you live theatre, you live in emotion, you live in hope, you dream, you have hope, hope, like live theatre, is an ontological need (Freire 1999, p. 8). We seek reconciliation, healing, not shaming or punishment, or harm to the other, yet we stand up for the rights of the oppressed.
SKEPTIC: Too much philosophy for me. Somebody is always hurt. Don't kid yourself. Harm is always done.
PAULO: We must invent new ways of living, and living with others. I have a dream, a belief, I am driven by the hope of remaking the world. a dream of a world where there is freedom from oppression, where persons are united

in solidarity. We are ethical beings, nothing can justify the degradation of another human being. We are called to intervene in the world (Freire 1998, pp. 93, 99).

AUGUSTO: You always say hopelessness is hope that has lost its footing.

PAULO: Hopelessness is a sickness. The powerful are beyond shame, corruption is gaining the upper hand, crimes go unpunished, starving people cry out.

JOKER: So your ethical injunctions are meant to be about recovering hope. I don't want to be too cynical, but I see a huge distance between your injunctions and actual everyday experiences.

Lights dim, curtains lower

Act Three: Scene Five: Hope

Lights dim, curtains rise

PAULO, AUGUSTO, ANNA, SOYINI, WITH THE FORUM THEATRE PERFORMERS: (in unison):

hope is a need
hope seeks truth
hope is ethical
hope is moral
hope is nonviolent
hope is love
hope rejects terrorism
hope seeks peace

hope turns
oppression into freedom
despair into hope
hatred into love
doubt into trust
oppression into justice

HOPE IS

In conclusion

I seek an autoethnographic theatre for social justice. I seek a social theatre that pushes back against the structures of neoliberalism. With Augusto Boal and Paulo Freire I seek a pedagogy of the unfinished, new horizons of hope, pedagogies of solidarity (Freire 2007).

Augusto Boal said that in order to exist he needed Paulo Freire. It's not clear this was the case for Paulo.[25] In the next chapter Paulo comes back on stage. Reading Pedagogy of the Oppressed through Theatre of the Oppressed, using techniques from Theatre of the Oppressed, I put Paulo and Augusto in dialogue with one another. I call this "Performing Critical Pedagogy: Learning from Paulo" (Freire and Faundez 1989; Freire 1999/1992, 1998, 1996, 2007; Freire, Freire and de Oloveria 2014; also Darder 2002; McLaren 2002; Gadotti 1994; Schugurensky 2014).

Notes

1 Augusto Boal, Diane Conrad, Barbara Dennis, Paulo Freire, Greek Chorus, Forum Clowns, Joker, Skeptic, Ms Coyote, Anna Deavere Smith, Mady Schutzman, Jan Cohen-Cruz, Dwight Conquergood, Victor Turner, Soyini Madison, Richad Schechner, Michael Taussig, Johnny Saldana, Tami Spry, Joe Norris.

2 The **Joker** (from the joker, or wild card in a deck of playing cards) is the director/ master of ceremonies of a TO workshop. In forum theatre the joker sets up the rules for the audience, facilitates the spectator's replacement of the protagonist and summarizes the essence of each solution proposed by the spect-actor. The **Joker System** mixes fact and fiction, and the shifting of identities so that all actors play all characters. The joker is used as a narrator who address the audience directly, a "wild card" actor able to jump in and out of any role in the play at any time (Schutzman and Cohen-Cruz 2006b, p. 237; Boal 1985, pp. 168–181). According to George (1995, pp. 41–43) much ado about nothing has been made of Boal's concept of the joker, that it in fact was extracted from Brecht, and when first put in practice it failed (but see Boal 2001, pp. 242, 248–249). McMahon (2005, pp. 77–78) provides a reading of Boal's use of the joker in his plays (e.g. *A Lua* and *Arena Conta Zumbi*). Throughout I use the joker as a wild card, a disruptive actor, a critic.

3 The lived experiences behind the *generally agreed upon facts* of an event (see Vidal 1989).

4 See www.asu.edu/tour/tempe/lyc.html

5 See   www.youtube.com/watch?v=3BsK4nFo9Sc;   www.youtube.com/watch?v= I71sLJ-j5LE;   www.youtube.com/watch?v=NbYx01re-ec;   https://en.wikipedia.org/ wiki/Theatre_of_the_Oppressed#/media/File:Augusto_Boal_nyc5.jpg

6 Boal offers no details concerning this particular experience.

7 Boal Dates: 1956-1971: Arena Theatre in Sao Paulo, Brazil, develops TO, forum theatre, the "Joker" system; 1971–1976: in exile: Peru, Argentina; develops image theatre and invisible theatre; 1976–1986: exile in Europe, Parisian Center for Theatre of the Oppressed formed; develops therapeutic techniques – Cop-in-the-Head; 1986 – returns to Brazil, offers workshops throughout Latin America, Africa, Europe and North America, continuing to develop therapeutic techniques, including Rainbow of Desire.

8 See www.google.com/#q=augusto+boal+forum+theatre+for+teachers–notes+from +athens+conference%2C+2000. I thank ElizaBeth Simpson for clarifying this model and the place of the oppressor, protagonist, spect-actor and joker in it.

9 The Jewish Wife is a playlet, from Brecht's *Fear and Misery of the Third Reich* (German: *Furcht und Elend des Dritten Reiches*), also known as *The Private Life of the Master Race*. This is one of Bertolt Brecht's most famous plays and the first of his openly anti-Nazi works. It was first performed in 1938. The production employed Brecht's epic theatre techniques to defamiliarize the behaviour of the characters and to make explicit the play's underlying message. The play consists of a series of playlets, portraying National Socialist Germany of the 1930s as a land of poverty, violence, fear and pretence. Nazi anti-Semitism is depicted in several of the sketches, including "the Physicist," "Judicial Process," and "the Jewish Wife" (https://en.wikip edia.org/wiki/Fear_and_Misery_of_the_Third_Reich). In the playlet the Jewish wife

calls a number of people (doctor, reporter, friend), as she agonizes over how to tell her husband, Fritz, she is leaving to save his career and to escape the violence and racism of Nazi anti-Semitism. She asks her friends to look after Fritz when she leaves (Brecht 1965, pp. 11–13).

10 The audience is invited to replace a protagonist and to act out their own solutions to a problem, thus rehearsing action for revolution.

11 See http://infed.org/mobi/augusto-boal-animation-and-education/

12 Spect-actors identify new laws which provide interventions into situations of oppression.

13 Agit-prop

14 Rehearsing a scene in a pubic space where actions could really happen, the improvised scene becomes reality (Boal 1995, p. 185)

15 Daily news items are transformed into materials for theatrical performances (Boal 1985, p. 143).

16 Performance technique in which one person, acting as a sculptor, moulds one or more people acting as statues, using only touch and resisting the use of words or mirror-image modeling.

17 Rainbow of Desire uses Theatre of the Oppressed Image and Forum techniques to investigate internalized oppression. It asks participants to discover how external oppression causes us to support our own oppression and, through creative exploration, helps to identify and deconstruct the contributing systems of power. Through fun games and intense images we will explain the process by which theatre can address internalized oppression and fight the Cops in the Head (http://theforumproject.org/offerings/rainbow/)

18 Of course this is an exaggeration!

19 On disability and crip theory see Berger, Feucht and Flad 2014, pp. 2–5; also Berger 2013, p. 5.

20 Shorter two-day workshops are also common.

21 See http://infed.org/mobi/augusto-boal-animation-and-education/

22 I steal this title from Dennis (2009); also Madison (2010, pp. 235–326).

23 See www.goodreads.com/quotes/528986-you-write-in-order-to-change-the-world-knowing-perfectly

24 As previously noted, in the post-performance-phase Mienczakowski' ethnodramas involve audiences as active co-participants. Norris' mirror theatre, playbuilding project also involves active audience participation.

25 I can find no reference to Boal in Freire's writings, although Boal cites Pedagogy of the Oppressed and its influence on this work (see Schugurensky 2014, p. 199). Peter McLaren (e-mail, February 17, 2016) confirms this. McLaren also reports that in 1996 he "was privileged to share the platform with Paulo and Augusto Boal (who developed the 'theater of the oppressed' based on Freire's work) at the Rose Theater in Omaha, Nebraska. It was the first time the three of us had ever presented together. In fact, I think it was the first time Paulo and Augusto spoke publicly together."

6 Performing critical pedagogy

Prologue

NARRATOR: (to audience): We are back center stage at Lyceum Theatre on the campus of Arizona State University, Tempe, Arizona. Please welcome returning members from the Forum Theatre Performers who will perform a four-act play based on Paulo Freire's Pedagogy of the Oppressed (1970/2000), and his semi-autobiographical (bio-text) work, Letters to Cristina (1996). Paulo and Gloria Anzaldua taught us that critical pedagogy takes many different forms: indigenous, queer, critical race, critical social disability, red, black, endarkened, performance, postcolonial, feminist, standpoint, transnational, non-Western, Asian, African. Tonight we will visit many of these forms. The ethnodrama moves back and forth in time. It is a story formed out of the crucible of war, exile, terror and imprisonment. The curtains are drawn back slowly.

***

Stage left: A spotlight shines on a huge photograph of Paulo Friere.[1]

***

MARCELO DIVERSI AND CLAUDIO MOREIRA: (to audience): The ghosts of Paulo Freire
are everywhere.
This play is written
in and through his language,
his words, his dreams:
resisting oppression, critical pedagogy,
praxis, freedom, hope, love,
justice, decolonizing knowledge, justice
terror, live as an exile (2016, p. 19, paraphrase)

(Paulo appears dressed in black throughout play)

PAULO: Once, in a TV report about landless rural workers in the interior of Sao Paulo, the reporter asked a country adolescent:

REPORTER: Do you usually dream?

YOUNG MALE: No, I only have nightmares.

PAULO: Without dreams there are only nightmares, darkness, silence (Freire 2007, p. 45).

DANIEL F. JOHNSON-MARDONES: For Paulo the words
and the silences
are the world (Johnson-Mardones 2015, p. 61, paraphrase).

Act One: Scene One: The many ghosts of Paulo Freire

PAULO: I am a Catholic. I am Brazilian. I am an educator. I am a writer, a son, a father, a husband, a brother. I was a lawyer, a welfare official, an administrator, a high school teacher. I wore black clothes to protest the tragedy of World War II. From 1947–1957 I coordinated education and culture programs directed to workers. In 1960 I founded Recife's Popular Culture Movement, and in 1963 became the director of the literacy program for the University of Recife's Cultural Extension Service. I defined myself as a progressive educator, a researcher, an advocate. I have an ethical obligation to be a writer, to make my ideas clear to others, to communicate, to proclaim what I discover (Schugurensky 2014, pp. 20–21; Freire 1998, p. 35, paraphrase; Duwe 2016. p. 628). My books are written in rage and love and hope. As a radical inquirer, I am committed to serious political analysis, to do work that makes hope possible. I have a moral obligation to struggle, to resist, to say no to the totalizing discourse of the neoliberal present (Freire 1999, pp. 10–11).

HENRY GIROUX: Paulo's critical pedagogy is dangerous to those in power because central to its very definition is the commitment to educate oppressed persons (workers, students) to become critical agents who actively question the systems of oppression in their own lives (2011, p. 157).

PAULO: We have a simple project, to help the oppressed develop a pedagogy of liberation. In 1962 in only 45 days we taught 300 formerly illiterate pupils to read and write. In 1963 we issued a call for 600 students to serve as literary tutors. Six thousand volunteers showed up. We had to move the interviews to a soccer stadium. We were training literacy teams to work in every Brazilian state. Our goal was for 5 million adult Brazilians to become literate and politically aware (Schugurensky 2014, pp. 22–23).

***

Stage right: spotlight shines on a poster listing the three stages in Paulo's literacy program

The three stages in Paulo Freire's literacy program

1   Stage One: Investigative Stage: Fieldworker mixes with people in a local community, recording the words, phrases, expressions people use to describe their world.

2   Stage Two: Thematization Stage: Themes from stage one are codified, and placed on cards in phonetic groups.

3   Stage Three: Problematization Stage: Themes are now connected to concrete actions and problems: wages, holidays, worker rights. The final objective is *conscientization*, wherein oppressive reality is named, experienced as a process which can be overcome.

The challenge of the road sweeper

I found it very difficult
to read and write.
But now I can write my name
and other things.
I'm a road sweeper,
a student and a worker,
I enjoy studying.
I'm learning and
I'm going to carry on.
I have to struggle to learn.
I like coming here (Gadotti 1994, pp. 20–23, 28, paraphrase).

***

Stage left: spotlight shines on a poster listing the key points in Paulo's literacy project which implement his three stages

Implementing literacy education

1   Literacy education is an act of knowing.

2   Literacy education must challenge learners to take on the role of subjects learning to read and write.

3   Literacy education must use the vocabulary of the universe of learners.

4   Literacy education must be characterized as a dialogue.

5   Literacy education must use words and sentences that are connected to concrete situations.

6   Literacy education must not dichotomize reading and writing.

7   Literacy education must teach adults how to write with pencils.

8   Literacy education must respect the insecurity of illiterate adults (1996, pp. 128–129).JOKER: This system worked. Three hundred new readers in 45 days! But then the military coup of 1964 shut it down, and silenced the teachers who were seen as threats to the new regime's power.

Act One: Scene Two: Terror, the military coup and jail

***

Stage right: spotlight shines on this newspaper headline:

In 1964, the Brazilian military dictatorship rolled in like a bad dream, kicking off a brutal twenty-year-long military dictatorship. President João Goulart fled to Uruguay, and with him went the hopes of progressive reforms.Yesterday and today mark the 50-year-anniversary of the U.S.-backed military coup d'état in Brazil. The coup kicked off a brutal twenty-year-long military dictatorship. Similar military coups would follow in Bolivia, Chile, Uruguay, and Argentina. Together with the support of the U.S. government and Paraguay, under General Alfredo Stroessner, the region would organize Operation Condor, a political repression and terror campaign to suppress opposition to their governments. The first of seventeen military decrees, or Institutional Acts (AI), were issued. Institutional Act 5, decreed by military president Artur da Costa e Silva on December 13, 1968, suspended habeas corpus and disbanded congress. Inspired by the 1959 Cuban revolution, and insurgent guerrilla movements in Argentina, Colombia, Guatemala, Peru, Uruguay, and Venezuela, Communist Party militants went underground and formed armed movements against the dictatorship, including the National Liberation Alliance and the Popular Revolutionary Vanguard, which would later become the Revolutionary Armed Vanguard Palmares (VAR-Palmares). Dissidents were tracked down, arrested, imprisoned, tortured, disappeared, or worse.[2]

***

PAULO: **June 16, 1964:**
Two policemen came
to my house,
and arrested me.
I was imprisoned
for seventy days.
This was just after the coup
and after our success
with the literacy programs.
They brought me
before the court.
They kept asking the same questions:
JUDGE: Do you deny that your method is similar to that of Stalin, Hitler, Peron, and Mussolini?
Do you deny that with your method you want to make Brazil a Bolshevik country?

Do you deny that you are an international subversive?
Do you deny that you are
a traitor to Jesus Christ
and the people of Brazil
(Schugurensky 2014, p. 23; Gadotti 1994, pp.
34–35, paraphrase)?

PAULO: (to judge): Your questions are stupid.
My love for Christ led me to Marx.
My love for Marx never demanded
that I abandon Christ.
I love Brazil and
I want her people to be free (1996, p. 87).

PAULO: (to audience): This line of questioning went on for seventy days. I soon decided it was too risky to remain in Brazil. I had no desire to die as a hero. I sought exile. That was the price I had to pay. To be free I had to leave my homeland.

DOM HELDER CAMARA (CATHOLIC BISHOP OF RECIFE): They could have said of Paulo, what they said of me. When I fed the poor, they called me a saint, but when I asked why the poor were hungry, they called me a communist. In effect this is what they said about Paulo (Schugurensky 2014, p. 46, paraphrase).

PAULO: I was welcomed by the Bolivian Ministry of Education. While in prison I had started work on my first book, *Education as the Practice of Freedom*. Writing this book carried me forward in exile.

JOKER: Meanwhile U.S.-Brazilian relations became tighter than ever, as the United States worked to turn Brazil into a "success story" in the fight against communism.[3] A failed project.

PETER: This is painful. The U.S. supported this regime of terror which forced Paulo and others to become exiles. There was no safe place for a pedagogy of the oppressed in Brazil at this time.

COYOTE: Is there today?

Act One: Scene Three: Life as an exile

AUGUSTO: Ah, life in exile: Prisoners in freedom. Dead Man Walking. Take your pick:
Solitary suicides,
disintegrated families,
nightmares at mid-day,
nails dug into the memory of
clawing out
chunks of the future,
daggers in the chest,
neighbors who drowned
themselves in confusion, relatives,

surrounded by the present,
looking into the future,
seeing nothing
kill themselves by
jumping out of very high windows
(Boal 2001, p. 306, paraphrase).

PAULO: We lived in constant fear of persecution not only for those of us who were exiled, but for those we left behind, many of whom were tortured and imprisoned. Brazil's secret intelligence listened in on our telephone conversations, intercepted letters we mailed home to our families, lifted passports, challenged our love of Brazil, called us traitors in the press (1996, p. 6, paraphrase).

ANA MARIA ARAUJO FREIRE (NITA): [4] They exiled Paulo for fifteen years when he was only forty-three years of age. He could not go home. He was forced to live outside Brazil: Chile (1964–1969), Cambridge (1969–1970), Geneva (1970–1979). He knew about silence, about violence and terror, his dreams had turned into nightmares.

PAULO: For too many years after I was an exile I felt silenced.

PETER MCLAREN: At this time Paulo understood that there had never been a greater need for critical self-consciousness (*consciensization*), for a critical pedagogy of freedom and liberation, a pedagogy which would use every media and communication tool available to help persons create dialogues of freedom and resistance.

AUGUSTO: Oppressed people are in danger of internalizing a part of the oppressor within themselves. I call this having the "cop in your head." We need educational practices that help people remove the cop in their head.

COYOTE: No liberation is ever permanent!
The cop never really leaves forever.

AUGUSTO: The men and women who lived
through the tragic experiences of exile
should tell the youth of today
that these things are true.
They did happen,
all these things and much more.

PAULO: My Pedagogy of Oppression
was born out
of these experiences. It was written in
the blood of those
persons who were
beaten until they bleed,
and then returned
to their cells,
half alive,
stumbling,
their frail

emaciated bodies
full of dignity,
walking naked down
filthy dark halls past their friend's cells (1996, p. 7, paraphrase).

PAULO: (*continued*): A small frail young was woman taken from her husband and young daughter and imprisoned for her political activities. She was repeatedly beaten, whipped, ridiculed and scorned by the guards. But not once did she or her husband dwell on the violence, the cruelty, the injustice she had experienced. They refused to accept that there was nothing to do but cross their arms and place their heads on the chopping block. Deep down they had hope, and faith and a rock solid belief that justice was possible. I carry her faith with me everyday (Freire 1996, p. 10, paraphrase).

PETER MCLAREN AND HENRY GIROUX: In his more optimistic moment Paulo saw himself engaging in a pedagogy of liberation, a pedagogy of happiness, a pedagogy of joy, a pedagogy of laughter, a belief in history as a possibility (McLaren and Giroux 1994, pp. xvi–xvii, paraphrase).

PAULO: But there were few happy moments.
This is why I wear black.
I am in mourning.

Act One: Scene Four: Lessons from Paulo

DANIEL SCHUGURENSKY: For Paulo inquiry is a political act which focuses on economic and educational institutions. His critical pedagogy is anchored in schools, classrooms, adult literacy and rural extension programs. These are the places where the foundations of a democratic society are nurtured.

PAULO: Using another language, I try to combine critical ethnography, with action research and collaborative inquiry. We interview, observe, use focus groups. I would like to videotape training groups and then share training tapes between groups, asking groups to tape their reactions to the activities of other groups. A Canadian movie director did this in Tanzania, filming the discussion between a farming community and an agronomist about the crops of the next growing season. He showed this film to another community 100 kilometers away. He then filmed the debate about the previous community's debate. He returned to the first community and showed them the reactions of the friends that they didn't know they had. In this way he lessened the distance between communities and created networks of shared meaning (Freire 2005, pp. 152–153; also Kamberelis and Dimitriadis 2011, p. 549, paraphrase).

GEORGE KAMBERELIS AND GREG DIMITRIADIS: This is the essence of Paulo's critical pedagogy; creating the spaces and opportunities for dialogue, interaction, and critical self-awareness.

MOACIR GADOTTI: This is a restless, ethical epistemology, an action praxis. It honors the other, it intervenes, it educates, it is on the side of the oppressed. It is always humble, open to revision and criticism.

TAMI SPRY: Paulo whispers in my ear.
He tells me
that I can only speak
from the spaces
inhabited by my
privileged material body (2016, p. 37, paraphrase).
PAULO: I work with one simple principle.
How can I help the
oppressed as they struggle
to take control
of their own lives (1998, pp. 35, 43, 62, 102)?

Act Two: Scene One: Performing hope, love, peace

MARC SPOONER: (to audience): We have a global problem. As democratic systems allow themselves to become subsumed by market logics, we must counter with the urgent demand for public spaces, public metaphors, new accountabilities, new pedagogies of resistance, reaffirmations of our shared democratic vision (Spooner 2017, p. 544).
THE GHOST OF PAULO: I hunger for
active peace on a global scale.[5]
I dream of a world without exploitation.
I imagine a radical ethic
of love, an ethic that condemns violence,
condemns the exploitation of labor,
condemns the fabrication of
illusions and lies,
I honor an ethic that is affronted
by racial, sexual, and
class discrimination (Freire 1998, pp. 24–25).
This is a radical pedagogy
of the heart, a pedagogy of hope and love.
JESUS GOMEZ AND AITOR GOMEZ: Radical hope emerges from acts of kindness. It requires acts of daring. It requires a willingness to resist tradition. Radical love dares to imagine new ways of being. Persons have the courage to create loving, passionate, caring, sharing relationships.
ANTONIA DARDER: I carry this one step further. This is a revolutionary love, a pedagogy of love. It is equalitarian, utopian. It is committed to transformation, liberation and equality (Darder 2002, p. 31; Gomez 2015, pp. 126–127; Kincheloe 2005, p. xlvii).
PAULO: A pedagogy of hope requires courage, humility, sincerity, a tolerance of difference. It requires a willingness to be criticized and a willingness to learn from criticism (McLaren 2005, pp. xxx–xxxii; Freire 1998, p. 128). It demands a respect for people's dreams and hopes. It mocks the two-faced morality of the ruling classes. It scorns the audacity of their shamelessness.

It challenges the indecent salaries paid to teachers. It contests the lack of respect shown for public property and the environment. It questions the excesses of government, and cries out against high unemployment, destitution, hunger, poverty and homelessness. It challenges the powerful to justify these shameless acts.

NITA: Paulo worked hard to counter the depression that came from bearing witness to these gross social injustices. He always said, "I must dream. Like every other dreamer I have a right to dream and a right to protest" (Freire 1998, pp. 127–128; 2007, p. 106).

HENRY GIROUX: Paulo taught us that critical pedagogy
is a performative practice.
It offers a language for struggle and transformation.
It is a pedagogy that connects
knowledge to critical awareness,
to struggles for justice and democracy (Giroux 2011, pp. 152, 157).

PETER MCLAREN: Personal experience is the foundation of the pedagogy of the oppressed. That is persons must be able to connect their experiences with personal troubles to concrete situations. Experience becomes the focus for the interrogation of broader issues (Giroux 2011, pp. 152, 157). The experience becomes the starting point for acts of resistance. Acts of resistance require acts of kindness, acts of love, acts which inspire hope, justice, freedom.

C. WRIGHT MILLS: Paulo grounds his project in the intersection of biography and society, that historical place where each person realizes his or her universal singularity, where each person reproduces him or herself as an instance of this historical moment (Sartre 1971/1981, p. ix–x). In this space the personal becomes political.

Act Two: Scene Two: An autoethnographic aside

COYOTE: So how does this happen?

PAULO: Let me answer with a little theory and a story. Theory first. There are several steps in this dialogical process:

1   The oppressed need a new pedagogy. Sadly, they have experienced defeat, depression and pain. They must use these experiences as reasons to organize against the oppressor. They must be moved to resist. They must be willing to engage in political and psychological struggle. They need a new language, a language of resistance which will help them become conscious of their own oppression and their place in it. They make their oppression a concrete object to act upon.

2   In doing this they excavate the archaeology of their own pain. They make it visible. They feel it and understand it in a new way (Freire 1999, pp. 30–31).

3   Leaders can help them localize the oppressor outside themselves, in their everyday worlds of experience. These leaders nurture a politics of

possibility, the hope that oppressive worlds can be remade. (2000, p. 164; 2016, p. 151; Madison 2012, p. 182; 1998, p. 284).

4   Still, a critical understanding of oppression does not produce liberation. The situation producing the oppression must be transformed. Political and psychological struggle is required. The world must be confronted and then remade. Then the oppression can be buried (Freire 1999, p. 31).

5   This desire to change can not be superficial. It must come from deep within the person, from their very core, a profound commitment to change.

PAULO: (*continued*, NB: this monologue can be broken up into several sections into different speakers):

These are the steps I followed, almost to the letter, when I overcame my depression, which I had suffered from the ages of twenty-two to twenty-nine. This happened in the 1950s while I was working as an organizer with peasants. I had no control over when I would be hit by a dark sense of despair and sadness. I was helpless in these moments. It would come on slowly, sometimes quickly, some times attacking me without warning. It would get the best of me. I'd feel wounded. I'd feel bored with the world. Nothing meant anything anymore. Sometimes I could barely move (1999, p. 27, paraphrase).

Then, at some point these experiences started coming more and more frequently. Sometimes I could see it coming, sometimes not. I started keeping track, a kind of diary, what happened the day before, what had been said, what had I done. I learned to take the depression as an object of curiosity. I stepped back from it, to learn its "why," its rhythms, its how. I treated it like a living thing, I discovered that these episodes occurred more frequently in the rainy season and mostly when I made trips to the Zona da Mata to speak to teachers and pupils' families in SESI schools (Social Service of Industry). It soon became clear that it wasn't the trips that caused the depression. It was the rain, but more than the rain, it was also the bright green land, the dark sky, the mud of the black earth, soaking up the rain (1999, pp. 29–30, paraphrase).

I worked hard to put these elements together: the rain, mud, the green land. I was seeking the "why" of my depression, the case of my pain. You could say I was excavating my situation, laying it bare, making it visible. And so it was one rainy afternoon in Recife, under a dark sky, I paid a visit to the house in which I had lived, the house where my father died in the late afternoon of October 21, 1934. You could say I went in quest of my childhood. Perhaps unconsciously, I was going back to the source of my pain. In doing this I was transforming the situation, changing it, re-claiming it. I saw the long lawn that extended in front of our house. I saw the green fronds of the mango trees. I saw my feet in the muddy earth. I saw my feet going up the hill. I could hear my family talking (1999, p. 29, paraphrase).

The rain poured down. I was soaked to the skin. I saw before me, as if on a large canvas, a painting, a family portrait. I was in the painting and I was looking at the painting. I saw my self as a young child. I saw my dying father. I saw my sobbing mother. I saw my entire family lost in sorrow. I saw myself step outside the painting. I looked up at the dark sky. I walked down the hill to the area under the trees where I hunted innocent little birds with my slingshot. I heard birds singing. I went back up the hill and walked around the house where in the shade of the mango trees my father taught me to read and write. My chalk was the twigs of the mango tree. My blackboard was the ground. This was my first school. I was the pupil and I was the teacher.

In that moment, imagining myself in that painting, and outside the painting, my life flashed in front of me. I discovered the essence of my depression. I saw the relationship between my childhood, the rain, the green, the mud, my sadness, my father's death, our family's poverty, the constant hunger, losing four grades in school, wearing ill-fitting clothes, my unsuccessful work with poor workers. I buried my depression that day. I vowed to devote myself to my work with rural and urban workers (1999, p. 30, paraphrase).

ELZA FREIRE: [6] Paulo, this had to be very painful.

PAULO: No, I felt great relief. I've come to understand that the moments we re-live are either glimpses from the past, or they set in motion a new process, which takes us back to something in the past. This is what happened that day at my parents' home. I set in motion a new way of looking at the past, at myself, at my work, at who I was and what my mission in life was to be.

AUGUSTO AND PAULO: Looking at our lives up to now we can say there has been coherence. Our project has always been moral. We wanted to speak in our own voice and we did and we paid a great price to do so.

PAULO: I rose above my depression. I took my knowledge of my experience with my depression back to my experiences with the workers. I moved from my theories about reading the world to actually working with rural and urban workers. I began listening to them, hearing their voices, their pain, I visited their homes. I saw their poverty. I felt it. I listened to them talking about coming home hungry, tired, to a house with no heat, electricity, or water, no kitchen, no maid's bedroom, no garden. I heard them talk about getting up at four in the morning and starting all over again, feeling sad, hopeless, hungry, tired, kids dirty, hungry, crying. If people hit their kids it is not because they are bad people, or don't love them, it is because life is so hard, and they may know nothing different. I looked into their eyes. I learned how to speak with them, talking with them, not at them.

ELZA: Using your imagery, you unraveled the fabric which contained the facts of your depression. This was an unmasking of the "why" of your suffering. This unmasking allowed you to get closer to the workers. To get to this place you had to navigate your own pain, to discover its meanings.

PAULO: I became willing to make changes.

But for this to happen

I had to return to the site

of my early childhood suffering,
my family's pain,
the loss of my father (1999, pp. 29-31, paraphrase).

Act Two: Scene Three: Performing resistance

PAULO: In the 1960s the Movement for Popular Culture (MCP), staged theatrical plays. We would debate political, social, economic, cultural and historical issues for audiences at a theatrical play. We created a mobile circus that went from neighborhood to neighborhood offering theatrical presentations and movies. After the shows we invited people to stay and debate and discuss, and they did (1996, p. 130, paraphrase).

AUGUSTO: (aside, to audience): My friendship with Paulo must have dated from 1960 when, for the first time, I and my Teatro de Arena de Sao Paulo went to Recief where he was trying his method. There we met. Paulo was ten years older then me (Boal 1998, p. 126). They were doing political theatre too.

***

Stage right: spotlight shines on photograph of Paulo and Augusto from Boal (2001, p. 316)

***

PAULO: The Movement for Popular Culture (MCP) was born of the political will of Miquel Arres, Mayor of Recife, and the equally strong political will of a group of workers' leaders, artists, and other intellectuals. I was part of the group, which the mayor had invited to meet in his office. He had a dream. Could there be an agency which would work with the popular classes and not above them (1996, p. 228, note 1)?

HENRY: This was a dialectical and anti-deterministic view of culture in the historical process.

PAULO: Unknowingly we were following in the footsteps of Antonio Gramsci with his dialectical views of culture, hegemony and ideology. It is no accident the words *culture* and *popular* were so frequently present in the movement's vocabulary: Popular Culture Movement, Cultural Centers, Popular Theatre, Popular Festivals (Freire 1996, pp. 109, 111, 116–117).

COMMUNITY MEMBER: We came to these events because they spoke to us. We were motivated to learn more about how we could push for our rights to participate against the repressive authoritarian Brazilian government. We were able to act out different forms of protest and resistance.

PAULO: The MCP subscribed to the school of thought that political-educational practice and action contributed to the construction of critical consciousness. With this consciousness the popular classes could engage in collective efforts to transform Brazil into a more just and more open society (Freire 1996, p. 120). This is the utopian dream we all embraced.

JOKER: To realize this dream, one of our strategies with MCP was to honor the people's popular culture traditions, their festivals, stories, mythic figures, their religious beliefs. Still, the relation between popular culture, resistance and oppression is complicated. At any moment in time, for any popular cultural form, there can be expressions of defeat and resignation alongside acts of resistance. Embedded in these stories and myths are expressions of the very oppression the oppressed wish to resist.

DONALD MACEDO: Ideally these cultural, aesthetic forms and practices became resources in the struggle against oppression. They can be as concrete as making a ceramic bowl, or a simple painting, or a bracelet, or weaving a scarf, or learning a new word in a new language, or writing a poem or a song. Anyone can make art and making art can be a revolutionary act of self-expression. Making art is not the privilege of a few elite (Freire 1996, p. 117).

AUGUSTO: But there are always personal and political contradictions. How do you reconcile the repressive racial and gender practices of the Catholic Church, including its religious art, with a love for Christ when Christ was the light that Paulo said led him to Marx (Freire 1996, pp. 86, 87, 88, 120, paraphrase).

Act Two: Scene Four: Nothing lasts forever

PAULO: Unraveling oppressor-oppressed relationships is difficult. The cop in the head means the oppressed think like the oppressor. The cop is internalized and becomes like a shadow in one's inner life. The oppressed become their own oppressors. But their cultural creations, their art, language, stories, myths "make a kind of muffled cry of resistance of the rebel in them" (Freire 1996, p. 118).

PETER: The goal is to nourish
    and exploit this
    rebel within,
    to facilitate the
    transformation of a
    rebellious consciousness
    into a revolutionary consciousness (Freire 1996, p. 180).

PAULO: The intent is to be radical
    but not doctrinaire,
    to be strategic but not cynical,
    or opportunistic,
    to be ethical but not puritanical,
    to be fearless,
    but not terrified
    in the face of opposition.

AUGUSTO: Here is where I learned from Paulo. There was no separation between his critical pedagogy, his theory of the oppressed, his methodologies, his politics and his theories of action and intervention.

NITA: It was a seamless system. But victories always exist side by side with sacrifice, happiness lies in cutting through the fences of illiteracy, ignorance and fatalism. Happiness is learning that freedom lies within our grasp (Freire 1996, p. 119).

PAULO: There were many victories, many advances: the literacy programs, curriculum reform, school councils, the land rights movement, the development of community schools, parent-teacher circles, expanding health services in rural areas.

AUGUSTO: Nothing lasts forever.

NITA: Shutting down Paulo's program was doomed to fail. Shutting it down did not provide an answer because the problems for our society remained: illiteracy, poverty, hunger, violence, repression.

Act Two: Scene Five: Our only weapon

PAULO: If you ask me whether I have a solution. No one has a solution, but I know the way forward is through the democratic struggle for a fair, open, decent humane society. We used cultural circles and cultural centers as ways of bringing people together in shared space, in libraries, theatres, at sporting events, soccer clubs, neighborhood associations, markets, churches, bars, barber shops. In these spaces dialogue, teaching and learning took place. These were the places where knowledge was produced, not just transmitted. Our volunteer educators lead discussions around select themes: voting rights, reading, literacy, education, wages, health care.

NITA: A dialogical approach was taken in the groups. In a dialogical performance self and other come together. Persons question, debate, challenge one another. They are committed to keeping dialogue and conversation alive (Conquergood 1985, p. 10; Madison 2012, p. 253). This was the spirit we brought to the groups. Reading and writing were treated as opposite sides of the same coin. We created a newspaper, and a university radio station.

JOKER: We were not really stopped by the 1964 coup d'état. Just slowed down (Gadotti 1994, p. 34).

PAULO: While in prison. I told anyone who would listen a story about one of my literacy students named Joaquim (my father's name and one of my sons' name). One day Joaquim wrote his first word, "NINA," and then burst into loud laughter. I asked him,

"Joaquim what's the matter. Why are you being so emotional? This is not like you"

"Nina, Nina," he replied, as if he had just discovered a new word. "Nina" is my wife's name. It's my wife." I just wrote my wife's name.

PAULO: (*continued*): I still feel that moment, being there to share

in the happiness
of a man who wrote
for the first time
his wife's name.
I have carried this
memory with me.
It sustained me in prison
and does so to this day.
This is what literacy
is all about,
helping people gain
the power to shape their own world, their own lives (Freire 1996, p. 138,
paraphrase).

PAULO: (*continued*): Critical pedagogy, dialogue, love, respect, hope, these were
the weapons we had. We were committed to helping people deal with the
deep injustices in Brazilian society. We had a belief in the power of progressive education to turn history around. Teaching people to read gave
them a new way to question and confront the injustices in their lives. This
is why our literacy programs were so important, and so threatening to the
power elite (Freire 1996, p. 116).

AUGUSTO: This is what a critical methodology, call it participatory action
research, is all about.

***

Stage left: spotlight shines on huge photograph of Gloria Anzaldua, Paulo
Freire and Augusto Boal
Lights dim, curtain lowers.

Notes

1 See https://en.wikipedia.org/wiki/Paulo_Freire
2 See http://nacla.org/news/2014/4/1/remembering-brazils-military-coup-50-years-later
3 See http://nacla.org/news/2014/4/1/remembering-brazils-military-coup-50-years-later
4 Second wife.
5 I thank Consuelo Chapela for the phrase active peace.
6 First wife, who died in 1986.

7   Tangled up in praxis

Act One: Scene One: Tangled up in theory

Stage left: spotlight shines on huge photograph of Gloria Anzaldua, Paulo Freire and Augusto Boal
Lights dim, curtain lowers.
Lights come back on. Curtain rises.

PAULO FREIRE: (to audience): I have been inserted into history and I embody my historical moment (Freire 1996, pp. 2–3, paraphrase).

GLORIA: Paulo, my history is not your history. But like you I grew up between two cultures. I am a border woman. All my life I've been straddling the *tejas*-Mexican border. Hatred, anger, resentment, violence and exploitation define these borderlands, as they must have for you (Anzaldua 1987, p. vii, paraphrase).

PAULO: Our borderlands are very much alike. We share the same desire: freedom from hatred and violence for all oppressed persons.

MARCELO AND CLAUDIO: We are two friends from the borderlands of European-colonized Brazil who came to the borderlands of the United States to learn about Paulo Freire's conscientization and postcolonial inquiry. We are treated as white in Brazil and as colored in the United States of America. We can speak street vernacular as Brazilian natives, yet have trouble discussing Pedagogy of the Oppressed in its original language – our mother tongue, Portuguese. In Brazil, where we were born, we are called gringos. In the U.S.A., where we live, we are called [illegal] aliens. We call ourselves *betweeners*, our unconscious bodies experiencing life in and between two cultures. This is the fluid dialogical space we occupy.

Our betweeness is all tangled up in theory, in decolonizing performances, in indigenous pedagogies. queer methodologies, resistance narratives, in clashes between regimes of power, truth and justice.

COYOTE: Be more specific.

CLAUDIO AND MARCELO: We offer workshops at the International Congress of Qualitative Inquiry on *Decolonizing Classrooms and Epistemologies*. Here is how we describe our workshop:

***

Stage right: spotlight shines on workshop abstract

This workshop is thoroughly grounded in the worlds of both the colonizer and colonized and it focuses primarily in the political space of a classroom. We, the authors situated between the world of northern academe and our southern origins, try to create a dialogue that works back and forth across Paulo Freire, Gloria Anzaldúa, Soyini Madison, Dwight Conquergood, Linda T. Smith, Third World feminisms, Indigenous Methodologies and Though, Postcolonialism and Decolonization. This workshop evokes the form of a manifesto, an invitation to indigenous, non-indigenous, betweeners, and allied scholars to think through the implications of connecting theories of decolonization and the postcolonial and indigenous epistemologies with emancipatory discourses, critical theory, critical pedagogy and/in performance.

It is designed around the central idea of co-constructing, with students in higher education, a dialogical collaboration in the processes of interpretation and production of decolonizing scholarship. We, facilitators and participants, will share our humble, and humbling, experiences with resisting colonizing rituals (e.g., use of titles and other power markers), exploring decolonizing possibilities of being (e.g., unconditional human rights), and with critiquing teaching while teaching. We believe that decolonizing methodologists, can – in concert with indigenous methodologies – speak to oppressed, colonized persons living in postcolonial situations of injustice: women of all colors, situations, and ethnicities; queer, lesbian, transgendered individuals; Aboriginal, First Nation, Native American, South African, Latin American, Pacific and Asian Islander persons. We seek the utopia of social justice and see this workshop as an opportunity to share our decolonizing imagination and to learn from others'. At the end, we hope participants will have new language, narratives, and ideas for advancing decolonizing pedagogies from within our colonizing educational system.

***

MARCELO AND CLAUDIO: We work to subvert the logics of neoliberalism, neopositivism and the new social media technologies of race (Clough 2016, p. 439).

CLAUDIO AND MARCELO: Paulo and Augusto taught us that our decolonizing acts must be performed in the occupied spaces controlled by the colonizer. These are the spaces we seek to decolonize. This is where we flourish as in-betweeners, in the new borderlands, in classrooms, hallways, bathrooms, parking lots, school playgrounds, street corners, coffee shops, inside the belly of the beast.

AISHA DURHAM: On the block

U.S. home girls huddle

to talk crap and take shots of cheap wine to chase

the Uncle Willie boogiemen and the 40 oz. spirits that haunt us.
we drink for an excuse to cut a fool
to be the 13-year-girls we really are. We sit around retelling the
'remember when' stories so many times they turn into project folklore
(Durham 2014, pp. 57–58, paraphrase).

PAULO: My opponents said
I was not an educator.
They said I politicized
the classroom.

AISHA: They said this of me as well. But in denying me the status of educator
because of my politics they were being political too.

Act One: Scene Two: Writing decolonizing autoethnographies

GLORIA: The struggle, in each instance, is inner: Chicano, indio, American
Indian, mojado, mexicano, immigrant Latino, queer, Anglo in power,
working class Anglo, Black, Asian – our psyches resemble the bordertowns
and are populated by the same people (Anzaldua 1987, pp. 3–4,
paraphrase).

DWIGHT CONQUERGOOD: Everything is always, already performative. Each of
these indigenous pedagogies exists on the public performance stage –
moving from decolonizing discourses, toward decolonizing praxis, toward
dreams of freedom and liberation towards spaces where we each become
experts in our own struggles to be free.

AUGUSTO: Paulo's critical pedagogy addresses forms of violence that come from
the intersections of race, class, gender, religion and sexual orientation. It
confronts the experiences of misery, violence, poverty, hatred and self-
loathing.

CLAUDIO AND MARCELO: We witnessed brutal inequalities while growing up in
Brazil. We were not innocent bystanders. No one is ever an innocent
bystander in their own life.

TAMI: I write autobiography to place myself in history. I wear dreadlocks. Are
dreadlocks on a white body a disruption of dominant narratives of race
and beauty, or are they the ultimate act of white privilege cooptation.
  Does it matter that my hair is so kinky that as a girl I used to get called
'nigger hair' on the playground and that none of the white teachers said a
damn thing, thereby schooling all of us white kids on race, beauty, power,
and how to be the consummate polite silent racist (Spry 2016, p. 68,
paraphrase).

GLORIA: As long as I have to accommodate
the English speakers rather
than having them accommodate me,
my tongue will be illegitimate (Anzaldua 1987, p. 8, paraphrase).

GLORIA: (*continued*): To write and live in the Borderlands means to
Put chile in the borscht,

speak Tex-Mex with a Brooklyn accent
It means you are the battleground
where enemies are kin to each other
and you are at home, a stranger
but to survive in the Borderlands
you must live in *sin fronteras* (without borders),
you must be crossroads (Anzaldua 1987, pp. 193–194, paraphrase).

AISHA DURHAM: Critical performance indigenous autoethnography unearths, excavates, exposes, performs. It is mind-mining excavation of experience exhumed from repressed memories of survival, suffering, violence, pain, love, hatred, bodies, border-crossings, love, desire, lost, and found, home again (Durham 2014, p. 19, paraphrase).

MS COYOTE: How do you go from misery and hatred to all this stuff about queering and engendering methodology? What does it mean to embrace indigenous pedagogies and methodologies, indigenous poetics?

KEN PLUMMER: Queer life today: postmodern fragmentation, post-humanism, post-materialist realities, reflexive queer/quare critiques, polyphonic narratives destroy/erase conventional categories of sexuality and gender.

BRYANT ALEXANDER: Queer Manifesto: Be transgressive, gothic, romantic, embrace queer/quare-worldmaking, live the queer critique of color, study quare studies, honor indigenous queers, and two-spirit persons, write quare-queer theories of resistance, embrace embodied praxis, think outside the box (Alexander 2017).

GLORIA: I seek a queer-free zone.
This is not new. Colored, poor, white,
latent queer passing for white, seething with
hatred, anger, unaware of its source, rage, crazed with not
not knowing who you are,
let me pick at the masks (Anzaldua 1987, p. 171, paraphrase).

AISHA: We write our way
back home again.
Lost and found.

GLORIA: Until I can take pride in my language,
I cannot take pride in myself, Until I can
accept as legitimate Chicano Texas Spanish,
Tex-Mex and all the other languages I speak
I cannot accept myself (Anzaldua 1987, p. 59, paraphrase).

CLAUDIO: I am trying to write in a way that places my body in history, my body with its muscles, blood, anger, and hunger. I am rewriting my life to create the conditions for changing myself and my past.

COYOTE: As Gloria says, I may be mad, but I choose this madness.

GLORIA: 145 acres for sale
the Indians safely locked up in reservations
or urban ghettos.
There's a forest fire in the Cuyamaca Peaks,

a sign: 4 parcels For Sale,

the Indians safely locked up in reservations

and Til'pu behind glass in the museum (Anzaldua 1987, p. 183 paraphrase).

COYOTE: How do you decolonize

a sign that says

'4 parcels for sale and

Indians behind glass in museums'?

GLORIA: Remember dear friends, theory never got me anywhere.

Until I got free of theory I was tied up in knots. I had no voice.

Act One: Scene Three: The many pedagogies of Paulo Freire

PAULO: The capitalist system, and globalization theory which speak of ethics, hide the fact that their ethics are those of the neoliberal marketplace and not the universal ethics of the human person. It is for these matters that we ought to struggle courageously if we have, in truth, made a choice for a humanized world (Freire 1998, p. 114, paraphrase).

SANDY GRANDE (RED PEDAGOGY): We are the children

of Paulo and Augusto

who gave us the

gift of critical pedagogy.

Now what do we do with it?

NARRATOR: Critical indigenous pedagogy rests on emancipatory, participatory views of ethics science, empirical research, democracy and community. Indigenists craft their own understandings of science, research, democracy and the decolonization process. They always ask what research do we want done? For whom? What difference will it make? Who will own the research? Who will benefit (L. Smith 2000, p. 239; G. Smith 2000)? Each pedagogy is grounded in an oppositional conscience that resists neocolonial, neo-liberal formations.

RUSSELL BISHOP (MAORI): When talking about indigenous rights we must always begin with treaties. Take New Zealand. Despite the guarantees of the Treaty of Waitangi, the colonization of Aotearoa/New Zealand and the subsequent neocolonial dominance of majority interests in social and educational research have continued. The result has been the development of a tradition of research into Maori people's lives that addresses concerns and interests of the predominantly non-Maori researches own making, as defined and made accountable in terms of the researchers' own cultural worldview (s) (Bishop 1998, p. 110).

RUSSELL BISHOP: (*continued*): Speaking as a Kaupapa Maori, we need to work through an indigenous politics of critical inquiry. We are about to enter the third Decade of Critical Indigenous Inquiry. In this decade there will be a thorough-going transition from discourses about and on method, to discourses centering on power, ethics and social justice. This discourse will bring new meanings to these terms. It will also involve a rethinking of terms like democracy, science and education.

SANDY GRANDE (RED PEDAGOGY): From the standpoint of red pedagogy the primary lesson is pedagogy, education, teaching. We are poised to raise yet another generation in a nation at war and at risk. We must consider how conceptions of citizenship, sovereignty and democracy affect young Native American young children. We must be willing to be agents of transgression and resistance. We must be advocates of decolonization, champions of equity, emancipation, and cultural sovereignty.

This is the basis of Red pedagogy which is political, cultural, and spiritual. It is rooted in praxis and hope. It is inspired by Gerald Vizenor's concept of survivance; that is living with dignity while actively rejecting racism and the legacies of colonialism.

GERALD VIZENOR (RED PEDAGOGY): I seek a Postindian Other, a radical Native American free of colonial stereotype. Never forget, the Indian is a simulation, a ruse of the colonial imaginary. And there are many different forms of simulation, including playing Indian in Wild West shows, being an Indian hobbyist, or painting red Indians on canvases that can be turned into advertisements in slick magazines enticing tourists to visit art galleries in Taos, New Mexico.

The postindian embraces
survivance,
The postindian resists colonial images
of playing the indigenous Indian Other
The postindian rejects simulations of redness
that turn Indians into victims
and toys for the white imagination.
The postindian always asks,
"Whose history, whose memory,
whose Indian (Vizenor 1999, 2008).

LINDA TUHIWAI SMITH (MAORI PEDAGOGY): I agree with Sandy, Gerald and Russell. We Maori want a set of proactive understandings aimed at giving Maori increased self-determination and autonomy in their own lives. Kaupapa Maori is an indigenous theory. It asks that individuals be free to determine their own goals and make sense of their world in terms of culturally meaningful terms. This call for autonomy is not a call for separatism, but rather is an invitation for a dialogue between Maori and non-Maori. It asks that work done with Maori be initiated by Maori, benefit them, represent them without prejudice, be legitimated in terms of key Maori values, and be done by researchers who are accountable for the consequences of their work.

COYOTE: This translates into a culturally responsive pedagogy. This pedagogy is implemented in the classroom, but it also extends into family, community, Maori culture and language. A culturally responsive pedagogy involves trust, care, love, patience, kindness.

RUSSELL BISHOP: This involves collaborative storytelling, the co-construction of counter-narratives, and the creation of classrooms as discursive, sacred spaces where Maori values were experienced. Out of these practices emerge students who were able to exercise self-determination in their own education, students able to achieve their own sense of cultural autonomy and healthy well-being (Bishop 1998).

CLAUDIO AND MARCELO: But where are the subjugated embodied bodies in the classrooms, administrator offices, faculty meetings, the hall ways, locker rooms, playing fields, marching bands? How do we decolonize these spaces?

NARRATOR: Culturally responsive pedagogy moves in several directions at the same time. It critiques the historical legacies and material realities of colonized indigenous life, including the loss of land and sacred sites, the destruction of natural resources (earth, air, water), and the plundering, and pollution of the environment.

MICHAEL YELLOW BIRD (INDIGENOUS SOCIAL JUSTICE THEATRE): I use social justice theatre, and Augusto Boal's Theatre of the Oppressed to help my students think about the connection between Paulo Freire, critical pedagogy and critical consciousness (Yellow Bird 2005, p. 13; also quoted in Diversi and Moreira 2009, p. 7). My students write their own scripts around themes of injustice, including oppression, racism, sexism and colonialism. They develop characters and plot, do stage design, build stages, produce posters and invite faculty, family and friends to performances.

One class did a play about discrimination against gay men and lesbian women, racial profiling and hate crimes. Another class wrote and performed a play focused on the illegal acts committed by the U.S. Government during the arrest, trial, conviction and imprisonment of American Indian Movement (AIM) member Leonard Peltier (Yellow Bird 2005, p. 13).

Act Three: Scene Four: Sovereignty, and governance

TIM BEGAYE (RED PEDAGOGY): Indigenous models of governance rest on inclusion, and the free and full participation of all members of a society in civic discourse. The architects of American democracy subverted this full-inclusion model when they wrote the U.S. constitution. They denied citizenship rights to Native Americans, African Americans and women.

MS COYOTE: From 1778 to the present, the sovereign rights of tribal groups were continually violated and eroded under U.S. law. In 1830, the U.S. Supreme court ruled that all tribal groups would be considered domestic dependent nations In 1934, Congress passed the Indian Reorganization Act, giving the government the right approve or disapprove all activities of tribal governments.

TIM BEGAYE: There is a need to return full sovereignty to all Native Americans. Their indigenous models of democracy should be allowed to flourish under full federal financial sponsorship. In a truly legitimate democratic society, the discussion of democracy and education would be irrelevant because everyone would be free to participate and express themselves regarding the welfare of the community. Sadly, this has not been the case for Native Americans in the United States (Begaye 2008, p. 465).

SANDY: The miseducation of American Indians precedes the birth of this nation. Before the first shots of the Revolutionary War were fired, American education was being used weapon in the American arsenal, of American imperialism. Where was Paulo Freire when we needed him?

GLORIA (BORDERLAND/MESTIZA): My Chicana identity is grounded in the Indian woman's history of resistance. The Aztec female rites of mourning were rites of defiance. When I leave home I do not lose touch with my origins. *Lo mexicano* is in my system. I am a turtle. Wherever I go I carry home on my back (Anzaldua 1987, p. 21, paraphrase).

GERALD: Resistance, memory, carrying our cultures on our backs. This is what survivance is all about, never letting go of our identities.

COYOTE: Given stories like this, can colonizer and colonized ever speak to one another?

ALISON JONES (PAKEHA COLONIZER) MARORI KUNI JENKINS (INDIGENE, MAORI, COLONIZED): Who speaks for whom here? Can there be a collaboration between indigenous and settler colleagues? It is never straight-forward. There is an inevitable tangle of passion, ignorance, ambivalence, desire and power which shapes the indigene-colonizer collaborating relationship. For example, the hyphen that connects Maori and non-Maori defines a colonial relationship. Each term forces the other into being. The hyphen can never be erased. There may be, however, an impulse for indigenous (and non-indigenous) persons to write from both sides of the hyphen – the outsider-within.

MS COYOTE: This is an impossibility.

ALISON AND KUNI: Nonetheless, collaborative inquiry can be guided by a set of ethical principles that include respect, care, equity, empathy, a commitment to fairness and a commitment to honoring indigenous culture and its histories.

JOKER: So the colonized goes over to the other side and becomes just like the colonizer.

CLAUDIO AND MARCELO: Well, not always. Indigene-coloniser collaboration can then become a site of "learning from difference rather than learning about the Other." Such a commitment respects and upholds difference. Remember, the Other is fundamentally unknowable, visible only in their cultural performances.

TAMI: We only know the other through her acts of resistance.

ALISON AND KUNI: We all stand exposed in these spaces that connect us to one another (Jones and Jenkins 2008).

Act Three: Scene Five: Exposed

MARIE BATTISTE (FIRST NATION; THE MI'KMAW ETHICS WATCH): Exposed! Tell me about exposed. Let's get down and dirty and talk about Indigenous

Ethics. Indigenous people must have control over their own knowledge. They must have mechanisms which protect them when research is being done on, among or with them. How can you create ethical mandates and ethical behavior in a knowledge system contaminated by colonials and racism (Battiste 2008).

MARCELO AND CLAUDIO: Marie gives us some principles, some ethical guidelines. Indigenous persons should be the guardians and interpreters of their culture. They have the right and obligation to exercise control to protect what is theirs. All research should be approached as a negotiated partnership, and all participants should be treated as equals.

COYOTE: Research ceases to be research within an ethical social justice perspective. It becomes, instead, a transformative practice, a form of social justice theatre where utopian models of empowerment are explored.

LESLIE AND PATRICIA: Hey, we are back! This involves a huge struggle, a commitment to principles before personalities, a non-judgmental commitment to respect, kindness, caring and love for the other, an honoring of personal experience, a belief in practical wisdom, the desire to heal and end pain.

WANDA MCCASLIN (METIS FROM NORTHERN SASKATCHEWAN) AND DENISE BRETON (WHITE AMERICAN OF CELTIC ANCESTRY): We work with another model of social justice, justice as healing. We want to get outside the colonizer's legal cage where "might makes right." We want to embed justice within a moral community. Legal positivism, a cousin of epistemological positivism, oppresses indigenous persons. It has caused great harm and destruction in Native communities by undermining indigenous concepts of community and natural law.

COYOTE: Tell me more. This is another form of justice.

WANDA AND DENISE: We advocate a restorative view of justice which is based on indigenous ways of healing, not scapegoating and punishing offenders. Restorative justice represents a paradigm shift, violations to persons and their properties are regarded as violations of relationship and only secondarily of the law. Punishment of offenders is not practiced. We do healing circles.

COYOTE: How do you implement this model?

WANDA AND DENISE: The key features include speaking the truth, healing, respect of the other person, an honoring of their voice, the prevention of future harm. Restorative justice can be achieved through various practices, including mediation, sentencing circles, healing circles and community conferencing.

MS COYOTE: So restorative justice is like a spiritual process. It celebrates balance, harmony, making persons whole again. It honors the intrinsic worth and good of each person.

WANDA AND DENISE: Exactly. It is dialogic. Healing is not about fixing persons, or getting even. It is about transforming relationships, about being good relatives and good neighbors. Healing is spiritual, involving sincere and genuine efforts by all those involved to practice values such as fairness, honesty, compassion, harmony, inclusiveness, trust, humility, openness and, most importantly, respect.

PAULO FREIRE: I get it. Healing, in combination with restorative justice, works to restore dignity. It refuses to engage in negative labeling, including applying harmful labels to disempowered youth. This is the core challenge; that is to confront the colonizing cage that traps both indigenous and non-indigenous people in genocide, fraud, theft, institutional racism and abuse.

WANDA AND DENISE: Yes! But restorative justice should not become yet another tool of colonizing institutions. The goal is to remove the cage altogether, and to rebuild our long house, hogans, iglus, pueblos, wikiups, earth lodges, wigwams, plank houses, grass houses or chickees.

COYOTE: Justice as healing has some similarities with the South African Truth and Reconciliation Commissions. In those commission hearings there was an attempt to hear the voices of the persons who suffered under Apartheid.

Act Three: Scene Seven: Pain

ANTJIE KROG, NOSISI MPOLWENI-ZANTSI AND KOPANO RATELE (SOUTH AFRICAN SCHOLAR/ACTIVISTS): We worked with Mrs. Konile, a native South African whose son was killed by military security forces. Mrs. Konile testified before the Truth and Reconciliation Commission (TRC). Her narrative, which included a dream episode and an incident with a goat, was hard to understand. Mrs. Konile testified in her mother tongue. Difficulties arose when it was translated and an official transcript was produced. Her testimony seemed ill-fitting, strange, incoherent. The court was inclined to disregard her testimony. But a deeper interpretation suggested that her narrative was coherent, and that she was resisting other frameworks that were imposed on her (Krog, Mpolweni-Zantsi and Ratele 2008, pp. 531–32).

MRS. KONILE: There was this goat looking up, this one next to me said oh! Having a dream like that with a goat looking up is a very bad dream. Just when we were approaching the houses there was Peza (a South African activist). I said what are you going to say to me? Say it, say it now! And then he told me about the death of my son. And this was a very scary time for me, the goat looking up at me, having this goat looking up at me (Krog, Mpolweni-Zantsi and Ratele 2008, p. 535).

COYOTE: Within a colonizing post-colonial context a woman like Mrs. Konile may appear incoherent because of severe suffering, or intelligible because of oppression – while in fact she is neither.

ANTJI: The goat, death, Peza, the dream, foreboding, death of son. Incoherent? NO.

SOUTH AFRICAN AMNESTY HEARING ATTORNEY: It happened fifteen years ago, now they fucking cry for the first time (Krog, Mpolweni-Zantsi and Ratele 2008, p. 531).

ANTJI, NOSISI AND KOPANO: Within her indigenous framework Mrs. Konile is logical and resilient in her knowledge of her loss and its devastating consequences in her life. The court was unable to hear her testimony. Her dream with the goat connects her to her culture, to her ancestral worlds, far from the world where her son was killed in the struggle to liberate his and her country (Krog, Mpolweni-Zantsi and Ratele 2008, p. 542).

COYOTE: So hearing her voice in this way allows us to better understand how the TRC operated for and against indigenous South African persons.

ANTJI: It is perhaps too late for Mrs. Konile. With this reading of her dream and the goat, justice has perhaps been served, but long after the fact. Too late? Healing? Justice? Pain.

LUIS MIRÓN: The case of Mrs. Konile is instructive. She is trapped. She occupies multiple spaces within the discourses of the TRC and yet they could not, rather would not hear her.

MS COYOTE: She is not a passive subject. She is not trapped in the iron cage of globalization.

LUIS, ANTJI, NOSISI AND KOPANO: Mrs. Konile uses her agency – her narrated dream – to resist racial and political oppression. Her courtroom story reinforces the need for a critical pedagogy framed around the tenets of restorative justice, justice as healing.

COYOTE: It took special listeners to hear her story!

LESLIE AND PATRICIA: Allow us to become pedagogical for a minute. This is how ethically responsible inquiry should work. Antji, Nosisi and Kopano helped us understand what Mrs. Konile was saying. They located the court, the hearings and the transcribes as sites of intervention. They challenged the ways in which the court was treating her TRC testimony. They initiated change for social justice purposes. They used this story as a model of change for others. The end.

Act Four: Scene One: Hope

MAHMOUD DARWISH: Where should we go after the last frontier?
Where should the birds fly after the last sky?
Where should the plants sleep after the last breath of air?
(Mahmoud Darwish 1984, p. 13; also quoted in A. Roy 2009, p. iv).

COYOTE: Is there hope?

MS COYOTE: We have a global organization, a network that extends around the world. Delegates from nearly 500 institutions. Fourteen international congresses. A journal, a book series. Templates for our own code of ethics. Emerging frameworks for evaluating our work.

SANDY, CLAUDIO AND MARCELO: We need a politics of hope. We are the children of Paulo Friere. We believe hope is an ontological need.

YVONNA S. LINCOLN: Write what you believe should be written. Dare to take chances.

SANDY, MARCELO AND CLAUDIO: We want to write in an in-between space. We are in a transitional moment with new decolonizing narratives. Resistance stories written over, around and behind the hyphen, hopeful, utopian narratives, narratives that dare to dream, stories that imagine pedagogies of freedom. Narratives that create new spaces of resistance – classrooms, courtrooms, nursing homes, hospitals, bus stations, street corners, faculty meetings, the hallways of the academy, sporting fields, cyberspace, treatment centers, journals, conferences, churches, books, new battlegrounds. A brand new morning.

PAULO FREIRE: Hope, faith and hard work will transform the world. This is a hope grounded in the belief that the demand for basic human rights, and the demand for social justice will prevail. But it requires a fight, and an investment of great emotion and passion.

ELISE DUWE: Joy Haro once told me, "People who cross borders become dangerous, because they exist in the dangerous in-between-spaces." Being dangerous means one has been wounded and is capable of wounding. Something wounded my soul. I wander into interstices, trying to heal (Duwe 2016, p. 629, paraphrase).

MS COYOTE: Paulo says change is difficult, but it is possible. Healing is always a goal (Freire 2007, p. 79, paraphrase).

PAULO: Remember. A pedagogy of hope enacts a politics of resistance and imagines a utopian future. Hope makes radical cultural critique and racial social change possible.

AUGUSTO: Hope alone will not produce change. First there must be pain, and despair. Persons must make pain the object of conscious reflection, the desire to resist, to change. This is what I try to do in my Theatre of the Oppressed. This desire must be wedded to a conscious struggle to change the conditions that create the pain in the first place.

KRIS KRISTOFFERSON: Hey I know about this stuff. I know about hope. Hope makes change possible. But listen, real change, I mean real change, does not occur without deeply felt pain, and without surrender. A willingness to fight oppression and pain from deep within the soul. All must be lost before change can occur. Freedom is just another word for nothing left to lose, and with that understanding hope is born, and radical change becomes possible. You can call this Paulo's pedagogy of hope.

MS COYOTE: Let's come full circle. Back to the beginning. A social justice agenda for qualitative inquiry is based on a politics of hope. Scholars who follow this fork in the road experience transformations in their own lives. These transformations lead them to embrace pedagogies of hope.

Act Four: Scene Two: Lunch in Lisbon, 1976

AUGUSTO BOAL: Paulo and I had lunch in Lisbon in 1976. We were two exiles from Brazil, full of hope in Portugal. My mother had recently arrived from

Brazil with a cassette letter from an old friend Chico Baurqe. We listened
in silence to Chico's words, "Do not come back, it is not time yet." We
wept. We felt tremendous emotion for the exiled, and the banished. We felt
a solidarity with those who stayed in the country. Those who have been
never been exiled have no idea how much good it did us when people
wrote, even telling of the everyday, the banal. Imagine, a sung letter. I
never threw the letter away (Boal 2002, pp. 317, 319–320),

PAULO: No one leaves this world
    without having been transfixed
    by its roots, or with a vacuum
    for a soul. We carry with us
    the memory of many fabrics,
    a self soaked in our history.
    We experience a tumult in our soul,
    a relief at the absence of the
    inquisitor, a guilt-feeling
    at leaving one's world,
    the scent of one's soul, one's folks.
    The pain of the broken dreams,
    utopia lost, the danger of
    losing hope. There is a reluctance
    on the part of the exiled to even
    buy a piece of furniture for their homes,
    even after five years in exile.
    Their half-empty houses
    speak to their loyalty
    to a distant land. Being an exile
    in a strange land is a difficult experience
    They cling to the idea of hope,
    which calls them home.
    They hang on by a thread
    (Freire 1998, pp. 31–32, paraphrase).

NORMAN DENZIN: I was in a 'series of dreams' where nothing made sense.[1]
    I felt like an extra in a scene in a movie,
    but what was I doing there?
    Gloria, Paulo and Augusto were the stars.
    The movie was a documentary about the time Paulo and Augusto
    were given honorary awards at the University of Nebraska.
    In the dream I wanted to be standing next to them.
    But there was no space on the stage, so I sat next to Gloria.
    I was in a series of dreams where nothing made sense.
    There was 'this movie I seen one time about a man and a woman
    and they wouldn't let them up on stage.[2]

GLORIA, MAGGIE, SANDY, MARCELO, CLAUDIO: Don't listen to Norman Denzin.
    As we join hands, the

sun eclipses the moon
The four winds hold our kindred spirits
The enemy is at the gate
Walking in the borderlands
of the academy means
you are never home,
but never alone.

Coda

INDIGENOUS INQUIRY CIRCLE: Dear reader, let there be hope.
We encourage you to take up
the Nehiyawewin (Cree)
notion of miskasowin,
go to your origins,
to the centre of yourself and
begin a new story of
healing relationships.
We offer our support and help for you
to cut a new trail so that we walk together
in a good way toward healing and reconciliation.[3]
MAHMOUD DARWISH: We have found a new frontier.
The birds now fly into a new sky.

The End.

Notes

1 Bob Dylan, "Series of Dreams." 1991, Special Rider Music, Bob Dylan's Greatest Hits, Volume 3, Columbia.
2 Bob Dylan, "Brownsville Girl." 1986. (With Sam Shepard), Special Rider Music, Bob Dylan's Greatest Hits, Volume 3, Columbia.
3 Excerpted from letter to Chancellor Robert J. Jones from the Indigenous Inquiries Circle (IIC), a special interest group (SIG) of the International Congress of Qualitative Inquiry (ICQI) hosted by the University of Illinois at Urbana-Champaign, September 27, 2016.: signatees: Elder Joseph Natytowhow, Knowledge Keeper, Treaty 6 Sturgeon Lake SK, Canada Dr. Margaret Kovach, University of Saskatchewan, Canada Dr. Patrick Lewis, University of Regina, Canada.

Part III

Toward a performative social science

8 The cinematic society and the reflexive interview

We inhabit a secondhand televisual world, one already mediated by social media, cinema, television and the other surveillance apparatuses of the fascist,[1] authoritarian predatory post-postmodern society (Gubrium and Holstein 2001, 2003).[2] As Bratich (2017) argues,

> The notion that we are in a *surveillance era* is as pervasive as the sci-fi depictions of surveillance itself ... Marketers recruit tweens to be info gatherers on their peers, calling it trendspotting. Reality TV, which permeates the airwaves, is a transformation of television programming in the service of naturalizing surveillance. Self-disclosure and peer monitoring are valorized as cornerstones of participatory culture. We experience an Internet visual culture replete with YouTube micro-videos, citizen journalists, camgirls, and a social media ecology of "selfies" ... Online performances of self depend on a hope and expectation that an Other is observing and will react with (positive) evaluation.

We are sliding into a complex space. Democracy is under assault. We are witnessing the emergence of a new mode of authoritarianism, one that threatens to shut down avenues for social justice and civil rights, as the 2016 Republican candidate for president shouted that the election was RIGGED! (see Giroux 2016b). In such a world, the usual distinctions between fact, fiction and truth disappear. They go up in smoke. Such a world is driven more and more by the interactive conventions of dramaturgy, live TV, split-TV screens, instant replay, virtual selves (selfies), Skype performance and social media formats, from Twitter to Facebook, from YouTube, to LinkedIn. Today our lives are lived on tiny handheld screens which we carry in our pockets. Consider the following scene. Hillary Clinton is on the 2016 Presidential campaign trail:

> Outside her plane after a speech in Tampa, Fla, Clinton stopped for a few minutes under a wing to chat and take pictures with the photographers in the press corps. This produced a classic through-the looking-glass scene: Clinton posing for pictures with the photographers who normally

photograph her, while the rest of her media contingent were photographing her posing for photos with her photographers.

(Leibovich 2016, p. 45, paraphrase).

A pure postmodern moment. Selfies, virtual and real selves, whose picture is being taken by whom? Photographers taking pictures of photographers taking pictures of photographers taking pictures. Does it really even matter any more? We engage this world, the only world we have, indirectly, through the tele-visual, from GPS maps, to Google links, from Google to GoDaddy hosted websites, from websites to Amazon.com, the world's largest shopping mall. We have no direct access to these worlds, even as our fingers and eyes move across keyboards and touch screens, bringing them into focus. The reflexive interview and the video and the photographic image are central components of this interpretive project.

In this chapter and the next, I examine the nexus of the surveillance society and the interview society. I show how post-postmodern society has become an interview society, how our very subjectivity "comes to us in the form of stories elicited through interviewing" (Holstein and Gubrium 2000, p. 129; see also Atkinson and Silverman 1997). The interview, whether conducted by social researchers, television hosts, political commentators, television journalists, therapists or counselors, is now a ubiquitous method of self-construction (Holstein and Gubrium 2000, p. 129).

I will discuss the concept of the active, dialogic interview, anchoring this complex formation in the cinematic society. A society which is increasingly mediated by online communities where individuals can put an identity or an experience online before it is even fully formed or understood (Leibovich 2016, p. 45). In these spaces feelings, taboos and interactional lines can be crossed, identities confused, trusts betrayed, relationships destroyed, emoticons expressing sadness.

The reflexive interview is simultaneously a site for conversation, a discursive method and a communicative format that produces knowledge about the self and its place in the dramaturgical society – the society that knows itself through the reflective technological gaze of the split screen tele-visual apparatus.

A single two-part question organizes my argument: First, how does the post-postmodern, cinematic world mediate the ways in which we represent ourselves to ourselves? And second, what is the place of the interview-interviewer relationship in this production process? I begin the discussion by outlining the central features of the post-postmodern, cinematic-interview society. I then show how the interview and the interviewer, as a voyeur, are basic features of this society. I thicken this argument by demonstrating how popular media representations shape and define situated cultural identities. I show how these representations become anchor points for the post-postmodern self – that is, how they occupy a central place in the background of our cultural conscious-ness. They mediate structures of meaning in the cinematic-interview society. A circular model of interpretation is thus created. Interviews, interviewers and storytellers are defined in terms of these dominant cultural images and under-standings. Thus the cinematic society structures the interview society and vice versa. I conclude with a series of epistemological observations on the significance of the relationship between the cinematic society and the reflexive interview.

The post-postmodern, cinematic society

Members of the postmodern society know themselves through the reflected images and narratives of cinema and television. On this, Altheide (1995) observes, "Culture is not only mediated through mass media ... culture in both form and content is constituted and embodied by the mass media" (p. 59). The postmodern landscape is distinguished, as Gottschalk (2000) argues, by "its constant saturation by multiple electronic screens which simulate emotions, interactions, events, desires ... From TV screens to computer terminals, from surveillance cameras to cell phones, we increasingly experience everyday life, reality ... via technologies of spectacle, simulation and 'telepresence'" (p. 23).

Consider the following exchange between ESPN sports journalist Sal Paolantonio and Kurt Warner, quarterback of the St. Louis Rams, who was named Most Valuable Player in the 2000 Super Bowl:

SAL.: There's a minute and 54 seconds left in the game. The Titans have just tied the score. Now look, let me show you your 73-yard winning pass to Isaac Bruce. Kurt, what were you thinking when Isaac caught that pass?

KURT: [Looks up at replay] We'd called the same play earlier and Isaac was open. So we thought it would work. It was a go route. We thought we could get a big one right off the bat. I just thought it was meant to be, it was meant to work.

SAL.: This has been a terrific year for you. Five years ago you were sacking groceries in the IGA. Two years ago you were playing arena football in Cedar Rapids, Iowa. This is better than a Hollywood script. Tell me how you feel about what has happened to you this year?

KURT: I don't think of it as a Hollywood story. It's my life. I take it one day at a time.[3]

Kurt's self-narrative is grafted onto the replay of the winning touchdown pass. Indeed, this Super Bowl victory symbolizes the larger-than-life-triumph that he has experienced over the course of the preceding five years. Sal elicits this self-story by asking Kurt how he feels about his award-winning year, comparing it to a Hollywood script. Kurt complies by giving him a socially acceptable answer.[4]

The ingredients of the postmodern self are modeled in the media. The post-modern self has become a sign of itself, a double dramaturgical reflection anchored in media representations on one side and everyday life on the other. These cultural identities are filtered through the individual's personal troubles and emotional experiences in interactions with everyday life. These existential troubles connect back to the dominant cultural themes of the postmodern era. The electronic media and the new information technologies turn everyday life into a theatrical spectacle where the dramas that surround the decisive performances of existential crises are enacted. This creates a new existential "videocy," a language of crisis coded in electronic, media terms. The everyday existential world connects to the cinematic apparatus.

The birth of cinematic surveillance

In the space of the period from 1900 to 1930, cinema became an integral part of American society. Going to the movies became a weekly pastime for millions of Americans. Motion pictures became a national institution. Hollywood stars became personal idols, fan clubs were formed, and movie theatres, with their lighted marquees, were a prominent part of virtually every American community.

The cinematic, surveillance society soon became a disciplinary structure filled with subjects (voyeurs) who obsessively looked and gazed at one another, as they became, at the same time, obsessive listeners, eavesdroppers, persons whose voices and telephone lines could be tapped, voices that could be dubbed, new versions of the spoken and seen self. A new social type was created: the voyeur, or Peeping Tom, who would, in various guises (ethnographer, social scientist, detective, psychoanalyst, crime reporter, investigative journalist, innocent bystander, sexual pervert), elevate the concepts of looking and listening to new levels.

With the advent of color and sound in film in the mid-1920s, there was a drive toward cinematic realism. This impulse to create a level of realism that mapped everyday life complemented the rise of naturalistic realism in the American novel and the emergence of hard-nosed journalistic reporting by the major American newspapers and radio (and later TV) networks (Denzin 1997, pp. 21–22). During the same period, an ethnographic, psychoanalytic and life history approach was taking hold in the social sciences and in society at large. Like journalists, sociologists, market researchers and survey researchers were learning how to use the interview to gather and report on the facts of social life (Fontana and Frey 1994, pp. 362, 2000; Denzin 1997, p. 129).

Robert E. Park (1950), a founder of the Chicago school of ethnographic research (Vidich and Lyman 1994, pp. 32–33), clarifies the relationships among journalism, social science and the use of the interview:

> After leaving college, I got a job as a reporter ... I wrote about all sorts of things ...
>
> My interest in the newspaper had grown out of the discovery that a reporter who had the facts was a more effective reformer than an editorial writer ...
>
> According to my earliest conception of a sociologist he was to be a kind of super-reporter ... He was to report a little more accurately, and in a little more detail.

And so, although sociologists and journalists both used interviews, the duties and practices of the two occupational groups were separated, and the groups organized surveillance in distinctly different ways.

The interview society

The interview society emerges historically as a consequence, in part, of the central place that newspapers and cinema (and television) came (and continue) to occupy in daily life. The media, human services personnel, market researchers and social scientists "increasingly get their information via interviews" (Holstein and Gubrium 1995, p. 1). The interview society has turned the confessional mode of discourse into a public form of entertainment (Atkinson and Silverman 1997, pp. 309–315; Holstein and Gubrium 2000, p. 129). The world of private troubles, the site of the authentic, or real, self, has become a public commodity.

The interview goes to Hollywood

It remained for Hollywood to authorize the interview as a primary method of gathering information about social issues, selves and the meanings of personal experience. Soon Hollywood was telling stories about newspaper reporters (*The Front Page*, 1931), detectives and private eyes (*The Maltese Falcon*, 1931, 1941), psychoanalysts and psychiatrists (*Spellbound,* 1945), spies and secret agents (*Saboteur,* 1942) and market researchers (*Desk Set,* 1957; *Sex and the Single Girl,* 1964). More recently, the movies have offered spoofs of sociologists (*The Milagro Beanfield War,* 1988) and anthropologists (*Krippendorf's Tribe,* 1998).

Each of these film genres glamorized the interview as a form of interaction and as a strategy and technique for getting persons to talk about themselves and others (see Holstein and Gubrium 1995, p. 3). Journalists, detectives and social scientists were presented as experts in the use of this conversational form. Hollywood led us to expect that such experts will use this form when interacting with members of society. Furthermore, it led us to expect that persons, if properly asked, will reveal their inner selves to such experts.

And thus the key assumptions of the interview society were soon secured. The media and Hollywood cinema helped to solidify the following cluster of beliefs: Only skilled interviewers and therapists (and sometimes the person) have access to the deep, authentic self of the person; sociologists, journalists and psychoanalysts know how to ask questions that will produce disclosures, often discrediting, about the hidden self; members of the interview society have certain experiences that are more authentic then others, and these experiences are keys to the hidden self (these are the experiences that have left deep marks and scars on the person); adept interviewers can uncover these experiences and their meanings to the person; nonetheless, persons also have access to their own experiences, and this increases the value of first-person narratives, which are the site of personal meaning.

When probing for the inner self, or when seeking information from an individual, an interviewer is expected to use some method to record what is said in the interview. In the film *True Crime* (1999), Clint Eastwood plays Steve Everett, a burned-out, alcoholic reporter who becomes convinced that Frank Beachum, a black man due to be executed within 24 hours, is innocent. Eastwood tracks down Mr. Porterhouse, the man whose testimony led to Beachum's conviction. Everett and Porterhouse meet in a café and the following exchange unfolds:

EVERETT: Let me get this straight, you didn't really see the murder?
PORTERHOUSE: I never said I did.
EVERETT: What did you see?
PORTERHOUSE: I can't tell you how many times I've been over this. I went into Pokeums to use the phone. My car had overheated. Beachum jumped up from behind the counter. He was covered with blood and had a gun in his hand. He was bending over, stealing her necklace. He got one good look at me and then he ran out the store. My concern was for the girl. So I immediately dialed 911. I figured why should I run after a killer, when the police should do their job.
EVERETT: And they sure did it, didn't they.
PORTERHOUSE: Aren't you gonna take some notes, or somethin'? Or use a tape recorder? Usually when I'm talkin' to a reporter they wanta keep some sort of record of what I've been sayin'.
EVERETT: I have a photographic memory [points to head]. I have a notebook right here [pulls a notebook and pen out of his jacket pocket].Everett refuses to write anything in his notebook, and Porterhouse challenges him: "I did some checking on you. You're the guy who led the crusade to get the rapist released. That lying what's his name? Had all your facts straight on that one too, didn't you?"

Everett next interviews Beachum in his prison cell. Beachum's wife, Bonnie, is there too. (The reporter who had originally been assigned to the case was killed in a car accident.)

BEACHUM: I guess you wanta hear how it feels to be in here.
EVERETT: Yeah, it's a human interest piece.
BEACHUM: I feel isolated. I feel fear, pain, fear of prison, fear of being separated from my loved ones. All those fears rolled up into one.

[Everett takes notebook out of pocket.]

BEACHUM: I want to tell everyone that I believe in Jesus Christ, our Lord and Savior.

[Everett scribbles on page of notebook: BLV, JC.]

BEACHUM: I came into my faith late in life. Did a lot of bad things ... I believe that the crooked road remains straight, that's what the Bible says.

[Everett scribbles on page of notebook: LORD, SAV, CARO, STRAIT.]

BEACHUM: Is there any more that you want?
EVERETT: You don't know me. I'm just a guy out there with a screw loose. Frankly I don't give a rat's ass about Jesus Christ. I don't even care what's right or wrong. But my nose tells me something stinks, and I gotta have my faith in it, just like you have your faith in Jesus ... I know there's truth out there somewhere ... I believe you.
BONNIE BEACHUM: Where were you?
EVERETT: It wasn't my story.

Beachum clearly expected Everett to ask him how he felt about being on death row. He expected to tell a reporter a deeply personal story about what this experience means to his inner, authentic self. Indeed, Everett's presence in the prison elicits such a story from Beachum. To paraphrase Holstein and Gubrium (2000, p. 129), the prison interview with a journalist is now a natural part of the death row identity landscape. But Everett, through his note taking, mocks this assumption. He has no desire to record the inner meaning of this experience for Beachum. This is unlike the desire illustrated in the excerpt from the *SportsCenter* interview above, in which Sal Paolantonio sought and got from Kurt Warner a self-validating, self-congratulatory story about hard work and success in American life.

The interview machine as an epistemological apparatus

The interview society uses the machinery of the interview methodically to produce situated versions of the self. This machinery works in a systematic and orderly fashion. It structures the talk that occurs in the interview situation. There is an orderly mechanism "for designating who will speak next" (Holstein and Gubrium 2000, p. 125). Using the question-answer format, this mechanism regulates the flow of conversation. Talk occurs in question-answer pairs, for the asking of a question requires an answer. Turn taking structures this give-and-take. The rule of single speakership obtains: One person speaks at a time. Interviews, in this sense, are orderly, dramaturgical accomplishments. They draw on local understandings and are constrained by those understandings. They are narrative productions; they have beginnings, middles and endings.

The methodology of asking questions is central to the operation of this machine. Different epistemologies and ideologies shape this methodological practice. Four epistemological formats can be identified: the objectively neutral format, the entertainment and investigative format, the collaborative or active interview format, and the reflexive, dialogic interview format.[5] In each format, the asking of a question is an incitement to speak, an invitation to tell a story;

in this sense the interview elicits narratives of the self (Holstein and Gubrium 2000, p. 129).

The place of the interviewer in this process varies dramatically. In the *objectively neutral format,* the interviewer, using a structured or semi-structured interview schedule, attempts to gather information without influencing the story that is being told. Holstein and Gubrium (2000) correctly observe that the demands of ongoing interaction make the "'ideal' interview a practical impossibility, because the interview itself always remains accountable to the normative expectancies of competent conversation as well as to the demand for a good story to satisfy the needs of the researcher" (p. 131).

In the *entertainment and investigative format,* the interviewer often acts as a partisan, seeking to elicit a story that will sell as an entertainment commodity or can be marketed as a new piece of information about a story that is in the process of being told. In this format, the interviewer asks leading, aggressive questions as well as friendly questions, questions that allow the subject to embellish on a previous story or to give more detail on the meanings of an important experience. Paolantonio's interview with Warner employs the entertainment format. This is a friendly interview that shows both participants in a good light. Steve Everett's interview with Mr. Porterhouse in *True Crime* illustrates the investigative version of this format. Everett is aggressive and hostile; he seeks to discredit Porterhouse as a witness.

In the *collaborative or active format,* interviewer and respondent tell a story together (see Holstein and Gubrium 1995, pp. 76–77). In this format a conversation occurs. Indeed, the identities of interviewer and respondent disappear. Each becomes a storyteller, or the two collaborate in telling a conjoint story. The *SportsCenter* interview excerpt above also illustrates this format, as together Sal and Kurt tell a story about the meaning of this victory for Kurt's life.

In the *reflexive interview format,* two speakers enter into a dialogic relationship with each other. In this relationship, a tiny drama is played out. Each person becomes a party to the utterances of the other. Together, the two speakers create a small dialogic world of unique meaning and experience. In this interaction, each speaker struggles to understand the thought of the other, reading and paying attention to such matters as intonation, facial gestures and word selection (see Bakhtin 1986, pp. 92–93).

Consider the following dialogue excerpted from the 1982 film *Chan Is Missing,* directed by Wayne Wang. Set in contemporary San Francisco, the film mocks popular culture representations of stereotypical Asian American identities. It also mocks social science and those scholars who point to language as an answer to cultural differences. The following Lily Tomlin-like monologue is central to this position. In the monologue, racial and ethnic identities are constructed. This construction is directly connected to the use of the objective interview format. The speaker is a female Asian American attorney. She is attempting to find Mr. Chan, who had an automobile accident just days before he disappeared. She is speaking to Jo, a middle-aged Chinese American cab driver, and Jo's young "Americanized" nephew, Steve. They are at Chester's

Cafe. The young attorney is dressed in a black masculine-style suit, with a white shirt and dark tie.

You see I'm doing a paper on the legal implications of cross-cultural mis-understandings. [nods head] Mr. Chan's case is a perfect example of what I want to expose. The policeman and Mr. Chan have completely different culturally related assumptions about what kind of communication [shot of Steve, then Jo] each one was using. The policeman, in an English-speaking mode, asks a direct factual question – "Did you stop at the stop sign?" He expected a yes or a no answer. Mr. Chan, however, rather than giving him a yes or a no answer, began to go into his past driving record – how good it was, the number of years he had been in the United States, all the people that he knew – trying to relate different events, objects, or situations to what was happening then to the action at hand. Now this is very typical … The Chinese try to relate points, events, or objects that they feel are pertinent to the situation, which may not to anyone else seem directly relevant at the time … This policeman became rather impatient, restated the question, "Did you or did you not stop at the stop sign?" in a rather hostile tone, which in turn flustered Mr. Chan, which caused him to hesitate answering the question, which further enraged the policeman, so that he asked the question again, "You didn't stop at the stop sign, did you?" in a negative tone, to which Mr. Chan automatically answered, "No." Now to any native speaker of English, "No" would mean "No I didn't stop at the stop sign." However to Mr. Chan, "No I didn't stop at the stop sign" was not "No I didn't stop at the stop sign [Jo shakes head, looks away]. It was "No, I didn't not stop at the stop sign." In other words, "Yes I did stop at the stop sign." Do you see what I'm saying? [camera pans room]

Then, in a voice-over, Jo comments, "Chan Hung wouldn't run away because of the car accident. I'm feeling something might have happened to him" (see Denzin 1995a, p. 105).

Here the speaker, the young attorney, attempts to dialogically enter into and interpret the meanings that were circulating in Mr. Chan's interview with the policeman. In so doing, she criticizes the concept of cross-cultural communica-tion, showing through her conversation that meanings are always dialogic and contextual.

This text from Wang's film is an example of how the reflexive, dialogic interviewer deconstructs the uses and abuses of the interview – uses that are associated with the objectively neutral and entertainment/investigative formats. This text suggests that interpretations based on the surface meanings of an utterance sequence are likely to be superficial. To paraphrase Dillard (1982, p. 46), serious students of society take pains to distinguish their work from such interpretive practices.

At another level, reflexively oriented scholars, such as Bakhtin, contend that there is no essential self or private, real self behind the public self. They argue that there are only different selves, different performances, different ways of being a gendered person in a social situation. These performances are based on different interpretive practices. These practices give the self and the person a sense of grounding, or narrative coherence (Gubrium and Holstein 1998, p. 165). There is no inner or deep self that is accessed by the interview or narrative method. There are only different interpretive (and performative) versions of who the person is.

Steve Everett embodies one version of the reflexive interviewer. He has no interest in the inner self of the person he is interviewing, no interest in right or wrong. He only seeks the truth, the truth that says an injustice may have been done. Wang's Asian American attorney is another version of this interviewer; she understands that the self is a verbal and narrative construction.

The interview and the dramaturgical society

The text from the Kurt Warner interview presented above suggests that the metaphor of the dramaturgical society (Lyman 1990, p. 221), or "life as theater" (Brissett and Edgley 1990, p. 2; Goffman 1959, pp. 254–255), is no longer a metaphor. It has become interactional reality. Life and art have became mirror images of each other. Reality, as it is visually experienced, is a staged, social production.

Raban (1981) provides an example of how life and television coincide. In a TV ad "beamed by the local station in Decorah, an Iowa farmer spoke stiffly to the camera in testimony to the bags of fertilizer that were heaped in front of him" (p. 123). Here the personal testimony of the farmer, a hands-on expert, authorizes the authenticity and value of the product. This message is carried live, staged in the frame of the TV commercial; a real farmer says this product works. The farmer's awkwardness comes, perhaps, from the fact that he must look at himself doing this endorsement, knowing that if he sees himself looking this way, others will as well.

The reflected, everyday self and its gendered presentations are attached to the cinematic/televisual self. Blumer (1933) provides an example. An interview respondent connects her gendered self to the Hollywood screen:

> *Female, 19, white, college freshman.* – When I discovered I should have this coquettish and coy look which all girls may have, I tried to do it in my room. And surprises! I could imitate Pola Negri's cool or fierce look. Vilma Banky's sweet and coquettish attitude. I learned the very way of taking my gentlemen friends to and from the door with that wistful smile, until it has become a part of me.
>
> (p. 34)

Real, everyday experiences are judged against their staged, cinematic, video counterparts. The fans of Hollywood stars dress like the stars, make love like the stars and dream the dreams of the stars. Blumer provides an example:

Female, 24, white, college senior. – During my high-school period I particularly liked pictures in which the setting was a millionaire's estate or some
such elaborate place. After seeing a picture of this type, I would imagine
myself living such a life of ease as the society girl I had seen. My day-dreams
would be concerned with lavish wardrobes, beautiful homes, servants,
imported automobiles, yachts, and countless suitors.

(p. 64)

With this dramaturgical turn, the technology of the media "disengages subjects
from their own expressions ... Individuals become observers of their own
acts ... Actions come to be negotiated in terms of a media aesthetic, both actor
and spectator live a reality arbitrated by the assumptions of media technicians"
(Eason 1984, p. 60). Altheide and Snow (1991) provide an example from
Richard Nixon's presidency. In a memo to H. R. Haldeman dated December 1,
1969, Nixon wrote:

We need a part- or full-time TV man on our staff for the purpose of seeing
that my TV appearances are handled on a professional basis. When I think
of the millions of dollars that go into one lousy 30-second television spot
advertising deodorant, it seems to me unbelievable that we don't do a
better job of seeing that Presidential appearances [on TV] always have the
very best professional advice.

(Quoted p. 105; see also Oudes 1989, p. 46)

And because of the same media aesthetic, Kurt Warner has learned how to talk
the form of sports talk that Ron Shelton mocks in his 1988 film *Bull Durham*.
So, too, does Frank Beachum expect Steve Everett to record his moral story.

The main carriers of the popular in postmodern society have become the very
media that are defining the content and meaning of the popular; that is, popular
culture is now a matter of cinema and the related media, including television, the
press and popular literature. A paradox is created, for the everyday is now
defined by the cinematic and the televisual. The two can no longer be separated.
A press conference at the 1988 Democratic National Convention is reported thus:

A dozen reporters stood outside CBS's area, and as was so often the case at
the convention, one began interviewing another. A third commented wryly
on the interview: "Reporter interviews reporter about press conference."

(Weiss 1988, pp. 33–34; quoted in Altheide and Snow 1991, p. 93)

Reporters are reporting on reporters interviewing reporters.

Studying the interview in the cinematic society

The cinematic apparatuses of contemporary culture stand in a twofold relationship to critical inquiry. First, the cultural logics of the postvideo cinematic

culture define the lived experiences that a critical studies project takes as its subject matter. How these texts structure and give meaning to the everyday must be analyzed. At the same time, critical ethnographies of the video-cinematic text must be constructed, showing how these texts map and give narrative meaning to the crucial cultural identities that circulate in the postmodern society.

Consider race, the racial self and Hollywood cinema. Lopez (1991) reminds us that "Hollywood does not represent ethnics and minorities; it creates them and provides an audience with an experience of them" (pp. 404–405). Consider her argument in terms of the following scene from Spike Lee's highly controversial 1989 film *Do the Right Thing*. Near the film's climax, as the heat rises on the street, members of each racial group in the neighborhood hurl vicious racial slurs at one another:

MOOKIE: [to Sal, who is Italian, and Sal's sons, Vito and Pino] Dago, wop, guinea, garlic breath, pizza slingin' spaghetti bender, Vic Damone, Perry Como, Pavarotti.

PINO: [to Mookie and the other blacks] Gold chain wearin' fried chicken and biscuit eatin' monkey, ape, baboon, fast runnin', high jumpin', spear chuckin', basketball dunkin' ditso spade, take you fuckin' pizza and go back to Africa.

PUERTO RICAN MAN: [to the Korean grocer] Little slanty eyed, me-no speakie American, own every fruit and vegetable stand in New York, bull shit, Reverend Sun Young Moon, Summer 88 Olympic kick-ass boxer, sonofabitch.

WHITE POLICEMAN: You goya bean eatin' 15 in the car, 30 in the apartment, pointy red shoes wearin' Puerto Ricans, cocksuckers.

KOREAN GROCER: I got good price for you, how am I doing? Chocolate egg cream drinking, bagel lox, Jew asshole.

SWEET DICK WILLIE: [to the Korean grocer] Korean motherfucker… you didn't do a goddamn thing except sit on your monkey ass here on this corner and do nothin. (See Denzin 1991, pp. 129–130.)

Lee wants his audience to believe that his speakers are trapped within the walls and streets of a multiracial ghetto that is the Bedford-Stuyvesant area of New York City. Their voices reproduce current (and traditional) cultural, racial and sexual stereotypes about blacks (spade, monkey), Koreans (slanty eyed), Puerto Ricans (pointy red shoes, cock-suckers), Jews (bagel lox) and Italians (dago, wop). The effects of these in-your-face insults are exaggerated through wide-angle, close-up shots. Each speaker's face literally fills the screen as the racial slurs are hurled.[6]

Lee's film presents itself as a realist, ethnographic text. It asks the viewer to believe that it is giving an objectively factual, authentic and realistic account of the lived experiences of race and ethnicity. The film performs race and ethnicity (e.g., Pino talking to Mookie) and does so in ways that support the belief that objective reality has been captured. The film "realistically" reinscribes familiar (and new) cultural stereotypes – for example, young gang members embodying hip-hop or rap culture. Lee's text functions like a documentary film. Lee's film needs to be read against the debates about Black Lives Matter, Blue Lives Matter, All Lives Matter, and police and citizen attitudes about civil and human rights that raged during the 2016 United States presidential election cycle (Spencer et al. 2017).

The cinematic society and the documentary interview

It is this documentary impulse and its reliance on the objectively neutral interview format that I now examine through an analysis of Trinh T. Minh-ha's 1989 film *Surname Viet Given Name Nam*. This is a film about Vietnamese women, whose names change or remain constant depending on whether they marry foreigners or other Vietnamese. In this film, Trinh has Vietnamese women speak from five different subject positions, representing lineage, gender status, age status, leadership position, and historical period. This creates a complex picture of Vietnamese culture (see Trinh 1992, p. 144).

The film is multitextual, layered with pensive images of women in various situations. Historical moments overlap with age periods (childhood, youth, adulthood, old age), rituals and ceremonies (weddings, funerals, war, the market, dance) and daily household work (cooking) while interviewees talk to offscreen interviewers. There are two voice-overs in English, and a third voice sings sayings, proverbs and poetry in Vietnamese (with translations into English appearing as texts on the screen). There are also interviews with Vietnamese subtitled in English and interviews in English synchronized with the onscreen images (Trinh 1992, p. 49). The interviews are reenacted in Trinh's film by Vietnamese actresses, who are then interviewed at the end of the film about their experiences of being performers in the film (Trinh 1992, p. 146).

Trinh's film allows the practice of doing reflexive interviews to enter into the construction of the text itself, thus the true and the false, the real and the staged intermingle; indeed, the early sections of the film unfold like a traditional, realist documentary (Trinh 1992, p. 145). The viewer does not know that the women onscreen are actresses reenacting interviews. Nor does the viewer know that the interviews were conducted in the United States, not Vietnam (this becomes apparent only near the end of the film).

In using these interpretive strategies, Trinh creates a space for the critical appraisal of the politics of representation that structures the use of interviews in the documentary film. In undoing the objectively neutral interview as a method for gathering information about reality, Trinh takes up the question of truth (see Trinh 1992, p. 145). Whose truth is she presenting – that given in the onscreen interview situation or that of the women-as-actresses who are interviewed at the end of the film?

Trinh begins by deconstructing the classic interview-based documentary film, which enters the native's world and brings news from that world to the world of the Western observer. In its use of the traditional, nondialogic interview method, documentary film starts with the so-called real world and the subject's place in that world. It uses an aesthetic of objectivity and a technological apparatus that produces truthful statements (images) about the world (Trinh 1991, p. 33). Trinh (1991, p. 39) argues that the following elements are central to this apparatus:

- The relentless pursuit of naturalism, which requires a connection between the moving image and the spoken word
- Authenticity – the use of people who appear to be real and locating these people in "real" situations
- The filmmaker/interviewer presented as an observer, not as a person who creates what is seen, heard, and read
- The capture only of events unaffected by the recording eye
- The capture of objective reality
- The dramatization of truth
- The presentation of actual facts in a credible way, with people telling them.

Along with these elements, the film-interview text must convince spectators that they should have confidence in the truth of what they see. These aesthetic strategies define the documentary interview style, allowing the filmmaker-as-interviewer to create a text that gives the viewer the illusion of having "unmediated access to reality" (Trinh 1991, p. 40). Thus naturalized, the objective, documentary interview style has become part of the larger cinematic apparatus in American culture, including a pervasive presence in TV commercials and news (Trinh 1991, p. 40).

Trinh brings a reflexive reading to these features of the documentary film, citing her own texts as examples of dialogic documentaries that are sensitive to the flow of fact and fiction, to meanings as political constructions (see Trinh 1991, p. 41). Such texts reflexively understand that reality is never neutral or objective, that it is always socially constructed. Filmmaking and documentary interviewing thus become methods of "framing" reality.

Self-reflexivity does not translate into personal style or a preoccupation with method. Rather, it centers on the reflexive interval that defines representation, "the place in which the play within the textual frame is a play on this very frame, hence on the borderlines of the textual and the extra-textual" (Trinh 1991, p. 48). The film becomes a site for multiple experiences.

A responsible, reflexive, dialogic interview text embodies the following characteristics (Trinh 1991, p. 188):

- It announces its own politics and evidences a political consciousness.
- It interrogates the realities it represents.
- It invokes the teller's story in the history that is told.
- It makes the audience responsible for interpretation.
- It resists the temptation to become an object of consumption.

- It resists all dichotomies (male/female and so on).
- It foregrounds difference, not conflict.
- It uses multiple voices, emphasizing language as silence, the grain of the voice, tone, inflection, pauses, silences, repetitions.
- It presents silence as a form of resistance.

Trinh creates the space for a version of the cinematic apparatus and the interview machine that challenges mainstream film. She also challenges traditional ethnography and its use of objective and investigative interview formats.

Reflexive texts question the very notion of a stable, unbiased gaze. They focus on the pensive image, on silences, on representations that "unsettle the male apparatus of the gaze" (Trinh 1991, p. 115). This look makes the interviewer's gaze visible. It destabilizes any sense of verisimilitude that can be brought to this visual world. In so doing, it also disrupts the spectator's gaze, itself a creation of the unnoticed camera, the camera that invokes the image of a perfect, natural world, a world with verisimilitude (Trinh 1991, p. 115). In using these interpretive strategies, Trinh creates the space for the viewer (and listener) to appraise critically the politics of representation that structures the documentary text.

Cultivating reflexive listening

Learning from Trinh, I want to cultivate a method of patient listening, a reflexive method of looking, hearing, and asking that is dialogic and respectful. I want to treat listening is an active, reflexive process (McRae 2015, p. 5). There must be, Salvo reminds us, a time made for listening, for listening is more than hearing. It involves being attentive to and giving meaning to narrative itself, an act that breathes the other into being (Salvo, 2019). Through listening I connect meaning to discourse, to speech, to the sounds of the other's presence. Listening becomes a performance, an ethical act. In listening I make ourselves vulnerable to the sounds and meanings of the other's voice. Listening, hearing the sounds of your voice, is an interiorizing experience for me. I am moved by your vocal co-presence. You become present to me (Conquergood 1991, p. 183).

I become a co-constructor of meaning in this dialogic relationship. As an active listener (Bourdieu 1996; McRae 2015) I treat dialogue as a process of discovery. I will attempt to function as an empowering collaborator. I will use the reflexive interview as a tool of intervention (Burawoy 1998). I will use it as a method for uncovering structures of oppression in the life worlds of the persons I am interviewing. As a reflexive participant, I will critically promote the agendas of radical democratic practice. In so doing, I hope to cultivate a method of hearing and writing that has some kinship with the kinds of issues Gloria Naylor (1998) discusses in the following passage:

> Someone who didn't know how to ask wouldn't know how to listen. And he coulda listened to them the way you been listening to us right now.

Think about it: ain't nobody really talking to you ... Really listen this time; the only voice is your own. But you done just heard the about the legend of Saphira Wade ... You done heard it in the way we know it, sitting on our porches and shelling June peas ... taking apart the engine of a car – you done heard it without a single living soul really saying a word.

(p. 1842)

But this is also a sociology that understands, here at the end, that when we screen our dreams and our crises through the canvases and lenses that the cinematic and electronic society makes available to us, we risk becoming storied versions of somebody else's version of who we should be. More deeply, Bratich (2017) cautions about the increasing dangers inherent in the surveillance society:

As surveillance society begins to creep into all spaces and absorb observation for its own ends, it is important to retain the antagonism within this long-contested practice. Preserving antagonism prevents the totalizing impulse of surveillance and protects the spaces for a democratic, popular expansion of observation as a weapon in the struggle for justice ... Needed now is a democratic notion of observational gazes rooted in and furthering popular justice.

The cinematic society undone.

Notes

1 I define fascism as a conservative, extreme right-wing political, economic and socio-legal state formation characterized by authoritarian forms of government, extreme nationalism, manufactured consent at key levels of public opinion, racism, a large military-industrial complex, foreign aggressiveness, anticommunism, state-supported corporate capitalism, state-sponsored violence, extreme restrictions on individual freedom and tendencies toward an "Orwellian condition of perpetual war... [and] a national security state in which intelligence agencies and the military replace publicly elected officials in deciding national priorities" (Rorty 2002, p. 13).
2 I thank Jay Gubrium and Jim Holstein for their comments.
3 See *SportsCenter*, ESPN, January 31, 2000; see also Vecsey (2000).
4 The underlying logic of the sports interview is mocked in the following dialogue from Ron Shelton's 1988 film *Bull Durham*. Kevin Costner, who plays an aging pitcher named Crash Davis, says to his protégé, played by Tim Robbins, "Now you are going to the Big Show. You have to learn how to talk to interviewers. When they ask you how it feels to be pitching in Yankee Stadium, you say, 'I just thank the good Lord for all his gifts. I owe it all to him. I just take it one game, one pitch at a time.'"
5 These interview formats blur with the three types of relationships between interviewer and interviewee that Mishler (1986) identifies: informant and reporter, collaborators and advocates.
6 Although prejudice crosses color lines in this film, racial intolerance is connected to the psychology of the speaker (e.g., Vito). It is "rendered as the *how* of personal bigotry" (Guerrero 1993, p. 154). The economic and political features of institutional racism are not taken up. That is, in Lee's film, "the *why* of racism is left unexplored" (Guerrero 1993, p. 154).

9 Toward a performative social science

I have argued that we perform culture; we do not write it.[1] Furthermore, our performances are not innocent practices. They are always ideological, carrying the traces and scars of global capitalism and white patriarchy. Still, if we know the world only through our representations of it, then to change the world, we must change how we write and perform it.

Throughout the twentieth century and well through the second decade of this new century, the transcribed interview remains the basic information-gathering tool and one of the major writing forms used by scholars in the social sciences. This model presumed a view from outside society and the possibility of an objective observer. The transcribed interview allowed the writer to create a discourse that suspended, even did away with, the presence of a real subject in the world. It made social experience and human character irrelevant to the topic at hand. It created an interpretive structure that said social phenomena should be interpreted as social facts. It shifted discussions about agency, purpose and meaning from the subject to the phenomena being discussed. It then transformed these phenomena into texts about society, giving the phenomena a presence that rested in the textual description (D. Smith 1989, p. 45.) Real people entered the text through excerpts from field notes and transcribed interviews (Denzin 1997, p. 55; D. Smith 1989, p. 51). Transcribed words did this work.

Performance writing challenges this model of inquiry. Building on the performance interviews of Anna Deavere Smith (1993, 1994, 2000, 2003/2004), in this chapter I introduce the concept of performance interviewing. I connect this form of the interview to performance writing and performance [auto] ethnography (see Pollock 1998a, p. 74). This chapter is a "writing performance" (Pelias 1999, p. xiv); in these pages, I take up the multiple ways in which writing can perform itself.

I begin the chapter with a discussion of the performative sensibility and the interview as an interpretive practice. I then turn to the topics of the performance interview, performative writing and performance [auto] ethnographies. I next explicate Anna Deavere Smith's project, especially her concepts of performance and the poetic text. I move from Smith's arguments to a performance text of my own based on a reflexive interview with a woman who led the battle to desegregate the schools in her city in the mid-1960s. I conclude the chapter by returning to my utopian themes, the promises of performance writing and the reflexive interview for helping to nurture a free and just society.

This chapter is a part of a utopian project. I search for a new interpretive form, a new form of the interview, which I call the *reflexive, dialogic* or *performative* interview. The reflexive interview is not an information-gathering tool per se. It is not a commodity that one person can hire another to collect or pay someone to produce. It belongs to a moral community. On this point I borrow from Leopold (1949), who says of the land, "We abuse land because we regard it as a commodity belonging to us. When we see land as a community to which we belong, we may begin to use it with love and respect" (p. viii). We do not own the land; the land is a community to which we belong. Substitute the words *interview* and *research* for the word *land*. As researchers we belong to a moral community. Doing interviews is a privilege granted to us, not a right that we have. Interviews are living things that belong to everyone. They should not be bought and sold. Interviews are part of the dialogic conversation that connects all us to the larger moral community. Interviews arise out of performance events. They transform information into shared moral experience.

This reflexive project presumes that words and language have a material presence in the world; that is, words have effects on people. Recall the words of Mary Weems (2002, p. 4) in her poem, "This Evolution Will Not Be Televised":

> One million poems, and blood
> paintings pressed between fingers
> not leaving prints....
> Our image, our braids, our music, our mistakes,
> our asses, our rhythms are played on TV
> like a long 78 album in commercial after commercial.

Words matter.

Those who perform culture critically are learning to use language in a way that brings people together. The goal is to create critically empowering texts that "demonstrate a strong fondness ... for freedom and an affectionate concern for the lives of people" (Joyce 1987, p. 344). These texts do more then move audiences to tears – they criticize the world the way it is and offer suggestions about how it could be different.

Interpretive framework

I want to reread the interview, to look at it not as a method of gathering information, but as a vehicle for producing performance texts and performance autoethnographies about self and society (see Richardson 1997, pp. 135–136). I want to locate this reading within a postexperimental period of writing and representation. The present moment is defined by a performative sensibility, by a willingness to experiment with different ways of presenting interview texts.

The performative sensibility turns interviews into performance events, into poetic readings, spoken-word poetry. It turns interviewees into performers, into persons whose words and narratives are then performed by others. As Richardson (1997, p. 121) argues, in the postexperimental period no discourse has a privileged place, and no method or theory has a universal and general claim to authoritative knowledge.

The interview as interpretive practice

The interview, as an interpretive practice, has had a different set of meanings in each historical period. Its meanings, forms and uses change from moment to moment, moving from the structured, semi-structured and open-ended objective formats of the traditional and modernist periods to the feminist criticisms of these formats in the third and fourth moments (see Oakley 1981; Reinharz 1992), to autoethnographic uses of the method in the fifth and sixth moments (DeVault 1999), as well as the more recent postexperimental performative turn. The present moment is further defined by increased resistance from persons of color to the interviews done by white university and government officials. The modernist interview no longer functions as an automatic extension of the state, as an interpretive practice to which persons willingly submit.

The interview is a way of writing the world, of bringing the world into play. The interview is not a mirror of the so-called external world, nor is it a window into the inner life of the person (see Dillard 1982, pp. 47, 155). The interview is a simulacrum, a perfectly miniature and coherent world in its own right (see Dillard 1982, p. 152). Seen thus, the interview functions as a narrative device that allows persons who are so inclined to tell stories about themselves. In the moment of storytelling, teller and listener, performer and audience, share the goal of participating in an experience that reveals their shared sameness (Porter 2000).

The interview's meanings are contextual, improvised, and performative (Dillard 1982, p. 32). The interview is an active text, a site where meaning is created and performed. When performed, the interview text creates the world, giving the world its situated meaningfulness. Seen thus, the interview is a fabrication, a construction, a fiction, an "ordering or rearrangement of selected materials from the actual world" (Dillard 1982, p. 148). But every interview text selectively and unsystematically reconstructs that world, tells and performs a story according to its own version of truth and narrative logic.

As I have argued previously, we inhabit a performance-based, dramaturgical culture. The dividing line between performer and audience, fact and fiction, reality and illusion is blurred. Everything has become a dramatic performance, pure pretense. This is a gendered racialized queer culture with nearly invisible boundaries separating everyday theatrical performances from formal theatre, dance, music, MTV, video and film. But the matter goes even deeper than blurred boundaries. The performance has become reality. On this, speaking of gender and personal identity, Butler (1990) is certain. Gender is performative, gender is always doing, "though not a doing by a subject who might be said to preexist the deed ... there is no being behind doing ... the deed is everything ... there is no gender identity behind the expressions of gender ... identity is performatively constituted by the very 'expressions' that are said to be its results" (p. 25). Further, the linguistic act is per-formative, embodied, a bodily act, and words can hurt (Butler 1997, p. 4).

Gender performances in the interview are shaped performatively, through the acts, gestures and symbols persons use to bring a gendered self into play. The coherence of the self is given in these performances; that is, "body, sex and gender are all performed [and regulated] through the fiction of heterosexual coherence" (Butler 1990, p. 137; 2015, p. 27; see also Clough 2000b, p. 760). Power, Foucault (1980, p. 93) reminds us, is a process located in a field of forces. Power works through unstable systems of discourse, producing, according to Butler, gendered differences, differences that have the potential to bring about disruption and political change (Clough 2000b, p. 760).

Performance interviews are situated in complex systems of racialized gendered discourse. Behind every interview, in the figure of the interviewer, lurks the power of the state. And in the figure of the interviewee lurks the illusion of a reflexive, unified self reporting on his or her opinions and beliefs. The meanings of lived experience and subjectivity are inscribed and made visible in these dramaturgical illusions.

A politics of possibility

I want a per-formative social science, a social science and a public ethnographic theatre that embraces racial diversity and social difference. Borrowing from Anna Deavere Smith (1993), this performative discipline asks: "Who has the right to ask whom what questions?" "Who has the right to answer?" "Who has the right to see what?" "Who has the right to say what?" "Who has the right to speak for whom?" (p. xxviii). The questions Smith raises are the ones that "unsettle and prohibit a democratic theatre in America" (p. xxix). Bringing together "these relationships of the *unlikely* ... is crucial to American theater and culture if theater and culture plan to help us assemble our obvious differences" (p. xxix). Perhaps more deeply, these are the questions that unsettle the discourses of a democratic social science in North America and the rest of the world today. Can performance (auto)ethnography do what Smith asks of theatre?

Performing the interview

A performative social science discourse uses the reflexive, active interview as a vehicle for producing moments of performance theatre, a theatre that is sensitive to the moral and ethical issues of our time (Smith 1993, p. xxix). This interview form is gendered and dialogic. In it, gendered subjects are created through their speech acts. Speech is performative. It is action. The act of speech, the act of being interviewed, becomes a performance itself (Smith 1993, p. xxxi; see also Butler 1990, p. 25).[2] The reflexive interview, as a dialogic conversation, is the site and occasion for such performances; that is, the interview is turned into a dramatic, poetic text.[3] In turn, these texts are performed, given dramatic readings. In such events, as Phelan (1998) puts it, "performance and performativity are braided together by virtue of iteration; the copy renders performance authentic and allows the spectator to find in the performer 'presence'... [or] authenticity" (Phelan and Lane, 1998, p. 10).

Listen to Laurel Richardson's (1997, p. 131) Louisa May introduce her life story:

> The most important thing
> to say is that
> I grew up in the South.
> Being Southern shapes
> aspirations shapes
> what you think you are...
> ...
> I grew up poor in a rented house
> in a very normal sort of way on a very normal sort of street
> with some very nice middle-class friends.

Louisa May comes alive as a person in these lines. She comes off the page, and if her words are spoken aloud softly, with a middle-Tennessee twang, you can feel her presence in the room.

The reflexive interview is simultaneously a site for conversation, a discursive method and a communicative format that produces knowledge about the post-postmodern cinematic society. This interview form furnishes the materials that are fashioned into critical performance texts, critical narratives about community, race, self and identity (Smith 1993, p. xxiii).

One of the young black men whom Smith (1994, pp. xxv–xxvi) interviewed after the 1992 Los Angeles riots reflects on the meanings of race, ethnicity and identity in his life:

> Twilight is the time of day between day and night
> limbo, I call it limbo,
> and sometimes when I take my ideas to my homeboys
> they say, well Twilight, that's something you can't do right
> now...
> I affiliate darkness with what came first,
> because it was first,
> and relative to my complexion,
> I am a dark individual
> And with me being stuck in limbo
> I see the darkness as myself.

The interview society

Atkinson and Silverman (1997) remind us that the postmodern is an interview society, a society of the spectacle, a society of the personal confession. The interview society, according to these authors, is characterized by the following features and beliefs:

1   The confessional mode of discourse has become a form of public entertainment.
2   The private has become a public commodity.
3   While persons are assumed to have private and public and authentic selves, the private self is the real self.
4   Skilled interviewers and therapists (and sometimes the person) have access to this real self.
5   Certain experiences, epiphanies, are more authentic then others, leaving deep marks and scars on the person.
6   Persons have access to their own experiences.
7   First-person narratives are very valuable; they are the site of true personal meaning (pp. 309–315).

The reflexive interviewer deconstructs these uses and abuses of the interview (Atkinson and Silverman 1997; Holstein and Gubrium 2000, pp. 227–228).[4] Indeed, to paraphrase Dillard (1982, p. 46), serious students of society take pains to distinguish their work from these popular interpretive practices. In the surveillance society, journalists, social scientists, psychiatrists, physicians, social workers and the police use interviews to gather information about individuals. Interviews objectify individuals, turning lived experiences into narratives. The interview is the method by which the personal is made public. The interview turns transgressive experience into a consumable commodity. These narratives are bought and sold in the mass-media and academic marketplaces. Thus the interview society affirms the importance of the speaking subject and celebrates the biographical. Nothing is private any longer.

Of course, there is no essential self or private, real self behind the public self. There are only different selves, different performances, different ways of being a gendered person in a social situation. These performances are based on different narrative and interpretive practices. These practices give the self and the person a sense of grounding, or narrative coherence (Gubrium and Holstein 1998). There is no inner or deep self that is accessed by the interview or narrative method. There are only different interpretive (and performative) versions of who the person is. At this level (to borrow from Garfinkel 1996, p. 6), there is nothing under the skull that matters.

Narrative collage and the postmodern interview

The postmodern or contemporary modernist interview builds on narrative collage, the shattering of narrative line.[5] Dillard (1982) compares narrative collage to cubism:

Just as Cubism can take a roomful of furniture and iron it into nine square feet of canvas, so fiction can take fifty years of human life, chop it to bits and piece these bits together so that, within the limits of the temporal form, we can consider them all at once. This is narrative collage.

(p. 21)

In the postmodern interview, storied sequences do not follow a necessary progression. Narrative collage fractures time; speakers leap forward and backward in time. Time is not linear; it is not attached to causal sequences, to "fixed landmarks in orderly progression" (Dillard 1982, p. 21). Time, space and character are flattened out. The intervals between temporal moments can be collapsed in an instant. More than one voice can speak at once, in more than one tense. The text can be a collage, a montage, with photographs, blank spaces, poems, monologues, dialogues, voice-overs and interior streams of consciousness.

In *montage,* the artist makes a picture by juxtaposing several different images. In a sense, montage is related to pentimento, in which something painted out of a picture (an image the painter "repented," or denied) becomes visible again, creating something new. What is new is what had been obscured by the previous image.

Montage and pentimento, like modern jazz, which are pure improvisation, create the sense that images, sounds and understandings are blending, bending. Blurring together, overlapping, forming a composite, a new creation. The images seem to shape and define one another, and an emotional, gestalt effect is produced. Often the images in film montages are combined in swiftly paced sequences, with dizzily revolving collections of images around a central or focused picture or sequence. Directors often use such effects to signify the passage of time.

In narrative collage or montage, the narrative can "shatter time itself into smithereens" (Dillard 1982, p. 22). Points of view and style collide, switch back and forth, commingle. Now and then the writer intrudes, speaking directly to the reader. Sentences may be reduced to numbered lines. As Dillard (1982) puts it, the "arrow of time shatters, cause and effect may vanish and reason crumble" (p. 22). No one can say which sequence of events caused what, and the text makes no pretense about causality. Time, effect and cause operate, as Borges would say, in a "garden of forking paths" (Dillard 1982, p. 22). Space is no longer fixed, confined to walled-in, three-dimensional sites. It moves back and forth, sometimes randomly, between the public and private realms, which may be only temporary resting places. As space shifts, so too do forms of discourse, character, voice, tone, prose style and visual imagery (Dillard 1982, pp. 22–23).

In these ways narrative collage allows the writer, interviewer and performer to create a special world, a world made meaningful through the methods of collage and montage. These uses lay bare the structural and narrative bones of the reflexive, post-postmodern interview. In text and in performance, this form announces its reflexivity. No longer does the writer-as-interviewer hide behind apparatuses of the interview machine, including the question-answer format.

The interview and the world

The interview elicits interpretations of the world, for it is itself an object of interpretation. But the interview is not an interpretation of the world per se. Rather, it stands in an interpretive relationship to the world that it creates. This created world stands alongside the so-called bigger and larger world of human affairs, of which this creation is but one tiny part. The lifelike materials of the interview absorb us and seduce us. They entice us into believing that we are seeing the "real world" being staged. But this is not so – there is no real world. There are no originals. There is no original reality that casts its shadows across the reproduction. There are only interpretations and their performances.

Nonetheless, the reflexive interviewer gives special attention to those performances, spaces, and sites where stories that cross and recross the borders and boundaries of illness, race, class, gender, religion, and ethnicity are told (Gubrium and Holstein 1998). I turn now to a consideration of the work of Anna Deavere Smith.

Anna Deavere Smith's project

Over the last three decades Anna Deavere Smith (1993, 1994, 2000, 2003)[6] has created a series of one-woman performance pieces about race and racism in America (1993, p. xvii; 2004). She deploys a documentary theatre style, speaking in the voice and manner of historical figures (living and dead) who are present in her plays (President Clinton, Thomas Jefferson, Sally Hemings, Monica Lewinsky, Anita Hill).[7] In the performances of her plays gender and race do not need to match those of the characters (2004, p. 7). This does not mean race and gender are insignificant. "Rather an actor's race and gender is on one side of the bridge, and the other they pursue is across the bridge. The effort to cross the bridge is the drama. And it should not be denied" (2004, p. xviii).

Anna Deavere Smith knows how to listen. She says of her project, "My goal has been to find American character in the ways that people speak. When I started this project, in the early 1980s, my simple introduction to anyone I interviewed was, 'If you give me an hour of your time, I'll invite you to see yourself performed'" (Smith 1993, p. xxiii). Smith has transformed her project into the production of a series of one-woman performance pieces about race in America (Smith 1994, p. xvii). She is drawn to those racialized moments, spaces and places where there is tension "between those on the margins and those in the center" (Smith 1993, p. xxxviii). In those liminal spaces, she seeks to find American character, asking whether the tension experienced in such sites will be productive or explosive, and if it explodes, will it "kill and maim those who happen to be in the wrong place at the wrong time" (1993, p. xxxvii).

In her search for American character, Smith observes, she has found that Americans lack a language that incorporates and transcends racial difference, a language that would bring communities together in productive ways while honoring difference. We need, Smith (1994, p. xxii) contends, a theatre that will show us how to create and embrace diversity, a theatre that includes new characters of color, characters previously excluded.

Since 1992 Smith has created performances based on actual events in a series she has titled "On the Road: A Search for American Character." As Smith (1994) describes her process, each of these performances "evolves from interviews I conduct with individuals directly or indirectly ... Basing my scripts entirely on this interview material, I perform the interviewees on stage using their own words" (p. xvii). In May 1992, Smith was commissioned to create a performance piece about the recent civil disturbances in Los Angeles. *Twilight: Los Angeles, 1992,* is the result of her search "for the character of Los Angeles in the wake of the initial Rodney King verdict" (1994, p. xvii).

Chronologically, Smith's *Fires in the Mirror* (1993) precedes her Los Angeles project. In *Fires,* she offers a series of performance pieces based on interviews with people who were involved in or otherwise connected to a racial conflict that took place in Crown Heights, Brooklyn, on August 19, 1991. The conflict was set in motion when a young black Guyanese boy was accidentally hit and killed by a car that was part of a police-escorted entourage carrying Lubavitcher Grand Rebbe Menachem Schneerson. Later that day, a group of black men fatally stabbed a 29-year-old Hasidic scholar. This killing was followed by a racial conflict that lasted three days and involved many members of the Crown Heights community. Smith's play has speaking parts for gang members, police officers, anonymous young girls and boys, mothers, fathers, rabbis, the Reverend Al Sharpton, playwright Ntozake Shange and African American cultural critic Angela Davis.

The theatre that Smith creates mirrors and criticizes society; she says that hers is a project that is "sensitive to the events of my own time" (Smith 1993, p. xxii). In fashioning her performance texts, she uses *dramaturges,* "persons who assist in the preparation of the text of a play and offer an outside perspective to those who are more active in the process of staging the play" (Smith 1993, p. xxii).

Smith, like Saldana, turns interview texts into scripts. She fashions an interview text "that works as a *physical, audible, performable* vehicle" (Smith 1993, p. xxiii). Words become a means or a method for evoking the character of a person. Smith has learned how to listen carefully. She has learned how to inhabit the words of the other, to use that person's manner of speech as a mark of individuality. She sees that a person can be completely present in his or her speech, and this is a gift (Smith 1993, pp. xxvii, xxxi).

Here is how Smith (1993, p. 19) renders her interview with the Reverend Al Sharpton:

James Brown raised me
Uh...
I never had a father.
My father left when I was ten.
James Brown took me to the beauty parlor one day

And made my hair like this.
And made me promise
to wear it like that
'til I die.
It's a personal family thing
between me and James Brown.
I always wanted a father
And he filled that void.

Smith (1993) says that her goal is to create "an atmosphere in which the interviewee would experience his/her own authorship" (p. xxxi). If this space is
created, "everyone... will say something that is like poetry. The process of
getting to that poetic moment is where 'character' lives" (p. xxxi).

Playwright, poet, and novelist Ntozake Shange reveals her character to Smith
(1993, p. 3) thus:

Hummmm.
Identity –
it, is, uh ... in a way it's, um ... it's sort of, it's uh ...
it's a psychic sense of place
it's a way of knowing I'm not a rock or that tree?
I'm this other living creature over here?
And it's a way of knowing that no matter where I put
Myself
that I am not necessarily
what's around me.

Smith (1993) asserts that an unavoidable and painful tension exists in the
United States today, a tension that has been taken up by women and people of
color, a tension that surrounds race, identity and gender; it is "the tension of
identity in motion" (p. xxxiv). This tension turns, in part, as indicated above,
on the question of "Who can speak for whom?" A profound danger exists,
Smith (1993) points out: "If only a man can speak for a man, a woman for a
woman, a Black person for all Black people, then we, once again, inhibit the
spirit of theatre, which lives in the bridge that makes unlikely aspects seem
connected" (p. xxix), and we cannot construct a bridge that will connect diverse
racial and gendered identities to discourse in the public arena. Democratic
discourse and a new racial politics are threatened.

In Piano (2004), she was looking for a time in American history in which
people of all different races could be in one living room. She comments:

In Piano we see the turning of a servant class into a powerful class. We see
those who are the subjects strive to become the authors of their history ...
These two plays react to history and are dedicated to encouraging those
who produce, direct, design, market, and perform them to get closer and

closer to caring passionately about what the truth is and was. They invite research and passionate debate ... Ultimately the goal is to involve the audience in that passion. These two plays, based on facts, take dramatic license and are not offered as truths, but as fictions that attempt to tell other truths, the kinds of truths that live in fiction and in imaginary worlds.

(2004, p. xix)

By interrogating and performing the facts of history her plays enact a politics of possibility. She takes dramatic license with history. Servants become part of the ruling class. She deals with truths that matter using fictionalized histories as a way to expose the truths of past injustices. She worries about those who write the facts. She quotes James Baldwin on facts and history. He is speaking to Margaret Mead:

JAMES BALDWIN: I do not care what the facts are.
    I cannot afford to care.
    You, historically write the facts which
    I
    Am expected to believe.
    The difference is that you
    Historically,
    Generically,
    Have betrayed me so often
    And lied to me so long
    That no
    Number of facts
    According to you
    Would ever convince!(2004, p. xv)

When the facts have been exhausted, "we must imagine a future and work to make it real, to go beyond the evidence, to make history present, to make the not yet now real" (p. xvi, paraphrase). For Baldwin and Smith history belongs to those who record the true facts, the fictions that are truths. Smith impersonates her interview subjects by finding the trick of their voices. She lets the verbatim testimonies do the talking and rebutting.

For the recent Berkeley production of "Notes From the Field," Smith has been conducting an experiment with her audience. In the second act, theatregoers are divided into groups that are led by a facilitator in the lobby and courtyard areas. Questions are raised to get the audience to link the material to their own lives. Pads and pens are distributed, along with snacks, and audience members are invited (though not compelled) to share their thoughts on what change might look like (McNulty 2016).

Before reconvening inside the theatre for the coda, everyone is asked to make a commitment to do something tangible. The Twitter account @adspipeline and the hashtag "NotesFromTheField" have been set up so that these pledges can be shared on social media. "There are so many opportunities to be passive," said Smith, who describes herself as the author of the second act and the audience as the actors. "You can watch television or a play and say, 'Isn't this awful?' But we need a lot more right now. What we're doing in Berkeley is an outgrowth of what I did last year, when I found that people standing up at the mike and talking isn't productive" (McNulty 2016).

"The facilitators are telling me that connections are starting to be made," she said. "That's what the goal is. I'll come out of this and maybe logistically design it a little differently. But just the fact that a friend of mine wrote to thank me for providing pads – how many people at intermission write something down they saw onstage? You talk to your friend, get a cup of coffee, go to the bathroom. Interrupting the evening like this asks you to have a different way of processing."[8]

As in Saldana's and Mienczakowski and Morgan's work, postperformance discussions informants and audience members are important for Smith's project. These discussions, she reports, are often quite emotional and pedagogical. They are ethnodramas in their own right, and they are important for several different reasons (Smith 1994, p. xxiii). For one thing, Smith's performances often bring into theatres persons who would not normally be together, including whites, blacks, Latino/as, public officials, police officers, politicians, members of the press and representatives of other mass media (1993, p.xxxviii). In these emotionally charged situations, interactants explore racial differences. They bring different interpretations to the experiences and events that Smith performs. These postperformance pedagogical exchanges provide Smith and her dramaturges with feedback. The interactions that take place bring participants into events that they may never have experienced directly. Participating in these performances gives them a form of ownership they would not otherwise have.

Cornel West (1993) observes that *Fires in the Mirror* is a "grand example of how art can constitute a public space that is perceived by people as empowering rather than disempowering" (p. xix). Thus blacks, gang members, the police and members of the Jewish community all come together and talk in this play. The drama crosses racial boundaries. As West observes, Smith's text shows that "American character lives not in one place or the other, but in the gaps between places, and in our struggle to be together in our differences" (p. xii).

In a scene from *Fires in the Mirror* (Smith 1993, pp. 79–80), one character, "An Anonymous Young Man # 1Wa Wa Wa," a Caribbean American with dreadlocks, describes the auto accident:

What I saw was
she was pushin'
her brother on the bike like
this,

right?
She was pushin'
him
and he keep dippin' around
like he didn't know how
to ride the bike ...
So she was already runnin'
when the car was comin' ...
we was watchin' the car
weavin',
and we was goin'
"Oh, yo
it's a Jew man.
He broke the stop light, they never get arrested."

In presenting this young man's words, Smith's text becomes performative; that is, the young Caribbean American narrates a street performance. The text works like a piece of montage, with many different things going on at once. It includes multiple points of view. Time moves back and forth, from past to present, present to past. More than one notion of causality (and blame) operates. In this text, Jews come up against blacks, young against old, as a small child's bike weaves its way down the sidewalk until it rolls in front of an oncoming car.

In Smith's public-voice theatre there are no cultural custodians or identity police who assert that only blacks can understand and perform black experience. Smith's antiessentialist performance aesthetic bridges the spaces that separate gender, race and ethnic identity. It accepts the fact that our so-called post-racial society is a myth, and to think otherwise is to engage in racist nostalgia.

Performance writing

Smith engages in a form of performance writing (see Pollock 1998a, 1998b; see also Phelan 1998, pp. 12–14; Pelias 2013). Using the methods of narrative collage, performance writing shows rather than tells. It is writing that speaks performatively, enacting what it describes. It is writing that does what it says it is doing by doing it. Performative writing "is an inquiry into the limits and possibilities of the intersections between speech and writing ... [It] evokes what it names" (Phelan 1998, p. 13). Performative writing is not a matter of formal style per se, nor is it writing that is avant-garde or clever (Pollock 1998a, p. 75). As Pollock (1998a, pp. 80–95) suggests, performative writing is evocative, reflexive and multivoiced; it cuts across genres and is always partial and incomplete. But in performative writing things happen; it is writing that is consequential, and it is about a world that is already being performed.

A performance writing text may contain pictures, such as photographs or drawings. It may look distinctive on the page, perhaps set in double or triple columns and using unusual spacing between words and lines. It may be deeply citational, with footnotes or endnotes. It may be broken into sections that are separated by rows of asterisks or dingbats. It may combine several different types of texts, such as poetry, first-person reflections, quotations from scholarly works and the daily newspaper.

Performative writing requires performative reading, an active, collaborative form of reading. As Jones (1997) observes, performative reading creates a union between reader and writer that is "seriate, simultaneous, sketch-driven, impro-visational, incorporative, circular, and transformative" (p. 72). In performative reading, the reader finds "a point of interest on the page, and lingers or moves on to another" (p. 72). The reader scans, fast-forwards, gazes at a line, and then turns back.

Ron Pelias describes the desire to write performatively:

> I turn to the poetic, the performative in the hope that I might pursue the possibilities of disappearance and the power of presence. I want to write in another shape. I seek a space that unfolds softly, one that circles around, slides between, swallows whole. I want to live in feelings that are elusive, to live in doubt, I want my writing to be a performance
>
> (Pelias 1999, pp. xii–xiii, paraphrase).

Tami Spy provides an example:

> My dad never quite understood what I did unless I was performing and I never consciously understood that it was a jazz swing of hope and pain and desire that made me want to get up here in the first place. At the hospital, I was smoothing his thick long clean white hair. Occasionally, my hand would find the heartbeat at his neck. His heart began to talk to my finger tips. Jazz coursing through his veins and into mine. And, sometimes, his heart would stop altogether, struck speechless at the sight of my radiant mother on the other side saying, "Hurry up, Kurt. We haven't got all day!" But he was not ready yet to go gently, not ready yet to cease the jazz riffing of his heart.
>
> (Spry 2016, pp. 26–27, paraphrase)

To say that Smith, or Spry or Pelias write performatively and that they ask for per-formative readers is to say that their scripts (like Trinh's and Saldana's) allow persons to experience their own subjectivity in the moment of perfor-mance. Performance writing recovers what appears and then disappears, the performance itself, the original and the copy. In this sense, performance writing is behavior that is twice behaved (Schechner 1998, pp. 361). Even as it dis-appears into thin air, the performance has an afterlife; quietly resting in the text, it awaits its next performance, riffing off of the next heartbeat.

Performance writing is poetic and dramatic, embodied. As Phelan (1998) notes, such writing lies at the "intersections between speech and writing" (p. 13). It is writing that is meant to be read, performed. It is transformative. It is a way of happening, a way of becoming (p. 10). It dwells in the spaces of liminality (pp. 8, 11). It is writing that refuses "the impossibility of maintaining the distinction between temporal tenses ... between beginning and ending, between living and dying" (p. 8). Performance writing transforms literal (and transcribed) speech into speech that is first person, active, in motion, processual. In such texts, performance and performativity are intertwined, the done and the doing; each defines the other. The performer's performance creates a space that the audience enters.

In this postmodern, liminal, posttheoretical age, performance writing teaches us how to rehearse events that have passed, allowing us to learn how to play the past when it happens again in the future (Phelan 1998, p. 7). And in this sense, like all writing, performance writing is ideological. Transgressive performance texts, based on performance writing, politicize and criticize the violent worlds we inherit from global capitalism. Through mimicry, iteration, simulations and repetition, twice-behaved behaviors interrupt the "strange temporal economy in which we live... [and] challenge the violence and illusionary seductions of colonialist and capitalist enterprises" (Phelan 1998, p. 9).

The writer's job

The actor's job, the ethnodramatist's job, the autoethnographer's job, is double-sided, to make the past and the future present at the same time. The task is to embrace the "murky truth as tragic, as absurd, and if we are lucky, as inspiring" (Smith. 2004, p. xvi). When the past and the future collide in the present, the possibilities of change and hope are created. Performed dramatic works become catalysts for social change (p. xviiii).

Paraphrasing Smith (2004) and Miles (1997, p. 164), the value of politicized theory, of activist art, like critical performance ethnography, lies in the ability to initiate a continuing process of social criticism in the public sphere. This form of theatre and art engages defined publics on issues from the pipeline that moves black males from schools to prison, homelessness to the survival of the rain forests, and domestic violence (Miles 1997, p. 164, paraphrase). It transgresses "the confines of public and domestic domains" (Miles 1997, p. 167). It shows how public laws and policies influence personal decisions. It shows how the limits of the public sphere shape changes in the private sphere (Miles 1997, p. 169).

However, as previously argued there are no privileged identities, no deep or essential selves connected to inner structures of meaning. There are only different performances, different ways of being in the world. And so, in her performances, Smith performs and presents the poetic texts of men and women of color. Smith's plays and performances interpret what she has learned and heard in sites of racial disturbance and racial violence (Smith 1993, p. xxiv). Her performances model a politics of possibility.

I now present a performance text of my own.

Performing racial memories

On July 28, 1966, Edge City desegregated its ten elementary schools. According to the local newspaper, Edge City was the first town in Illinois to do this. In 1965–1966 there were 456 African American children in elementary school in the district; 95% of these children attended the virtually all-black Martin School in the north end of town. To accomplish desegregation, the school district bused all but 100 of the African American students from Martin School to its nine other previously all-white schools. It then sent 189 international children to Martin School. These children lived with their parents in a university housing complex. The school board called this "cross-busing," but the newspaper said that no white children were bused, just the kids from university housing (see Denzin 1997).

Mrs. Anderson was the only woman member of the all-white school board that made the decision to desegregate. I had read stories about her in the local newspaper, seen her picture. I knew that she has been a secretary at one of the grade schools, and that she had worked at the Citizens Building Association. I did not know that she has been a single parent when she served on the board, nor did I know that her daughter eventually married a black man, making her the grandmother of biracial children. I learned these things later.

The newspaper said that Mrs. Anderson died in her home at 6:35 P.M. on November 10, 1996. She was 81 years old, a victim of old age and emphysema. For some time before her death, a long, clear-plastic air hose connected her to an oxygen machine. She breathed with great effort and had brief spells of intense coughing. She had the look of a patrician, a commanding presence, tall and graceful, but slow in her movements, held back by the hose. She had crystal-clear blue eyes. She was elegant in her velvet floor-length blue robe. Her chair faced a picture window that looked out on her small, well-cared-for backyard garden; from the window, she could see roses, bird feeders, evergreens and a dying river birch.

There is a jar of jellybeans on the coffee table in front of the sofa, where I sit. I put the tape recorder next to Mrs. A's chair and pin its microphone to the collar of her robe, being careful not to disturb the oxygen tube. She begins to speak, to tell her story about how desegregation happened in Edge City. Her story moves from the mid-1960s to the present. The point of view in her story changes as she takes on different voices.[9]

MRS A: It started with two people,
  James and Marilyn Daniels.
  They led a group of their neighbors
  in the black neighborhood.
  They said:
  Look, you're moving all those kids

from university housing by bus to school.
Why don't you take Martin School
and bring them up here and take
King School kids out to the various neighborhoods?

[Pause]

MRS A: And thirty years later
I look back and wonder
at what kind of courage it took
for those people to say that.
And so after some talking about it back and forth ...
we had a six-to-one vote ...
But they came to us.
I don't think we were actually
aware of the fact that
there was a segregated school over there...
I think probably at heart
we didn't know how racist
we were behaving by allowing
the school to stay there.

She coughs. She gets up and goes to the kitchen and gets a glass of water.
She comes back and looks out the window. The phone rings. She ignores it.
She returns to her thoughts:

MRS A: I remember the night
we voted on it. I remember –
It's stupid,
you remember what you thought,
not what you said.
I said,
Well we're only twelve years late.
Let's go.
And I said
Something
stupid and female,
like
I'd be honored.
I sat there and said to
myself,
This is historic.
We are doing something historic.
Of course this did not happen all at once.

There were community meetings
before the board voted,
one meeting involved the parents from university housing.
We met with people at Martin School.
That was ghastly.
We sat up front.
The board and the people
asked us questions and then they
got a little nasty.
I was not frightened,
but I was so unhappy.
A graduate student
stood up
and said,
"Those people
those African-
Americans
don't want to leave their homes
and
their schools ..."
"Those people"
has haunted me for thirty years.

[Pause]

MRS A: We only had one outspoken
racist
on the board
at that time
he is
dead now
and
we can speak ill of the dead.
He happened to be a National
Guard,
that was his
bread and butter.
The night we voted,
he had just come
back
from Chicago,
where the Guard had been sent
to hold down some of
the riots.
And he turned to me

and said,
"You haven't been in Chicago and
listened to those black bastards
calling you names."
No was his vote.
I had a different upbringing than many folks
I guess.
For years
I can remember my mother saying,
The happiest years of my life
were the 10 years we lived next door
to a Negro family down in Joliet.
And I don't know if that impressed me
that Negroes were people
or what,
but I remembered it and felt it
and
I have some black
friends today.
See the picture on the VCR?

I cross the room and remove the large family photo from the top of the VCR and hand it to Mrs. Anderson, who hands it back to me. It is one of those close-up color photos, a blow-up, of four people: mother and father in the back and two children, two little girls, in the front. The father is black, the children mixed, the mother white. Mrs. Anderson explains:

MRS A: That is my older daughter
and her
husband
and
my two beautiful grandchildren.
Aren't they pretty?
I swear
they had the best of both worlds!
The young man
graduated from Columbia
and
played basketball for four years.
Now he's taking his M.B.A. at UCLA.
The young lady, my daughter,
graduated from Wesleyan.
She's now at Indiana University
in the school of law.

Another set of memories

As we prepared to leave Mrs. Anderson's house, one more question came to mind. It concerned the school board elections in 1968. I asked Mrs. Anderson about a black woman named Mrs. Caroline Adams Smith, who was part of an all-white coalition that ran against Mrs. Anderson and her fellow board members. The paper had said that Mrs. Smith's group felt that the incumbents on the board did business behind closed doors, that the busing decision had not been made in public. There were other issues as well. In the summer of 1968, the Martin parents walked out of a school board meeting because they felt that the board members were not considering their complaints. Mr. Daniels's group wanted more representation of African American teachers; the group also wanted an African American principal at Martin and more after-school programs for their children. In 1972, there was a report about desegregation and, according to Mr. Daniels, the report ignored the efforts of the Martin parents in the desegregation project. The president of the board apologized to Mr. Daniels. I reminded Mrs. Anderson that the newspapers called the summer of 1968 "Edge City's Summer of Discontent." She was quick to respond:

MRS A: They must have taken the Summer of Discontent
    from the John Steinbeck novel. -
    They had to have taken it from
    someone.
    They were not that clever.
    Were you reading last night's paper?
    I said that
    the wrong way.
    Still the same old things,
    30 years later.
    But I just flat out don't remember those complaints.
    Caroline Adams Smith.
    She never did like us very much.
    I'm having a problem
    bringing up the story though.
    Probably
    it was not nice and
    I turned it off and
    didn't want to remember it.
    I have one habit
    that is really very well
    ingrained,
    and that is if it was distasteful,
    I put it away and don't remember it.
    My mind is horrible. I don't remember this.
    I'm remembering the report now.
    But I pitched it.

Another memory

Six days after the interview, Mrs. Anderson called me at home. It was early evening.

MRS A: Hello, Dr. Denzin,
      this is Alice Anderson.
      After you left last week
      I remembered
      I kept a scrapbook of the years
      I was on the school board.
      I think you should have it.
      I want someone
      to tell my story,
      now that I am getting so old.
      You are welcome to it,
      if you want it.

When I arrived at her home, she directed me to her kitchen table. There lay a large scrapbook, 12 by 14 inches, and two folders, as well as a large manila envelope with press clippings inside. The scrapbook carried the label "School board, 6/66–4/67" (the first year of her first term on the board). Two collie puppies were pictured on the cover of the scrapbook, one sitting in a red wheelbarrow. Out of the folders fluttered newspaper clippings, pictures, and notes that congratulated Mrs. Anderson on her victorious re-election to the board in 1968.

Mrs. Anderson had remembered what she had forgotten. She hadn't pitched her files. She had kept all of them. Her scrapbook was a record of the past. But not everything was there. She had indeed forgotten to clip those stories about the "Summer of Discontent," and she had no record of the 1972 desegregation report that ignored Mr. Daniels and his group. These were painful experiences, and Mrs. Anderson had the habit of not remembering distasteful things. Thirty years ago, a lot of distasteful things surrounded desegregation in Edge City.

Reading Mrs. Anderson's performance

I have attempted to turn Mrs. Anderson's interview into a dramatic, poetic text. As Smith notes, such a text should evoke the character of the speaker; it should allow the speaker to be fully present in his or her speech.

Mrs. Anderson uses irony to convey her views of the world, a racist world she disdains. With her words she creates a narrative montage. Inside this world of jumbled images and memories she looks back, locating herself in the summer of 1966. Thirty years after the fact, she sees courage in the eyes and words of James and Marilyn Daniels. She sees that she and her colleagues allowed themselves to not see the segregated school "over there," and she applies the term *racist* to this gaze. But when she voted, she voted as a woman, and said something "stupid and female," as if a white woman in Edge City could not have a voice on race matters in 1966.

She recalls the graduate student who spoke harshly of "those people." She willingly speaks harshly herself of the one outspoken racist on the board. The 1966 Chicago race riots are evoked by the images behind the words she quotes, "You haven't been to Chicago and listened to those black bastards calling you names." So, for one man, Edge City's desegregation vote was a vote to give a voice to those "black bastards."

In her montage, Mrs. Anderson separates herself from other white people. Her mother had spoken to her of happy times living next door to a Negro family in Joliet, and she came to see that Negroes are people too. She passed this understanding along to her daughter, as the family photo dramatically demonstrates.

All did not go well in Edge City's desegregation experiment. There was a summer of discontent. The white school board ignored the black parents. Mrs. Anderson's scrapbook, with its pictures and clippings, tells part of this story, but the most painful part she did not keep. And in her obituary, there was no mention of her part in this history. The paper did not even record the fact that she had served on the school board.

Conclusion

Anna Deavere Smith (1993) contends that Americans have difficulty "talking about race and talking about [racial] differences. This difficulty goes across race, class and political lines" (p. xii). There is, she says, "a lack of words ... we do not have a language that serves us as a group" (p. xii). Smith's plays are attempts to find that language. Her performance texts allow us to see more clearly the limits of the language we now use.

Performances like Mrs. Anderson's create spaces for the operation of racial memories. They create occasions for rethinking the politics of race and racism. Mrs. Anderson's text shows that in the 1960s a wide gulf existed between whites and blacks in Edge City. White male voices reproduced racial stereotypes. When a white women spoke out, she felt uncomfortable. But a white woman did speak out in 1966, and she crossed racial boundaries. Listening to Mrs. Anderson's story today reminds us that we still need performers (and performances) like her if we are ever to achieve the promise of a democracy for all races in the United States.

I seek an interpretive social science that is simultaneously autoethnographic, vulnerable, performative and critical. This is a social science that refuses abstractions and high theory. It is a way of being in the world, a way of writing, hearing and listening. Viewing culture as a complex performative process, it seeks to understand how people enact and construct meaning in their daily lives. This is a return to narrative as a political act, a social science that has learned how to use the reflexive, dialogic interview. This social science inserts itself into the world in an empowering way. It uses the words and stories that individuals tell to fashion performance texts that imagine new worlds, worlds where humans can become who they wish to be, free of prejudice, repression and discrimination.

This is the promise of a performative social science in a postcinematic, postvisual society. This social science refuses to treat research as a commodity that can be bought and sold. As researchers, we belong to a moral community. The reflexive interview helps us to create dialogic relationships with that community. These relationships, in turn, allow us to enact an ethic of care and empowerment. This is the kind of ethic Mrs. Anderson sought to create in Edge City in the summer of 1966. In performing her interview, we learn a little more about how we can do the same in our own communities.

Notes

1 Portions of this chapter draw from Denzin (2014, pp. 51–68).
2 I want to avoid the debate about whether it is "really possible, even in theory, to divide utterances between the performative and the constative" (Sedgwick 1998, pp. 106–107), to distinguish utterances that merely say from those that do. Words have material effects on people. Subjects, as gendered selves, are constituted in and through their performative acts – that is, acts that both do and say something (e.g., "With these words I thee wed"; see Sedgwick 1998, p. 107). There is "no abiding, gendered subject" (Butler 1990, p. 140) who precedes a performance (see also Butler 1990, pp. 25, 141).
3 To repeat, a performance is an interpretive event. A performance, such as an interview, is a bounded, theatrical social act, a dialogic production (on the interview as a social act, see also Kuhn 1962, pp. 196–197).
4 Recall the earlier discussion of interview formats and types. Each type is produced by the apparatuses connected to the machinery of the interview apparatus.
5 I borrow the term *postmodern interview* from Fontana and Frey (1994, pp. 368, 2000).
6 Since 2008 she has had a series of one-woman shows: The Arizona Project (2008), On Grace (2014), Never Givin' Up (2015), Notes from the Field (2016).
7 Her current project is *The Pipeline Project*, a work in progress about the "school-to-prison pipeline" www.philly.com/philly/entertainment/arts/20150503_Probing_the_pipeline_with_Anna_Deavere_Smith.html#QTRF4Ds5CW8rc9es.99
8 See www.latimes.com/entertainment/arts/la-ca-cm-anna-deavere-smith-20150726-column.html
9 This interview was conducted with my colleagues Belden Fields, Walter Feinberg and Nicole Rioberts.

10 Reading and writing performance[1]

For many the turn to performance autoethnography texts poses two problems: first the problem of performative criteria; namely how these texts and their performances are to be critically analyzed in terms of epistemological, aesthetic and political criteria. Second, following Pelias (above) how do we write performance in such a way that it comes off the page and moves into the emotional life of the reader?

Building on recent discussions of interpretive criteria (Jones, Adams and Ellis 2013; Bochner and Ellis 2016; Spry 2016; Madison 2012; Manning and Adams 2015; Faulkner 2009; Leavy 2015; Jones 2017). I foreground subversive, resistance narratives, dramatic, epiphanic performances that challenge the status quo. My topics, reading, writing and judging performances, producing autoethnographic performances that move history.

My argument unfolds in four parts. I begin with a discussion of criticisms of the genre and responses to the criticisms. Of course criteria and criticisms vary, depending on the type of autoethnography that is being written and performed: analytic/scientific, evocative, interpretive, critical, artistic (Bochner and Ellis 2016, p. 212).[2] I then turn to the problem of setting criteria for experimental writing (Gingrich-Philbrook 2013; Clough 2000a, 2000b, 2007; Bochner 2000; Bochner and Riggs 2014; Faulkner 2009; Pelias 1999, p. xiii). This leads to a discussion of feminist and communitarian criteria, as they apply to resistance performance texts. I next discuss alternative modes of assessing narrative and performance texts, concluding with commentary on the politics of interpretation in the performance community.

Criticisms and responses: part one

Autoethnography has been criticized for being non-analytic, self-indulgent, irreverent, sentimental and romantic. The focus on the narrative, not the performative "I" has also been criticized (Jackson and Mazzei (2008, p. 299). Autoethnography has been criticized for being too artful. It has been criticized for not being scientific, for having no theory, no concepts, no hypotheses. It has been criticized for not being sufficiently artful (Ellis, Adams and Bochner 2011). It has been dismissed for not being sufficiently rigorous, theoretical or analytical. Critics contend that a single case only tells one story, narrative inquiry is not scientific inquiry.

Some charge that autoethnographers do too little fieldwork, have small samples, use biased data, are navel-gazers and are too self-absorbed, offering only verisimilitude, and not analytic insights. Others say it is bad writing. Some contend it reflects the work of a writer who sits in front of a computer, never leaving a book-lined office to confront the real world (see Ellis, Adams and Bochner 2011 for a review of these criticisms and Bochner and Ellis 2016, pp. 212–213). And of course poststructuralists contend that such key terms as experience, voice, presence and meaning are under-theorized.

A deconstructive autoethnography

Jackson and Mazzei (2008, p. 300) extending the familiar arguments of Scott (1991, 1992, 1993), in evocative autoethnographies. They content that often leads to a focus on the myth of the self with a unproblematic window to its inner feelings, a self with a clear voice anchored in past experience (Jackson and Mazzei 2008, p. 300).

In contrast, a deconstructive autoethnography makes experience, voice and presence problematic (see below). The performative "I" puts experience under erasure (Jackson and Mazzei 2008, p. 305). A deconstructive reading of the "I" in autoethnography de-centers the knowing "I," challenges the writer's voice, unsettles the concept of past experiences as the site of subjectivity, and opens the door for multiple voices and perspectives to be heard and performed and seen. Listen to Tami Spry's Performative I.

TAMI SPRY: I am in the bathroom of a disco, circa 1980.
    I am white, 19, 110 pounds, blonde ...
    In this mostly Black disco.
    Four Black women
    follow me into the bathroom.
    Standing in front of the mirror ...
    which we use as our looking glass...
    we reify our versions of womanhood:
    Black, White, Pretty, Sexy,
    race in a mirror.

(Spry 2011, p. 146, paraphrase)

It's all here, mirrors, racialized selves, fragmented identities, the white gaze, the Black gaze, race and gender in the bathroom, circa 1980. It could have been yesterday.

The unified speaking subject with full access to her thoughts and intentions is a myth. Even though "performance appears to express prior intention, a doer behind the deed, the prior agency is only legible as the effect of that utterance" (Butler 1995, p. 227, also quoted in St. Pierre 2009, p. 227). Accordingly a deconstructive autoethnography problematizes the writer's presence in the text. Devices which unsettle the writer's presence in the text are employed: shifting counter-voices, split texts, stuttering voices, repetitions, silences, mimicry, exaggerations, mischief-making talk that disrupts, and disguises itself (Lather 2009, p. 22; 2013).

SOPHIE TAMAS ON THE PHONE: I am 29 years old, washing dishes in a rented run-down three bedroom row house on a small Canadian town ... Dora is drooling beside me an ExerSaucer. The phone rings. I dry my hands...
Hello?
Is Joe there?
It's a woman, around my age.
He's away on business ...
Who's this?
That's rude.
His wife. Can I help you?
Are you serious? You can't be.
I put my hand on the counter.
I am using my best reasonable voice.
I have been for ten years. He lives here ...
Three days later she calls again.
Hello?
I'm so sorry (she is in tears)...
He bought me a ring. He sends me money.
I don't remember the rest of the conversation. I am cold...
She is crazy, almost hysterical ... My hands are shaking. He never bought me a ring.... It's not true, I decide. So it isn't ...
SOPHIE: Why didn't I leave?
METASOPHIE: You're ... a dependent idiot.
SOPHIE: Why am I such a basket-case.
METASOPHIE: Pathetic.
UBERSOPHIE: You could use some help.

(Tamas 2011, pp. 11, 15, 16, 19 paraphrase)

Although the language is deceptively simple and direct, Tamas offers a text filled with complexity, confusion, doubt, selves reflecting on selves. Tamas tells herself a lie which she believes. She becomes the other talking to herself.

The evidence of experience

To repeat. Lived experience is a performance. It is socially constructed. It does not have an ontological reality independent of language and interaction.[3] Persons and their lives, and their experiences are constituted through performative discourse. Subjects' accounts of experience, including their stories and performances, cannot be taken ipso facto as true or accurate renderings of the real. Individuals "do not have experience, rather individuals as subjects are constituted through experience [and performance]" (Scott 1991, p. 779, paraphrase). To think of experience this way is to interrogate the practices that give identities the appearance of being real and authentic. Experience, at this level, is already performative, it is "at once already an interpretation, and something that needs to be interpreted" (Scott 1991, p. 797).

Performance as experience

Extending Scott's arguments, performance which is the expression of experience cannot be appealed to as uncontestable evidence for the meaning of an experience (Scott 1991, p. 777). Rather, performances are constitutive of experience. Performances are the practices that allow for the construction of situated identities in specific sites. They are the embodied co-performatives that actually do something in the world (Conquergood 1998, p. 32; Hamera 2011, p. 320). Subjects as performers are constituted in and through their co-performative practices. These acts relationally connect subjects to others, to their yearnings, desires, fears, fantasies (Madison 2012, p. 186; Hamera 2011, p. 322).[4] Performative acts have material and affective effects (Clough 2007). At the sensory level they are felt, and have sounds, specific looks, rhythms, movements, gestures, glances, smells (Hamera 2011, pp. 318–319).

A performative theory of everyday life "celebrates performance as imitation, construction, and resistance" (Conquergood 1998, p. 31). Agency is made visible in performative acts of resistance, as well as in mimesis, when imitation functions as criticism or intervention, or disruption. We move then from body, to paper, to stage (Spry 2011; 2016). Embodied performance is the stand-in-for and the site of experience. When fused with a social justice initiatives, these co-performances become vehicles for resisting "regimes of oppressive power" (Madison 2012, p. 189).

CLAUDIO MOREIRA: (in Diversi and Moreira 2009, p. 189):
   My job is not making the co-performer agree with me.
   My job is to articulate a clear text of my moral position that
   contains in itself all the arguments needed to
   understand the event.

Experience as performance

This view of experience and the performative makes it difficult to sustain any distinction between "appearances and actualities" (Schechner 1998, p. 362). Further, if, as Butler (1993, p. 141) reminds us, there are no original performances, then every performance establishes itself performatively as an original, a personal, and locally situated production.

An extended quote from Goffman (1959) summarizes my position.

> The legitimate performances of everyday life are not "acted" or "put on" in the sense that the performer knows in advance just what he [she] is going to do, and does this solely because of the effect it is likely to have. The expressions it is felt he [she] is giving off will be especially "inaccessible" to him [her] ... but the incapacity of the ordinary individual to formulate in advance the movements of his [her] eyes and body does not mean that he [she] will not express him [her] self through these devices in a way that is dramatized and pre-formed in his [her] repertoire of actions. In short, we all act better than we know how.
>
> (pp. 73–74)

Criticisms and responses: part two

Critics claim that autoethnographies lack reliability, generalizability and validity. Of course these terms come from a positivist framework, and have specific meaning within that discourse. Naturally reliability, generalizability and validity have different meanings (if any) for the autoethnographer (Ellis, Adams and Bochner 2011; also below). This is not traditional ethnography, nor is it performance art.

For the autoethnographer reliability refers to the narrator's credibility as a writer-performer-observer; that is has an event been credibly remembered and described. Is the writer a credible observer of those events? What does credible even mean? Is the report pure fiction, or a truthful account? Autoethnographers assert that narrative truth is based on how a story is used, understood and responded to. Memory is fallible. People tell different stories of the same event or experience.

Validity means that a work has verisimilitude. It evokes a feeling that the experience described is true, coherent, believable and connects the reader to the writer's world. Stake calls this naturalistic generalization; the reader "comes to know some things told, as if he or she had experienced them" (Stake 1994, p. 240). Generalizability is determined by how a reader responds to a representation. Does it speak to them as an universal singular (Ellis, Adams and Bochner 2011)?

Apples and oranges again. Autoethnography cannot be judged by traditional positivist criteria. The goal is not to produce a standard social science performance. The goal is to write performance texts that move others to ethical action. Such works implement Conquergood's third triad: imagination, intervention; artistry, activism; critique. Performances are judged by their ability to enact a politics of possibility, every performance is a moral act.

Performance is:
A moral act

An intervention,
An invention
An entanglement with the Other

Setting criteria for performance autoethnography

Clough (2000, p. 278) rightly warns that setting criteria for judging what is good and what is bad experimental writing, or performance autoethnography, may only conventionalize the new writing, "and make more apparent the ways in which experimental writing has already become conventional" (p. 278). More deeply, in normalizing this writing, and the performances connected to it, we may forget that this kind of writing was once "thought to be 'bad' writing, improper sociology ... It might be forgotten that experimental writing was strongly linked to political contentions over questions of knowledge" (p. 278). And, the new writing, in, one moment, was taken to be a form of cultural criticism, a way of also criticizing traditional ethnography.

Bochner (2000, p. 268) elaborates, observing that today "no single, unchallenged paradigm has been established for deciding what does and what does not comprise valid, useful, and significant knowledge." Furthermore, it is impossible to fix a single standard for deciding what is good or bad, or right, there are only multiple standards, temporary criteria, momentary resting places (Bochner 2000, p. 269). Too often criteria function as policing devices. The desire to authorize one set of standards can take our attention away from "the ethical issues at the heart of our work" (p. 269).

On this point Christians (2000) agrees with Bochner, all inquiry involves moral, political and ethical matters. Clough goes one level deeper. She reminds us that, from the beginning, the criticisms of standard ethnographic writing in sociology were linked to identity politics and feminist theory, and in anthropology to postcolonial criticisms. These criticisms involved a complex set of questions, namely who had the right to speak for whom, and how? (Clough 2000a, p. 283).

The need to represent postcolonial hybrid identities became the focus of experimental writing in ethnography, just as there has been "an effort to elaborate race, classed, sexed, and national identities in the autoethnographic writings of postcolonial theorists" (Clough 2000a, p. 285; Madison 2012, pp. 236–37). These debates about writing, agency, self, subjectivity, nation, culture, race and gender unfolded on a global landscape, involving the transnationalization of capital and the globalization of technology (p. 279). Thus from the beginning, experimental, autoethnographic writing has been closely connected to gender, race, family, nation, politics, capital, technology, critical social theory and cultural criticism; that is to debates over questions of knowledge, and its representation and presentation.

The drive to performance autoethnography within Western ethnography, the drive to the personal, and the autobiographical, Clough suggests, reflects a growing sensitivity to issues surrounding agency and the new media technologies. But, the subjectivity and forms of selfhood performed and examined in the new autoethnography are linked to "the trauma culture of the tele-technological" (Clough 2000a, p. 287; Halley 2012, pp. 5–6). Clough observes that much of the new autoethnography involves persons writing about the "experiences of drug abuse, sexual abuse, child abuse, rape, incest, anorexia, chronic illness, and death." She goes on, "autoethnography is symptomatic of the trauma culture that has been most outrageously presented in television talk shows" (Clough 2000a, pp. 2, 87; 2007, pp. 2–3, 5).

This trauma culture exposes and celebrates the erasure of traditional barriers separating the public and the private in American life. In a pornography of the visible, the violent side of intimate family life is exposed, and the contradictions in capitalism as a way of life are revealed. Much of the new autoethnography focuses on trauma, on injuries, on troubled, repressed memories, inabilities to speak the past, the search for a new voice, shattered, damaged egos seeking new histories, new forms of agency. But in speaking from the spaces of trauma, autoethnographers do not "critically or self-consciously engage enough the technical substrata of their own writing form" (Clough 2000a, p. 287; also 2000b).[5]

Clough does not mean to trivialize the trauma written about, rather she wants to read it as symptomatic of something else that requires attention, namely how the new television, computer and media technologies, in conjunction with global capital on a transnational scale, are creating new forms of sub-jectivity. "I think it is these figures of subjectivity appearing in autoethnography which cultural criticism must now attend" (2000a, p. 287).

Thus Clough comes back to a single criterion for evaluating experimental writing, namely cultural criticism and theoretical reflection. Staying close to these two terms allows "experimental writing to be a vehicle for thinking new sociological subjects, new parameters of the social" (p. 290). She is fearful that the search for new criteria will silence cultural criticism (p. 290). I agree. However, indigenous scholars remind us that in native communities interpretive practices must be contextual, congruent with tribal epistemology, ethics, ritual, story telling traditions and tribal values (Kovach 2009, pp. 44–45, 125–126).

Mindful of the above distinctions, discussions of criteria move in three directions at the same time: the moral, political and the ethical; the literary and the aesthetic; trauma and the politics of experience. Indeed the word criteria should be placed under erasure.

An aside on criteria

After Schwandt, we might go so far to say farewell to criteriology (1996). Indeed in the spaces of the ontological turn and post-foundational epistemologies and (Lather 2016) searches for stable criteria are suspended. Nothing is any longer certain. Alternative models for evaluating inquiry are now debated, from Schwandt's view of inquiry as practical philosophy,[6] to MacLure's call for post-materialist work that honors disruption, confusion and unruly interpretive practices (Schwandt 1996, pp. 58–59; MacLure 2015; Lather 2016; Taylor and Hughes 2016). At the same time performance autoethnographers and Arts-Based Researchers explore alternative ways of judging performance inquiry (Leavy 2013, 2015; Faulkner 2014, 2009).

We can never say farewell to criteria. We can only suspend the notion of fixed standards of evaluation, perhaps replacing the word criteria with the term interpretive practice. A single question can then be asked: what performance practices, including interpretive standards, produce acts of activism that lead to hope and positive social change? What stories, what performances foster these experiences? How do these stories remind us of who we are (Kovach 2009, p. 94)?

We also want practices that allows us to take a situation up to a crisis and then stop and let spectators/readers intervene, and make up their own lines, write their own script, perform their lives into the crisis. This is what Boal did.

Listen to Anzaldua as she announces her queer Chicana identity, she confronts crisis and writes here way through it:

> For the lesbian of color, the ultimate rebellion she can make against her native culture is through her sexual behavior. Being lesbian and raised Catholic, indoctrinated as straight *I made the choice to be queer.*
>
> > (1987, p. 19, italics in original, paraphrase)

Her painful text is a performance, a call to action, an invitation to others to consider the ultimate act of resistance, to turn against her culture and her church. She puts her life, her gender and her sexual identity on the line, no greater commitment. There is more

> This is not new,
> Colored, poor, white, latent queer
> passing for white
> seething with hatred, anger …
> I am the only round face,
> Indian beaked, off-colored
> in the faculty line-up …
> I am the flesh you dig your fingernails into …
> I risk your sanity
> and mine (1987, pp. 19, 171, paraphrase.)
> who are they.
> > (Anzaldua 1987, p. 171, paraphrase)

Feminist, communitarian interpretive practices

Building on Clough, and Madison, the interpretive practices for evaluating critical performance events combine aesthetics, ethics and epistemologies.[7] Several models can be outlined. Like hooks's black aesthetic (1990, p. 111), and

Giroux's public pedagogy (2000b, p. 25; also 2000a), these performance criteria erase the usual differences between ethics, politics and power (Giroux 2000b, p. 25). This erasure creates the possibilities for a practical, performative pedagogy, a call for performances which intervene and interrupt public life. Such interruptions are meant to unsettle and challenge taken for granted assumptions concerning problematic issues in public life. They create a space for dialogue and questions, giving a voice to positions previously silenced, or ignored.

Ideologically, this performance aesthetic refuses assimilation to white middle class norms, and the traumas of that culture. It resists those understandings that valorize performances and narratives centered on the life crises of the humanistic subject. In contrast, this aesthetic values performance narratives that reflexively go against the grain, and attack the dominant cultural ideologies connected to nation, race, class, family and gender. These performances expose cracks in the ideological seams in these dominant cultural mythologies.

Three interconnected criteria (with parallels to Conquergood's three triads) shape these representations of the world. Interpretive sufficiency is the watchword (Christians 2000, p. 145).[8] Accounts should possess that amount of depth, detail, emotionality, nuance and coherence that will permit a critical consciousness, or what Paulo Freire (2000) terms conscientization to be formed. Through conscientization the oppressed gain their own voice, and collaborate in transforming their culture (Christians 2000, p. 148).

Second, these accounts should exhibit a representational adequacy and be free of racial, class or gender stereotyping (Christians 2000, p. 145). Finally texts are authentically adequate when three conditions are met: they (1) represent multiple voices; (2) enhance moral discernment; and (3) promote social transformation (p. 145). Multi-voiced ethnographic texts should empower persons, leading them to discover moral truths about themselves, while generating social criticism. These criticisms, in turn should lead to efforts at social transformation (p. 147).

This is a dialogical epistemology and aesthetic. It involves a give and take, an on-going moral dialogue between persons. It enacts an ethic of care, and an ethic of personal and communal responsibility (Collins 1991, p. 214). Politically, this aesthetic imagines how a truly democratic society might look, including one free of race prejudice and oppression. This aesthetic values beauty and artistry, movement, rhythm, color and texture in everyday life. It celebrates difference and the sounds of many different voices. It expresses an ethic of empowerment.

This ethic presumes a moral community that is ontologically prior to the person. This community has shared moral values, including the concepts of shared governance, neighborliness, love, kindness and the moral good (Christians 2000, pp. 144–149). This ethic embodies a sacred, existential epistemology that locates persons in a noncompetitive, nonhierarchical relationship to the larger moral universe. This ethic declares that all persons deserve dignity and a sacred status in the world. It stresses the value of human life, truth telling and nonviolence (Christians 2000, p. 147).

Under the principle of authentic adequacy (above), this aesthetic enables social criticism, and engenders resistance (see below). It helps persons imagine how things could be different. It imagines new forms of human transformation and emancipation. It enacts these transformations through dialogue. If necessary, it sanctions nonviolent forms of civil disobedience (Christians 2000, p. 148). In asking that interpretive work provide the foundations for social criticism, and social action this ethic represents a call to action.

This aesthetic understands that moral criteria are always fitted to the contingencies of concrete circumstances, assessed in terms of those local understandings that flow from feminist, communitarian understandings. This ethic calls for dialogical research rooted in the concepts of care, and shared governance. How this ethic works in any specific situation can not be given in advance.

Literary and aesthetic criteria

I turn now to the work of Ellis, Bochner and Richardson. Collectively these scholars offer a subtly nuanced set of criteria that emphasize the literary, substantive and aesthetic dimensions of the performance writing. In the main, these scholars and their students have focused on what Clough calls the experiences embedded in the culture of trauma. Their works (especially Ellis and Bochner) destigmatize the experiences of damaged egos.

Ellis (2000, p. 273; 2009, pp. 14–17), Ellis, Adams and Bochner (2011), and Jones Adams and Ellis (2013) offer a fully developed literary aesthetic. Ellis and her co-authors want writing that conforms to the criteria of interpretive sufficiency, and authentic adequacy. They want works that are engaging, and nuanced, texts that allow readers to feel. They want a story that immerses readers in another world, a story that stays with the readers after they have read it. Ellis privileges evocation over cognitive contemplation. If a writer can not write evocatively, she recommends they write in another genre. She asks that a story tell her something new: "About social life, social process, the experience of others, the author's experience, my own life. Is there anything 'new' here?" (2000, p. 275).

To the criteria of interpretive sufficiency, and authentic adequacy, Ellis adds a third, what might be called literary value, or what Richardson (2000a, p. 937; 2000b, p. 254; 2017) calls aesthetic merit. Ellis wants stories to have a good plot, to have dramatic tension, to be coherent, logically consistent, to exhibit balance, flow and an authenticity of experience, to be lifelike. She asks that authors show and not tell, that they develop characters and scenes fully, but that there not be too many characters or scenes.

She wants careful editing, an economy of words, but vivid pictures, sounds, smells, feelings, conversations that feel like real life, surprise endings that challenge her to see things in a new way. She asks if analysis has been connected closely to the story, and to the relevant literature. She asks if the story is worth fighting for, even if it is unconventional (2000, p. 276).

She wants to know what the author's goals are, what they are trying to achieve, and asks if the goals are achievable, and if they are worthwhile. She asks if another writing form would better serve the author's purposes. She wonders if the writer learned anything new about him-or herself, about other characters in the story, about social processes and relationships (p. 275).

A relational ethics is advocated, an ethic that asks researchers to act from their hearts and minds, to be caring, open inquirers, to bring respect and dignity to the researcher relationship.[9] A relational ethic encourages mindful self-reflection, recognizes that relationships change over time, and that ethnical obligations change accordingly (2009, p. 308; Ellis, Adams and Bochner 2011; Bochner and Ellis 2016, p. 139). This means that are obligated to share their work with those others who are implicated in their texts, including giving them space to talk back (Ellis 2000, p. 275; Bolen and Adams 2017).[10]

Bochner's narratives of self

Ellis's literary realism compliments Bochner's vision of poetic social science and alternative ethnography. Bochner (2000) also emphasizes issues surrounding interpretive sufficiency. He asks if these new narratives of self use language in a way that allows the reader (and writer) to extract meaning from experience, "rather than depict experience exactly as it was lived" (p. 270). Bochner isolates seven criteria.

First, he looks for abundant, concrete detail, for the "flesh and blood emotions of people coping with life's contingencies; not only facts but also feelings" (p. 270; 2007, p. 205). Second, he likes structurally complex narratives, stories told in the curve of time, weaving past and present together in the nonlinear spaces of memory work. Memory work, Giorgio argues, "memorializes the past and the present, creating new spaces for community and collective memory" (Giorgio 2013, p. 407).

Third, Bochner judges authors in terms of their emotional credibility, vulnerability and honesty. He wants texts that comment on those "cultural scripts that resist transformation ... squeezing comedy out of life's tragedies" (p. 270), texts that take a "measure of life's limitations" (p. 270). Fourth, he wants stories of two selves, stories of who I was to who I am, lives transformed by crisis.

Fifth, he holds the writer to "a demanding standard of ethical self-consciousness" (p. 271). Like Ellis, he wants the writer to show concern for those who are written about, concern for their place in the story and concern for how telling the story changes the writer's (and reader's) self, concern for the "moral commitments and convictions that underlie the story" (p. 271). Sixth, also like Ellis, he wants a story that "moves me, my heart and belly as well as my head" (p. 271). He does not demean a story if it is confessional or erotic, or pornographic, because every story is a dare, a risk.

Seventh, consistent with the criteria of authentic adequacy, Bochner wants narratives of the self that can be used as "a source of empowerment and a form of resistance to counter the domination of canonical discourses" (p. 271). He values those works that devictimize stigmatized identities, works that "confirm and humanize tragic experience by bearing witness to what it means to live with shame, abuse, addiction, or bodily dysfunction and to gain agency through testimony" (p. 271).

These criteria do not actively engage the issues surrounding authentic adequacy, including ethical discernment and social transformation. It is perhaps not enough, Clough would argue, to just bear witness to tragic experience, to just make public the traumas of the trauma culture.

Richardson's five criteria

Laurel Richardson asks for more, offering five criteria that move back and forth across the dimensions of interpretive sufficiency, representational adequacy and authentic adequacy. Her first criterion is substantive contribution: does the piece contribute to our understanding of social life? Is the work grounded in a social scientific perspective? Second, she asks if the work has aesthetic merit, does it succeed aesthetically, is it artistically shaped, is it satisfying, complex, not boring? (2000b, p. 254). Her third criterion is reflexivity, it involves several separate issues. She asks if the author is familiar with the epistemology of postmodernism. She wants to know how the information in the text was gathered, were ethical issues involved in this process (2017)? She asks if the author's subjectivity is in the text, is their point of view clear, is there adequate self-awareness, and self-exposure. Is the author held accountable to standards of knowing and telling (2000b, p. 254)?

The fourth criterion assesses impact. Richardson asks how the work affects her, emotionally, intellectually, and as a scholar. She asks, does it generate new questions? Does it move her to try new research practices? Does it move her to action? Fifth, she wants to know how the work expresses a reality. "Does this text embody a fleshed out, embodied sense of lived-experience? Does it seem 'true'—a credible account of a cultural, social, individual, or communal sense of the 'real'?" (2000a, p. 937).

Together, Ellis, Bochner and Richardson offer a set of interpretive criteria that emphasize the literary and aesthetic qualities of a work, as well as its substantive contributions to an area of knowledge. Ethically, they focus on the dialogical relationship between the writer and the subject, asking that this be an honest and open relationship. Each of these scholars wants to be moved emotionally and intellectually by a work. Each values reflexivity, and texts that empower.

A new aesthetic criterion emerges in this reading of Ellis, Bochner and Richardson. It might be termed the dialogical requirement. In asking that readers be moved by a text, these writers want works that invite us into another person's world of experience. The reading experience is a performance. It enlivens the written text, which is also a performance. Performance writing must be personal, raw, visceral, and evocative. It must move to the heart of the performance experience itself (Pelias 2013, p, 388).

Leavy's criteria

Not all inquiry can be effectively represented within a literary format. A single interview may not be appropriate for a dramatic reading involving multiple characters. A fictionalized short story might work well in a social work classroom but be completely ineffective in a presentation to policy makers. The writer must ask, "Does the literary format effectively communicate knowledge about the subject matter at hand? Would a traditional format do better?" If so, then the literary format is not warranted.

A somewhat ambiguous set of criteria should operate. Leavy (2015, pp. 21–28, 79–90, 96–97) drawing on the work of Faulkner (2009, p. 89; 2014), Richardson (2000a, 2000b), Ellis (2000), Bochner (2000), Clough (2000), Pelias (2011) and others, sets out three criteria for evaluating arts-based research, with an emphasis on research poetry:[11]

> Scientific criteria: depth, authenticity, trustworthiness, understanding, emotional verisimilitude, reflexivity, usefulness, crystallization, articulation of method, ethics, makes substantive contribution, problem solves, unsettles, describes;
>
> Poetic criteria: artistic concentration, embodied experience, discovery, conditional, narrative truth, and coherence, empathy, transformation;
>
> Artistic criteria: compression of empirical materials, understanding of craft, moral truth, emotional verisimilitude, sublime, empathy.

Leavy's first two categories are applied to any form of critical qualitative inquiry.

The third category can be extended. Is the literary, poetic statement effective aesthetically? Does it exhibit accessible literary qualities? Is it dramatically evocative? Is it lyrical? Does it invoke shared feelings, images, scenes and memories? Does it express emotion effectively, economically? Does it establish objective correlatives for the emotions the writer is attempting to evoke (see Eliot 1922)? Does it meet the criteria attributed to Emily Dickenson, " If I read a work and it makes my whole body so cold no fire can ever warm me, I know it is poetry." I add a fourth category:

> Social justice criteria: creates critical awareness concerning social justice, moves persons to action, promotes public dialogue (Leavy 2015, p. 22; Bochner and Ellis 2016, pp. 60–62,212–213; Sughrua 2016, p. 3).

Sughrua is quite explicit. Critical autoethnographers have a responsibility to address issues of social injustice (Sughrua 2016, p. 3; also Madison 2012, p. 3). End of story.

Performative criteria

Building on the above normative understandings, I value those autoethnographic performance texts that:

1   Unsettle, criticize and challenge taken for granted, repressed meanings;
2   Invite moral and ethical dialogue, while reflexively clarifying their own moral position;
3   Engender resistance; and offer utopian thoughts about how things can be made different;
4   Demonstrate that they care, that they are kind;
5   Show, instead of tell, while using the rule that less is more;
6   Exhibit interpretive sufficiency, representational adequacy, and authentic adequacy;
7   Are political, functional, collective and committed.

In asking if a performance event does these things, I understand that every performance is different. Further, audiences may or may not agree on what is caring, or kind, or reflexive, and some persons may not want their taken for granted understandings challenged. Performance writing turns back on itself, hesitates, refuses to stand still, "moves nervously across the page ... is nothing more than water leaking through the fingers of cupped hands" (Pelias 2013, p. 400, paraphrase).

Ethics for performance studies

Any consideration of performance ethics must move in three directions at the same time, addressing three interrelated issues: ethical pitfalls, traditional ethical models and indigenous performance ethics connected to political theatre (Boal 1995). Conquergood (1985, p. 4; see also Madison 2012, pp. 142–146) has identified four ethical pitfalls/stances that performance ethnographers must avoid. He terms them "The Custodian's Rip-Off," "The Enthusiast's Infatuation," "The Skeptic's Cop-Out" and "The Curator's Exhibitionism." Conquergood presents a fifth stance, the dialogical performance, which avoids the above pitfalls.

Cultural custodians, or cultural imperialists, ransack their biographical past looking for good texts to perform and then perform them for a fee often denigrating a family member or a cultural group who regard such experiences as sacred. The enthusiast's infatuation, or superficial stance, occurs when the writer (and the performer) fail to become deeply involved in the cultural setting which they re-perform. Conquergood (1985, p. 6) says this trivializes the other because their experiences are neither contextualized, nor well understood.

Modifying Conquergood, the skeptic or cynic values detachment and being cynical. This position refuses to face up to the "ethical tensions and moral ambiguities of performing culturally sensitive materials" (Conquergood 1985, p. 8). Finally the curator or sensationalist, like the custodian, is a performer who sensationalizes the cultural differences that supposedly define the world of the other. He or she stages performances for the voyeur's gaze, perhaps telling stories about an abusive, hurtful other (Conquergood 1985, p. 7).

These ethical stances make problematic the questions of "How far into the other's world can the performer and the audience go?" Of course we can never know the mind of an other, only the other's performances. We can only know our own minds, and sometimes not well. This means that the differences that define the other's world must always be respected. There is no null point in the moral universe (Conquergood 1985, pp. 8–9).

The second issue is implicit in Conquergood's four ethical pitfalls. He presumes a researcher who is held accountable to a set of universal ethical principles that are both duty-based and utilitarian. Duty-based ethics assume researchers and performers who are virtuous, have good intentions and are committed to values like justice, honesty and respect. This is Conquergood's ideal performer. However, Conquergood is concerned with more than good intentions, he is concerned with the effects, or consequences, of a performance on a person or a community. Thus he appears to implicitly endorse a utilitarian ethics based on consequences and pragmatic effects, not good intentions. This is the cost-benefit utilitarian model used by Human Subject Review Boards when they ask how this research will benefit society.

Both of these models have deficiencies. Carried to the extreme the duty position can result in a moral absolutism, requiring that persons live up to an absolute standard, regardless of its human consequences (Edwards and Mauthner 2002, p. 20; Kvale 1996, pp. 121–122). But who holds these values; whose values are they? The utilitarian model is predicated on the belief that the ends justify the means (Kvale 1996, p. 122), thus the "wrongness or rightness of actions are judged by their consequences, not their intent" (Edwards and Mauthner 2002, p. 20). Whose consequences are being considered, whose means are being used, best for whom?

It is necessary to contrast these two universalist models with feminist and critical pedagogically informed ethical models (Edwards and Mauthner 2002, p. 21). Contingent feminist ethical models work outward from personal experience, and from local systems of meaning and truth, to social contexts where experience is shaped by nurturing social relationships based on care, respect and love. The researcher is an insider to the group, not an outsider (Smith 1999, p. 139). The desire is to enact a locally situated, contingent, feminist, communitarian ethic that respects and protects the rights, interests and sensitivities of those one is working with, including ideas specific to the cultural context (Smith 1999, p. 119; 2012, p. 124; Denzin 1997, p. 275).

Contingent ethical models have been adopted by social science professionals associations that often navigate between universal normative models and contingent ethical directives (Edwards and Mauthner 2002, p. 21). Such guidelines are then meant to guide the researcher when the kinds of pitfalls and dilemmas Conquergood identifies are encountered.

These professional guidelines do not include a space for culturally specific ethical ideas and values. Within specific contexts, for instance the Maori, specific ethical values and rules are prescribed in cultural terms. These understandings include showing respect for others, listening, sharing, and being generous, cautious and humble. Smith is quite explicit. "From indigenous perspectives ethical codes of conduct serve partly the same purposes as the protocols which govern our relationships with each other and with the environment" (Smith 2012, p. 25).

In contrast to social science codes of ethics and the protocols used by human subject review boards, critical pedagogy seeks to enact a situationally contingent ethic that is compatible with indigenous values. This ethic is predicated on *a pedagogy of hope*. It is based on values shared in the group. It blends intentions with consequences. It presumes that well-intended, trusting, honest, virtuous persons engage in moral acts that have positive consequences for others. This is a communitarian dialogical *ethic of care* and responsibility. It presumes that performances occur within sacred aesthetic spaces where research does not operate as a dirty word. It presumes that performers treat persons, their cares and their concerns with dignity and respect. Indeed, the values that structure the performance are those shared by the community and its members. These values include care, trust and reciprocity. Because of these shared understandings this model assumes that there will be few ethical dilemmas requiring negotiation.

A feminist, communitarian performance ethic is utopian in vision. While criticizing systems of injustice and oppression, it imagines how things could be different. It enacts a *performance pedagogy of radical democratic hope*. For example, "What African American minstrels created was a new form of theater based in the skills of the performers, not their ability to conform to stereotypes" (Bean 2001, pp. 187–188).

An empowering performancepedagogy frames the third issue that must be addressed. The multivoiced performance text enacts *a pedagogy of hope*. A critical consciousness is invoked. The performance event engenders moral discernment that guides social transformation (Denzin 2003, p. 112; Christians 2000). The performance text is grounded in the cruelties and injustices of daily life. Like Boal's forum theatre, a documentary-drama format may be used, drawing on current events and media accounts of these events. A radical performance ethic is grounded in a politics of resistance. The performance must be ethically honest. It must be dialogical, seeking to locate dialogue and meaningful exchange in the *radical center*.

The other always exists, as Trinh (1989) would argue, in the spaces on each side of the hyphen (Conquergood 1985, p. 9; also Fine 1994). The hyphen is not neutral. Nor are the colonized and gendered spaces on either side of the hyphen neutral. This is why the performance text should be dialogic, a text that does not speak about or for the other, but which "speaks to and with the other" (Conquergood 1985, p. 10). It is a text that reengages the past, and brings it alive in the present. The dialogic text attempts to keep the dialogue, the conversation – between text, the past, the present, performer and audience – ongoing and open-ended (p. 9). This text does more than invoke empathy, it interrogates, criticizes and empowers. It critiques existing cultural practices, embraces the writer's vulnerability, breaches silences, bears witness to injustice, creates spaces for the other. This is dialogical criticism. The dialogical performance is the means for pedagogies of hope which are grounded in "honest intercultural understandings" (Conquergood 1985, p. 10).

The politics of interpretation

We are continually reminded that writing, is not an innocent practice, although in the social sciences and the humanities there is only interpretation, only performance (Richardson 2001 p. 87). Nonetheless Marx (1888/1983, p. 158) continues to remind us that we are in the business of not just interpreting but of changing the world. Clough asks that writers transcend the traumas celebrated in a mass-mediated trauma culture. She asks for works that go more deeply into cultural criticism, into the politics of interpretation.

Each text, each performance, should be valued for the collective and individual reflection and critical action it produces, including conversations that cross the boundaries of race, class, gender and nation. We should ask how each performance text promotes the development of human agency, "resistance... and critical consciousness" (hooks 1990, p. 111).

This aesthetic also seeks and values beauty and looks to find beauty in the everyday, especially in "the lives of poor people" (hooks 1990, p. 111). Here is an illustration from bell hooks, who recalls the houses of her childhood, especially the house of Baba, her grandmother. Looking back into her childhood, hooks observes that she now sees how this black woman was struggling to create, in spite of poverty and hardship, an oppositional world of beauty. Baba had a clean house that was crowded with many precious objects. Baba was also a quilt maker. She turned everyday, worn-out clothing into beautiful works of art, and her quilts were present in every room of her small house.

Late at night, hooks would sit alone in an upstairs room in Baba's house. In the stillness of the night, in reflections from the moon's light, hooks came to see darkness and beauty in different ways. Now, in a different time, late at night, she and her sisters "think about our skin as a dark room, a place of shadows. We talk often about color politics, and the ways racism has created an aesthetic that wounds us, we talk about the need to see darkness differently ... in that space of shadows we long for an aesthetic of blackness – strange and oppositional" (hooks 1990, p. 113).

Aesthetics, art, ethics, performance, history, culture and politics are thus intertwined, for in the artful, interpretive production, cultural heroes, heroines, mythic pasts and senses of moral community are created. It remains to us to chart the future – to return to the beginning, to reimagine the ways in which performance autoethnography can advance the agendas of radical democratic practice, to ask where these practices will take us next.

Into the future

A new postinterpretive, postfoundational paradigm is emerging. This framework is attaching itself to new and less certain interpretive criteria. A more expansive framework shaped by an aesthetics of color, gender and critical race theory principles informs these criteria.

Epistemologies and aesthetics of color will proliferate, building on indigenous, Afrocentric, Chicana/o, Native American, First Nation, Maori, Asian American and Third World perspectives. More elaborated epistemologies of gender (and class) will appear, including queer theory and feminisms of color. These interpretive communities and their scholars will draw on their group experiences for the texts they will write, and they will seek texts that speak to the logics and cultures of these communities. In so doing, they will challenge those representations that have come before (see Cook-Lynn 1996, pp. 37–38, 71). They will be committed to advancing the political, economic, cultural and educational practices of critical race theory. These practices will be embedded in the everyday world, in the worlds of oppression. New forms of critical pedagogy will not be reduced to arguments or explanations "bounded by the Western tradition" (Bishop 1998, p. 209).

This new generation of scholars will be committed not just to describing the world, but to changing it. Their texts will be performance based. They will be committed to creating civic transformations and to using minimalist social theory. They will inscribe and perform utopian dreams, dreams shaped by critical race theory, dreams of a world where all are free to be who they choose to be, free of gender, class, race, religious and ethnic prejudice and discrimination. The next moment in qualitative inquiry will be one in which the practices of performance autoethnography finally move, without hesitation or encumbrance, from the personal to the political.

In the end, then, to summarize: I seek an existential, interpretive social science that offers a blueprint for cultural criticism. This criticism is grounded in the specific worlds made visible in the writing and performing process. It understands that autoethnography is never theory- or value-free. There can be no objective account of a culture and its ways. Taking our lead from 20th-century African American cultural critics (Du Bois, Hurston, Ellison, Wright, Baldwin, Hines), we now know that the autoethnographic, the aesthetic and the political can never be neatly separated. Autoethnography, like art, is always political.

Accordingly, after Ford ([1950] 1998), we seek a critical, civic, literary ethnography that evidences a mastery of literary craftsmanship, the art of good writing. It should present a well-plotted, compelling but minimalist narrative, a narrative based on realistic, natural conversation, with a focus on memorable, recognizable characters. These characters should be located in well-described, "unforgettable scenes" (p. 1112). Such work should present clearly identifiable cultural and political issues, including injustices based on the structures and meanings of race, class, gender and sexual orientation. The work should articulate a politics of hope. It should criticize how things are and imagine how they could be different. It should locate and represent the gendered, sacred self in its ethical relationships to nature. Finally, it should do these things through direct and indirect symbolic and rhetorical means. Writers who create such texts are fully immersed in the oppressions and injustices of their time. They direct their ethnographic energies to higher, utopian, morally sacred goals.

The truth of these new texts is determined pragmatically, through their truth effects, through the critical, moral discourse they produce, the "empathy they generate, the exchange of experience they enable, and the social bonds they mediate" (Jackson 1998, p. 180). The power of these texts is not a question of whether "they mirror the world as it 'really' is" (Jackson 1998, p. 180) – the world is always already constructed through our performances. Rorty (1980) is firm on this point. There is no mirror to nature.

And so we must learn how to enact an enabling, performative auto-ethnography, an autoethnography that aspires to higher goals. We can scarcely afford to do otherwise. We are at a critical crossroads in the histories of our disciplines and our nation. As Cornel West (1994) reminds us (paraphrasing), "We simply cannot end the second decade of twenty-first century at each other's throats" (p. 159). But, with West, we must ask, "Do we have the intelligence, humor, imagination, courage, tolerance, love, respect, and will to meet the challenge?" (p. 159). As a community of scholars we can not afford to do otherwise. We have an ethical responsibility to act together as a "we" in a moral community. This is an obligation to articulate an ethic of freedom, to act, that is in, concert, becoming a plural body, one that speaks, thinks, and moves together, in harmony and dissent (Jones 2017).

Notes

1 This chapter extends arguments in Denzin (2009, pp. 151–173; 2014, pp. 69–83).
2 Criteria by type: analytic: data, validity, generalizing; evocative: emotion, temporality, concern (see below).
3 Scott reviews different meanings of experience, including experience as a process that is internal, external, objective, subjective, or constitutive of consciousness (1991, p. 782).
4 Madison (2012, p. 186) recasts performance ethnography as co-performance ethnography.
5 Salvo (2017) outlines two autoethnographic ethics, an ethic of disclosure and an ethics of communicating epiphany. For Salvo (2017) much autoethnography addresses the trauma that we experience in the context of suffering and being with intimate others. Autoethnography is at bottom a discourse about removing the shame that has been silenced and experienced in the trauma culture, about revealing the secrets that have been hidden, about an ethics of disclosure. For Salvo autoethnography is at bottom a discourse about finding our way back home, how we can flourish with happy lives.
6 Rather than using the term criteria, Schwandt suggests the concept of guiding ideal and the related notion of enabling conditions (dialogue, shared community of knowers, etc.) that shape such practices, and the outcomes of such action (generate useful knowledge, critical intelligence, and critical judgment).
7 Definitions: **Aesthetics**: Theories of beauty; **Ethics**: Theories of ought, of right; **Epistemology**: Theories of knowing. **Anti-Aesthetic**: denies a privileged aesthetic realm, is political. This section draws from Denzin (2000, pp. 326–327). I seek a radical anti-aesthetic that operates as political critique, challenging at every turn the aestheticization of everyday life, and modernist ethical models (Eagleton 1990, p. 119; Featherstone 1991, p. 67; Jameson 1981, p. 299).
8 I thank Clifford Christians for clarifying these principles.

9 Relational ethics are an extension of Joseph Fletcher's situational ethics, which are grounded in the particularities of each situation. The goal is to create an ethical relationship with each research participant by "recalling past experiences, learning from each event as it happens, imagining future sequences of events and considering consequences of actions" (Bochner and Ellis 2016, p. 139).

10 As Bolen and Adams (2017, p. 618) note, issues of truth, memory, privacy, ownership and privilege arise in the context of narrative ethics – the ethics of telling stories about self and other.

11 She uses the term research poetry to reference "poems that are crafted from research endeavors" (2009, p. 20), work that turns interviews, transcripts, observations and personal experience into poetic form (on found poetry see also Prendergast 2006).

Part IV

Performance texts: bone deep in landscapes

11 Grandma's story

Trinh (1989, p. 150) urges us to value the stories grandmothers tell us. My grandmother, Leota Bell Johnston Townsley (1891–1975) was a tiny woman. She was a graduate of the Iowa City Academy, a college preparatory school for those intending to attend the University of Iowa. In a 1912 photo she comes off the page, sparkling eyes, short dark curly hair frames her smiling face. She is wearing a high-necked lace bodice and a long formal skirt, a wide belt around her waist. She is holding a small dress purse. Her legs are crossed. She is smiling at the cameraman.

In another photo, on her 50th wedding anniversary, she is wearing a fur stole, a silk dress and a fashionable hat with a feather through it. She is smiling, as she stands proudly next to Waldo William Townsley (1890–1980) who is wearing his new dark grey dress suit.

In another photo (Indianola, 1953) she stands next to my father, Ken Denzin (1920–1995). My brother and I look on. Mother, Betty Townsley Denzin (1917–1996), is not in the picture. Ken is wearing a cowboy shirt and cowboy boots. Leota is wearing one of her semi-formal everyday working dresses, a v-necked, gingham dress, with black pumps. Underneath she would have been wearing a corset, which she washed three times a week and dried on a rack in her bedroom. She is smiling at Ken.

But I am getting ahead of myself. Grandmother was a storyteller, and Mark and I were her audience. I correct myself. She was a bedtime storyteller. From 1946–1956 Mark and I spent weekends and every summer with Grandpa and Grandma. Every night Grandma read stories to us, one page at a time, at least an hour every night, or until we fell asleep. She read us the Bobbsey Twins stories. We learned all about Nan and Bert and their mysteries. She read us the Hardy Boys mysteries, and the Nancy Drew mysteries. We lived inside these stories, and each day, as we worked side-by-side in her flower and vegetable gardens we would talk about Nan or Bert, or the Hardy Boys, or Nancy Drew. In taking us into these worlds and I suppose at one level she knew she was taking us a way from the pain we felt at home with our parents, where there was a lot of fighting, drinking and partying.

I would say today that Grandma lived a life that embodied the stories she told us, or rather, she lived the live of a grandmother who had the patience to read stories to her grandsons. And in reading us those stories she told us stories about how to be storytellers ourselves, how to lose yourself in another person's story, how to listen, to care.

Her story was interrupted by two key moments. On 28 October 1917, at the age of 26 Leota and Waldo became the parents of an adopted daughter, Betty Rachel (1917–1996). From 1925–1927 Betty and Leota live in expansive Kansas City hotels while Waldo markets Serval, his accounting system across the U. S. The family retires to the family farm in 1937. In 1938 Betty graduates from Stephen's College, marries Kenneth Denzin (1920–1980) two years later and has two sons, born in 1941 and 1944.

***

1973: I'd received a call. Grandma was not doing well and Grandpa could no longer take care of her. She had been moved to a cot in the TV room, just off the kitchen. She was frail, she did not recognize me. She had been sleeping. Grandpa was crying, "Grandma is not doing well." The TV was on, barely visible images flickered across the yellow-green screen.

With a jolt, Grandma sits up straight in the cot. She turns, looks at Grandpa:

GRANDMA: Waldo, Ike died, there is Mamie in that open-air car. Who will take care of Mamie now that Ike is gone? You never took care of Betty and I when you left us in Kansas City. Waldo, I could never forgive you for that. I feel for Mamie. You know Ike cheated on her too.

She fell back down on the cot, closed her eyes and went to sleep. To the best of my knowledge she never spoke again. When we visited Grandpa in the nursing home he would say, Grandma does not talk any more. There it was, in the TV room, a Grandma story that had never been told before.

I stayed inside this story for a long time. What did it mean? I drifted off. I was caught in a series of dreams, painful moments about Grandma, Grandpa, Mother, my father. Mother was talking to me. She was talking to my grandfather, and to my father. Grandma was looking on, I was watching. It was all mixed up.

Mother says to Grandpa:

MOTHER: Daddy, you never told me you were my real father. You lied and told Momma that you got me from a poor family in Muscatine. Why didn't you tell the truth! Why did you leave us in that fancy hotel in Kansas City and go off with that other woman? Momma never forgave you.

Silence fills the room. Grandma is crying. My father has his back turned away from mother. Grandpa is slouched in his chair.

***

An Iowa farm house. Late spring. I'm sitting at the top of the stairs, outside Grandma's bedroom, two doors down from Mother's old bedroom, the bedroom where Mark and I slept when Grandma read us bedroom stories. Grandma is dead now. I'd come back to settle affairs. I'd found a letter in her safe. I was drunk. The letter was dated October 28, 1917. It was to Grandma and Grandpa. It was from a women with a Muscatine, Iowa address "Please take good care of my baby girl. Elizabeth Rachel. God bless you."

***

At this point in my dreams there was no exit. We were all trapped in the same room, and Mother has having her fury out on all of us. I had that letter in my hand. There was no place to run. Grandma was crying. Grandpa was yelling, "Now Leota, you know that letter is a lie. Why did you ever keep it?" My father was crying.

I had witnessed a crime, a series of crimes against Mother and Grandma. We were all trying to run away. In a flash I saw Grandma in a different light. She was doubly betrayed. It started in 1917 when Grandpa gave her a baby, the day Grandpa denied he was the father of that child. That betrayal was compounded when Grandpa, like Ike, had affairs with other women.

The betrayal cut deep. Mother was never able to give Grandma or Grandpa the love they wanted, for she lived their betrayal, in a way they could not. She had never been properly loved, just as Grandpa had never properly loved Grandma. Mother's response was to punish, punish herself, punish those she might have one day loved. She did not attend the funeral of Grandma and Grandpa.

In their dreams, Mother and Grandma were was always wounded, surrounded by weak unfaithful men who needed to be controlled, controlled through guilt, illness, guile.

I remember Grandma to this day, the prim, controlled beautiful woman, smiling from a photograph taken in 1912. In a sense it all went down hill from then. Although I believe when she read us bedtime mystery stories she found a love she could share, that she read mysteries suggests too that she knew somewhere the truth about the past, any past, could be discovered,

And I remember Mother, from better days, a phone call from Arizona, "Hello, this is your Mother," and I close my eyes and I see a Liz Taylor smile, winks, a toss of the head, cowboy boots, tight-fitting blue jeans, and silver belts, hello, this is your mother.

12 A family tradition

About the time Mother was being cremated I was at Ted Peterson's memorial in the Faculty Center listening to a local classical jazz group play a version of Louis Armstrong's "When the Saints Come Marching In."

This was the afternoon of October 24, 1997. Ted had died two months earlier. He loved jazz. Mother loved Louis Armstrong. It seemed fitting that I was listening to Louis' song when Mother was cremated. There was a pattern at work here. Twenty minutes after I left, everything fell into place.

When I got home and walked into the kitchen, my wife Kathy said, "I have some pretty big news for you. Where have you been?"

"Ted Peterson's memorial," I said, "Remember, I told you? What's up?" I thought maybe something had happened to one of the kids, Rachel, or Johanna, or Nate. We were a little worried about Nate in Seattle.

Kathy got right to it. "Your mother died. Johanna has been trying to reach you before you came home and played the message from your brother Mark. She was cremated an hour after she died."

I was stunned. Mother was dead. Kathy got down to the details. "Mark told Johanna your mother planned this event pretty carefully. She was very explicit, 'I want no funeral, and I want to be cremated immediately after I die.' Mark said she died at 1:00 in the nursing home outside Lone Tree, Iowa. She had a stroke, and never came out of it."

I couldn't believe it. How could Mother die and do this to me?

Lone Tree is 30 miles from Muscatine where Mother was born 76 years earlier. The nursing home is a little over 10 miles from my grandparents' old home where mother had been taken by my grandfather when she was three days old. He gave her to my grandmother, and said, "Here's the baby we can't have." Grandpa and Grandma told Mother that she had been adopted. Mother never knew who her real mother was, but she sure suspected that Grandpa was her real father. She never forgave him for going behind Grandma's back. Neither did Grandma, for that matter.

I started to cry. I went in to my study and put Nat King Cole doing "Sweet Lorraine" on the CD player. Mother liked "Sweet Lorraine."

All I could think of was machines, messages and death, how Mother hated machines. She never used any of those new kitchen appliances, like ovens with timers. She would not allow an answering machine in her house, but she was sure good on the phone. This is what I thought, until the last time we talked.

We'd gotten into a pattern, especially in the fall of 1988. She'd call me every morning before I left for campus to teach a 10:00 class. I got so I expected the call. Looked forward to it, even.

This pattern started about 6 months after she and George moved to Champaign. She and I had gotten back together, after not talking for 15 years. It all started with a phone call, mid-January, 1987. "Hello, Norman, this is Mother. How are you?" One thing led to another. Before you knew it she was calling every Saturday at 11:00 from Cottonwood, Arizona. George was retired from Bell, so he had free long distance calls. We'd talk about an hour every week. She got to know Kathy this way.

Mother and George came up to Champaign to visit in the fall of 1987. I helped them find a house. After all these years of being apart Mother wanted to buy one around the corner from us on Crescent Drive. George thought maybe that was a little too close. Instead they bought a nice brick two-bedroom ranch about two miles away.

It didn't take too long, before we were talking back and forth every day. She didn't want me to tell Johanna and Rachel to call her. I could tell them that Grandma Campbell had moved to town. If they wanted to call her they could. I followed her instructions. But the girls never called her. They could not remember who she was. It had been 15 years since they had heard from her.

Mother put us all in a double bind. If the girls called her, she would say it was because I told them to. If the girls did not call her it was because they did not love her. If I had been a good father, they would have loved her and wanted to call her. This is how Mother worked family relationships. It's easy to understand why Johanna and Rachel never got around to calling her.

I'd drive out and visit once or twice a week. Once I came in unannounced at 4:30 in the afternoon. They were eating dinner on little rugs in front of the TV in the living room. They were watching "Wheel of Fortune." I guess the rugs protected the carpet from the food, if they spilled any. Mother was stretched out, propped up on her elbows, eating franks and baked beans and a tossed salad with Russian dressing. I felt kind of awkward. I stayed for a couple of spins of the big wheel and left.

This happened in the middle of the summer. As I said, that fall I was teaching the morning class at 10:00 and Mother was calling every morning between 9 and 9:15. If it got to be 9:20 and she hadn't called, I'd call her. She'd say she was running a little late with breakfast, but that she was just getting ready to call. We'd chat around a little bit, and I'd say I had to run, to get to campus. Rather than say good-bye, we'd say we loved each other, and then hang up.

It kept getting closer to the holidays. Mother had always been big on the Holidays. At least she said she had been, I couldn't remember, because 15 years without doing them together is a long time. That Thanksgiving Dad, and Lesley, my step-mother, were coming over from Amana, Iowa for a short visit. They had been doing this for several years. It was a family tradition.

I told Mother that this is what we were doing. Kathy invited Mother and George over for Thanksgiving Day dessert, but she said no. She thought they would go out of town for the holiday, maybe drive to Lone Tree, and look at the old homestead. I said, "If you change your minds let us know." I had this uncomfortable mental image of Mother and George passing Dad and Lesley on Interstate 80, somewhere around Davenport, Iowa.

So we did Thanksgiving with Lesley and Dad. The next week the phone calls started up again, as if nothing had happened. But we both knew that something had happened. Mother had returned to Iowa and had not had a family holiday dinner with her family in Champaign. I felt pretty bad about this.

Christmas was just around the corner. I kept putting off inviting her. Kathy and I did not quite know how to get Mother and the girls all together in the same room. We had invited Steve and Brian for Christmas dinner. We'd been doing this for several years. On the Thursday before Christmas, which was on Sunday, I called Mother and asked her if she and George had plans, and if not would they join us for Christmas dinner? She said they would be honored. I told them to come at 12:30. I also told her we had invited Steve and Brian.

At 11:30 Christmas Day Johanna and Rachel panicked. They did not have a present for Grandma. Kathy got out a calendar she was giving to me. The girls wrapped it and put Grandma's name on it.

At 12:30 sharp I looked out the front door window. Mother and George were coming up the walk. I stepped outside. Mother was in her Southwestern splendor, hand carved cowboy boots, tight fitting blue jeans with a big silver belt buckle, Navajo necklace, blue cowboy shirt, a bright red scarf around her neck, blazing black hair, with a trace of white, a short bobbed cut, Mamie Eisenhower bangs, those twinkling blue eyes. She stood still for a moment, frozen in my memory. She looked me in the eye. She looked down and kicked a frozen clump of snow. She looked up and spoke, "Good day sir, and how are you? We are so pleased to be invited into your home for this holiday." As I remember it today there was more than a bit of sarcasm in her voice.

We did the gift exchange before sitting down. Mother gave the kids gifts she had made by hand, an apple with cloves in it for Nate, a crumbling chocolate cake for Johanna and Rachel. Kathy and I didn't get anything.

Dinner did not go well. I still think it was because Steve and Brian were there. Steve played the waiter, "May I serve you dessert Madame?" I think Mother resented this. She tried to talk to the kids. Nobody knew what to say. Eventually everything was reduced to chit chat back and forth between Kathy and me, and Steve and Brian. George never spoke.

As soon as dessert was over they left. I helped them on with their coats. As she stepped down into the snow, Mother turned, smiled, and said, "Thank you so much."

About 40 minutes later the phone rang. It was Mother, "Hi honey, it's me, we had a wonderful time. I will remember this for ever. Thank you so much. Good bye." I thanked her for calling and said the girls loved it, that they really like Grandma Betty and Grandpa George. This was the last time we ever talked.

She didn't mean it, and she didn't say I love you. I knew she had not had a good time. And I kicked myself. I was not sure what I had done wrong. Kathy said I did nothing wrong, that Mother was just weird.

I didn't expect any call that week, because there were no classes going on. In fact it would be three weeks before classes started up again. I thought about calling Mother, but decided to wait until classes started. Besides I didn't want to talk to her.

Classes started and on that first Tuesday the phone didn't ring at 9:00 or at 9:15. I thought, "Oh, well, she doesn't know classes have started up." There was no call at all that week. By the following Monday, I was inside the lyrics of an old Jimmy Buffett Song, "If The Phone Doesn't Ring, It's Me." The phone was not ringing at 9:00, and Mother was not calling.

This went on for a month. No calls. And I didn't call her. So I couldn't just blame her. I think I didn't want to talk her. I knew something important was happening. I was not willing to start up again, with an apology, and take the responsibility for not talking. I had done this when she had started calling and talking in the spring and summer of 1987.

Right after Valentine's Day we ran into Mother and George in the IGA parking lot. That is we saw them. They were in their car, and we were in my Cressida. It was like a movie. I watched them look at us, and they must have watched us look at them. Nobody blinked, nobody waved. Then George drove off. We parked and went into the store.

On the way home I started to cry. Kathy said, "Let's go do something nice for you. What would you like?"

Frank Sinatra was in the air. He was 75 years old. In celebration of his birthday, the four-disc Reprise Collection of his works had just been released; all those great arrangements of Gershwin, Mercer, Mandel, Arlen from "Sweet Lorraine" to "Second Time Around." I liked Sinatra's voice, so did Mother. She didn't approve of his life-style, neither did I. Anyway, I went out and bought that new Sinatra collection.

Second time around, Mother and I didn't do so well, or was it the third time around? Fifth? Sixth? Had we always been doing this, making up and breaking apart?

I never saw her again. That fall when we were visiting my father he mentioned that Bobby Lentz said he saw Mother and George in Lone Tree. Bobby said Mother told him they had moved back home.

In the summer of 1964 Mother spent the money she had saved from her part-time job at Fuchs' Jewelry Store. She had enough money for a seven-day vacation. She and I were pretty close back then. Dad had left the family in the spring of 1960. It had taken her about three years to get back on her feet. She took up with an on and off again boyfriend named Jim, an oil field worker with a wife back in Oklahoma. We'd all get together two or three times a week at the American Legion, shoot pool and get drunk on 10 High bourbon.

That summer Mother and Jim were fighting. He had gone back to his wife. She said she needed some time off from everything. So she took the train from Iowa City to New Orleans. She stayed at the Seven Sisters just off Basin Street. She went to the little bars where Dixieland spills out into the street. She missed Satchmo by a week.

Part V

Pedagogy, politics and ethics

13 Critical performance pedagogy

Announcement: Richard Rorty's 1998 Book Predicts 2016 U.S. Presidential Election

Members of labor unions, and unorganized unskilled workers, will sooner or later realize that their government is not even trying to prevent wages from sinking or to prevent jobs from being exported. Around the same time, they will realize that suburban white-collar workers – themselves desperately afraid of being downsized – are not going to let themselves be taxed to provide social benefits for anyone else.

At that point, something will crack. The nonsuburban electorate will decide that the system has failed and start looking around for a strongman to vote for – someone willing to assure them that, once he is elected, the smug bureaucrats, tricky lawyers, overpaid bond salesmen, and postmodernist professors will no longer be calling the shots. ... One thing that is very likely to happen is that the gains made in the past 40 years by black and brown Americans, and by homosexuals, will be wiped out. Jocular contempt for women will come back into fashion. ... All the resentment which badly educated Americans feel about having their manners dictated to them by college graduates will find an outlet.

(Rorty 1998, quoted in Senior 2016)

Prologue

It remains, then, to return to the beginning, to take up again the task of offering a critical framework for reading performance ethnography's place in a progressive discourse that advances a pedagogy of freedom and hope in this new century. It is not enough just to do performance autoethnography or qualitative inquiry. Of course we seek to understand the world, but we demand a performative politics that leads the way to radical social change.

***

It started before the election of Donald J. Trump to the office of president of the United States on November 9, 2016. You could go back 15 years to the terrorist attacks of September 11, 2001 when the U.S., under the Bush administration, invaded Iraq under great pretense (there were no weapons of mass destruction) and put in place the permanent War on Terror. Loneliness, anxiety, uncertainty, and a culture of fear followed. Every American was turned into a potential terrorist (Giroux 2016c, p. 65). A new generation, fearful, resentful and angry, was created. Its members were ready to gravitate to a cult of personality, a celebrity, the woman or man who promised a new day, an escape from fear, from terror. Welcome to Donald Trump's America. We have fallen prey to a politics of extremism, misogyny and ultra-nationalism (Giroux 2016c).

We are participants in, and witnesses to the performances of a politician-entertainer-reality TV president who uses the social media (twitter) to offer easy solutions to America's problems. He has elevated incivility to a performance, a pedagogy of self-righteous indignation which fuels resentment and anger, hatred and bigotry (Giroux 2016c). A dis-eased, embodied pedagogy of fear and war, based on fake- news is fitted to a post-9/11 ISIS world (Garorian and Gaudelius 2008; Giroux 2016c; Altheide 2010). Manufactured ignorance reinforces bullying and violence (Giroux 2016c). Hate crimes are on the rise. We are living under a managed democracy which everyday looks more and more like fascism.[1] Meanwhile the social fabric unravels. Intolerance, misogyny, racism, ugliness, anger and authoritarianism gain ground, and the new president promises to be the master of the art of the deal. "I'll make America great again" he says (Giroux 2016c, pp. 69–70, 80).

Recalling C. Wright Mills (1959, p. 3), everyone today is looking for a new hero, a new savoir. People are losing their homes, their jobs, their children, their marriages and families are collapsing. Many feel a loss of control over what is important, including sanity itself. They no longer trust their political leaders. Wages are falling. Health care costs are rising. Demagogues, appealing to popular desires and prejudices, paint apocalyptic scenes: undocumented immigrants – rapists and murders– are pouring through the nation's borders... Blacks, Mexicans and Muslins are taking over neighborhoods and schools; violent gangs are roaming the streets. Racist comments against President Obama occur without apology. Hate groups target women, and persons of color. Leaders embrace a survival of the fittest ideology, reject mainstream science and contend that human-caused climate change is a hoax (Giroux 2016c, p. 73).

The dividing line between private troubles and private lives and public issues has disappeared. Surveillance cameras are everywhere. There is no privacy. There is no e-mail or telephone conversation that cannot be made public. Life in the private sphere has become a public nightmare. People are trapped in a never-ending nightmare of violent world events, unrest, war, suicide bombings, drone attacks, mass murders, from Palestine to Afghanistan, Israel to Iraq, Paris to Istanbul, Aleppo to Seoul. The world has gone mad. Paranoia is rampant. Conspiracy theories focus on radical Islamic terrorists (ISIS/Al-Qaeda) who are threatening our borders, invading our communities and murdering our community members. Politicians are no help. And mothers have to explain to their young daughters how a man known for groping women was just elected

President of the United States, the man who will end abortion rights, deport millions of immigrants and go after ISIS-controlled oil fields in Iraq and "bomb the s– out of 'em."

Henry Giroux reminds us that America is at war with itself, indeed the world is at war with itself (Giroux 2016c). Multiple wars: the war on democratic ideals, the war on dissent, the war on youth, on women, on minorities, on healthcare, the environment, the criminalization of social problems, the militarization of everyday life. The moral and ethical foundations of our democracy are under assault. The politics may be local, but the power is global, the fear is visceral. We are global citizens trapped in a world we neither created nor want any part of.

Democratic public life is under siege. A culture of fear and paranoia spreads around the world. Crony capitalism reigns. Conservative politicians tied to global capitalism advocate free markets defined by the languages of commercialism. Neoliberals contend that what is good for the economy is good for democracy. The gap between rich and poor widens. Social injustices extending from "class oppression to racial violence to the ongoing destruction of public life and the environment" have become commonplace (Giroux 2003).

We live in a new garrison state. Since September 11, 2001, America's public spaces have become increasingly militarized (Bratich 2017). Armed guards and openly visible security cameras are everywhere, in airports and pedestrian malls, outside hospitals and schools, even on college campuses. President Trump is poised to authorize war tribunals, water boarding and detention camps for suspected terrorists. Civil liberties are disappearing. Racial profiling operates behind the guise of protecting national security. A multi-level civil-defense alarm system remains in place. Soon, in response to perceived threats from terrorists (Islamic) there will be calls for a national curriculum. This is already happening in the United Kingdom. It is being used to promote fundamental national values and reassert a more pure UK identity (Brexit) (Stronach 2017).

Public unions, education and civic, participatory social science are in jeopardy. Academics and pacifists critical of the public order under President Trump are branded traitors or cry babies. Critical qualitative, interpretive research will be stifled by pro-Trump federal administrators who define what constitutes acceptable science. Right-wing politicians stifle criticism while implementing a "resurgent racism… [involving] punitive attacks on the intellectuals, the poor, urban youth, and people of color" (Giroux 2000a, p. 132; 2016c, p. 221). A new website, *Professor Watch list*, a project of *Turning Point USA*, targets "Leftist professors who advance a radical agenda in lecture halls" (Mele 2016).[2]

***

Pedagogies of oppression

In 2015 almost 1,200 people, mostly minorities, were killed by US police, the majority of whom were "people of color." Refusing to accept this fact, the ultraright Breitbart news service alleged that more blacks killed blacks than the police.[3]

> Because the ugly truth behind #BlackLivesMatter is that black people kill-ing other black people does nothing to advance its political power in the same way that one white cop killing a black criminal can. Despite the media's overindulgence on white cops killing blacks, there is still a far-larger amount of black bodies being sent to morgues by black killers. Here's five devastating facts, liberals can't deny, that prove it.[4]
>
> (Hudson 2015)[5]

Two weeks after the Charleston Church massacre of nine Blacks, Breitbart News ran an article talking about how people should proudly fly the Confederate flag.[6]

We live in dark and bitter times (see Hall and Goehl 2016; Pitt 2016; Good-man 2016; Giroux 2016a, 2016b; Jay 2016). The election of Trump is part of a world-wide phenomenon, a global political movement framed by violent racist right-wing, anti-democratic conservative authoritarian ideologies: Marine Pen's populist National Front in France, Greece's Golden Dawn politics party, Zhirinovsky's Liberal Democratic Party of Russia (Giroux 2016c, p. 61).

Consider these remarks of Trump on race in America:

> Mexicans are rapists, drug dealers and murderers.
> We need a federal registry of all Muslims living in the United States.
> Laziness is a trait in blacks.
> Illegal immigrants will be given Obama Care and free college tuition but nothing has been mentioned about our VETERANS.
> Let's take a closer look at that birth certificate. @BarackObama was described in 2003 as being "born in Kenya."

***

In the 2016 U.S. Presidential election tens of millions of Americans voted for a policy platform that included:

> profiling Muslims; expelling millions of unauthorized immigrants; building Donald Trump's wall along the U.S.-Mexico border; supporting faith-based institutions; opposing the Common Core; open opposition to planned parenthood and marriage and legal protection for gay and transgender people; transferring all federally controlled lands to states; treating pornography as public health crisis while making no such des-ignation for guns; referring to coal as a "clean" energy source; repealing the Affordable Health Care Act of 2010; opposing measures to lower global warming.
>
> (Porter 2016, p. B1, B 3; also Republican Party 2016)

Richard Rorty predicted this outcome in 1998, and railed against another demagogue, Pat Buchanan, who in 1991 talked about building a wall at the Mexican border (Senior 2016). While a functionally meaningless messaging document, the Republican platform is a signal of where Republicans, and the international neo-liberal conservative movements, are at the present time. We are trapped in deep divisions of race, gender, sexual orientation, class, religion, immigration and education. These divisions will manifest themselves in conflicts and anxiety long after the 2016 U.S. election dust-up has settled (Anderson 2016).

America not at war with itself[7]

We need a dignified politics that is open to the possibilities of nonviolent ways of living (Giroux 2016c, p. 219). We need a community centered democracy that promotes civic literacy, and encourages alignments between protest movements led by youth, women, Latinos, Muslims, LGBT persons, the poor, perhaps modeled after the Black Lives Matter movement. Now, more than ever we need reasons to believe the citizens can reclaim their voice in the public sphere, where they can speak out, protest, express their outrage and voice their utopian dreams of peace and justice.

The tools of critical pedagogy are of great importance. We must use our analytical skills to imagine more equitable and just societies, while shaping democratic ideals, and inspiring civic courage (Giroux 2016c, p. 222). Any global system that inflicts violence on young people cannot be supported. We need a public pedagogy that emphasizes an ethics of trust, compassion, care and solidarity. We need to fight off despair, self-pity and fear. We must model creative resistance.

Young people cannot inherit a future marked by intimidation, militarism and suicide bombers. We cannot give them a world where human rights, and social justice have been emptied of substantive meaning (Giroux 2016c, p. 223). We must work to imagine better futures, and new ways of sustainable living in "one world in which many worlds fit" as the Zapatista of Mexico envision it (Giroux 2016c, p. 223). We must forge a banner of solidarity for real ideological and structural change. This would be a discourse willing to unite the fragmented Left around the call for a resurgent insurrectional democracy. The good news is that the type of hateful ideology and harsh economic politics that Trump embraces cannot support a democratic society at all (Giroux 2016c, p. 58).

We must encourage the development of critical historical memories. We must mobilize against the violence of organized forgetting. We must stop the willful erasure and distortion of radical discourses which encourage critical thinking (Giroux 2014, p. 26). We must mobilize students to be critically engaged historical agents, attentive to important social issues. Critical pedagogy teaches students how to critique a social order, like the Tuscon school district that banned Paulo Freire's Pedagogy of the Oppressed and dismantled its Mexican

American/Studies Program (Giroux 2016c, p. 235). Students must be taught that inquiry is always about power, about what is knowledge, about what is truth, that is inquiry is always a form of moral intervention in the service of liberation. We cannot separate theories, values, inquiry from moral and ethical and political being (Giroux 2016c, p. 237). The challenge is to inspire people to become critical inquirers and critically engaged citizens willing to fight for democracy, liberation and solidarity (Giroux 2016c, p. 241).

What kind of society allows economic injustice, and environmental violence towards its children and persons of color? What kind of society punishes transgender students? What kind of society elects as president a man who mocks the disabled? We seek students and researchers who embrace a politics of emancipation. We seek leaders who will help us enact a pedagogy of educated hope. We need teachers who as public intellectuals will teach students how to be critical historical agents. We need students who are not afraid to raise their voices in solidarity with those who struggle to translate personal troubles into public issues (Giroux 2016c, p. 248; Mills 1959).

As the public collapses into the private, the private and the personal becomes the site of the political. Individual fate and personal troubles are now a matter of individual responsibility. They are no longer a problem for the common good (Giroux 2016c, pp. 225, 230). The civic cultures that make social responsibility and community central to democratic public life are undermined. If we are lucky, we become self-isolated automatons, linked to the world by our mobile devices, sharing selfies, chattering away on Facebook, updating our blogs on a daily basis.

America is at war with itself. Critical pedagogy and critical inquiry have an essential role in helping us fight back (Giroux 2016c, p. 55). We must defend the public sphere. We need history lessons, remembering moments in the past when resistance was required – the labor strikes of 1930s; the civil rights movement of the 1950s and 1960s; the anti-war new left movement of the 1960s; the women's liberation movement of the 1960s and 1970s; the LGBT rights movement of the 1960s and 1970s; the contemporary Black Lives Matter movement. We need to reclaim a radical democratic imagination which sees democracy as a never-ending struggle. We need an ongoing language of critique, of hope, a broad-based democratic liberation movement with many rhizomatic roots, trunks, and branches (Giroux 2016c, p. 267). We need a new *geography of hope* to help our suffering souls in these times of spiritual crisis, hate crimes, swastikas, and racial intolerance (Stegner 1980a).

***

These are the troubled spaces that radical performance autoethnography must enter. The interpretive methods, democratic politics and feminist, communitarian ethics of performance (auto)ethnography offer progressives a series of tools for countering reactionary political discourse. At stake is an "insurgent cultural politics" (Giroux 2000a, p. 127) that challenges neofascist state apparatuses. This cultural politics encourages a critical race consciousness that flourishes within the free and open spaces of a "vibrant democratic public culture and society" (Giroux 2000a, p. 127). But more is involved, for performance autoethnography is more than a tool of liberation. It is a way of being moral and political in the world. Performance autoethnography is moral discourse. In the discursive spaces of performativity there is no distance between the performance and the politics that the performance enacts. The two are intertwined, each nourishing the other, opposite sides of the same coin, one and the same thing.

Within the spaces of this new performative cultural politics a radical democratic imagination redefines the concept of civic participation and public citizenship.[8] This imagination turns the personal into the political. Struggle, resistance and dialogue are key features of its pedagogy. The rights of democratic citizenship are extended to all segments of public and private life, from the political to the economic, from the cultural to the personal. This pedagogy seeks to regulate market and economic relations in the name of social justice and environmental causes.

A genuine democracy requires hope, dissent and criticism. Performance (auto)ethnography is a strategic means to these political ends. Democratic hope resists organized forgetting. It questions, challenges, refuses commodification, and inspires resistance (Giroux 2014, pp. 224, 226). Democratic hope is subversive, defiant. It places the voices of the oppressed at the center of inquiry. It exposes corruption, inspires activism, critiques social policy. Hope has to be nurtured, educated, inspired, modeled, performed, praised. Democratic hope makes power visible and interrogates the tructuress that prop it (Giroux 2014, p. 227).

This project celebrates the autoethnographer as a public intellectual who produces and engages in meaningful cultural criticism. Like McLaren's (1997) postmodern flaneur, the performance autoethnographer critically inspects everyday urban life under late capitalism. Through resistance texts, critical ethnography, forum theatre and ethnotheatre, the performance autoethnographer offers moral tales that help men and women endure and prevail in the frightening environment of this new century. It is our obligation to future generations – we must make our voices heard. When we do so, we speak and perform as critical autoethnographers. We align our selves with Schechner, Conquergood, Freire, Madison, Boal, Saldana, we use performance and theatre to awaken and change the world.

The critical imagination and pedagogies of hope

The need for a civic, participatory social science – a critical ethnography that moves back and forth among biography, history and politics – has never been greater. Such a performative discourse, grounded in the sociological and ethnographic imagination (Mills 1959), can help individuals to grasp how the fascist structures of the neoliberal world order, the new global empire, relate to one another. These discourses help to locate this new form of fascism within recent world history, including its previous European and American formations during and after World War II.

Following C. Wright Mills (1959, p. 7), the critical autoethnographer seeks to identify the varieties of men, women and children that prevail in this current historical moment, including refugees, war widows and orphans, Afghan tribal lords, filthy-rich CEOs, homeless persons, Texas politicians, Palestinian refugees, militant Islamics, right-wing Christians, white supremacists, skinheads, bisexuals, transgendered persons, gays and lesbians, African American feminists, Latinos, First Nations persons and "twice-hyphenated" Americans (from Asian-American-Japanese to Hispanic-American-Bolivians). The autoethnographer connects these varieties of personhood to the experiences of racism, sexism, violence, oppression and injustice. The critical imagination moves dramatically back and forth between the personal troubles experienced under global crony capitalism and public responses to terrorism, violence and private troubles in the private sphere.

Today, however, as argued above and as Bauman (1999, p. 4) and Giroux (2016c, p. 221) have observed, the connections between the public and the private are being dismantled. This means that in neoliberal societies such as the United States it is becoming increasingly more difficult, except under the most superficial of conditions, to translate private troubles into public issues. Indeed, today public issues trump private troubles. For example, there was a wide-scale social response to the loss of lives after the attacks of 9/11, from newspaper stories to the outpouring of financial aid. But this humane response was quickly enveloped in patriotic flag-waving and the display of the American flag on automobiles, on homes and in schoolrooms across the country. The loss of lives was used as an excuse for gearing up the American war machine.

When there is a disconnect between the public and the private, notions of the good society and the public good are eroded or turned into political capital. The pursuit of private satisfaction and the consumption of consumer goods become ends as well as goals for the good life. Human lives fall by the wayside.

The critical imagination is radically democratic, pedagogical and interventionist. To build on arguments made by Freire (1998, p. 91), this imagination dialogically inserts itself into the world, provoking conflict, curiosity, criticism and reflection. It advocates a "rigorous 'ethical grounding' in a commitment to combat 'racial, sexual and class discrimination'" (Arónowitz 1998, p. 12). It aspires to radical social change in such areas as "economics, human relations, property, the right to employment, to land, to education, and to health" (Freire 1998, p. 99). Its ethics challenge the ethics of the marketplace; it seeks utopian transformations committed to radical democratic ideals.

These ideals embrace a democratic-socialist-feminist agenda. This agenda queers straight heterosexual democracy (Butler 1997). It is always relational, temporary and historically specific. It is founded on its own conditions of hope and impossibility (Fraser 1993). This agenda asserts capitalism's fundamental incompatibility with democracy while thinking its way into a model of critical citizenship that attempts to unthink whiteness and the cultural logics of white supremacy (Roediger 2002). It seeks a revolutionary multiculturalism that is grounded in relentless resistance to the structures of neoliberalism. It critiques the ways in which the media are used to manufacture consent (Chomsky 1996). It sets as its goal transformations of global capital, so that individuals may begin to "truly live as liberated subjects of history" (McLaren 1997, p. 290).

A moral crisis

Indigenous discourse, as discussed in Chapter One, thickens the argument, for the central tensions in the world today go beyond the crises in capitalism and neoliberalism's version of democracy. Of course, as Cameron, Fast, Helferty and Lewis note "indigenous methodologies and paradigms have existed for a long time, managing to survive colonization, war, genocide, and a host of colonizer practices. Only recently has the academy taken an interest in them" (2016, p. 273).

The central crisis in the world today, as defined by a Red Pedagogy, is spiritual, "rooted in the increasingly virulent relationship between human beings and the rest of nature" (Grande 2000, p. 354). Smith (1999), writing as an indigenous Maori woman from New Zealand, discusses the concept of spirituality within indigenous discourse, giving added meaning to the crisis at hand:

> The essence of a person has a genealogy which could be traced back to an earth parent ... A human person does not stand alone, but shares with other animate ... beings relationships based on a shared "essence" of life ... [including] the significance of place, of land, of landscape, of other things in the universe ... Concepts of spirituality which Christianity attempted to destroy, and then to appropriate, and then to claim, are critical sites of resistance for indigenous peoples. The value, attitudes, concepts and language embedded in beliefs about spirituality represent... the clearest contrast and mark of difference between indigenous peoples and the West. It is one of the few parts of ourselves which the West cannot decipher, cannot understand and cannot control ... yet.
>
> (p. 74)

A respectful, radical performance pedagogy must honor these views of spirituality. It works to construct a vision of the person and the environment that is compatible with these principles. This pedagogy demands a politics of hope, of loving, of caring nonviolence grounded in inclusive moral and spiritual terms. Yet it will not do to simply fold radical indigenous discourse into critical theory and performance pedagogy. As Grande (2008), Kovach (2009), Smith (2012) and Rinehart (2017) note, key terms in critical theory like emancipation must be proactively fitted to the values of local indigenous communities. Terms like respect, mutuality and honor must become part of the researcher's moral fiber, not just scripts, lines to be read and performed (Rinehart 2017). By proactively framing participatory views of science, democracy and community, indigenous people can take control of their own fates and not be sidetracked by non-indigenous others' attempts to define their life situations (G. Smith 2000).

Performance autoethnography as a pedagogy of freedom

Within this framework, to extend Freire (1998) and elaborate Glass (2001, p. 17), performance autoethnography contributes to a conception of education and democracy as pedagogies of freedom. As praxis, performance auto-ethnography is a way of acting on the world in order to change it. Dialogic performances, enacting a performance-centered ethic, provide materials for critical reflection on radical democratic educational practices. In so doing, performance ethnography enacts a theory of selfhood and being. This is an ethical, relational and moral theory. The purpose of "the particular type of relationality we call research ought to be enhancing... moral agency moral discernment, critical consciousness, and a radical politics of resistance " (Christians 2002, p. 409; see also Lincoln 1995, p; 287),

As Freire (1998), Marx ([1888] 1983), Mead (1934), Dewey ([1922] 1930) and Glass (2001) have observed, praxis is a defining feature of human life and a "necessary condition of freedom" (Glass 2001, p. 16). Human nature is expressed through intentional, meaningful conduct that is anchored in historically specific situations. The desire for freedom is basic. Freire reminds us that "there is no such thing is freedom without risk. It is not possible to live ethically without freedom" (1996, p. 250). Further, freedom must always accept limits, freedom is never solely a freedom, it is a duty, a responsibility (1998, p. 87).

People make history and culture through their performative acts, and these acts enable the "realization of freedom" (Glass 2001, p. 16), the opening up of choices, often in the face of oppression and resistance. Freedom is never given. Race, class and gender oppressions limit the real and perceived degrees of freedom that individuals in any given instance. Freedom is always contingent – contingent on a pledge to struggle and resist, and contingent on individuals' willingness to accept the consequences of their actions. The practice of democratic freedom requires a condition of permanent struggle, the promise to transform the world in the name of freedom itself.

A position of militant nonviolence is paramount. The struggle for freedom and for democracy must honor human life. As Glass (2001) writes, the "certitude of death demands that those who take life possess a level of certitude... that is perhaps beyond reach, especially in the case of death on the scale of war" (p. 23). Violence is not justified. A commitment to nonviolence structures struggles of liberation, and these struggles always occur within contested terrains. In turn, the permanent struggle for freedom and liberation gives to "all equally the power to seek self-determined hopes and dreams" (p. 23). Performance autoethnography performs these struggles and becomes, in the process, the practice of freedom itself.

Indeed, performance autoethnography enters the service of freedom by showing how, in concrete situations, persons produce history and culture, "even as history and culture produce them" (Glass 2001 p. 17). Performance texts provide the grounds for liberation practice by opening up concrete situations that are transformed through acts of resistance. In this way, performance autoethnography, like Boal's Theatre of the Oppressed, and Saldana's ethnotheatre advance the causes of liberation.

Hope, love, joy, pedagogy and the critical imagination

As an interventionist ideology, the critical imagination is hopeful of change. It seeks and promotes an ideology of hope that challenges and confronts hopelessness (Freire [1992] 1999, p. 8). It understands that hope, like freedom, is an "ontological need" (Freire [1992] 1999:8). Hope is the desire to dream, the desire to change, the desire to improve human existence. As Freire ([1992] 1999) says, hopelessness is "but hope that has lost its bearings" (p. 8).

Hope is ethical. Hope is moral. Hope is peaceful and nonviolent. Hope is joyful. Hope seeks the truth of life's sufferings. Hope gives meaning to the struggles to change the world. Hope is grounded in concrete performative practices, in struggles and interventions that espouse the sacred values of love, care, community, trust, and well-being (Freire [1992] 1999, p. 9). Hope, as a form of pedagogy, confronts and interrogates cynicism, the belief that change is not possible or is too costly. Hope works from hopelessness to rage to love. Hope articulates a progressive politics that rejects "conservative, neoliberal postmodernity" (Freire [1992] 1999, p. 10). Hope rejects terrorism. Hope rejects the claim that peace must come at the cost of war. Hope rejects the re-birth of the Neo-Nazi-Fascist threat (1996, pp. 187–188), the threat which does not tolerate doubt, loves authoritarianism, exploits difference, celebrates whiteness, represses free speech and uses violence and terror to manipulate public opinion.

The pedagogies of hope enable persons to develop their own languages of resistance, respect and of joy. This politics of possibility imagines utopian futures, new worlds, and opposes the racist "authoritarian gobbledygook" of the ruling class (Freire 1998, p. 69). This is a hope that inspires joy, sharing, collaboration, the belief that something new and empowering can be produced together. But hope, while always unfinished, can be smashed, turned into hopelessness, despair. A pedagogy of love and joy allows me to fight off despair, to maintain a belief in Paulo's utopia of hope (Darder 2002, p. 88). This is a love for the world and the other "from which a revolutionary praxis of dialogue and solidarity emerges" (Darder 2002, p. 89). A pedagogy of love frames a deep "commitment to social justice and economic democracy, a revolutionary commitment to release our humanity from the powerful death grip of crony capitalist domination" (Darder 2002, p. 89). Without hope we are nothing.

The critical democratic imagination is pedagogical in four ways. First, as a form of instruction, it helps persons think critically, historically, and sociologically. Second, as critical pedagogy, it exposes the pedagogies of oppression that produce and reproduce oppression and injustice (see Freire 2000, p. 54). Third, it contributes to an ethical self-consciousness that is critical and reflexive. It gives people a language and a set of pedagogical practices that turn oppression into freedom, despair into hope, hatred into love, doubt into trust. Fourth, in turn, this self-consciousness shapes a critical racial self-awareness. This awareness contributes to utopian dreams of racial equality and racial justice.

For persons who have previously lost their way in this complex world, using this imagination is akin to being "suddenly awakened in a house with which they had only supposed themselves to be familiar" (Mills 1959, p. 8). They now feel that they can provide themselves with critical understandings that undermine and challenge "older decisions that once appeared sound" (Mills 1959, p. 8). Their critical imagination enlivened, such persons "acquire a new way of thinking.... in a world by their reflection and their sensibility, they realize the cultural meaning of the social sciences" (Mills 1959, p. 8). They realize how to make and perform changes in their own lives, to become active agents in shaping the history that shapes them.

Recall how Boal's Theatre of The Oppressed puts Freire's Pedagogy of The Oppressed into action. His forum theatre transforms spectator-actors into agents who confront history by acting out moments of oppression and violence. The performance of such stories empowers persons and helps them experience a kind of dignity that had previously been denied. This form of political theatre redresses past misdeeds while criticizing specific institutional patterns of discrimination. In so doing, it maps pathways of praxis that help create a progressive citizenship. The critical, autoethnographic imagination becomes the vehicle for helping persons realize a politics of possibility.

If critical performance autoethnography is to the join the "fight against neo-liberal authoritarianism in the United States its practioners will need to connect private troubles to public issues, and broader structural and systemic problems within neo-liberalism" (Giroux 2016c, p. 262). As discussed in Chapter Four, the dialogical, dramaturgical methods of playacting (Norris 2009), forum theatre, ethnodrama and performance autoethnography are well suited to confront the intersection between private troubles and public issues. Social theatre helps persons remember, forget and to perform actions which heal, inspire action and create community. Painful experience is dramatically transformed into social critique (Thompson and Schechner 2004, pp. 14–15). Such performances use theatre to reveal sites for change and activism, encouraging persons to ask "What can I do now about this social injustice?"

A performative critical inquiry

I have attempted to retheorize the grounds of critical autoethnography, rede-fining the political and the cultural in performative and pedagogical terms. Diawara' twenty-year-old argument (1996) remains relevant. The racialized black public sphere "needs both an economic base for young people and defi-nitions and discussions of the culture it is producing daily" (p. 306).[9] Diawara suggests that these discussions will take place from within a model that uses performance "as a mode of interpolating people in the black cultural sphere, positioning the people of the black good life society as its 'ideal readers'" (p. 306). For Diawara the cultural is always performative and pedagogical, and hence always political, and too frequently racist and sexist. The performative practices that enact pedagogy are the very practices that bring meaning and power into play. They shape the "performative character ... of identity" (p. 302) as it is socially constructed.

History is the unwritten word in Diawara's argument. Today the cultures of predatory capitalism hover like dark shadows over the pedagogical and performative features of a progressive performance studies. To repeat, Americans live under the Orwellian structures of a government whose motto seems to be "Perpetual war brings perpetual peace." This self-same government brings new meanings to fascism. In fashioning free-market, state-supported millennial capitalism, neoliberalism makes the corporate marketplace primary (Comaroff and Comaroff 2001, p. 7). It encourages consumption by redefining citizens as consumers and equating freedom with the choice to consume.

The concepts of multiple democratic public spheres, civic space, citizenship and democratic discourse disappear in the pedagogical practices and spaces of millennial capitalism. In these deregulated corporate spaces a dismantling of the structures of public education, welfare, housing and affirmative action occurs. Corporate and (ad)venture capitalists define the new public morality, some call it the art of the deal. They know no shame. This is a racist Darwinian morality, celebrating the survival of the fittest. It refuses any commitment to the values of environmentalism, social justice, nonviolence, grassroots democracy, feminism, affirmative action and the rights of indigenous persons everywhere.

These are the situations a performative interpretive studies confronts. People in Diawara's racialized black public sphere face almost insurmountable odds as they attempt to fashion democratic ideologies and identities in these violent racist spaces.

Of course, culture and power are experienced in the pedagogical performances that occur in these spaces. Viewed thus, culture *is* public pedagogy, a set of recurring interpretive practices that connect ethics, power and politics (Giroux 2000b, p. 25). Obviously, cultural performances cannot be separated from power, politics or identity. In cultural performances, identities are forged and felt, agency is negotiated, citizenship rights are enacted and the ideologies surrounding nation, civic culture, race, class, gender and sexual orientation are confronted.

Power and culture are opposite sides of the same coin. The conditions under which they are joined and connected are constantly changing. Power (like culture) is always local, contextual and performative, linking ideologies, representations, identities, meanings, texts and contexts to "existing social formations [and] specific relations of power" (Giroux 2000b, p. 169).

Pedagogy-as-performance is central "to the theory and practice of ... radical cultural politics" (Giroux 2000b, pp. 158–159). The performative side of culture shows how the pedagogical is always political. That is, through their

performances persons represent, disrupt, interpret, "engage and transform...
the ideological and material circumstances that shape their lives" (Giroux
2000b, p. 166).

Radical cultural critique and radical social change occur at the intersection of
the pedagogical, the performative, and the political. In these sites, in these
moments Spry's utopian performatives are made visible. Repression occurs in
the same sites. In the spring, summer and fall of 2002 and continuing into 2003,
the Bush administration placed the United States in a permanent state of war
against terrorism, a war that extends to the present day. Many on the left were
critical, fearing the rapid development of a neofascist state. Supporters of the
administration argued that Bush's critics were being unpatriotic; they said that
in a time of war, it is every citizen's duty to support the president. When those
in power attempt to shut down the performances of those who question their
power, they are engaging in power politics. Through these articulations, they
are attempting to govern public culture, to set the terms around which discourse
on war, peace and terrorism will occur.

Fast forward to December 2016. President-elect Trump vows to implement a
new war on terrorism. By threatening to deport illegal Mexican immigrants, he
places millions of families and their children under permanent threat of being
removed from their homes and communities. Muslim families are told to leave
the U.S. and President Trump says he will bring back water boarding as a form
of torture for eliciting confessions from alleged terrorists.

What to make of this. What kind of country do we life in? Is this what we
teach our students, that torture is a valid form of conduct by our government
officials. Critique and criticism begin in those places where violence and official
torture intersect, those places "where people actually live their lives, where
meaning is produced... and contested" (Giroux 2000b, p. 170). These meanings
are filtered through the systems of representation that are produced by the
media. Cultural criticism treats these texts as forms of public pedagogy (Garoian
and Gaudelius 2008). They shape and give meaning to lived experience within
specific historical moments. The autoethnographer works back and forth
between the contexts and situations of lived experience and the representations
of those experiences. The critical ethnographer criticizes the pedagogical structures of capitalism, using radical pedagogy to undermine the very authority of
capitalism's central ideological arguments.

In an article published in late autumn 2002, which could gave been written
yesterday, Rorty addresses Washington's appetite for war, just change the
names of the country and the dictator:

> On some days Washington tells us that we need to go after Iraq for reasons
> that were present before 9/11, and are quite independent of that event. On
> others we are told that the plan to depose Saddam Hussein is part of "the
> war on terrorism" that began on 9/11. This rapid alteration produces a
> blur. This blur helps conceal the fact that neither of the two arguments for
> attacking Iraq has been laid out in terms that would justify the sort of

resolution (the equivalent of a War Powers Act ...) that a spineless Congress was, as of this writing, about to pass.

(p. 11)

Critically interrogating the Bush administration's arguments, Rorty exposes the contradictions in its ideological position. This unraveling of official pedagogy creates the space for protest that connects the personal and the political in acts of resistance. *New York Times* columnist Maureen Dowd wrote this commentary on political discourse in Washington just after the House and Senate voted to give the president war powers in Iraq:

> This has always been the place where people say the opposite of what they mean. But last week the Capital soared to ominous new Orwellian heights ... Mr. Bush said he needed Congressional support to win at the U.N., but he wants to fail at the U.N. so he can install his own MacArthur as viceroy of Iraq ... The Democrats were desperate to put the war behind them, so they put it front of them ... Senator Hillary Rodham Clinton voted to let the president use force in Iraq because she didn't want the president to use force in Iraq ... The C.I.A. says Saddam will use his nasty weapons against us only if he thinks he has nothing to lose. So the White House leaks its plans about the occupation of Iraq, leaving Saddam nothing to lose.[10]

Extending Tyler (1986), Diawara (1996) and Conquergood (1998), I have suggested that the discourses of postmodern (auto)ethnography provide a framework against which all other forms of writing about the politics of the popular under the regimes of global capitalism are judged. Within this model, a performative, pedagogical critical cultural studies becomes autoethnographic. The autoethnographer becomes a version of McLaren's (1997) reflexive flaneur/flaneuse and Kincheloe's (2001) critical *bricoleur*, the "primordial ethnographer" who lives "within postmodern, postorganized, late capitalist culture" (McLaren 1997:144) and functions as a critical theorist, an urban ethnographer, an ethnographic agent, a Marxist social theorist (see McLaren 1997, pp. 164, 167; 2001, pp. 121–122).

Listen to McLaren (1997):

> Thursday, May 9, 1996, Florianopolis, Brazil. Each time I give a speech here I realize how partial my knowledge is compared to the students or the workers. Today during my visit with Father Wilson, I was reminded of the terrible beauty among the people in the *favela* ... Father Wilson made me a wonderful fish stew. The tires of his car have recently been slashed, the windows broken ... Father Wilson is not popular with the *favela* drug dealers.

(p. 172)

The radical performance (auto)ethnographer functions as a cultural critic, a version of the modern antihero, who, as Spender (1984) describes, "reflect[s] an extreme external situation through his own extremity." The performance ethnographer's autoethnography is like the antihero's story, which "becomes diagnosis, not just of himself, but of a phase of history" (p. ix). Because the critical autoethnographer is a reflexive flaneur/flaneuse or *bricoleur,* his or her conduct is justified; the story he or she tells is no longer just one individual's case history or life story. Within the context of history, the autoethnography becomes the "dial of the instrument that records the effects of a particular stage of civilization upon a civilized individual" (Spender 1984, p. ix). The autoethnography is both dial and instrument. The autoethnographer functions as a universal singular, a single instance of a more universal social experience (Sartre 1981, p. ix) Every person is like every other person, but like no other person. The autoethnographer inscribes the experiences of a historical moment, universalizing these experiences in their singular effects on a particular life.

Using a critical imagination, the autoethnographer is theoretically informed in poststructural and postmodern ways. He or she has a commitment to connect critical ethnography to issues surrounding cultural policy, cultural politics, and procedural policy work (Willis and Trondman 2000, pp. 10–11). The commitment, as McLaren (1997) argues, is to a theory of praxis that is purposeful, "guided by critical reflection and a commitment to revolutionary praxis" (p. 170). This commitment involves a rejection of the historical and cultural logics and narratives that exclude those who have previously been marginalized. This is a reflexive, performative ethnography. It privileges multiple subject positions, questions its own authority, and doubts those narratives that privilege one set of historical processes and sequences over another (p. 168).

Critical performance pedagogy

A commitment to performance pedagogy and critical race theory gives critical inquiry studies a valuable lever for militant, utopian cultural criticism. In his book *Impure Acts* (2000a), Giroux calls for a practical, performative view of pedagogy, politics and cultural studies. He seeks an interdisciplinary project that would enable theorists and educators to form a progressive alliance "connected to a broader notion of cultural politics designed to further racial, economic, and political democracy" (p. 128). This project anchors itself in the worlds of pain and lived experience and is accountable to these worlds. It enacts an ethic of respect and hope.

Critical race theory

Such a project embraces critical race theory and engages a militant utopianism, a provisional Marxism without guarantees, a cultural studies that is anticipatory, and interventionist. It does not back away from the contemporary world in its multiple global versions, including the West, the Third World, the

North, the South, the moral, political and geographic spaces occupied by First Nation and Fourth World persons, persons in marginal, or liminal, positions (Ladson-Billings 2000, p. 263; Ladson-Billings and Donner 2005; Donnor and Ladson-Billings 2017). Rather, it strategically engages this world in those liminal spaces where lives are bent and changed by the repressive structures of neo-liberal conservatism in all its *alt. right* forms. This project pays particular attention to the dramatic increases around the world in domestic violence, rape, child abuse and violence directed toward persons of color (Comaroff and Comaroff 2001, pp. 1–2; Giroux 2016b).

As Jamel Donnor and Gloria Ladson-Billings (2017) note, critical race theory (CRT) appeared in legal journals and texts more than 20 years ago. Its genealogy is one of both scholarship and activism. Extending critical legal theory, critical race theory theorizes life in these liminal spaces, offering "pragmatic strategies for material and social transformation" (Ladson-Billings 2000, p. 264). Critical race theory assumes that racism and white supremacy are the norms in U.S. society. Critical race scholars use performative, storytelling autoethnographic methods to uncover the ways in which racism operates in daily life. Critical race theory challenges those neoliberals who argue that civil rights have been attained for persons of color. It also challenges those who argue that the civil rights crusade is a long, slow struggle (Ladson-Billings 2000, p. 264). Critical race theorists argue that the problem of racism requires radical social change, and that neoliberalism and liberalism lack the mechanisms and imaginations to achieve such change (Ladson-Billings 2000, p; 264).

Critical race theorists contend that whites have been the main beneficiaries of civil rights legislation. Strategically, critical race theory examines the ways in which race is performed, including the cultural logics and performative acts that inscribe and create whiteness and nonwhiteness. In an age of globalization and diasporic, postnational identities, the color line should no longer be an issue, but, sadly, it is.

CRT is committed to social justice and a revolutionary habitus. CRT is a set of theories – not one unified theory. These theories rely on intersectionality (i.e., the nexus of race, gender, class, etc.), a critique of liberalism, the use of critical social science, a combination of structural and post-structural analysis, the denial of neutrality in scholarship, and the incorporation of storytelling or, more precisely, "counternarratives" to speak back against dominant discourses. Donnor and Ladson-Billings use counternarratives as a qualitative research strategy in this era which they term "the postracial imaginary."

They direct our focus to the meaning of the "call," those epiphanic moments when people of color are reminded that they are locked into a hierarchical racial structure. Critical race theorists experiment with multiple interpretive strategies, ranging from storytelling to autoethnography, case studies, textual and narrative analyses, traditional fieldwork and, most important, collaborative, action-based inquiries and studies of race, gender, law, education and racial oppression in daily life. Inquiry for social justice is the goal.

CRT scholars take observations (of classrooms, of interactions, of communities, etc.) and close readings (of journals, of letters, of official documents, etc.) and provide muted and missing voices that ask questions and propose alternative explanations. The use of a CRT lens is not meant to twist or distort reality. Rather, CRT is meant to bring an alternative perspective to racialized subjects so that voices on the social margins are amplified. Critical race theory is not about special pleadings or race baiting, as some may argue. It is also not the "hot," "new" or "sexy" paradigm that makes a scholar seem more cutting edge or avant-garde. It is about the serious business of permanent and systemic racism that ultimately diminishes the democratic project. It is about dispelling notions of color-blindness and postracial imaginings so that we can better understand and remedy the disparities that are prevalent in our society. It is one of the tools we can use to assert that race still matters.

For justice to happen, the academy must change; it must embrace the principles of decolonization. A reconstructed university will become a home for racialized others, a place where indigenous, liberating empowering pedagogies have become commonplace (Diversi and Moreira 2009).

Participatory, performance action inquiry

Drawing on the complex traditions embedded in participatory action research (PAR) as well as the critical turn in feminist discourse and the growing literature for and by indigenous peoples, critical performance pedagogy implements a commitment to participation and performance *with,* not *for,* community members (Smith 1999, 2012, Kemmis and McTaggart 2000; Fine et al. 2003; Fine 2003; Denzin & Lincoln 2017). Amplifying the work of Fine et al. (2003, p. 176–77) and Denzin & Lincoln (2017), this project builds on local knowledge and experience developed at the bottom of social hierarchies. Consistent with Smith's (1999, 2012) project, participatory, performance work honors and respects local knowledge, customs, and practices and incorporates those values and beliefs into participatory, performance action inquiry (Fine et al. 2003, p. 176).

Work in this participatory, activist performance tradition gives back to the community, "creating a legacy of inquiry, a process of change, and material resources to enable transformations in social practices" (Fine et al. 2003, p. 177). Through performance and participation, the scholar develops a "participatory mode of consciousness" (Bishop 1998, p. 208) and understanding.

This project works outward from the university and its classrooms, treating the spaces of the academy as critical public spheres, as sites of resistance and empowerment (Giroux 2000a, p. 134). Critical pedagogy resists the increasing commercialization and commodification of higher education. It contests the penetration of neoliberal values into research parks, classrooms and the curriculum. It is critical of institutional review boards that pass ever-more restrictive judgments on human subject research.

A commitment to critical pedagogy in the classroom can be an empowering, dialogic experience. The instructional spaces become sacred spaces. In them, students take risks and speak from the heart, using their own experiences as tools for forging critical race consciousness. The critical discourse created in this public sphere is then taken into other classrooms, into other pedagogical spaces, where a militant utopianism is imagined and experienced.

As a performative practice, this project interrogates and criticizes those cultural narratives that make victims responsible for the cultural and interpersonal violence they experience, thus blaming and revictimizing them. But performance narratives do more than celebrate the lives and struggles of persons who have lived through violence and abuse. They must always be directed back to the structures that shape and produce the violence in question. Pedagogically, the performative is political and focused on power. Performances are located within their historical moment, with attention given to the play of power and ideology. The performative becomes a way of critiquing the political, a way of analyzing how culture operates pedagogically to produce and reproduce victims.

Pedagogically, and ideologically, the performative becomes an act of doing, a dialogic way of being in the world, a way of grounding performances in the concrete situations of the present (Giroux 2000a, p. 135). The performative becomes a way of interrogating how "objects, discourses, and practices construct possibilities for and constraints on citizenship" (Nelson and Gaonkar 1996, p. 7; quoted in Giroux 2000a, p. 134). This stance connects the biographical and the personal to the pedagogical and the performative. It casts the cultural critic in the identity of a critical citizen, a person who collaborates with others in participatory action projects that enact militant democratic visions of public life, community and moral responsibility (Giroux 2000a, p. 141). This public intellectual practices critical performance pedagogy. As a concerned citizen, working with others, he or she takes positions on the critical issues of the day, understanding that there can be no genuine democracy without genuine opposition and criticism (Giroux 2000a, p. 136; see also Bourdieu 1999, p. 8).

In turn, radical democratic pedagogy requires citizens and citizen-scholars who are committed to taking risks, persons who are willing to act in situations where the outcomes cannot be predicted in advance. In such situations, a politics of new possibilities can be imagined and made to happen. Yet in these pedagogical spaces there are no leaders and followers; there are only coparticipants, persons working together to develop new lines of action, new stories, new narratives in a collaborative effort (Bishop 1998, p. 7). Participatory action research combines theory and practice in a participatory way. It presumes that knowledge generation is a collaborative process. "Each participant's diverse experiences and skills are critical to the outcome of the work" (p. 387). The goal of PAR is to solve concrete community problems by engaging community participants in the inquiry process.

Brydon-Miller and colleagues (2011) reviewed the several different traditions and histories of PAR, noting that much of the early development of PAR took place outside of traditional academic settings in the "south," or Third World. The history is dense, ranging from Paulo Freire's critical pedagogy project in Brazil, to Fals Borda's initiatives in Latin America, the Scandinavian folkschool movement, participatory action networks in Asia and Australia (Stephen Kemmis and Robin McTaggart), the global young people's initiatives of Michele Fine and associates, to the struggles of feminist, literacy, social justice, labor, civil rights and academic advocates. Traditionally, PAR challenges the distinction between theory and method. Strategies for collecting, analyzing, understanding and distributing empirical materials cannot be separated from epistemology, social theory or ethical stances. Inquire framed by PAR principles challenges and unsettles existing structures of power and privilege. It provides opportunities for those least often heard to share knowledge and wisdom. It encourages people to work together to bring about positive social change and to create more just social systems (Brydon-Miller et al. 2011, p. 396).

María Elena Torre, Brett G. Stout, Einat Manoff, and Michelle Fine (in Denzin & Lincoln 2017) move the PAR conversation forward into new spaces, the global movement for community-based critical participatory action research. This version of PAR references a form of public-oriented and coopera-tive science, like worker-owned cooperatives, community land trusts, municipal corporations and the expanding practice of participatory budget management. Critical PAR challenges the hegemony of elite interests as the dominant lens of science. It insists on social inquiry theorized, practiced and collectively owned by and for communities enduring state violence.

Torre and colleagues reflect on two cases of critical PAR, one in the South Bronx interrogating violent policing and the other in Miska in Israel/Palestine contesting the occupation (in Denzin & Lincoln 2017). They note that in moments of widening inequalities, waves of immigrants/refugees are landing on hostile shores. As this occurs, we witness more and aggressive state violence. Their version of critical participatory action research reveals the scars of state violence. The desire to tell and perform a different story is urgent. We need performances that reveal the limits and the terrors of neoliberalism in these times of violent inequality and social injustice.

Closer to home, Aisha Durham reminds is of what us at stake in these performances:

> i moved to digs park in 2000
> ten years from now i'll be
> owning a home
> letting my kids go in the back yard with their own things so
> they don't have to worry about when they go to the play-park,
> and pick up a hypodermic needle that might [be] AIDS infested
> you know
> i'm satisfied with just having a home.

With his recent poem, "Trump as strumpet: Three takes on the performance art of The Donald" Robert Rinehart (2017) brings us back to the current historical moment in America:

1.
Wrestlemania 23
2007: it was all about
faces and heels.
Trump strutted in,
one blonde on either arm,
the consummate
P. T. Barnum. No lions,
no tigers: no bears.
Just Trump,

3.
Trump, by Trump
"Losers, losers,
losers: they are
losers.
and you all know it!"

A reflexive critique of reflexive critical ethnography

Bourdieu and Wacquant (1992), Carspecken (1996), Kincheloe and McLaren (2000), Foley (2002), Willis (2000), Willis and Trondman (2000), Burawoy (1998, 2000), and Visweswaran (1994) all speak favorably of a global, reflexive, critical ethnography. The concept of reflexivity is critical to this discourse. Foley (2002), Marcus (1998) and Tedlock (2000) distinguish at least three types of reflexive ethnography. The first is a confessional reflexivity. The writer refuses to make a distinction between self and other, creating the space for autoethnography, for feminist, racial, indigenous and borderland standpoint theories and inquiries (Foley 2002, p. 475).

The second type of reflexivity is theoretical. It is associated with the work of Bourdieu and Wacquant (1992) and, to a lesser degree, that of Burawoy and Willis, all of whom advocate an epistemologically reflexive sociology and ethnography grounded in everyday cultural practices. The sociologist works back and forth between field experience and theory, cultivating a theoretical reflexivity that produces a detached, objective authoritative account of the world being studied (Foley 2002, p. 476). This form of reflexivity questions the value of autoethnography, suggesting that it is shallow textuality (Foley 2002, p. 475).

Burawoy (2000, p. 28) wants an extended, reflexive case method that takes observers into the field for long periods of time, across multiple sites. In the process, ethnographers learn how move back and forth between macro and micro processes while developing theory grounded in the data. Willis and Trondman (2000), influenced by Bourdieu, call for a "theoretically informed methodology for ethnography" (TIME). Also grounded in ethnographic data, this reflexive approach insists on recording lived experience while bringing that experience into a "productive but unfussy relation to 'theory' ... the criterion for relevance is maximum power in relation to the data for purposes of illumination" (p. 12). Such illuminations produce "aha" experiences and become the catalyst for "self-reflexivity and self-examination" (p. 14). The researcher maintains a self-reflexivity that emphasizes history and biography while producing objective ethnographic accounts that are as rigorous as possible (Willis 2000, pp. 113, 116).

Carspecken (1996) offers an elegant model for critical ethnography that deploys a critical, reflexive epistemology involving the collection of monologic data, dialogic data generation, the discovery of systems relations and using systems relations to explain findings. In Carspecken's model, truth is judged in terms of a set of regulative rules, including normative and intersubjective referenced claims that a statement must meet in order to be judged truthful.

Visweswaran (1994) anticipates a third type of reflexivity that complicates this picture by unsettling the notion of an objective, reflexive ethnographer. She criticizes the reflexive, normative ethnographic approach that presumes an observer and a subject with stable identities. She contrasts this stance with deconstructive ethnography, where the observer refuses to presume a stable identity for self or other. If Carspecken's reflexive ethnography questions its own authority, Visweswaran's deconstructive ethnography "forfeits its authority" (Kincheloe and McLaren 2000, p. 301). Deconstructive reflexivity is post-modern, confessional, critical, and intertextual.[11]

Foley (2002) can be read as extending Visweswaran. He calls himself a reflexive, realist, critical ethnographer. He critically reviews several complimentary reflexive practices: confessional, theoretical, intertextual and deconstructive. He situates his view of reflexive practices in Haraway and Harding's standpoint theories of science. Unlike Carspecken, Foley has little interest in developing a foundational scientific method for his ethnography. He states: "I am much more interested in expanding the notion of cultural critique by tapping into the genres of autobiography, new journalism, travel writing and fiction. Appropriating epistemologies and textual practices from these genres will help us create more public, useful ethnographic storytelling forms" (p. 486).

Still, Foley is contained within a scientific frame. He states that his science would "still subscribe to extensive, systematic fieldwork. It would speak from a historically situated standpoint" (p. 486). This science "would be highly reflexive ... I continue to use a quasi-scientific abductive epistemology, or what Paul Willis now calls an 'ethnographic imagination.'... But I am also trying to tap into introspection and emotion the way that autoethnographers and ethnic and indigenous scholars are" (p. 487). He is doing so because this "eclectic approach helps produce realist narratives that are much more accessible ... I feel a great need to communicate with ordinary people" (p. 487).

It is not enough to want to communicate with ordinary people. That is no longer an option. The critical performance ethnographer is committed to producing and performing texts that are grounded in and co-constructed in the politically and personally problematic worlds of everyday life. This ethnographer does not use words like *data*, or *abduction* or *objectivity*. These words carry the traces of science, objectivism and knowledge produced for disciplines, not everyday people. Bourdieu's theoretical reflexivity coupled with Willis's ethnographic imagination may produce detached accounts that satisfy the social theorist, but such accounts have little place in the pedagogical practices of performance ethnography.

McLaren's postmodern ethnographer does not fall into these linguistic traps. His critical, reflexive [auto] ethnographer is thoroughly embedded in the world of praxis and acts as an agent of change. His ethnographer holds to a radical pedagogy, a militant utopian vision that is missing from the larger group of scientifically oriented, contemporary, reflexive, critical ethnographers. McLaren's ethnography and pedagogy are the kinds that cultural studies needs today.

Reflexivity after the ontological turn

Maggie MacLure's (2017) "Thinking Reflexivity in the 'Ontological Turn" unsettles the discourse. She rightly notes that reflexivity has traditionally been a powerful concept for qualitative research. It has been used to challenge narrow definitions of "objectivity." It addresses the breach often posited between researchers, participants and knowledge. In conventional discourse reflexivity is offered as a method for addressing the so-called intrusive effects of the researcher on inquiry.

MacLure reconsiders the status of reflexivity from within the ontological or materialist "turn" in current theory. This "turn" previously discussed in Chapter Two, represents a loose collection of theoretical influences from Barad, Braidotti to Deleuze.[12] To quote MacLure "It prompts a radical rethinking of the methods and the conceptual architecture of qualitative inquiry itself. Can reflexivity be rethought within the new materialisms? Or, must we do away with the concept entirely, because it is irrevocably tainted through the excesses of the earlier traditions?"

Following Barad, MacLure proposes that inquirers are part of the research apparatus that engages the world and makes it visible: that is we are born from the "agential cut" that also produces the world and our relation to it. We are not outside observers of the world. We are part of the world (Barad 2003, p. 828). There is no exterior observational point from which reflexivity might be launched (Barad 2003, p. 828). Accordingly, we must ask, "What would an immanent reflexivity look like, and how would it work?" MacLure suggests that we might think of reflexivity as a kind of ontological or actual performance. It is perhaps akin to Spry's utopian performative, Madison's dialogic performative, or the performative-I turning back on itself? Or is, it something different?

The ontological turn blurs the distinction between what counts as reflexivity, what counts as performance and what counts as ontology. It embeds reflexivity in the performative moment. Reflexivity becomes an enactment that cannot be separated from agency; nor is it an attribute of observers, subjects or objects (Barad 2003, p. 826). It is an utopian performative, always lurking in the shadows of inquiry. It has no fixed presence, no certain protocol, no set of practices that can produce it. It is no where and somewhere, and everywhere at all times.

A posthumanist materialist account of reflexivity asks that we rethink what we mean by inquiry itself. A posthumanist materialist account of reflexivity forces us to return to the beginning, to begin a rethinking of canonical terms: observer, participation, inquiry, observation, voice. We might draw a Derridean-line of ~~erasure~~ through the word, and begin to think of it as a term that we inherited from an earlier moment. Or not?

The labor of reflexivity[13]

Whatever we do, reflexivity is a traveling concept, with a complex genealogy, moving across ontological, interpretive, ethnographic and epistemological spaces (Pillow 2015).[14] The term takes on different meanings in different historical moments and ethnographic formations, including those reviewed above. The recent autoethnographic turn introduces a collage of reflexive formations from the evocative to the performative, the queer to the feminist, the betweener to the generative autobiographical (Chawla 2007a; Moreira 2011; Alexander 2011; Berry and Clair 2011; Pillow 2015). In each instance the turn is away from reflexively writing about the other, to being the reflexive other who does the writing. We reflexively question the act of writing itself (Moreira 2011, p. 146). We reflexively write ourselves into those spaces were we imagine, perform and engage a practical progressive politics of difference (Moreira 2011, p. 146). We do not write about the other. We write about our selves in the spaces we share with the other (Madison 2011; Conquergood 1991).

At one level, reflexivity may be defined as turning back on experience and making experience an object of consciousness (Mead 1934, pp. 132–34; also Madison 2011, p. 131). I reflexively enter into my own experience. I turn back on myself and become an object to myself. I adjust my performance. I align my line of action with the action of the other who has become an object in my consciousness. I take her attitude toward me (Mead 1934, pp. 135–136, 225). She enters my experience and I experience her through her words, gestures, silences and mood. We experience ourselves as co-performative I's, caught up in dialogue, performance and interaction. We are drawn into a succession of co-performances in the present, a running current of intersecting moments, each of which implies a past, a present and a future. We catch glance of the performative-I only after it has occurred. We live in the present but are trapped in a past that unfolds as a new future. We are always one step ahead of our-selves and stumbling, one step back, in the horizon of a receding present (Mead 1934, p. 203).

Madison calls this the labor of reflexivity, asking what lingers after reflexivity has come and gone. What are reflexivity's lasting effects (2011, p. 129)? Is lasting effect even an appropriate question? The labor of reflexivity performs community, performs me, performs you. It creates the space where the ethnographer and the other (the subject/object of inquiry) come together in a dialogical space. Madison calls this, after Conquergood, a dialogical performative (Conquergood 1991; Madison 2011, p. 129; 2012, p. 145). The dialogical performative is a commitment to the reflexive interrogation of one's interpretive practices. But in the heat of performance, the performative-I takes over. Reflection recedes into the background. The performer becomes the performance, and loses herself in the moment. When she steps outside herself and reflects on what she is doing, she is creating another performative-I.

But wait when the person plays a part, or stages a performative-I she implicitly requests to be taken seriously (Goffman 1959, p. 17). The question arises, is she sincere, does she believe she is the person she presents herself as being, is she taken in by her performance? Or is she a cynic masquerading as someone she is not (Goffman 1959, pp. 17–18). Does it matter if she is sincere, or a cynic? The labor of reflexivity asks "To What End? is the performance being staged?" Of course it is staged, but what are the reflexive, ethical and moral consequences of the performance?

Madison illustrates, drawing on her 2005 ethnographic fieldwork on water rights in West Africa. She asks, "Did I have a right to be here?"

> The performative-I, within the ethnographic reflexivity of water democracy, required that I challenge my own reflection and ask myself the hard question of how I had the right or the authority to make judgments about a people, country, and problem of which I did not belong. The performative-I required that the question be staged as a rhetorical question where I was not only dramatically challenging my own claims but also laboring in an open and free public venue to convince audiences that access to clean water is a human right being threatened by local and global forces.
>
> (2011, p. 132)

In these gestures Madison dwells in a hopeful present, a present that pushes forward toward a multiplicity of futures, or utopian performatives. She imagines a politics of possibility, a world were people have free clean water, a world where water democracy is possible (2011, pp. 133, 136). Being reflexive, then, means to be utopian, transgressive, political, to bend time, to "embrace a greater material freedom for others, a freedom beyond the self" (Madison 2011, p. 16).

To summarize

Being reflexive means "circling back, beginning again, turning back on language, writing deja vu prose that makes the familiar hum with newness" (Adams and Jones 2011, p. 108). Being reflexive means stopping the flow of reflexivity long enough to grasp a glimpse of its movement (Foley 2002, p. 477). Being reflexive means to be reflexively queer, being reflexive means testing the limits of knowledge and certainty, being reflexive means listening to the silences, being reflexive means pushing back, being reflexive means only ever capturing a glimpse of the other, being reflexive means acting as an agent of change, being reflexive means bearing witness to violence, being reflexive means not hiding behind words and theory, being reflexive means telling stories, being reflexive means writing performatively, being reflexive means finding an opening, being reflexive means owning what I bring to the ethnographic present, being reflexive means exposing what is hidden, being reflexive means to engage in a political act, being reflexive means being tangled up in interpretation and genealogy, being reflective means writing with and for the Others, being reflective means to be performative, being reflexive means self-care, means catharsis, being reflexive means letting go (Alexander 2011, pp. 101, 104; Pillow 2015, p. 429; Chawla 2007; Berry and Clair 2011, pp. 199–200).

Conclusion

Performing [auto] ethnography reflexively and politically means putting the critical sociological imagination to work. This work involves pedagogies of hope and freedom. A performative autoethnography reflexively enacts these pedagogies. These practices require a performance ethics, the topic of my concluding chapter. Now, more than ever, we need reasons to believe in the possibilities of a dignified politics committed to nonviolent ways of living in a world that is at war with itself (Giroux 2016c, p. 222).

Notes

1 I define fascism as a conservative, extreme right-wing political, economic and socio-legal state formation characterized by authoritarian forms of government, extreme nationalism, manufactured consent at key levels of public opinion, racism, a large military-industrial complex, foreign aggressiveness, anticommunism, state-supported corporate capitalism, state-sponsored violence, extreme restrictions on individual freedom and tendencies toward an "Orwellian condition of perpetual war... [and] a national security state in which intelligence agencies and the military replace publicly elected officials in deciding national priorities" (Rorty 2002, p. 13; Arendt 2001).
2 See www.nytimes.com/2016/11/28/us/professor-watchlist-is-seen-as-threat-to-academic-freedom.htm; http://www.professorwatchlist.org
3 See www.huffingtonpost.com/entry/colin-kaepernick-police-killings_us_57e14414e4b04a1497b69ba6
4 See www.breitbart.com/big-government/2015/11/28/5-devastating-facts-black-black-crime/
5 Breithart News Network is a conservative news, opinion, commentary and website founded in 2007. Stephen Bannon is/was its current President and Chairman. Bannon was Donald Trump's presidential campaign manager and has been appointed Trump's Chief White House strategist and senior counselor (www.nbcnews.com/politics/2016-election/trump-s-pick-steve-bannon-chief-strategist-sparks-backlash-n683386). Under Bannon's leadership the site targeted blacks, Jews, women, Latinos and Muslins, and nationalist views. The site faced regular criticism for its close ties to the "alt right," an online-based counterculture movement associated with white nationalism. Critics argue that Breitbart is associated with is nothing more than the rebranding of white supremacy, and white nationalism, for the digital age.

6 The Charleston church massacre was a mass shooting that took place at the Emanuel African Methodist Episcopal Church in downtown Charleston, South Carolina, United States, on the evening of June 17, 2015.

7 Obviously stolen from Giroux (2016c); indeed this entire section is stolen from Giroux.

8 Here there are obvious political connections to Guy Debord's (2012) situationist project.

9 In 2016–2017 the Black Public Sphere can be re-phrased to read or include the racialized public sphere.

10 See www.nytimes.com/2002/10/13/opinion/texas-on-the-tigris.html

11 Elsewhere (Denzin 1997, pp. 217–227), I distinguish six levels of reflexivity: subjectivist, methodological, intertextual, standpoint, queer and feminist/ Materialist (See Alexander 2011, p. 101; also Pillow 2015).

12 Including posthumanist formations. Under the ontological turn agency is not confined to human beings.

13 Stolen from Madison (2011).

14 See Pillow (2015, pp. 420–421) for a discussion of the multiple meanings of reflexivity and a discussion of the difference between reflexivity and reflection.

14 A relational ethic for performance autoethnography, or in the forest but lost in the trees, or a one-act play with many endings[1]

Coming full circle, it is necessary to take up once again the practices of critical pedagogy, a performative cultural politics and a performance ethics based on feminist, communitarian assumptions. In this final chapter, I will attempt to align these assumptions with the call by First and Fourth World scholars for an indigenous research ethic (see Rinehart 2016).

My goal is to outline a code of ethics, an ethics of equity, a set of ethical principles for critical performative inquiry, a blueprint for the global community of qualitative researchers, an ethics, after Madison, and Freire, that re-imagines a world free of oppression. An ethic that turns inquiry into praxis, and praxis into critical consciousness. I want a large tent, one that extends across disciplines and professions, from anthropologists to archaeologists, sociologists to social workers, health care to education, communications to history, performance studies to queer and disability studies, a global community committed to social justice and human rights.

Following the arguments of Christians, Freire, Roy, Madison and the Human Rights Coalition of AAAS (above), this code will be informed by a human rights, social justice agenda. It will distinguish between duty-based, procedural, utilitarian and relational ethical systems. This interdisciplinary code will reflect the concerns of a core transnational constituency. It will exist alongside specific disciplinary codes. It will offer an alternative to state-sponsored regulatory systems, including Institutional Review Boards (IRB),[2] in the United States and IRB counterparts in the UK, Australia, New Zealand, Canada, Scandinavia and elsewhere (see Sikes & Piper 2010; Hammersley & Traianou 2012, p. 5; Israel 2015; Halse & Honey 2007; Dingwall 2008; Haggerty 2004; Becker 2004; Hedgecoe 2008; National Research Council 2014). It will be positive, not negative.

This will be an ethical code based on a moral contract, a relational ethics, an ethics of care. It will use process consent agreements, rather than traditional utilitarian informed consent forms (Ellis 2009, pp. 308–310).[3] It will presume that all inquiry is already moral and ethical, framed by an ethics of hope, care and liberation. It will be performative, using dramaturgy and social theatre to imagine new futures and a new politics of resistance.

There is more, and it is complicated. As repeatedly argued, performance autoethnography and social theatre involve taking the side of the oppressed. But there will always be multiple points of view. We must make an effort to hear everyone. McRae (2015) calls this performative listening, performative acts in which listeners ethnically engage in learning from others across difference. In performative listening the listener attempts to see and understand contradictions, understanding that ethical choices arise in moments of contradiction, crisis and conflict. These are the times for performative intervention. In these moments, in these spaces, harm has been done. Oppressors need to be exposed, challenged. Oppressors, in turn resist, push back, arguing that their actions are warranted, that they are misunderstood, or mis-represented. But Paulo Freire is firm on this point. Every oppressed person has the right to rebel against the ethical and moral transgressions committed by the oppressor. The oppressed must be encouraged to speak out and be given the resources to do so, even if this embarrasses the oppressor (Freire 1998, p. 93).

Augusto Boal extends the argument. When you live in performance, when you live in social theatre, you live in emotion, you live in hope, in politics, you dream. These are moral and ethical spaces. We seek reconciliation, healing, not shaming or punishment, or harm to the other, yet we stand up for the rights of the oppressed. We have an ethical calling to do so. Perfomance and social theatre become the vehicles for answering the call.

This moral-ethical code will serve the following purposes:[4]

1   Identify and implement a set of core values on which critical performance inquiry is based. These values include social justice, human rights, integrity, a belief in the dignity and worth of the person.
2   Summarize the broad ethical principles that embody and enact these core values. These principles outline our ethical responsibilities to ourselves, to our students, to stakeholders, clients, those we study, the broader society, other professionals, as well as our conduct in practice, performance and research settings.
3   Clarify and distinguish the relationship between guidelines framed by federal, national, and institutional regulatory agencies and specific disciplinary codes (see Sikes & Piper 2010; Hammersley & Traianou 2012).
4   Distinguish between federal, national and institutional regulatory agencies guidelines and guidelines grounded in human rights, social justice considerations.
5   Establish a set of specific ethical standards and procedures that should guide the research activity of critical inquiry performance scholars.
6   Provide ethical standards to which the general public and public officials can hold performance inquiry scholars accountable.
7   Socialize scholars new to the field to these values, ethical principles and ethical standards.
8   Articulate standards that performance inquiry scholars can use in defense of their work: performance is an object of inquiry, performance is an aesthetic practice, performance is always political, inquiry is always a performance, we know the world through performance. (Schechner 2013, pp. 1–2)

This code serves to implement the primary mission of the global qualitative inquiry community; namely to use the methods and principles of critical qualitative inquiry for social justice purposes. Members of this community seek an ethics of justice framed by human rights agendas, understanding that ethical decision-making is a dialogical process. However, code of ethics cannot guarantee ethical behavior (Stake & Jegatheesan 2008; Stake & Rizvi 2009).

***

The flaws in the current regulatory ethical apparatuses are well known, and have been extensively reviewed by others. The past is littered with controversy, acrimony, and struggle (see Denzin 2009, pp. 284–295 for a review; also Lincoln 2009; Lincoln & Guba 2013; Speiglman & Spear 2009). I do not want to become embroiled in conflict or critique, only to note the sites of tension. (There is even a humanities and IRB blog[5] where complaints are aired.)

Conflict has centered on the following topics:

1   Mission or ethics creep, or the over-zealous extension of ethical review procedures and regulations to interpretive forms of social science research, has been criticized by many, including Gunsalus and Associates (2007) and Dash (2007).[6]

2   In the USA communication and education scholars have contested narrow applications of the Common Rule and the Belmont Principles of respect, beneficence and justice (Title 45, Code of Federal Regulations, part 46; Christians 2005; Lincoln 2009). Respect is achieved through informed consent agreements, beneficence through perceived risks, or harm, and justice through assurances that subjects are not unduly burdened by being required to participate in a research project. But respect involves caring for others and honoring them. It is more then agreeing to sign an informed consent form. Beneficence cannot be quantified, and justice includes more then being randomly selected to be a subject in a research project.

3   Oral historians have contested the narrow view of science and research contained in current U.S. regulations (Shopes 2011; Shopes & Ritchie 2004).

4   Anthropologists and archaeologists have challenged the concept of informed consent as it impacts ethnographic inquiry where scientific inquiry is not a shared value, or, as in the case of the past, the question of who can give informed consent is problemaeic (see Fluehr-Lohban 2003a).

5   Journalists argue that blanket insistence on anonymity (often required by regulatory bodies) reduces the credibility of journalistic reporting which rests on naming the sources used in a news account (Dash 2007). Dash, for example, contends that IRB oversight interferes with the First Amendment rights of journalists and the public's right to know (Dash 2007, p. 871). A free press is often the last line of defense against a repressive political regimes.

6   Indigenous scholars Battiste (2008) and Smith (2005) assert that Western conceptions of epistemology and ethical inquiry have "severely eroded and damaged indigenous knowledge" and indigenous communities (Battiste 2008, p. 497; Fast, Cameron, Helferty and Lewis 2016). Knowledge, inquiry and ethics have been constrained by neocolonial discourse. Indigenous scholars seek to create indigenous models of ethics and inquiry within and without the academy, free of the neocolonial framework (Fast et al. 2016, p. 381).

We have much to learn from indigenous scholars about how radical democratic practices can be made to work. Indigenous communities demand an ethics of resistance that is defined from within the epistemological framework of the group (Fast et al. 2016, p. 381). Maori scholars Linda Tuhiwai Smith (1999) and Russell Bishop (1998) are committed to a set of moral and pedagogical imperatives and, as Smith expresses it, "to acts of reclaiming, reformulating, and reconstituting indigenous cultures and languages...to the struggle to become self-determining" (p. 142). Such acts lead to a research program that is committed to the pursuit of social justice. In turn, a specific approach to inquiry is required. In his discussion of a Maori approach to creating knowledge, Bishop (1998) observes that researchers in Kaupapa Maori contexts are

> repositioned in such a way as to no longer need to seek to *give voice to others*, to *empower* others, to *emancipate* others, to refer to others as *subjugated* voices, but rather to listen and participate ... in a process that facilitates the development in people as a sense of themselves as agentic and of having an authoritative voice ... An indigenous Kaupapa Maori approach to research ... challenges colonial and neo-colonial discourses that inscribe "otherness."
>
> (pp. 207–208)

This participatory mode of knowing privileges subjectivity, personal knowledge and the specialized knowledges of oppressed groups. It uses concrete experience as a criterion of meaning and truth. It encourages a participatory mode of consciousness that locates the researcher within Maori-defined spaces in the group. The researcher is led by the members of the community and does not presume to be a leader, or to have any power that he or she can relinquish (Bishop 1998, p. 205).

As a way of honoring the group's sacred spaces, the researcher gives the group a gift. In laying down this gift, the researcher rejects the ideology of empowerment. There is no assumption that the researcher is giving the group power. Rather, the laying down of the gift is an offering, a pure giving. And in this act, the researcher refuses any claim to anything the group might give him or her in return. If the group picks up the gift, then a shared reciprocal relationship can be created (Bishop 1998, p. 207). The relationship that follows is built on understandings involving shared Maori beliefs and cultural practices.

In turn, the research is evaluated according to Maori-based criteria, not criteria imported from the international literature, including Western positivist and postpositivist epistemologies, as well as certain versions of critical pedagogy that think in terms of grand narratives and "binaries" or "dialectical linear progressions" (Bishop 1998, pp. 209, 211).

Like Madison's, Conquergood's, Freire's and Boal's revolutionary pedagogy, the Maori moral position values dialogue as a method for assessing knowledge claims.

***

With respect to the USA it is clear that the existing Belmont and Common Rule definitions have little, if anything, to do with a human rights and social justice ethical agenda. Regrettably these principles have been informed by notions of value-free experimentation, and utilitarian concepts of justice (Christians 2005). They do not conceptualize research in participatory terms. In reality these rules protect institutions and not persons, although they were originally created to protect human subjects from unethical biomedical research. As currently deployed, these practices close down critical ethical dialogue. They create the impression that if proper IRB procedures are followed then one's ethical house is in order. But this is ethics in a cul de sac.

A new day

Clifford Christians locates the ethics and politics of qualitative inquiry within a broader historical and intellectual framework. He first examines the Enlightenment model of positivism, value-free inquiry, utilitarianism and utilitarian ethics. In a value-free social science, codes of ethics for professional societies become the conventional format for moral principles. By the 1980s, each of the major social science associations (contemporaneous with passage of federal laws and promulgation of national guidelines) had developed its own ethical code with an emphasis on several guidelines: informed consent, nondeception, the absence of psychological or physical harm, privacy and confidentiality, and a commitment to collecting and presenting reliable and valid empirical materials. Institutional review boards (IRBs) implemented these guidelines, including ensuring that informed consent is always obtained in human subject research.

However, Christians notes that in reality IRBs protect institutions and not individuals. Several events challenged the Enlightenment model, including the Nazi medical experiments, the Tuskegee syphilis study, Project Camelot in the 1960s, Stanley Milgram's deception of subjects in his psychology experiments, Laud Humphrey's deceptive study of gay and bisexual males in public restrooms. Recent disgrace involves the complicity of social scientists with military initiatives in Vietnam, and most recently the complicity of the American Psychological association with the CIA and national security interrogations involving military and intelligence personnel. In addition, charges of fraud, plagiarism, data tampering and misrepresentation continue to the present day.

Christians details the poverty of the Enlightenment model. It creates the conditions for deception, for the invasion of private spaces, for duping subjects, and for challenges to the subject's moral worth and dignity. Christians calls for its replacement with an ethics of being based on the values of a feminist communitarianism.

This is an evolving, emerging ethical framework that serves as a powerful antidote to the deception-based, utilitarian IRB system. The new framework presumes a community that is ontologically and axiologically prior to the person. This community has common moral values, and research is rooted in a concept of care, of shared governance, of neighborliness, or of love, kindness and the moral good. Accounts of social life should display these values and be based on interpretive sufficiency. They should have sufficient depth to allow the reader to form a critical understanding about the world studied. These texts should exhibit an absence of racial, class and gender stereotyping. These texts should generate social criticism and lead to resistance, empowerment, social action, restorative justice and positive change in the social world.

Social justice means giving everyone their appropriate due. The justified as the right and proper is a substantive common good. The concept of justice-as-intrinsic-worthiness that anchors the ethics of being is a radical alternative to the right-order justice of modernity which has dominated modernity from Locke to Rawls' *Theory of Justice* and his *The Law of Peoples* and Habermas' *The Postnational Constellations*. Retributive and distributive justice is the framework of modernists' democratic liberalism. Justice as right order is typically procedural, justice considered done when members of a society receive from its institutions the goods to which they have a right. For the ethics of being, justice is restorative.

A sacred, existential epistemology places us in a noncompetitive, non-hierarchical relationship to the earth, to nature, and to the larger world. This sacred epistemology stresses the values of empowerment, shared governance, care, solidarity, love, community, covenant, morally involved observers and civic transformation. As Christians observes, this ethical epistemology recovers the moral values that were excluded by the rational Enlightenment science project. This sacred epistemology is based on a philosophical anthropology that declares that "all humans are worthy of dignity and sacred status without exception for class or ethnicity" (Christians 1995, p. 129). A universal human ethic, stressing the sacredness of life, human dignity, truth telling and nonviolence, derives from this position (Christians 1997, pp. 12–15). This ethic is based on locally experienced, culturally prescribed protonorms (Christians 1995, p. 129). These primal norms provide a defensible "conception of good rooted in universal human solidarity" (Christians 1995, p. 129; also 1997, 1998). This sacred epistemology recognizes and interrogates the ways in which race, class and gender operate as important systems of oppression in the world today.

In this way, Christians outlines a radical ethical path for the future. He transcends the usual middle-of-the-road ethical models, which focus on the problems associated with betrayal, deception and harm in qualitative research.

Christians's call for a collaborative social science research model makes the researcher responsible, not to a removed discipline (or institution), but rather to those studied. This implements critical, action and feminist traditions, which forcefully align the ethics of research with a politics of the oppressed. Christians's framework reorganizes existing discourses on ethics and the social sciences.

Clearly the Belmont and Common Rule definitions had little, if anything, to do with a human rights and social justice ethical agenda. Regrettably, these principles were informed by notions of value-free experimentation and utilitarian concepts of justice. They do not conceptualize research in participatory terms. In reality, these rules protect institutions and not people, although they were originally created to protect human subjects from unethical biomedical research. The application of these regulations is an instance of mission or ethics creep, or the overzealous extension of IRB regulations to interpretive forms of social science research. This has been criticized by many, including Cannella and Lincoln (2011), as well as Kevin Haggerty (2004), C. K. Gunsalus et al. (2007), Leon Dash (2007), and the American Association of University Professors (AAUP 2006a, 2006b).

Disciplining and constraining ethical conduct

The consequence of these restrictions is a disciplining of qualitative inquiry that extends from granting agencies to qualitative research seminars and even the conduct of qualitative dissertations. In some cases, lines of critical inquiry have not been funded and have not gone forward because of criticisms from local IRBs. Pressures from the right discredit critical interpretive inquiry. From the federal to the local levels, a trend seems to be emerging. In too many instances, there seems to be a move away from protecting human subjects to an increased monitoring, censuring, and policing of projects that are critical of the right and its politics.

Yvonna S. Lincoln and William G. Tierney (2002) observe that these policing activities have at least five important implications for critical social justice inquiry. First, the widespread rejection of alternative forms of research means that qualitative inquiry will be heard less and less in federal and state policy forums. Second, it appears that qualitative researchers are being deliberately excluded from this national dialogue. Consequently, third, young researchers trained in the critical tradition are not being heard. Fourth, the definition of research has not changed to fit newer models of inquiry. Fifth, in rejecting qualitative inquiry, traditional researchers are endorsing a more distanced form of research, one that is compatible with existing stereotypes concerning people of color.

These developments threaten academic freedom in four ways: (1) they lead to increased scrutiny of human subjects research and (2) new scrutiny of classroom research and training in qualitative research involving human subjects; (3) they connect to evidence-based discourses, which define qualitative research as unscientific; and (4) by endorsing methodological conservatism, they reinforce the status quo on many campuses. This conservatism produces new constraints on graduate training, leads to the improper review of faculty research, and creates conditions for politicizing the IRB review process, while protecting institutions and not individuals from risk and harm.

Oral historians offer a solution

Oral historians have contested the narrow view of science and research contained in current reports (Shopes & Ritchie 2004). Anthropologists and archaeologists have challenged the concept of informed consent as it impacts ethnographic inquiry (see Fluehr-Lobban 2003a, 2003b). Journalists argue that IRB insistence on anonymity reduces the credibility of journalistic reporting, which rests on naming the sources used in a news account. Dash (2007, p. 871) contends that IRB oversight interferes with the First Amendment rights of journalists and the public's right to know. Marie Battiste (2008) and Linda Tuhiwai Smith (2005) assert that Western conceptions of ethical inquiry have "severely eroded and damaged indigenous knowledge" and indigenous communities (Battiste 2008, p. 497).

Since 2004, many scholarly and professional societies have followed the Oral History and American Historical Associations in challenging the underlying assumptions in the standard campus IRB model. A transdisciplinary, global, counter-IRB discourse has emerged (Battiste 2008; Christians 2007; Mertens and Ginsberg 2009; Lincoln 2009). This discourse has called for the blanket exclusion of non-federally funded research from IRB review. The AAUP (2006a, 2006b) recommended that

> exemptions based on methodology, namely research on autonomous adults whose methodology consists entirely of collecting data by surveys, conducting interviews, or observing behavior in public places should be exempt from the requirement of IRB review, with no provisos, and no requirement of IRB approval of the exemption.
>
> (p. 4)

The executive council of the Oral History Association endorsed the AAUP recommendations at its October 2006 annual meeting. They were quite clear: "Institutions consider as straightforwardly exempt from IRB review any 'research whose methodology consists entirely of collecting data by surveys, conducting interviews, or observing behavior in public places'" (Howard 2006, p. 9). This recommendation can be extended: Neither the Office for Human Resource Protection, nor a campus IRB has the authority to define what constitutes legitimate research in any field, only what research is covered by federal regulations.

Most recently the National Research Council of the National Academies published *Proposed Revisions to the Common Rule for the Protection of*

Human Subjects in the Behavioral and Social Sciences (2014). This report significantly increases the number of research approaches and research data that are excused from IRB review (2014, pp. 4–5).

Don Ritchie reports that in response to a call for a clarification on federal regulations

> On September 8 2015, the U.S. Department of Health and Human Services issued a set of recommended revisions to the regulations concerning human subject research. Oral history, journalism, biography, and historical scholarship activities that focus directly on the specific individuals about whom the information is collected be explicitly excluded from review by IRBs.[7]

The proposed revisions defined human subject research "as a systematic investigation designed to develop or contribute to generalizable knowledge that involves direct interaction or intervention with a living individual or that involves obtaining identifiable private information about an individual." Only research that fits this definition should be subject to IRB procedures and the Common Rule. Human subjects research studies would be placed in one of three review categories – *excused research, expedited review*, or *full review*. A new category, " *excused*," references research that does not require IRB review if it involve only informational risk that is no more than minimal. Examples of excused research could include use of pre-existing data with private information, or benign interventions or interactions that involve activities familiar to people in everyday life, such as educational tests, surveys and focus groups. The report notes that because the primary risk in most social and behavioral research is informational, much of this research would qualify as excused under the new regulations. The committee recommended that excused research remain subject to some oversight; investigators should register their study with an IRB, describe consent procedures and provide a data protection plan.[8]

With these recommendations, a nearly 30-year struggle involving federal regulations of social science research moves into a new phase. Ritchie notes that the federal government began issuing rules that required universities to review human subject research in 1980. At first, the regulations applied only to medical and behavioral research, but in 1991, the government broadened its requirements to include any interaction with living individuals.

We hope the days of IRB Mission Creep are over. We are not sanguine. As Cannella and Lincoln note, qualitative and critical qualitative researchers will continue to "take hold" of their academic spaces as they clash with legislated research regulation (especially, for example, as practiced by particular institutional review boards in the United States). This conflict will not end any time soon. This work has demonstrated not only that "legislated attempts to regulate research ethics are an illusion, but that regulation is culturally grounded and can even lead to ways of functioning that are damaging to research participants and collaborators" (Cannella and Lincoln 2011, p. 87)

Ethics and critical social science

Gaile Cannella and Yvonna S. Lincoln, building on the work of Michel Foucault, argue that a critical social science requires a radical ethics, an "ethics that is always/already concerned about power and oppression even as it avoids constructing 'power' as a new truth" (Cannella and Lincoln 2011, p. 97). A critical ethical stance works outward from the core of the person. A critical social science incorporates feminist, postcolonial and even postmodern challenges to oppressive power. It is aligned with a critical pedagogy and a politics of resistance, hope and freedom. A critical social science focuses on structures of power and systems of domination. It creates spaces for a decolonizing project. It opens the doors of the academy so that the voices of oppressed people can be heard and honored and so that others can learn from them. Aligned with the ethics of the traditionally marginalized, which could ultimately reconceptualize the questions and practices of research, a critical social science would no longer accept the notion that one group of people can "know" and define (or even represent) "others." This perspective would certainly change the research purposes and designs that are submitted for human subjects review. Furthermore, focusing on the individual and the discovery of theories and universals has masked societal, institutional, and structural practices that perpetuate injustices. Finally, an ethics that would help others "be like us" has created power for "us." This ethics of good intentions has tended to support power for those who construct the research and the furthering of oppressive conditions for the subjects of that research. A critical social science requires a new ethical foundation, a new set of moral understandings.

Path forward

Paths through the current ethical maze must be found. Researchers are invited become to become involved in the ethics review process within their own academic and research settings. For instance, I am the Institutional Review Board (IRB) officer for the College of Media, University of Illinois, Urbana-Champaign. This came about in the following way. In 2004 I asked our campus IRB officer if the 2003 Oral History Association (OHA) IRB exemption[9] was recognized on this campus,[10] and if so, could it be extended to interpretive research in my college.[11]

Our campus officer replied that the UIUC IRB generally upholds the OHA and American History Association (AHA) AHA positions on this. As such, the UIUC typically considers oral histories as exempted from IRB review, unless there are severe extenuating factors of some sort (e.g., interactions involving deception) that *may* increase the level of review.[12]

I then stated that interpretive media research involves historical research and open-ended, oral history interviewing. This research does not fit the type of research defined by federal regulations, namely: "A systematic investigation, including research development, testing and evaluation, designed to develop or contribute to generalizable knowledge."[13]

I contended that much of the research in my college is based on case studies, open-ended interviews, life histories and life stories. Each individual case is treated as unique. This category of social science research has historically been called idiographic or emic. Emic studies emphasize stories, narratives, collaborative performances and accounts that capture the meaning persons bring to experience. Nomothetic studies, in contrast, conform to the federal definitions of research. Researchers seek abstract generalizations, test hypotheses and use random sampling techniques, quasi-experimental designs, and so forth.

I requested that the Oral History exemption apply to interpretive research in the College of Communications, with these provisos:

1   The research is not federally funded.
2   The research does not place subjects at risk or harm.
3   Researchers demonstrate that this exclusion should be granted, because the research in question does not involve research as defined by the federal guideline. An exemption could be granted, if research does meet this definition.
4   Scholars define their work as scholarship, not research, and locate it within an artistic, humanistic paradigm, including: critical pedagogy, arts-based inquiry, narrative or performance studies (see below).

This request was granted. I then created an IRB website, linked to the University of Illinois, Urbana-Champaign College of Media website. I included the text of the original (2003) Oral History exemption, as well as application forms modeled after those used at the campus level. And today the College of Media IRB office annually processes 8–10 requests for expedited, or exempted IRB reviews. Concerned students and colleagues come to our office, asking if they have to go to the campus IRB. I direct them to our website, and ask if their project conforms to the oral history guidelines. I also ask if their work is federally funded, and if it places subjects at more then minimal harm or risk. I ask them if they are doing oral history inquiry, arts-based or performance inquiry. I ask if they are testing scientific hypotheses, drawing random samples, and using experimental or survey-research designs. Thus has getting IRB approval become one more step in the dissertation project in my college.

***

Ethical practices: a one act play

Characters

Speaker One
Speaker Two

Staging notes

Performers are seated around a seminar table on the third floor of Gregory Hall, a four story, 125-year-old brick classroom on the campus of the University of Illinois. There a twenty-five chairs along the walls and around a forty-foot long wood table. Two large nature paintings on loan from the art department hang on the north and east walls of the room. There is a pull down screen at the south end of the room for projecting video. Overhead lights are dimmed. Sun streams in through the two north windows. It is 1:00 in the afternoon. The time is the present. There are two voices, speaker one and speaker two. The text of the play is handed from speaker to speaker. The first speaker reads the text for speaker one. The second speaker reads the text for speaker two, and so forth, to the end.

Act One: Scene One: Getting unstuck

    (This dialogue starts stage left, then two speakers step forward, one at a time)

SPEAKER ONE: We gotta get out of this place. I have a serious headache. I thought we had a way out with that oral history exemption and the AAUP recommendations. Then I wasn't so sure, but now the 2014 Proposed Revisions in the Common Rule for the Protection of Human Subjects in the Behavioral and Social Sciences has the potential to radically change the entire IRB landscape.

SPEAKER TWO: We have to be aggressive. The new guidelines in fact implement the oral history proposals by placing interpretive inquiry in the excused category. However, we are still under the shadows of federal regulation.

SPEAKER ONE: We are in the side of justice. We are researchers committed to positive social change. We are social workers, health care and educational researchers, anthropologists, critical performance ethnographers, sociologists, archaeologists, activists. Ethics, politics and justice cannot be separated. Indigenous scholars have long understood this.

SPEAKER ONE: There needs to be significant regulatory reform at the national level (Levine and Skedsvold 2008, paraphrase). The scholarly societies must organize to make this happen.

SPEAKER TWO: We have to be hopeful. The revisions in existing ethical regulations give us directions on where we do not want to go. We need to formulate our own guidelines.

SPEAKER ONE: Okay. We can learn from the existing IRB models. If ethics cannot be separated from politics and power, then whose power, whose knowledge, and whose history is shaping what we are doing? Are we really on the side of the angels?

SPEAKER TWO: We must be critically self-reflective, and hold to the highest ethical values. Researchers put subjects at risk. Researchers lie, misrepresent, break promises, cheat, squander funds, misappropriate intellectual property, manipulate evidence, steal. No ethical code can prohibit this kind of conduct.

SPEAKER ONE: Ouch! So you're saying researchers with little integrity can always find some ethical principle to justify the violation of some other ethical principle (Stake and Rizvi 2009, p. 531).

SPEAKER TWO: Yes!

SPEAKER ONE: Ethical conduct has to be guided by an inner voice, by one's conscience, by the group's values ... Ultimately researchers are forced to rely on personal, situational judgments. Codes and institutional reviews cannot protect us from the need to be ethical, from the need to address complex ethical dilemmas (Stake and Rizvi 2009, p. 531).

SPEAKER TWO: We need a transdisciplinary, feminist communitarian ethical code, a normative model, a dialogical code that enables community transformation, empowers the oppressed, enacts a politics of resistance, recognition and difference, a code informed by human rights initiatives (Christians 2005, pp. 157–158). The information we present must be accurate, fair, through and based on integrity.[14]

SPEAKER ONE: Your ethical model embodies a set of methodological directives for conducting critical interpretive inquiry, so now methodology, ethics and inquiry are folded into one framework

SPEAKER TWO: Ethics in this framework generates social criticism. This leads to resistance and empowers persons to transformative action.

Act One: Scene Two: Core values

SPEAKER ONE: Remember, our mission is rooted in these interdisciplinary core values: service, social justice, the dignity and worth of the person, the importance of human relationships, integrity, and competence. We respect the inherent dignity and worth of the person, we honor people and their material culture (see Fluehr-Lobban 2003a, pp. 264–265).

SPEAKER TWO: We must minimize harm! But this is complicated. Journalists, for example, have First Amendment protection and a commitment to their profession, and to the public to tell the truth. That means they may harm people, because the truth can hurt (Dash 2007). So what does do no harm mean?

SPEAKER ONE: Treat subjects with respect. Have an honest relationship with those we engage in critical inquiry. Show compassion. Balance the need for information against potential harm. Weigh the consequences of making private information public.

SPEAKER TWO: **Watchwords:** No deception, full disclosure, empower, collaborate, care/

Act One: Scene Three: Conquergood's pitfalls

SPEAKER ONE: Performance ethnographers worry about the four ethical pitfalls identified by Dwight Conquergood: "the Custodian's Rip-Off," "the

Enthusiast's Infatuation," "the Curator's Exhibitionism," and "the Skeptic's Cop-Put" (Conquergood 1985, p. 4: Spry 2016, p. 32).

SPEAKER TWO: Custodians ransack their own and our past, searching for texts to perform for profit. Enthusiasts visit our cultures and become superficially involved, trivializing who we are. Skeptics are cynical and detached, acing as if they own our worlds. Curators sensationalize our worlds, staging performances for the voyeur's gaze. This is the "Wild Kingdom" approach, the fascination with the exotic other, the Nobel Savage (Conquergood 1985, p. 7).

SPEAKER TWO: Each of Dwight's ethical dilemmas pits the researcher, as an outsider, often a stranger, against the other. These pitfalls are based on the mistaken assumption that we can understand and appropriate the other's identity. But this is a colonial assumption, based on a false self-other binary. We can be co-present with the other, we can care for the other, be in the service of the other, but never be one with the other (Spry 2016, p. 32).

SPEAKER ONE: We want a dialogical ethic, texts, performances and inquiries that speak to and with the other. We write "from the entanglements of copresence, from the intimacy of dialogue, from the liminal spaces of inbetweeneness" (Spry 2016, p. 61). We can never appropriate the other's identity. We want works that reengage the past and bring it alive in the present. The dialogic text attempts to kept the dialogue alive, to keep the conversation between performer, inquirer and the audience ongoing and open-ended. The dialogic text enacts a dialogical ethic. It involves more than empathy: it interrogates, criticizes, empowers, and creates languages of resistance.

SPEAKER TWO: We want a dialogical ethic that honors the essential human freedoms of expression, worship, the freedom from want, from fear of violence. We want a code that is sensitive to the basic human rights, the rights to housing, health, the rights of indigenous people, of peoples with disabilities, the rights of children, the rights of workers, the right to sexual and gender self expression, language rights, cultural rights, environmental rights, the rights of prisoners, the right to freely participate in democracy.

Act One: Scene Four: A relational ethics

SPEAKER ONE: As an autoethnographer, I need a relational ethic. When I write autoethnography, I write about my own life and the lives of others who are close to me, intimate others. I have a responsibility to them. How do I tell the truth, do no harm, and honor and respect our relationship at the same time?

SPEAKER TWO: These issues are not acknowledged by IRBs! These are difficult ethical issues and no simple mandate or universal principle applies in all cases, and of course ethical work does not end with IRB approval (Ellis 2009, pp. 307, 310).

SPEAKER ONE: Right, there is a range of responses. Let's make a list

(holds up bulletin board with the following items listed)

1   do not publish, or delay publishing potentially harmful or painful material;
2   publish under a pseudonym, fictionalize the story, use pseudonyms or no names for participants;
3   publish without approval;
4   seek approval after publication;
5   work out with participants what will be contained in the story, change, or omit identifying details or problematic events;
6   use multiple voices;
7   seek consent beforehand;
8   use process consent (below) in addition to informed consent;
9   follow a socially contingent ethic.

SPEAKER TWO: So which option do I follow?

SPEAKER ONE: Your conscience. I don't always use recognizable people in my stories, other than myself, and a few family members and public officials. I focus on places, historical events, fictional dialogues, and performances with unnamed narrators, numbered voices, persons wearing masks. I have to take responsibility for what I write, whether I share or not with those I write about.

SPEAKER TWO: I tell my students to use process consent, not just informed consent. Relationships change during the course of a project, people change their minds, back out, stop talking. Practicing process consent means checking at each stage of inquiry to make sure participants still want to be part of the process. Relational ethics values mutual respect, dignity, connectedness, being true to one's conscience, one's values, an ethics of care (Ellis 2009, p. 310).

SPEAKER ONE: This is a socially contingent ethic, it works outward from shared personal experience, it is based on care, respect, love, it respects rights, and needs, and intimacies specific to a relational context.

SPEAKER TWO: Taking a story back to those you write about is not like sharing fieldnotes. Special care has to be taken when writing about thick family relations, parents, friends, and lovers. Taking a story back to an intimate can cause harm. It can destroy a relationship. It can place the writer in harm's way (Ellis 2009, p. 314; Bochner 2007, p. 199).

SPEAKER ONE: At the relational level it gets complicated. I have the right to write about my past, and my present relationships. But what can I decently write about other people? Whose permission do I have to ask? Will I change them, or hurt them? What can I decently reveal about myself? How can I write about the past, the dead are dead? What is the exact truth of a story, what is its emotional truth? Should I tell the truth if it hurts someone else?

SPEAKER TWO: Only I can decide whether or how to write about them, about me. And once I have written about them, we are all forever changed. This is my right, to write about the past and the present, and others have the same right. I believe in named sources, no hiding behind fictionalized, or made-up names. This keeps me honest (Blew 1999, pp. 6–7).

SPEAKER ONE: Our ethical principles are these: (1) honor and respect the dignity of the person; (2) assert the moral integrity of the researcher-practioner relationship; (3) enact the dialogical commitment to empowerment, and transformation; (4) implement the multiple agendas of social justice and human rights at the local level.

SPEAKER TWO: These relational and dialogical codes redefine the Belmont principles of respect, beneficence, and justice

SPEAKER ONE: We implement these principles by following the Oral History Association Guidelines. In this way we go beyond the Belmont guidelines concerning respect, beneficence, justice, harm, confidentiality, risk assessment and subject selection.

Act One: Scene Five: Oral historians

SPEAKER ONE: I think I can be of some help. I've been fighting this ethics battle between IRBS and historians for the last 20 years. Oral historians have their version of the Belmont Principles and practical ethical conduct. We have our own concepts of respect, beneficence, justice, informed consent, risk and the selection of subjects.

SPEAKER TWO: Oral historians respect and honor the rights of interviewees to refuse to discuss certain topics. We never randomly select interviewees. That would be unimaginable: We select people because of their oral histories and the stories they can tell. They are never anonymous. Anonymity violates a fundamental principle of oral history; that is anonymous sources lack credibility. Oral history interviews are copyrightable documents, owned by the narrator. He or she must sign over the rights to the interview via a legal release form. This release form is akin to process consent. It allows the narrator (interviewee) to define the terms of the research relationship. Oral history guidelines state that researchers should guard against possible exploitation of interviewees, and take care not to reinforce thoughtless stereotypes.

SPEAKER ONE: This is dialogical ... a give and take, back and forth between interviewer and interviewee.

SPEAKER TWO: We do not want IRBs constraining critical inquiry, or our ethical conduct. Our commitment to professional integrity requires awareness of one's own biases and a readiness to follow a story, wherever it may lead. We are committed to telling the truth, even when it may harm people.

SPEAKER ONE: When publishing about other people, my ethics require that I subject my writing to a fine-mesh filter: do no harm (Richardson 2007, p. 170).

SPEAKER TWO: So there we have it. A set of methodological guidelines, not regulations. The dignity of the person is honored through the terms of the research contract, which takes the place of an informed consent document. Beneficence, do no harm, is challenged in the oral history interview, for interviews may discuss painful topics, and they have the right to walk away at any time. Deception is never an option. It is assumed that telling the truth about the past is of great benefit to society.

The End

Act One: Scene Six: An ode to performance ethics in a minor key

> performance ethics
> provide the foundation for resistance,
> for critique, for understanding
> performance ethics
> inspire militant utopianism and pedagogies of freedom
> performance ethics imagine a world free of conflict and injustice

* * *

the autoethnographer's life is the topic, the site of inquiry

PAULO FREIRE: **enters** the text stage left (speaks softly):
> The words the dreams, the silences, the fear
> Why i wear black
> Rage, love, hope, pedagogy of liberation
> Terror, military coups, jail, revolutions, exiles,
> Two policeman came to my house
> To be free i had to leave my homeland
> Nightmares at mid day
> Emaciated bodies, my pedagogy was written
> in the blood of those who where were beaten
> How can i help the oppressed as they struggle to take control of their own lives?
> Am I doomed to be helpless?
> We perform hope, love, peace
> A radical ethic of love condemns violence,
> I seek an archaeology of my own pain,
> the desire to change comes must from my own biography
> I am required to push against the repressive brazilian government
> Ethics and performance are my only weapons
> i write to place my self in history
> I write to be transgressive, to write my way back home,
> Now it is clear, ethics' duty is to inspire critique,
> to bring dignity, to model acts of activism
> to be utopian, to be moral,

to perform the work of advocacy,
I witnessed moral acts of injustice and pain
I learned to turn witnessing into an intervention,
Into a performance which enacts the unimaginable
and opens the door for
social theatre for healing, for action, for community.
A performance ethic based on witnessing
honors the past, imagines new futures,
demands to be heard, gives a voice to performance
performance inhabits, imagines and bears witness to acts of activism
the ethics of radical performance demand that I pay
attention to the political economy of poverty, injustice, and human rights
performance makes injustice visible (Madison)
relational ethics offer guidelines: no harm,
tell the truth,
whose truth? Whose facts?
long live critical pedagogy,
long live the Theatre of the Oppressed
spect-actors, simultaneous dramaturgy, catharsis, forum theatre,
conscientization, anti-model, oppressed person, joker, legislative
theatre, authentic dialogue, image theatre,
helping people who are suffering imagine and enact change in
their lives through Theatre of the Oppressed
a poetics of the oppressed, social theatre
an end which is only a new beginning.

Notes

1 I thank Pat Sikes for her comments. Portions of this essay re-work and extend Denzin (2017), and pp. 298–305 in Denzin (2009); and pp. 71–84 in Denzin (2010). My examples draw primarily from the United States. For reviews from other national sites see Sikes and Pipes (2010) and Hammersley and Trainou (2012).
2 The Belmont principles and the so-called Common Rule regulate U.S. IRBs (see Christians 2005 for a discussion and National Research Council 2014).
3 Under this model inquiry is relational, and processual and collaborative. At each step in the process co-inquirers address moral and ethical issues that arise as a consequence of the inquiry process itself. See also discussion in Chapter Three, Act Three, Scene Two.
4 These guidelines draw from the revised 2008 Code of Ethics of the National Association of Social Workers (see www.socialworkers.org/pibs/code/code.asp; (also Reamer 2006; also National Research Council 2014).
5 See the blog: Institutional Review Blog News and commentary about Institutional Review Board oversight of the humanities and social sciences. See also IRBwatch – www.irbwatch.org/; also Irbideas.com; also see the *Journal of Empirical Research on Human Research Ethics* (*JERHRE*) which publishes research on IRBs.
6 Mission creep includes these issues and threats: rewarding wrong behaviors, a focus on procedures and not difficult ethical issues, enforcing unwieldy federal regulations, threats to academic freedom and the First Amendment (Gunsalus et al. 2007; also Haggerty 2004; Becker 2004). Perhaps the most extreme form of IRB mission is the

2002 State of Maryland Code, Title 13 – Miscellaneous Health Care Program, Subtitle 20 – Human Subject Research.

§ 13–2001, 13–2002: Compliance with Federal Regulations: A person may not conduct research using a human subject unless the person conducts the research in accordance with the federal regulations on the protection of human subjects.

7   See more at: http://historynewsnetwork.org/article/160885#sthash.Om3fectQ.dpuf

8   Read more at: http://phys.org/news/2014-01-common.html#jCp

9   Under the Common Rule (45 CFR.46) there are two categories, expedited reviews and exemptions. Expedited reviews are moved forward, quickly because they present no more than minimal risk to human subjects. There are several categories of expedited research, including categories 5 and 7. Category 5 focuses on research involving materials (e.g. archival) collected for nonresearch purposes. Category 7 involves research on individual or group characteristics or behavior (including, but not limited to, research on perception, cognition, motivation, identity, language, communication, cultural beliefs or practices, and social behavior) or research employing survey, interview, oral history, focus group, program evaluation, human factors evaluation, or quality assurance methodologies. Exempted proposals do not have to submit to review. The 2014 proposed revisions to the Common Rule (National Research Council 2014) create a new review category, for human-subjects research, "excused." Excused research includes information that can be observed in the public domain if individuals have no expectation of privacy, if investigators have no interactions with individuals, as long as proper ethical guidelines for handling such information are followed and as long as risks are minimal (National Research Council 2014, p. 4).

10 Oral historians establish their exclusion from IRB review on several grounds. Their research does not use large samples, nor is it designed for testing hypotheses, or forming statistical generalizations or generalizable knowledge. Unlike biomedical and behavioral science researchers, oral historians do not seek to discover laws or generalizations that have predictive value. Oral history interviewees and narrators are not anonymous individuals selected as part of a random sample for the purposes of a survey or experiment. Nor do they respond to standard questionnaire items. Oral history narrators engage in dialogues tailored to fit their unique relationship to the topic at hand (see Ritchie & Shopes 2003). See Shopes and Ritchie (2004), for later developments in this discourse.

11 There are four research paradigms or streams in my College: (1) experimental and survey-based research; (2) oral history and interpretive inquiry that does not require IRB review; (3) standard behavioral research that qualifies for expedited review within the College IRB; (4) journalist inquiries involving investigative, narrative and public affairs reporting. Such work is routinely exempted from review under the First Amendment. Proposed revisions to the common rule introduce a new category, excused from review (see National Research Council 2014, pp. 48–49). This is research involving methodologies familiar to people in every day life and where informational risk is at no more than the minimal level, when appropriate data security and information protection plans are in place.

12 The 2014 revisions discuss the problems surrounding data protection, and risks to subjects when harmful information is disclosed. Risks not necessarily associated with research are greater in a changing electronic technological environment where surveillance apparatuses are everywhere present. Corporate owners of social media platforms openly admit gathering personal data and using such data for interventions economic ends (see Bratich 2017; also Shildrick 1997).

13 Readers outside the USA should note that this definition of what constitutes research does not apply elsewhere. In UK universities for example, it is usually the case these days that all research which involves or refers to human subjects regardless of discipline or methodological approach, must undergo ethical review

14 See www.spj.org/ethicscode.asp; Society of Professional journalists code ethics, revised 9/6/2014.

15 Coda

In the beginning

To begin anew. This book has been about reading, writing and performing autoethnography, that writing form that places the writer's self and its experiences directly in the narrative. Autoethnography merges biography, ethnography and history. It treats each writer as an universal singular, as an universal instance of a historical moment and its contingencies. Autoethnography merges the personal and the political. It is writing, James Baldwin reminds us, that changes the world, one life, one word at a time.

In the beginning there was *ethnography (writing culture)*. Then there was *performance*, which allowed us to see ethnography as a performance. Further, every performance is performative, always unique, emergent, liminal, transformative, bound up in the presence of the other. The turn to autoethnography and performance autoethnography complicated matters. The performative I could not be escaped, making autoethnography a slippery topic. There are many different ways of reflexively writing the self into and through the ethnographic text, isolating that space where memory, history, performance and meaning come together. And there are multiple forms, the list is long: social scientific, interpretive, critical, artistic, poetic, analytic, evocative, dramaturgical, deconstructive, collaborative, feminist, interventionist, resistance, performative, social justice collaborative, political, postcolonial, transnational, relational, family, place, trauma. loss, illness, abuse, sexuality, race, death.

Stacy Holman Jones offers clarity, reminding us that

> Autoethnography is a blurred genre ... a response to the call ... it is setting a scene, telling a story, weaving intricate connections between life and art ... making a text present... refusing categorization ... believing that words matter and writing toward the moment when the point of creating autoethnographic texts is to change the world.
>
> (2005, p. 765)

Extending Holman Jones, autoethnography represents a new writing form:

> It is part cultural critique, part autobiography, part ethnography, a form that uses the techniques of a minimalist fiction: plot, characterization,

dialogue, more showing than telling. The writer writes from the scenes of cultural memory, taking up moments of injustice, racism, injury, intolerance, rearranging, suppressing, even inventing scenes, forging claims to exact truth, or factual accuracy, searching instead for emotional truth, for deep meaning, for texts that move persons to critical consciousness, and political action in the world. In so doing, I'm in the "boundaries of creative nonfiction [which] will always be as fluid as water."

(see Blew 1999, p. 7)

This book has been about performance, about social justice, about race, about writing utopian performatives that imagine a world free of injustice. It has been about acts of activism, ethnodramas that address real life trauma. It has been about re-thinking the word performance. It has been about locating ethnography and autoethnography in a social theatre framework, from Saldana's [auto] ethnodramas, ethnotheatre and reality theatre, to Victor Turner's ethnoscripts, to Boal's theatre of the oppressed (from forum to invisible), to Schechner's four types of social theatre (healing, action, community, art).

It has been about competing models of performance, from Saldana's embodied performances framed by a script, presented in front of an audience, to Conquergood's complicated performance triads: intervention, artistry, critique, fieldwork as an object of study, as a method of study, performance as a tactic of intervention, as poesis, mimesis, kinesis, as transgression, as pedagogy.

Goffman's dramaturgical theory treats all the world as a stage and everything as a performance. This argument frames Turner's theory of performance as ritual (breach, crisis, redress, reintegration), as liminality, as making not faking. Sechechner's argument that performance is twice-behaved behavior extends Turner's ritual model. In contrast, Madison's critical performance ethnography centers on the performative I (Spry) and a radical existential politics of resistance. Boal's theatre of the oppressed uses new terms, from simultaneous dramaturgy, to spectators as actors, to bring persons into performance spaces where acts of resistance can be imagined.

Boal and Freire's theatre's (and pedagogies) of the oppressed use performance, ethnography, theatre and dramatic theory to criticize neoliberal discourse, to inspire acts of activism. Here the theatrical, the performative and the ethnographic come together. The dramatist, with the assistance of spect-actors, uses the facts and experiences of oppression to change history. This is critical pedagogy in action, a politics of liberation, inquiry and theatre for justice. There is no going back.

Back to Mils and Goffman

The implications of the theatrical, performance turn are complicated, tangled up in biography, politics and acts of resistance. The implications bring us back to C. Wright Mills and Erving Goffman and the question addressed in our Introduction. What kind of [auto] ethnographic performance studies do we want today? Do we want Mills' richly theoretical sociological imagination, or do we want Goffman's cool, aloof, dramaturgical model which treats all the world as a stage? Although never showing me how to do it, Mills challenged me to link my biography to my historical moment. No theatre here, just flesh and blood human beings struggling to make do in their historical moment.

Goffman is all theatre, all pretense, illusion, masks, impression management, no historical moment. I said I was not prepared to accept Goffman's model in 1959. I've since turned the corner, if only momentarily, because under Donald Trump Baudrillard's simulacra has become our new reality. The simulacrum is never that which conceals the truth – it is the truth which conceals that there is none (Baudrillard 1983, p. 1). The simulacrum is true. There is no longer any certain truth, illusion prevails, truthiness if it looks truthy it is truthy, lies, forgeries prevail. A ministry of truth adjudicates, reads tweets, offers historical revisionism. Fake news circulates in daily discourse. Like other fascist dictators, Donald Trump, rose to power because of his ability to manipulate the media, to lie, to misrepresent, to create media spectacles complete with Greek choruses, cheering crowds, jesters, jokers, comedians, judges, protesters, activists, journalists and a 24-hour breaking infotainment news cycle which requires constant new news (Davies 2018).

Goffman helps me dismantle Trump's dramaturgical facade: front stage, back stage, props, scripts, performers in costume – butlers, masseuses, chauffeurs, chefs – face-work, impression management, staged productions, gaudy Trump Tower, Mar-a-Lago, Trump's pretend Winter White House, gold chandelier, gaudy art, theatrics and waving arms, the orange pompadour, slogans Make American Great Again.

Mills challenges me to use the tools of the critical sociological imagination to create performative autoethnodramas that unsettle and enact new utopias of possibility.

Here it is necessary to borrow from Durham:

> By revisiting spaces and places where we are, we reimagine … the dynamic possibilities of a feminist politics that can help homegirls survive, escape, and dismantle colluding exploitive systems that render us invisible. *By writing myself into a place called home, I have arrived at the end of a chapter of a new beginning where I can say I am here.*
>
> (2014, p. 128, italics added)

Amen. Home at last. I know the place for the first time.
The end

Appendix A: A genealogy of terms, moments and texts

1905	Avant-Garde art/theatre: dadism, futurism, surrealism
1912–1920	Civic Theatre Movement in US; National Women's Party suffrage parades
1915–	Little Theatre movement, local acting and local talent
1917–1935	Harlem Renaissance, combining art, politics, theatre, music and civic activism (Du Bois, Hurston, Hughes Du Bois)
1920–1930s	Working-class theatre movement, left-wing artists and playwrights lead protests: Brecht
1935–1939	Federal Theatre Project
1945–1960	The Dramaturgical turn: Burke, Goffman; art/performance as experience: Dewey
1955–	The Performative Turn, speech act theory: Austin, Searle
1960–1970	Civil Rights movement. Community-based performance groups engage anti-war, civil rights issues; Free Southern Theatre; Susanne Lacy and the Women's movement; El Teatro Campesino and Chicano Farm Workers struggles
1960s	The Linguistic, narrative, poststructural turn: Saussure, Wittgenstein, Derrida
1970s	Local political theatre; Black Arts movement (Neal); CETA and Neighborhood Arts Program funding for community-based art programs in schools, senior centers and prisons
1975, 1979	First use of the term autoethnography (Goldschmidt 1975; Heider 1975; Hayano 1979)
1970–1990	Alternative, feminist, queer, indigenous, experimental, community based applied theatre performance groups (Heider 1975; Hayano 1979)
1980s	The cultural turn: Writing Culture: Geertz, Clifford, Marcus
1980s	The performing culture, social drama, performative turn: Conquergood, Turner, Bruner, Kirschenblatt-Gimblett, Butler
1980	Performance as representation; performance ethnography: Schechner, Conquergood; multiple meanings/origins of performance: European theatre, historic, shamanism, play,

	everyday life, ritual, dialogic, experimental theatre (Schechner 2013, p. 18)
1980–	Contemporary performance art movement
1985	Theatre of the Oppressed; Forum Theatre: Boal; critical pedagogy: Freire
1980s	Performance Studies Departments/programs emerge: NYU, Northwestern (NW), Texas A & M, UC Berkeley, Liverpool Hope University; two main brands (NYU): theatre, dance, performance art, queer, critical race, postcolonial; (NW): global, critical ethnography, politics, identity
1985	Performance Studies division created in National Communication Association
1990–	Critical pedagogy turn: Garoian; critical theory informs critical ethnography (McLaren, Kincheloe, Giroux)
1990s	Performance Writing, after the literary turn: Pollock
2000–2010:	Queer, Critical Race, Feminist, Indigenous Critical Performance Ethnography
2002	Performance Studies: An Introduction, 1e/ (Schechner 2002)
2006	Sage Handbook of Performance Studies (Madison and Hamera 2006)
2006	Performance Studies: An Introduction, 2e/ (Schechner 2002)
2013	Handbook of Autoethnography (Jones, Adams & Ellis 2013)
2013	Performance Studies: An Introduction, 3/e/ (Schechner, 2013)
2010–2020:	Acts of activism (Madison 2010), hybridity: Paper, Body, Stage (Spry 2011); multiple strands of autoethnography; analytic, evocative, performance, critical, ethnographic, therapeutic, embodied, narrative, intersectional (Boylorn and Orbe 2014)

***

From this dateline it is clear that the performance turn in performance studies has been shaped by a recurring commitment to use performance, theatre and art in the name of social justice. From the 1900s forward local acts of protest in the United States have focused on inequities connected to gender, sexuality, violence race, class and nation. These protests have been situated within a theatrical, performative framework. The violence, the injustice is brought on stage, made visible through performance. The link between performance, ethnography, autoethnography, politics and cultural struggles runs deep. In times of need global citizens use the weapons of theatre, drama and performance to pursue social justice, This impulse is deeply embedded in the fabrics of culture and history.

The alliance between theatre, performance ethnography, personal narrative, pedagogy and performance studies can be traced to many sources, told in many different ways. Multiple turns: civic theatre, working-class theatre, dramaturgical, linguistic, narrative, performative, cultural, social drama, performance art, performance writing, critical pedagogy, autoethnography. Each telling, each turn establishes a different history, a different story of origin, but the broader, meta-narrative is unwavering, the theatrical backdrop is ever present.

In every instance each turn is inserted deeply in the social fabric. The dramaturgical, performative, linguistic and narrative turns are bracketed by the Second World War and the Korean War, the working-class theatre project and the Great Depression Federal Theatre project on one side and the anti-war, civil rights movements on the other. The autoethnographic, performing culture, critical pedagogy, performance ethnography turns appear as feminist, queer, indigenous applied theatre performance groups make their presence felt on the global stage in the 1980s and 1990s.

Each of these origin stories is required. In hindsight, it can now be seen that each turn needed to be taken. Each turn moved the project closer to its current critical performative, pedagogical moment. Each turn created a new space, a new set of openings, each space unsettled what had come before.

Most importantly, ethnography had to be taken out of a purely methodological framework and located first within a social justice performative arena, and then within the spaces of pedagogy where it was understood that the pedagogical was always political. It can now be seen that interpretive autoethnography's subject matter is set by a dialectical pedagogy. This pedagogy connects oppressors and the oppressed in capitalism's liminal, epiphanic spaces.

Bibliography

Adams, T. E. 2011. *Narrating the Closet: An Autoethnography of Same-Sex Attraction.* Walnut Creek, CA: Left Coast Press.

Adams, T. E. and S. Holman Jones. 2008. "Autoethnography Is Queer." Pp. 373–390 in N. K. Denzin, Y. S. Lincoln and L. T. Smith (Eds.) *Handbook of Critical and Indigenous Methodologies.* Thousand Oaks, CA: Sage.

Adams, T. E. and S. Holman Jones. 2011. "Telling Stories: Reflexivity, Queer Theory, and Autoethnography." *Cultural Studies? Critical Methodologies* 11(2), 108–116.

Adams, Tony, Stacy Holman Jones and Carolyn Ellis. 2013. "Conclusion: Storying our Future. " Pp. 669–677 in Stacy Holman Jones, Tony E. Adams and Carolyn Ellis (Eds.) *Handbook of Autothnography.* Walnut Creek: Left Coast Press.

Alasuutari, P. 2004. *Social Theory and Human Reality.* Thousand Oaks, CA: Sage.

Alexander, Bryant. 1999. "Performing Culture in the Classroom: An Instructional [Auto] Ethnography." *Text and Performance Quarterly* 19, 217–306.

Alexander, B. K. 2000. "Skin Flint (or, the Garbage Man's Kid): A Generative Performance Based on Tami Spry's Tattoo Stories." *Text and Performance Quarterly* 20, 97–114.

Alexander, Bryant. 2005. "Performance Ethnography: The Reenacting and Inciting of Culture." Pp. 411–442 in N. K. Denzin & Y. S. Lincoln (Eds.) *Handbook of Qualitative Research*, 3/e. Thousand Oaks, CA: Sage.

Alexander, B. K. 2011. "Standing in the Wake: A Critical Auto/ethnographic Exercise on Reflexivity in Three Movements." *Cultural Studies? Critical Methodologies*, 11(2), 98–107.

Alexander, Bryant Keith. 2012. *The Performativity Sustainability of Race: Reflections on Black Culture and the Politics of Identity.* New York: Peter Lang.

Alexander, Bryant. 2013. "Telling Autoethnography and Autoethnographic Pedagogy." Pp. 538–556 in Stacy Holman Jones, Tony E. Adams and Carolyn Ellis (Eds.) *Handbook of Autoethography.* Walnut Creek: Left Coast Press.

Alexander, Bryant. 2017. "Queer/Quare Theory: Worldmaking and Methodologies." Pp. 275–308 in N. K. Denzin and Y. S. Lincoln (Eds.) *Sage Handbook of Qualitative Research*, 5/e. Thousand Oaks: Sage. Alexander, Bryant Keith, Claudio Moreira and Hari Stephen Kumar. 2015. "Memory, Mourning, and Miracles: A Triple-Autoethnographic Performance Script." *International Review of Qualitative Research* 8(2), 229–255.

Alrutz, Megan. 2015. *Digital Storytelling, Applied Theatre & Youth: Performing Possibility.* London: Routledge.

Altheide, David L. 1995. *An Ecology of Communication*. New York: Aldine de Gruyter.

Altheide, David. 2010. *Terror Post 9/11 and the Media*. New York: Peter Lang.

Altheide, David L. and Robert P. Snow. 1991. *Media Worlds in the Postjournalism Era*. New York: Aldine de Gruyter.

American Association for the Advancement of Science. 2009. "AAAS Science and Human Rights Coalition Meeting Report." July 23–24. www.aaas.org/

American Association of University Professors (AAUP). 2006a. "Research on human subjects: academic freedom and the Institutional Review Board." www.aaup.org/AAUP/comm./rep/A/humansub.htm

American Association of University Professors, Committee A. 2006b. "Report on human subjects: academic freedom and the Institutional Review Boards." www.aaup.org/AAUP/About/committees/committee+repts/CommA/

Anderson, James. 2016 "Post-election Thoughts from Dean Anderson." Thursday, November 10, 2016 at 2:35 PM. College of Education Dean.

Anderson, L. 2006. "Analytic Autoethnography." *Journal of Contemporary Ethnography* 35, 373–395.

Anzaldua, Gloria. 1987. *Borderlands/La Frontera: The New Mestiza*. San Francisco: aunt lute books.

Arendt, Hannah. 2001. *The Origins of Totalitarianism*. New York: Houghton Mifflin Harcourt (originally published 1951).

Aronowitz, Stanley. 1998. "Introduction." Pp. 1–19 in Paulo Freire, *Pedagogy of Freedom: Ethics, Democracy, and Civic Courage*. Boulder, CO: Rowman & Littlefield.

Atkinson, Paul. 2015. *For Ethnography*. London: Sage.

Atkinson, Paul. 2017. *Thinking Ethnographically*. London: Sage. Atkinson, Paul and David Silverman. 1997. "Kundera's Immortality: The Interview Society and the Invention of the Self." *Qualitative Inquiry* 3, 304–325.

Atkinson, P., S. Delamont and A. Coffey. 2004. *Key Themes in Qualitative Research: Continuities and Changes*. Lanham, MD: Rowman Altamira.

Auden, W. H. 1940. "Funeral Blues." P. 40 in *Another Time: Poems by W. H. Auden*. London: Faber & Faber Limited.

Austin, J. L. 1962. *How To Do Things With Words*. Cambridge, MA: Harvard University Press.

Badley, Graham Francis. 2015. "Qualitative Ranting?" *Qualitative Inquiry* 21(9), 759–765.

Bagley, Carl. 2008. "Educational Ethnography as Performance Art: Towards a Sensuous Feeling and Knowing." *Qualitative Research* 8(1), 53–72.

Bakhtin, M. 1986. *Speech Genres and Other Essays* (V. McGee, Trans.). Austin, TX: University of Texas Press. (Original work published 1952–1953).

Baldwin, James Arthur. 1979. "Interview with Mel Watkins." *New York Times Book Review*, 23 September, 4.

Barad, K. 2003. "Posthumanist Performativity: Toward an Understanding of How Matter Comes to Matter." *Signs: Journal of Women in Culture and Society* 28(3), 801–831.

Barad, Karen. 2007. *Meeting the Universe Halfway: Quantum Physics and the Entanglement of Matter and Meaning*. Durham: Duke University Press.

Baraka, Amiri. 1998. "Black Art." Pp. 1501–1502 in Patricia Liggins Hill (Ed.) *Call & Response: The Riverside Anthology of the African American Tradition*. Boston: Houghton Mifflin. (Copyright 1969 Amiri Baraka).

Barthes, Roland. 1985. *The Grain of the Voice: Interviews: 1962–1980* (L. Coverdale, Trans.). New York: Hill & Wang.

Battiste, Marie. 2008. "Research Ethics for Protecting Indigenous Knowledge and Heritage: Institutional and Researcher Responsibilities." Pp. 497–510 in N. K. Denzin, Y. S. Lincoln and L. T. Smith (Eds.) *Handbook of Critical and Indigenous Methodologies*. Thousand Oaks: Sage.

Baudrillard, Jean. 1983. *Simulations*. New York: Semiotext(e).

Bauman, Zygmunt. 1999. *In Search of Politics*. Stanford, CA: Stanford University Press.

Becker, Howard S. 1967. "Whose Side Are We On?" *Social Problems* 14(2), 239–247.

Becker, Howard S. 1986. *Doing Things Together: Selected Papers*. Evanston, IL: Northwestern University Press.

Becker, H. S. 2004. "Comment on Kevin D. Haggerty. Ethics Creep: Governing Social Science Research in the Name of Ethics." *Qualitative Sociology* 27(4), 415–416. Bean, A. 2001. "Black Minstrelsy and Double Inversion, circa 1890." Pp. 171–191 in H. J. Elam, Jr. and D. Krasner (Eds.) *African American Performance and Theatre History*. New York: Oxford University Press.

Beebe, Rose Marie and Robert M. Senkewicz. 2015. *Junipero Serra: California, Indians, and the Transformation of a Missionary*. Norman: University of Oklahoma. Press.

Begaye, Tim. 2008. "Modern Democracy: The Complexities Beyond Appropriating Indigenous Models of Governance and Implementation." Pp. 459–469 in N. K. Denzin, Y. S. Lincoln and L. T. Smith (Eds.) *Handbook of Critical and Indigenous Methodologies*. Thousand Oaks: Sage.

Bently, Leslie. "A Brief Biography of Paulo Freire." http://ptoweb.org/aboutpto/a-brief-biography-of-paulo-freire/Pedagogy and Theatre of the Oppressed; http://ptoweb.org/gatherings/conference/conference-site-application/

Benjamin, Walter. 1969a. *Illuminations*, Edited and with an Introduction by Hannah Arendt, translated by Harry Zohn. New York: Harcourt, Brace & World, Inc.

Benjamin, W. 1969b. What Is Epic Theater? *Understanding Brecht*, 15–22.

Berger, Ronald J. 2013. *Introducing Disability Studies*. Boulder, CO: Lynne Rienner Publishers.

Berger, Ronald J., Jon A. Feucht and Jennifer Flad. 2014. *Disability, Augmentative Communication, and the American Dream: A Qualitative Inquiry*. Boulder: Lexington Books.

Berry, K. and R. P. Clair. 2011. "Contestation and Opportunity in Reflexivity: An Introduction." *Cultural Studies ☒ Critical Methodologies* 11(2), 95–97.

Bertaux, Daniel. 1987. "Review Essay of *L'illusion biographique* by Pierre Bourdieu" (*Acts de la recherche en sciences sociales* 62/63: 69–72). *Life Stories/Récits de vie* 3, 47–50.

Bhabha, Homi K. 1994. *The Location of Culture*. New York: Routledge.

Bial, Henry. 2004. "Introduction." Pp. 1–4 in Henry Bial (Ed.) *The Performance Studies Reader*. New York: Routledge.

Birringer, Johannes. 1993. *Theatre, Theory, Postmodernism*. Bloomington: Indiana University Press.

Bishop, Russell. 1998. "Freeing Ourselves from Neo-Colonial Domination in Research: A Maori Approach to Creating Knowledge." *International Journal of Qualitative Studies in Education* 11, 199–219.

Bishop, Russell. 2008. "Te Kotahitanga: Kauppa Maori in Mainstream Classrooms." Pp. 339–458 in N. K. Denzin, Y. S. Lincoln and L. T. Smith (Eds.) *Handbook of Critical and Indigenous Methodologies*. Thousand Oaks: Sage.

Blew, Mary Clearman. 1999. *Bone Deep in Landscape: Writing, Reading and Place*. Norman: University of Oklahoma Press.

Bloom, Leslie Rebecca. 2009. "Introduction: Global Perspectives on Poverty and Social Justice."*International Studies of Qualitative Studies in Education* 22(3), 253–261.

Bloom, Leslie Rebecca and Patricia Sawin. 2009. "Ethical Responsibilities in Feminist Research: Challenging Ourselves to do Activist Research with Women in Poverty." *International Studies of Qualitative Studies in Education* 22(3), 333–351.

Blumer, Herbert. 1933. *Movies and Conduct*. New York: Macmillan.

Blumer, Herbert. 1969. "Science Without Concepts." Pp. 153–170 in Herbert Blumer, *Symbolic Interaction: Perspective and Method*. Englewood Cliffs, N.J.: Prentice-Hall.

Boal, Augusto. 1985. *Theatre of the Oppressed*. New York: Theatre Communications group (originally published 1974).

Boal, Augusto. 1994. "She Made Her Brother Smile: A Three-minute Forum Theatre Experience." Pp. 81–83 in Mady Schutzman and Jan Cohen-Cruz (Eds.) *Playing Boal: Theatre, Therapy, Activism*. London and New York: Routledge.

Boal, Augusto. 1995. *The Rainbow of Desire: The Boal Method of Theatre and Therapy*. London: Routledge.

Boal, Augusto. 1998. *Legislative Theatre: Using Performance to Make Politics*London: Routledge.

Boal, A. 2000. *Theater of the Oppressed*. London: Pluto Press.

Boal, Augusto. 2001. *Hamlet and the Baker's Son: My Life in Theatre and Politics* (trans. Adrian Jackson and Candida Blaker). London: Routledge.

Boal, Augusto. 2002. *Games for Actors and Non-Actors*, second edition (trans. Adrian Jackson). London: Routledge (first edition 1992).Boal, Augusto. 2006. *The Aesthetics of the Oppressed* (trans. Adrian Jackson). London: Routledge.

Birringer, Johannes. 1993. *Theatre, Theory, Postmodernism*. Bloomington: Indiana University Press.

Bochner, Arthur P. 2000. "Criteria Against Ourselves." *Qualitative Inquiry* 5(2), 266–272.

Bochner, Arthur P. 2007. "Notes Toward an Ethics of Memory in Autoethnographic Inquiry." Pp. 197–208 in N. K. Denzin and M. D. Giardina (Eds.) *Ethical Futures in Qualitative Research: Decolonizing the Politics of Knowledge*. Walnut Creek: Left Coast Press.

Bochner, Arthur P. and Carolyn Ellis. 2016a. *Evocative Autoethnography: Writing Lives and Telling Stories*. New York: Routledge.

Bochner, Arthur P. and Carolyn Ellis. 2016b. "The ICQI and the Rise of Auto-ethnography." *International Review of Qualitative Research* 9(2), 208–217.

Bochner, Arthur P. and Nicholas Riggs. 2014. "Producing Narrative Inquiry." Pp. 23–45 in P. Leavy (Ed.), *Handbook of Qualitative Methods*. New York: Oxford University Press.

Bolen, D. M. and T. E. Adams. 2017. *Narrative Ethics. The Routledge International Handbook on Narrative and Life History*. New York: Routledge. Bourdieu, Pierre. 1986. "L'illusion biographique." *Acts de la Recherche en Sciences Sociales* 62/63, 69–72.

Bourdieu, Pierre. 1996. "Understanding." *Theory, Culture & Society* 13, 17–37.

Bourdieu, Pierre. 1999. *Acts of Resistance*. New York: New Press.

Bourdieu, P. and L. J. Wacquant 1992. *An Invitation to Reflexive Sociology*. Chicago: University of Chicago Press.

Boylorn, Robin M. and Mark P. Orbe (Eds.). 2014. *Critical Autoethnography: Intersecting Cultural Identities in Everyday Life*. Walnut Creek: Left Coast Press.

Brady, Sara. 2012. *Performance, Politics, and the War on Terror: "Whatever It Takes"*. New York: Palgrave Macmillan.

Bratich, Jack. 2017. "Observation in a Surveilled World." Pp. 526–545 in N. K. Denzin and Y. S. Lincoln (Eds.) *Sage Handbook of Qualitative Research*. Thousand Oaks: Sage.

Brecht, Bertolt. 1965. *The Jewish Wife & Other Short Plays*. English versions by Eric Bentley. New York: Grove Press, Inc.

Brissett, Dennis and Charles Edgley (Eds). 1990. *Life as Theater: A Dramaturgical Sourcebook*, 2/e. New York: Aldine de Gruyter.

Broadhurst, Susan. 1999. *Liminal Acts: A Critical Overview of Contemporary Performance and Theory*. New York: Cassell.

Bruner, Edward M. 1986. "Experience and Its Expressions." Pp. 3–30 in Victor M. Turner and Edward M. Bruner (Eds.) *The Anthropology of Experience*. Urbana: University of Illinois Press.

Brydon-Miller, M., M. Kral, P. Maguire, S. Noffke and A. Sabhlok. 2011. "Jazz and the Banyan Tree." *Handbook of Qualitative Research*, 387–400.

Buckley, Cara. 2017. "Exploring Racism in Intimate Terms." *New York Times, Arts & Leisure*, Sunday August 27, AR 12–13.

Burawoy, Michael. 1998. "The Extended Case Method." *Sociological Theory* 16, 4–33.

Burawoy, Michael. 2000. "Introduction: Reaching for the Global." Pp. 1–40 in Michael Burawoy, Joseph A. Blum, Sheba George, Zsuzsa Gille, Teresa Gowan, Lynne Haney et al., *Global Ethnography: Forces, Connections, and Imaginations in a Postmodern World*. Berkeley: University of California Press.

Burke, James Lee. 2009. *Rain Gods*. New York: Simon & Schuster.

Butler, Judith. 1990. *Gender Trouble*. New York: Routledge.

Butler, Judith. 1993. *Bodies that Matter*. New York: Routledge.

Butler, Judith. 1995. "For a Careful Reading." Pp. 127–143 in S. Benhabib, J. Butler, D. Cornell, & N. Fraser (Eds.) *Feminist Contentions: A Philosophical Exchange*. New York: Routledge.

Butler, Judith 1997. *Excitable Speech: A Politics of the Performative*. New York: Routledge.

Butler, Judith. 2004. *Undoing Gender*. New York: Routledge.

Butler, Judith. 2015. *Notes Toward a Performative Theory of Assembly*. Cambridge, Mass: Harvard University Press. Califia, P. 1997. *Sex Changes: The Politics of Transgenderism*. San Francisco: Cleis Press.

Cameron, Rose E., Elizabeth Fast, Anjali Helferty and Patrick Lewis. 2016. "Critical Reflexivity on Indigenous Knowledge as a Mode of Inquiry." *International Review of Qualitative Research* 9(3), 273–276.

Cannella, Gaile S. 2015. "Introduction: Engaging Critical Qualitative Science: Histories and Possibilities." Pp. 7–30 in Gaile S. Canella, Michelle Slazar Perez, and Penny A. Pasque (Eds.) *Critical Qualitative Inquiry: Foundations and Futures*. Walnut Creek: Left Coast Press.

Cannella, G. S. and Y. S. Lincoln. 2011. "Ethics, Research Regulations, and Critical Social Science." *The Sage Handbook of Qualitative Research* 4, 81–90.

Carnevale, Fulvia and John Kelsey. 2007. "Art of the Possible: An Interview with Jacques Ranciere." *Artforum*, March, 260–261.

Carspecken, P. F. 1996. *Critical Ethnography in Educational Research: A Theoretical and Practical Guide*. London: Psychology Press.

Carver, M. H. 2003. "Risky Business: Exploring Women's Autobiography and Performance." Pp. 15–29 in L. C. Miller, J. Taylor and M. H. Carver (Eds.) *Voices Made Flesh: Performing Women's Autobiography*. Madison, WI: University of Wisconsin Press.

Carver, Raymond. 1979. "The Calm." *The Iowa Review* 10(3), 33–37.

Catlin, George. 1848. *Catlin's Notes of Eight Years' Travels and Residence in Europe, with his North American Indian Collection, with Anecdotes and Incidents of the Travels and Adventures of Three Different Parties of American Indians Whom He Introduced to the Courts of England, France, and Belgium, In Two Volumes. Vol, I.* London: Published by the Author at his Indian Collection, No 6, Waterloo Place. Printed by William Clowes and Sons, London: Stamford Street.

Chang, Heewon, Faith Wambura Ngunjiri and Kathy-Ann C. Hernandez. 2013. *Collaborative Autoethography.* Walnut Creek: Left Coast Press. Charmaz, Kathy. 2005. "Grounded Theory in the 21st Century: A Qualitative Method for Advancing Social Justice Research." Pp. 507–535 in N. K. Denzin and Y. S. Lincoln (Eds.) *Handbook of Qualitative Research*, 3/e. Thousand Oaks: Sage. Charon, Rita. 2006. *Narrative Medicine: Honoring the Stories of Illness.* New York: Oxford University Press.

Chawla, D. 2007a. "Between Stories and Theories: Embodiments, Disembodiments, and Other Struggles." *Storytelling, Self, Society: An Interdisciplinary Journal of Storytelling Studies* 3(1), 16–30.

Chawla, D. 2007b. "The First Disciple: A Generative Autobiographical Performance from an Ethnographic field." *Cultural Studies? Critical Methodologies* 7(4), 357–377.

Chomsky, Noam. 1996. *Class Warfare: Interviews With David Barasamian.* Monroe, ME: Common Courage.

Christians, Clifford. 1995. "The Naturalistic Fallacy in Contemporary Interactionist-Interpretive Research." *Studies in Symbolic Interaction* 19, 125–130.

Christians, Clifford. 1997. "The Ethics of Being in a Communications Context." Pp. 3–23 in Clifford G. Christians and Michael Traber (Eds.) *Communication Ethics and Universal Values.* Thousand Oaks, CA: Sage.

Christians, Clifford. 1998. "The Sacredness of Life." *Media Development* 2, 3–7.

Christians, Clifford G. 2000. "Ethics and Politics in Qualitative Research." Pp. 133–155 in N. K. Denzin and Y. S. Lincoln (Eds.) *Handbook of Qualitative Research*, 2/e. Thousand Oaks, CA: Sage.

Christians, Clifford. 2002. "Introduction." In "Ethical Issues and Qualitative Research," special issue of *Qualitative Inquiry* 8(4), 407–410.

Christians, Clifford G. 2005. "Ethics and Politics in Qualitative Research." Pp. 139–164 in N. K. Denzin and Y. S. Lincoln (eds.) *Handbook of Qualitative Research*, 3/e. Thousand Oaks, CA: Sage.

Christians, Clifford G. 2007. "Neutral Science and the Ethics of Resistance." Pp. 47–66 in N. K. Denzin and M. D. Giardina (Eds.) *Ethical Futures in Qualitative Research.* Walnut Creek, CA: Left Coat Press.

Churchill, Ward. 1994. *Indians Are Us? Culture and Genocide in Native North American.* Monroe, Me: Common Courage Press.

Clarke, Adele E., Carrie Friese and Rachel Washburn. 2015. "Introducing Situational Analysis." Pp. 11–75 in Adele E. Clarke, Carrie Friese and Rachel Washburn (Eds.) *Situational Analysis in Practice: Mapping Research with Grounded Theory.* Walnut Creek: Left Coast Press.

Clifford, James, and George Marcus (Eds.). 1986. *Writing Culture: The Poetics and Politics of Ethnography.* Berkeley: University of California Press.

Clough, Patrica Ticineto. 1988. "Women Writing and the Life History: A Reading of Toni Morrison's "The Bluest Eye." Unpublished manuscript.

Clough, Patricia Ticineto. 1990. "The Deconstruction of Ethnographic Subjectivity and the Construction of Deliberate Belief." *Studies in Symbolic Interaction* 11, 35–44.

Clough, Patricia Ticineto. 2000a. "Comments on Setting Criteria for Experimental Writing." *Qualitative Inquiry* 6, 278–291.

Clough, Patricia Ticineto. 2000b. "Judith Butler." Pp. 754–773 in *The Blackwell Companion to Major Social Theorists* (ed. George Ritzer). Malden, MA: Blackwell.

Clough, Patricia Ticineto. 2007. "Introduction." Pp. 1–33 in Patricia Ticineto Clough with Jean Halley (Eds.) *The Affective Turn: Theorizing the Social*. Durham: Duke University Press.

Clough, Patricia Ticineto. 2016. "Rethinking Race, Calculation, Quantification, and Measure." *Cultural Studies – Critical Methodologies*, 16(5), 435–441.

Clough, P. T. and J. Halley (Eds.). 2007. *The Affective Turn: Theorizing the Social*. Durham: Duke University Press.

Cohen-Cruz, Jan. 2005. *Local Acts: Community-Based Performance in the United States*. New Brunswick: Rutgers University Press. Cohen-Cruz, Jan. 2006. "The Problem Democracy is Supposed to Solve." Pp. 427–445 in D. Soyini Madison and Judith Hamera (Eds.) *The Sage Handbook of Performance Studies*. Thousand Oaks: Sage.

Cohn, Ruby. 1988. "Realism." P. 815 in Martin Banham (Ed.), *The Cambridge Guide to Theatre*. Cambridge: Cambridge University Press.

Collins, Patricia Hill. 1991. *Black Feminist Thought*. New York: Routledge.

Collins, Patricia Hill. 2000. *Black Feminist Thought*, 2/e. New York: Routledge.

Comaroff, Jean, and John L. Comaroff. 2001. "Millennial Capitalism: First Thoughts on a Second Coming." Pp. 1–56 in Jean Comaroff and John L. Comaroff (Eds.) *Millennial Capitalism and the Culture of Neoliberalism*. Durham, NC: Duke University Press.

Conquergood, Dwight. 1985. "Performing as a Moral Act: Ethical Dimensions of the Ethnography of Performance." *Literature in Performance* 5(1), 1–13. (Reprinted as pp. 65–80 in Patrick Johnson (Ed.) 2013. *Cultural Struggles: Performance, Ethnography, Praxis: Dwight Conquergood*. Ann Arbor: University of Michigan Press.)

Conquergood, Dwight. 1986. "Performing Cultures: Ethnography, Epistemology and Ethics." *Scriptor*, 55–147. (Originally appeared in *Miteinander Sprechenand Handeln: Festschrift fur Hellmut Geissmer*, ed. Edith Slembek.)

Conquergood, Dwight. 1991. "Rethinking Ethnography: Towards a Critical Cultural Politics." *Communication Monograph* 58, 179–194.

Conquergood, Dwight. 1992a. "Ethnography, Rhetoric and Performance." *Quarterly Journal of Speech* 78: 80–97.

Conquergood, Dwight. 1992b. "Life in Big Red: Struggles and Accomodations in a Chicago Polyethnic Tenement." Pp. 95–144 in Louise Lamphere (Ed.), *Structuring Diversity: Ethnographic Perspectives on the New Immigration*. Chicago: University of Chicago Press.

Conquergood, Dwight. 1998. "Beyond the Text: Toward a Performative Cultural Politics." Pp. 25–36 in Sheron J. Dailey (Ed.), *The Future of Performance Studies: Visions and Revisions*. Annadale, VA: National Communication Association.

Conquergood, Dwight. 2002. "Performance Studies: Interventions and Radical Research." *The Drama Review*, 45, 145–156.

Conquergood, Dwight. 2006. "Rethinking Ethnography: Towards a Critical Cultural Politics." Pp. 351–365 in D. Soyini Madison and Judith Hamera (Eds.) *The Sage Handbook of Performance Studies*. Thousand Oaks: Sage.

Conquergood, Dwight. 2013. "Performance Studies: Interventions and Radical Research." Pp. 32–46 in Patrick Johnson (Ed.), *Cultural Struggles: Performance, Ethnography, Praxis: Dwight Conquergood*. Ann Arbor: University of Michigan Press (originally published 2002).Coole, Diane and Samantha Frost, 2010. "Introducing the

New Materialisms." Pp. 1–46 in Diane Coole and Samantha Frost (Eds.) *New Materialisms: Ontology, Agency, and Politics*. Durham: Duke University Press.

Cook-Lynn, Elizabeth. 1996. *Why I Can't Read Wallace Stegner and Other Essays*. Madison: University of Wisconsin Press.

Conrad, Diane. 2004. "Exploring Risky Youth: Popular Theatre as Participatory, Performative Research Method." *International Journal of Qualitative Methods* 3(1), 12–25.

Corey, Frederick C. 2015. "Editor's Introduction: Performance and Social Change." *Text and Performance Quarterly* 35(1), 1–3.

Dailey, Sheron J. (Ed.). 1998a. *The Future of Performance Studies: Visions and Revisions*. Washington, D.C.: National Communication Association.

Dailey, Sheron J. 1998b. "Editor's Note." Pp. ix–xii in Sheron J. Dailey (Ed.). *The Future of Performance Studies: Visions and Revisions*. Washington, D.C.: National Communication Association. Darder, Antonia. 2002. *Reinventing Paulo Freire: A Pedagogy of Love*. Boulder: Westview Press.

Darder, Antonia, Marta Baltodano and Rodolfo D. Torres. 2003. "Critical Pedagogy: An Introduction." Pp. 1–23 in Antonia Darder, Marta Baltodano and Rodolfo D. Torres (Eds.) *The Critical Pedagogy Reader*. New York: Routledge-Falmer.

Darwish, Mahmoud. 1984. "The Earth is Closing on Us." P. 13 in M. Darwish, *Victims of a Map* (trans. Abdullah al-Udhari). London: al-Saqi Books.

Dash, L. 2007. "Journalism and Institutional Review Boards." *Qualitative Inquiry* 13(6), 871–874.

Davies, Bronwyn, 2006. "Collective Biography as Ethically Reflexive Practice." Pp. 182–189 in Bronwyn Davies and Susanne Gannon (Eds.) *Doing Collective Biography: Investigating the Production of Subjectivity*. Maidenhead: Open University Press.

Davies, Bronwyn. 2018. "Seduction and Desire: The Power of Spectacle." ICQI Keynote Address, 2018.

Davies, Bronwyn and Susanne Ganno. 2006. "Prologue." Pp. iv–x in Bronwyn Davies and Susanne Ganno (Eds.) *Doing Collective Biography: Investigating the Production of Subjectivity*. Maidenhead: Open University Press.

Davidson, Judith and Silvana di Gregorio. 2011. "Qualitative Research and Technology in the Midst of a Revolution." Pp. 627–643 in N. K. Denzin and Y.S. Lincoln (Eds.) *Handbook of Qualitative Research*, 4/e. Thousand Oaks: Sage.

Debord, Guy. [1967] 1994. *The Society of the Spectacle* (trans. Donald Nicholson-Smith). New York: Zone Books.

Deloria, Vine, Jr. 1969. *Custer Died for Your Sins: An Indian Manifesto*. Norman: University of Oklahoma Press.

Deloria, Vine, Jr. 1997. "Vine Deloria, Native American Author and Teacher." Pp. 34–38 in Studs Terkel, *The Studs Terkel Reader: My American Century*. New York: The New Press. Democratic Party. 2016. "2016 Democratic Party Platform, July 21, 2016." Approved by the Democratic Platform Committee July 8–9, 2016, Orlando, Fl. www.demconvention.com/wp-content/uploads/2016/07/Democratic-Party-Platform-7.21.16-no-lines.pdf

Dennis, Barbara. 2009. "Acting Up: Theater of the Oppressed as Critical Ethnography." *International Journal of Qualitative Methods* 8(2), 61–96.

Denzin, N. K. 1984. *On Understanding Emotion*. San Francisco: Jossey-Bass.

Denzin, N. K. 1991. *Images of Postmodern Society: Social Theory and Contemporary Cinema*. London: Sage.

Denzin, N. K. 1995a. *The Cinematic Society: The Voyeur's Gaze*. Thousand Oaks, CA: Sage.

Denzin, N. K. 1995b. "Information Technologies, Communicative Acts, and the Audience: Couch's Legacy to Communication Research." *Symbolic Interaction* 18, 247–268.

Denzin, N. K. 1997. *Interpretive Ethnography: Ethnographic Practices for the 21st Century.* Thousand Oaks, CA: Sage.

Denzin, Norman K. 2000. "Aesthetics and the Practices of Qualitative Inquiry." *Qualitative Inquiry* 6, 256–265.

Denzin, N. K. 2001. *Interpretive Interactionism* (2nd edn). Newbury Park: Sage Publications.

Denzin, Norman K. 2003a. "Much Ado About Goffman." Pp. 127–142 in A. Javier Trevino (Ed.) *Goffman's Legacy.* New York: Roman & Littlefield Publishers, Inc.

Denzin, N. K. 2003b. *Performance Ethnography: Critical Pedagogy and the Politics of Culture.* Thousand Oaks, CA: Sage.

Denzin, N. K. 2005. "Indians in the Park." *Qualitative Research* 3, 9–33.

Denzin, N. K. 2008. *Searching for Yellowstone: Performing Race, Nation and Nature in the New West.* Walnut Creek, CA: Left Coast Press.

Denzin, N. K. 2009. *Qualitative Inquiry under Fire.* Walnut Creek: Left Coast Press.

Denzin, N. K. 2010. *The Qualitative Manifesto: A Call to Arms.* Walnut Creek: Left Coast Press.

Denzin, N. K. 2011. *Custer on Canvas: Representing Indians, Memory and Violence in the New West.* Walnut Creek: Left Coast Press.

Denzin, Norman K. 2012. "The Politics of Evidence." Pp. 645–659 in N. K. Denzin and Y.S. Lincoln (Eds.) *Handbook of Qualitative Research,* 4/e. Thousand Oaks: Sage.

Denzin, Norman K. 2013a. *Indians on Display: Global Commodification of Native America in Performance, Art, and Museums.* Walnut Creek: Left Coast Press.

Denzin, Norman K. 2013b. "Interpretive Autoethnography." Pp. 123–142 in Stacy Holman Jones, Tony E. Adams and Carolyn Ellis (Eds.) *Handbook of Autoethnography.* Walnut Creek: Left Coast Press.

Denzin, Norman K. 2014. *Interpretive Autoethnography,* 2/e. Thousand Oaks: Sage.

Denzin, Norman K. 2015a. *Indians in Color: Native Art, Identity, and Performance in the New West.* Walnut Creek: Left Coast Press.

Denzin, Norman K. 2015b. "Fragments of a Western Self." *Qualitative Inquiry* 22(1), 40–46.

Denzin, Norman K. 2016. "Grandma's Story." *International Review of Qualitative Research* 9(2), 218–221.

Denzin, Norman K. 2017. "A Relational Ethic for Narrative Inquiry, or in the Forest but Lost in the trees. Or a One-Act Play with Many Endings." Pp. 605–617 in Ivor Goodson, Ari Antikainen, Pat Sikes, and Molly Andrews (Eds.) *The Routledge International Handbook on Narrative and Life History.* Abingdon, England: Routledge.

Denzin, N. K. and Y. S. Lincoln (Eds.). 2005. *The Sage Handbook of Qualitative Research,* 3/e. Thousand Oaks, CA: Sage.

Denzin, Norman K. and Yvonna S. Lincoln. 2008. "Introduction: Critical Methodologies and Indigenous Inquiry." Pp. 1–20 in N. K. Denzin, Y. S. Lincoln, and L. T. Smith (Eds.) *Handbook of Critical and Indigenous Methodologies.* Thousand Oaks, CA: Sage.

Denzin, Norman K. and Yvonna S. Lincoln. 2011. "Introduction: The Discipline and Practice of Qualitative Research." Pp. 1–20 in N. K. Denzin and Y. S. Lincoln (Eds.) *Handbook of Qualitative Research,* 4/e. Thousand Oaks, CA: Sage.

Denzin, N. K. and Y. S. Lincoln (Eds.). 2017. *The Sage Handbook of Qualitative Research,* 5/e. Thousand Oaks, CA: Sage.

Derrida, Jacques. 1967/1973. *Speech and Phenomena.* Evanston, IL: Northwestern University Press.

Derrida, Jacques. 1967/1976. *Of Grammatology.* Baltimore, MD: Johns Hopkins University Press.

Derrida, Jacques. 1967/1978. *Writing and Difference.* Chicago: University of Chicago Press.

Derrida, Jacques. 1972. "Structure, Sign and Play in the Discourse of the Human Sciences." Pp. 247–265 in Richard Macksey and Eugene Donato (Eds.) *The Structuralist Controversy: The Languages of Criticism and the Sciences of Man.* Baltimore, MD: Johns Hopkins University Press.

Derrida, Jacques. 1972/1981. *Positions.* Chicago: University of Chicago Press.

Derrida, Jacques. 2001. "The Future of the Professional or the Unconditional Uncertainty." Pp. 245–260 in Laurence Simmons and Heather Worth (Eds.) *Derrida Downunder.* Auckland: Dunmore Press.

DeVault, Marjorie L. 1999. *Liberating Method: Feminism and Social Research.* Philadelphia: Temple University Press.

Dewey, John. 1922/1930. *Human Nature and Conduct.* New York: Modern Library.

Diamond, David. 1994. "Introduction" and "Out of the Silence: Headlines Theatre and Power Plays." Pp. 1–16 and 35–52 in Mady Schutzman and Jan Cohen-Cruz (Eds.) *Playing Boal: Theatre, Therapy, Activism.* New York: Routledge.

Diamond, Elin. 1996. "Introduction." Pp. 1–12 in Elin Diamond (Ed.) *Performances and Cultural Politics.* New York: Routledge.

Diawara, Mantha. 1996. "Black Studies, Cultural Studies: Performative Acts." Pp. 300–306 in John Storey (Ed.) *What Is Cultural Studies? A Reader.* London: Arnold.

Dillard, Annie. 1974. *Pilgrim at Tinker Creek.* New York: Harper & Row.

Dillard, Annie. 1982. *Living by Fiction.* New York: Harper & Row.

Dimitriadis, Greg. 2005. "Pedagogy on the Move: New Intersections in (Between) the Educative and the Performative." Pp. 296–308 in D. Soyini and Judith Hamera (Eds.) *The Sage Handbook of Performance Studies.* Thousand Oaks: Sage.

Dingwall, R. 2008. "The Ethical Case against Ethical Regulation in the Humanities and Social Science Research." *21st Century Society* 3, 1–12.

Diversi, Marcelo, 2015. "On Decolonizing: E-Mail." 9 April.

Diversi, Marcelo and Dan Henhawk. 2012. "(Re) Awakening, Together, From a Long Colonizing Slumber." *International Review of Qualitative Research* 5(1), 51–72.

Diversi, Marcelo and C. Moreira. 2009. *Betweener Talk: Decolonizing Knowledge Production, Pedagogy, and Praxis.* Walnut Creek, CA: Left Coast Press.

Diversi, Marcelo and Claudio Moreira. 2012. "Decolonizing Constructions of Childhood and History: Interrupting Narratives of Avoidance to Children's Questions About Social Justice." *International Journal of Qualitative Studies in Education* 25(2), 189–203.

Diversi, Marcelo and Claudio Moreira. 2016. "Performing Between Autoethnographies Against Persistent Us/Them Essentializing: Leaning on a Freirean Pedagogy of Hope." *Qualitative Inquiry* 22(7), 581–587. Donnor, Jamel K. and Gloria Ladson-Billings. 2017. "Critical Race Theory and the Post-Racial Imaginary." Pp. 195–213 in N. K. Denzin and Y. S. Lincoln (Eds.). *Handbook of Qualitative Research,* 5/e. Thousand Oaks: Sage.

Dolan, J. 2001. "Performance, Utopia, and the 'Utopian Performative'." *Theatre Journal* 53(3), 455–479.

Dolan, Jill. 2005. *Utopia in Performance: Finding Hope in the Theater.* Ann Arbor: University of Michigan Press.

Dos Passos, J. 1937. *U.S.A.: I. The 42nd Parallel; II. Nineteen Nineteen; III. The Big Money.* New York: Modern Library.

Driskell, Charles B. 1975. "An Interview with Augusto Boal." *Latin American Theatre Review* 9(1), 71–78.

Driskill, Qwo-Li, Chris Finley, Brian Joseph Gilley and Scott Luria Morgensen (Eds.). 2011. *Queer Indigenous Studies: Critical Interventions in Theory, Politics and Literature.* Tucson: University of Arizona Press.

Du Bois, W. E. B. 1903. *The Souls of Black Folk.* New York: Fawcett.

Du Bois, W. E. B. 1926. "Krigwa Players Little Negro Theatre: The Story of a Little Theatre Movement." *Crisis* 32, 134–136.

Du Bois, W. E. B. 1978. "The Problem of the Twentieth Century is the Problem of the Color Line." Pp. 281–289 in W. E. B. Du Bois *On Sociology and the Black Community,* Edited and with an Introduction by Dan S. Green and Edward Driver. Chicago: University of Chicago Press (originally published 1901).Durham, Aisha S. 2014. *HOME With Hip Hop Feminism.* New York: Peter Lang,

Duwe, Elise AnnGeist. 2016. "Toward a Story Powerful Enough to Reduce Health Inequities in Indian Country: The Case of Diabetes." *Qualitative Inquiry* 22(8), 624–635.

Dylan, Bob, 1965. "Gates of Eden" Released on Bringing It All Back Home. Columbia Records.

Dylan, Bob. 1991. "Series of Dreams." Special Rider Music. Colombia Records.

Dylan, Bob. 2004. Chronicles, Vol. 1. New York: Simon & Schuster.

Dylan, Bob. 2008. Tell Tale Tales, The Bootleg Series, Volume 8: Rare and Unreleased, 1999–2006.

Eagleton, Terry. 1990. *The Ideology of the Aesthetic.* Oxford: Blackwell.

Eason, David. 1984. "The New Journalism and the Image-World: Two Modes of Organizing Experience." *Critical Studies in Mass Communication* 1, 51–65.

Edwards, Rosalind and Melanie Mauthner. 2002. "Ethics and Feminist Research: Theory and Practice." Pp. 14–31 in Melanie Mauthner, Maxine Birch, Julie Jessop and Tina Miller (Eds.) *Ethics in Qualitative Research.* London: Sage.

Eisenhart, Margaret and A. Susan Jurow. 2011. "Teaching Qualitative Research." Pp. 699–714 in N. K. Denzin and Y. S. Lincoln (Eds.) *Handbook of Qualitative Research,* 4/e. Thousand Oaks: Sage.

Elam, H. J. and D. Krasner (Eds.). 2001. *African American Performance and Theater History: A Critical Reader.* Oxford University Press on Demand.

Eliot, T. S. 1922. *The Sacred Wood: Essays in Poetry and Criticism.* London: Methune.

Ellis, Carolyn. 1995. *Final Negotiations.* Philadelphia: Temple University Press.

Ellis, Carolyn. 1997. "Evocative Authoethnography: Writing Emotionally About Our Lives." Pp. 115–139 in Yvonna S. Lincoln and William Tierney (Eds.) *Representation and the Text: Reframing the Narrative Voice.* Albany: SUNY Press

Ellis, Carolyn. 2000. "Creating Criteria: An Autoethnographic Story." *Qualitative Inquiry* 5(2), 273–277.

Ellis, Carolyn. 2004. *The Ethnographic I: A Methodological Novel about Teaching and Doing Autoethnography.* Walnut Creek, CA: AltaMira.

Ellis, Carolyn. 2009. *Revision: Autoethnographic Reflections on Life and Work.* Walnut Creek: Left Coast Press.

Ellis, Carolyn. 2013. "Preface: Carrying the Torch for Autoethnography." Pp. 9–12 in Stacy Holman Jones, Tony E. Adams and Carolyn Ellis (Eds.) *Handbook of Autoethnography.* Walnut Creek: Left Coast Press.

Ellis, Carolyn. 2017. "Compassionate research: interviewing and storytelling from a relational ethics of care." Pp. 431–445 in I. Goodson, M. Andrews, A. Antikainen, and P. Sikes (Eds.) *The Routledge International Handbook of Narrative and Life History.*

New York: Routledge. Ellis, Carolyn and Arthur P. Bochner. 1996. "Introduction: Talking Over Ethnography." Pp. 13–45 in Carolyn Ellis and Arthur P. Bochner (Eds.) *Composing Ethnography: Alternative Forms of Qualitative Writing*. Walnut Creek, CA: AltaMira Press.

Ellis, Carolyn and Arthur P. Bochner. 2000. "Autoethnography, Personal Narrative, Reflexivity: Researcher as Subject." Pp. 733–768 in Norman K. Denzin and Yvonna S. Lincoln (Eds.) *Handbook of Qualitative Research*, 2/e. Thousand Oaks, CA: Sage.

Ellis, Carolyn, Tony E. Adams, and Arthur P. Bochner. 2011. "Autoethnography: An Overview." FQS: Forum: Qualitative Social Research. 12, 1 (January): 1–14: Http://www.qualitative-research.net/index.php/fqs/article/view/158

Ellis, Carolyn, Tony E. Adams and Arthur P. Bochner. 2011. "Autoethnography: An Overview." *Forum Qualitative Sozialforschun/Forum: Qualitative Social Research*, 112(1), ISSN 1438–5627.

Evans, Brad and Henry A. Giroux. 2015. *Disposable Futures: The Seduction of Violence on the Age of Spectacle*. San Francisco: City Lights Books.

Evans, Mike, Rachelle Hole, Lawrence D. Berg, Peter Hutchinson and Dixon Sookraj. 2007. "Common Insights, Differing Methodologies: Toward a Fusion of Indigenous Methodologies, Participatory Action Research, and White Studies in an Urbana Aboriginal Research Agenda." *Qualitative Inquiry* 15(5), 893–910.

Farago, Jason. 2017. "Cindy Sherman Takes Selfies (as Only She Could) on Instagram." *New York Times*, August 6.

Faulkner, Sandra L. 2009. *Poetry as Method: Reporting Research Through Verse*. Walnut Creek: Left Coast Press.

Faulkner, S. L. 2014. *Family Stories, Poetry, and Women's Work: Knit Four, Frog One (Poems)*. Rotterdam: Sense Publishers.

Fast, Elizabeth, Rose E. Cameron, Anjali Helferty and Patrick Lewis. 2016. "Indigenous Knowledges and a Relational Peer Review Process." *International Review of Qualitative Review* 9(4), 381–384.

Featherstone, Mike. 1991. *Consumer Culture & Postmodernism*. London: Sage.

Fenske, Mindy and Dustin Bradley Goltz. 2014. "Editor's Introduction: Disciplinary Dedications and Extradisciplinary Experiences: Themes on a Relation." *Text and Performance Quarterly* 34(1), 1–8.

Fernandez, Iscar. 1968 "Brazil's New Social Theatre." *Latin American Theatre Review* 9(1), 15–30

Filewood, A. 2009. "The Documentary Body: Theatre Workshop to Banner Theatre." Pp. 55–73 in A. Forsyth and C. Megson (Eds.) *Get Real: Documentary Theatre Past and Present*. New York: Palgrave Macmillan.

Fine, Michelle. 1994. "Working the Hyphens: Reinventing Self and Other in Qualitative Research." Pp. 83–98 in N. K. Denzin and Y. S. Lincoln (Eds.) *Handbook of Qualitative Inquiry*, 1/e. Thousand Oaks: Sage.

Fine, Michelle et al. 2003. "Participatory Action Research: From Within and Beyond Prison Bars." Pp. 173–198 in Paul M. Camic, Jean E. Rhodes, and Lucy Yardley (Eds.) *Qualitative Research in Psychology: Expanding Perspectives in Methodology and Design*. Washington, DC: American Psychological Association Books.

Finley, Susan. 2008. "Arts-Based Research." Pp. 71–81 in J. Gary and Ardra L. Cole. (Eds.) *Handbook of the Arts in Qualitative Research*. Thousand Oaks: Sage.

Finley, Susan. 2017. "Critical Arts-Based Inquiry: Performance of Resistance Politics." Pp. 561–575 in N. K. Denzin and Y. S. Lincoln (Eds). *Sage Handbook of Qualitative Research*, 5/e. Thousand Oaks: Sage.

Finley, S. 2000. "'Dream child': The role of poetic dialogue in homeless research." *Qualitative Inquiry* 6(3), 432–434. Fisher, Berenie. 1994. "Feminist Acts: Women, Pedagogy, and Theatre of the Oppressed." Pp. 185–197 in Mady Schutzman and Jan Cohen-Cruz (Eds.) *Playing Boal: Theatre, Therapy, Activism*. London and New York: Routledge.

Fletcher, Joseph F. 1966. *Situation Ethics: The New Morality*. Philadelphia: Westminster Press,

Fluehr-LobbanC. (Ed.) 2003a. *Ethics and the Professional of Anthropology*, 2/e. Walnut Creek: AltaMira.

Fluehr-LobbanC. 2003b. "Informed Consent in Anthropological Research." Pp. 159–177 in C. Fluehr-Lobban (Ed.) *Ethics and the Professional of Anthropology* 2nd Edition. Walnut Creek: AltaMira.

Foley, Doug. 2002. "Critical Ethnography: The Reflexive Turn." *International Journal of Qualitative Studies in Education* 15, 469–490.

Fontana, Andrea and James H. Frey. 1994. "Interviewing: The Art of Science." Pp. 361–376 in N. K. Denzin and Y. S. Lincoln, *Handbook of Qualitative Research*. Thousand Oaks, CA: Sage.

Fontana, Andrea and James H. Frey. 2000. "The Interview: From Structured Questions to Negotiated Text." Pp. 645–672 in N. K. Denzin and Y. S. Lincoln, *Handbook of Qualitative Research*, 2/e Thousand Oaks, CA: Sage.

Forber-Pratt, Anjali J. 2015. "'You're Going to Do What?' Challenges of Auto-ethnography in the Academy." *Qualitative Inquiry* 21(9), 821–835.

Ford, Nick Aaron. 1998. "A Blueprint for Negro Authors." Pp. 1112–1114 in Patricia Liggins Hill, *Call & Response: The Riverside Anthology of the African American Literary Tradition*. New York: Houghton Mifflin. (Originally published in Phylon, 1950).

45 CFR 46. 1974. Title II, National Research Act of1974, Title 45, Part 46. *Protection of Human Subjects, or the Common Rule*. Washington, D.C.: U.S. Government.

Foucault, Michel. 1980. *Power/Knowledge: Selected Interviews and Other Writings, 19721977*, edited by C. Gordon; translated by L. Marshall, J. Mepham and K. Soper. New York: Pantheon.

Fox, Margalit. 2015. "Brian Sutton-Smith, Scholar of What's Fun Dies at 90." *New York Times*, 15 March (Obituaries), 24.

Frank, Arthur. 1995. *The Wounded Storyteller: Body, Illness and Ethics*. Chicago: University of Chicago Press.

Frank, Arthur. 2004a. *The Renewal of Generosity Illness, Medicine, and How to Live*. Chicago: University of Chicago Press.

Frank, Arthur. 2004b. "Moral Non-fiction: Life Writing and Children's Disability." Pp. 174–194 in P. J. Eakin (Ed.) *The Ethics of Life Writing*. Ithaca, NY: Cornell University Press. Fraser, Nancy. 1993. "Clintonism, Welfare, and the Antisocial Wage: The Emergence of a Neoliberal Imaginary." *Rethinking Marxism* 6, 9–23.

Freire, Paulo. 1967. *Education as a Practice of Freedom*. Rio de Janeiro: Paz e Terra.

Freire, Paulo. 1996. *Letters to Cristina: Reflections on My Life and Work* (trans. Donaldo Macedo with Quilda Macedo and Alexandre Oliveira). London: Routledge.

Freire, Paulo. 1998. *Pedagogy of Freedom: Ethics, Democracy, and Civic Courage*. (trans. Patrick Clarke, Foreword by Donaldo Macedo, Introduction by Stanley Aronowitz). Boulder: Roman & Littlefield Publishers, Inc.

Freire, Paulo. 1999. *Pedagogy of Hope*. New York: Continuum (originally published 1992).

282   *Bibliography*

Freire, Paulo. 2000. *Pedagogy of the Oppressed* (30th Anniversary edition, Introduction by Donaldo Macedo. New York: Continuum (originally published 1970, fifth reprinting 2015).

Freire, Paulo. 2005. *Teachers as Cultural Workers: Letters to Those Who Dare Teach* (trans. Donaldo Macedo, Dale Koeike, and Alexandre Oliveria, with a foreword by Donaldo Macedo and Ana Maria Arujo Freire, and New Commentary by Peter McLaren, Joe L. Kincheloe, and Shirley Steinberg). Boulder: Westview Press. Freire, Paulo. 2007. *Pedagogy of the Heart.* New York: Continuum.

Freire, Paulo. 2016. *Pedagogy in Process: The Letters to Guinea-Bissau* (trans. Carman St. John Hunter). London: Bloomsbury Academic,

Freire, Paulo and Antonio Faundez. 1989. *Learning to Question: A Pedagogy of Liberation.* New York: Continuum. Freire, Paulo and Ana Maria Araujo Freire. 2007. *Daring to Dream: Toward a Pedagogy of the Unfinished* (trans. Alexandre K. Oliveria). Boulder: Paradigm Publishers.

Freire, Paulo, Ana Maria Arujo Freire and Walter de Oloveria. 2014. *Pedagogy of Solidarity.* Walnut Creek: Left Coast Press. Gadotti, Moacir. 1994. *Reading Paulo Freire* (trans. John Milton). Albany: SUNY Press.

Gale, Ken and Jonathan Wyatt. 2009. *Between the Two: A Nomadic Inquiry into Collaborative Writing and Subjectivity.* Newcastle upon Tyne: Cambridge Scholars Publishing,

Gale, Ken, Ron Pelias, Larry Russell, Tami Spry and Jonathan Wyatt. 2012. *How Writing Touches: An Intimate Scholarly Collaboration.* Newcastle upon Tyne: Cambridge Scholars Publishing,

Gale, Ken, Ron Pelias, Larry Russell, Tami Spry and Jonathan Wyatt. 2013. "Intensity: A Collaborative Autoethnography." *International Review of Qualitative Research* 6(1), 165–180.

Gannon, Susanne. 2017. "Autoethnography." *Oxford Research Encyclopedia of Education: Education, Cultures, and Ethnicities, Research and Assessment Methods* doi:10.1093/acrefore/9780190264093.013.71.

Garfinkel, Harold. 1996. "Ethnomethodology's Program." *Social Psychology Quarterly* 59, 5–21.

Garoian, Charles R. 1999. *Performing Pedagogy: Toward an Art of Politics.* Albany: SUNY Press.

Garoian, Charles R. 2013. *The Prosthetic Pedagogy of Art: Embodied Research and Practice.* Albany: State University of New York.

Garoian, Charles R. and Y. M. Gaudelius. 2008. *Spectacle Pedagogy: Art, Politics, and Visual Culture.* Albany: State University of New York.

Geertz, Clifford. 1968. "Thinking as a Moral Act: Ethical Dimensions of Anthropological Fieldwork in the New States." *Antioch Review* 18, 139–158.

Geertz, Clifford. 1973. *The Interpretation of Cultures.* New York: Basic Books.

Geertz, Clifford. 1983. *Local Knowledge: Further Essays in Interpretive Anthropology.* New York: Basic Books. Geertz, Clifford. 1988. *Works and Lives: The Anthropologist as Author.* Stanford, CA: Stanford University Press. Gencarella, Stephen Olbrys and Phaedra C. Pezzullo. 2010. "Introduction: Body Politics, Social Drama, and Public Culture." Pp. 1–12 in Stephen Olbrys Gencarella and Phaedra C. Pezzullo (Eds.) *Readings on Rhetoric and Performance.* State College, Penn.: Strata Publishing Incl.

George, David S. 1995. "Theatre of the Oppressed and Testro de Arena: In and Out of Context." *Latin American Theatre Review* 28(2), 39–54.

Gergen, Kenneth J. 2014. "Pursuing Excellence in Qualitative Inquiry." *Qualitative Psychology* 1, 49–60.

Gergen, Kenneth J. 2015. "From Mirroring to World-Making: Research as Future Forming." *Journal for the Theory of Social Behavior*, 45(3), 287–310.

Gergen, Mary M. and Kenneth J. Gergen. 2012. *Playing with Purpose: Adventures in Performative Social Science*. Walnut Creek: Left Coast Press.

Giardina, Michael D. and Josh I. Newman. 2011. "Physical Cultural Studies and Embodied Research Acts." *Cultural Studies – Critical Methodologies*, 11(76), 523–534.

Gilbert, H. 2003. "Black and White and Re (a)d All Over Again: Indigenous Minstrelsy in Contemporary Canadian and Australian Theatre." *Theatre Journal* 55, 679–698.

Gilroy, Paul. 1991. *There Ain't No Black in the Union Jack: The Cultural Politics of Race and Nation*. Chicago: University of Chicago Press

Gilroy, Paul, 2000. *Against Race: Imagining Political Culture Beyond the Color Line*. Cambridge: Harvard University Press.

Giorgio, Grace A. 2013. "Reflections in Writing Through Memory in Autoethnography." Pp. 406–424 in Stacy Holman Jones, Tony E. Adams and Carolyn Ellis (Eds.) *Handbook of Autoethnography*. Walnut Creek: Left Coast Press.

Gingrich-Philbrook, Craig. 2013. "Evaluating (Evaluations) of Autoethnography." Pp. 609–626 in Stacy Holman Jones, Tony E. Adams and Carolyn Ellis (Eds.) *Handbook of Autoethnography*. Walnut Creek: Left Coast Press.

Giroux, Henry. 2000a. *Impure Acts: The Practical Politics of Cultural Studies*. New York: Routledge.

Giroux, Henry. 2000b. *Stealing Innocence: Corporate Culture's War on Children*. New York: Palgrave.

Giroux, Henry. 2001. "Cultural Studies as Performative Politics." *Cultural Studies – Critical Methodologies* 1, 5–23.

Giroux, H. A. 2003. *The Abandoned Generation: Democracy beyond the Culture of Fear*. New York: Palgrave Macmillan.

Giroux, Henry. 2007. *Stealing Innocence*. New York: Palgrave.

Giroux, Henry. 2010. *Zombie Politics in the Age of Casino Capitalism*. New York: Peter Lang.

Giroux, Henry. 2011. *On Critical Pedagogy*. New York and London: Bloomsbury Academic.

Giroux, Henry. 2014a. *Neoliberalism's War on Higher Education*. Chicago: Haymarket Books.

Giroux, Henry. 2014b. *The Violence of Organized Forgetting*. San Francisco: City Lights Bookstore.

Giroux, Henry, 2014c. "Memory's Hope: In the Shadow of Paulo Freire's Presence." Pp. 7–12 in Paulo Freire, Ana Maria Arujo Freire, and Walter de Oloveria. *Pedagogy of Solidarity*. Walnut Creek: Left Coast Press.

Giroux, Henry A. 2015. "Fascism in Donald Trump's United States." *Truthout*, December 8 . www.truth-out.org/news/item/33951-fascism-in-donald-trump-s-united-states

Giroux, Henry. 2016a. "Donald Trump and the Plague of Atomization in a Neoliberal Age." *Truthout*, 8 August. www.truth-out.org/opinion/item/37133-donald-trump-and-the-plague-of-atomization-in-a-neoliberal-age

Giroux, Henry. 2016b. "Radical Politics in the Age of American Authoritarianism: Connecting the Dots." *Truthout*, Sunday 10 April. www.truthout.org/news/item/35573-radical-politics-in-the-age-of-american-authoritarianism-connecting-the-dots

Giroux, Henry. 2016c. *America At War with Itself*. San Francisco: City Lights Open Media.

Giroux, Henry. 2016d. "America." *Truthout*, Sunday November 13. www.truth-out.org/opinion/item/38351-the-authoritarian-politics-of-resentment-in-trump-s-america.Glass, Ronald David. 2001. "On Paulo Freire's Philosophy of Praxis and the Foundations of Liberation Education." *Educational Researcher* 30, 15–25.

Goodall, H. L., Jr. 2012. "Three Cancer Poems." *Qualitative Inquiry* 18(9), 724–727.

Goffman, Erving. 1959. *The Presentation of Self in Everyday Life*. New York: Doubleday.

Goldschmidt, W. 1975. "Anthropology and the Coming Crisis: An Autoethnographic Appraisal." *American Anthropologist* 79(2), 293–308.

Goodall, H. L. 2000. *Writing the New Ethnography*. Walnut Creek: AltaMira Press.

Goodall, H. L. 2008a. *Writing Qualitative Inquiry: Self, Stories and Academic Life*. Walnut Creek CA: Left Coast Press.

Goodall, H. L. 2008b. *A Need to Know: A Clandestine History of a CIA Family*. Walnut Creek CA: Left Coast Press.

Goodall, H. L., Jr. 2010. *Counter-Narrative: How Progressive Academics Can Challenge Extremism and Promote Social Justice*. Walnut Creek CA: Left Coast Press. Goodman, Amy. 2016. "Is Trump's Rise a Result of America Declaring War on Institutions that Make Democracy Possible? Interview with Henry Giroux." 14 October. www.democracynow.org/2016/10/14/is_trumps_rise_a_result_of

Gomez, Aitor, Lidia Puigvert and Ramon Flecha. 2011. "Critical Communicative Methodology: Informing Real Social Transformation Through Social Research." *Qualitative Inquiry* 17(3), 235–246. Special Issue: Critical Communicative Methodology, Guest Editor, Aitor Gomez.

Gomez, Jesus. 2015. *Radical Love: A Revolution for the 21st Century* (ed. Licia Puigvert). New York: Peter Lang.

Gorman, Geraldine. 2012. "Divorce: The Aftermath." *Qualitative Inquiry* 18(10), 843–844.

Gottschalk, S. 2000. "Escape From Insanity: 'Mental Disorder' in the Postmodern Moment." Pp. 18–48 in *Pathology and the Postmodern: Mental Illness as Discourse and Experience*, edited by Dwight Fee. Thousand Oaks, CA: Sage.

Grande, Sandy. 2008a. *Red /Pedagogy: Native American Social and Political Thought*. Lanham, MD: Rowman & Littlefield

Grande, Sandy. 2008b. "Red Pedagogy: The Uni-Methodology." Pp 233–254 in N. K. Denzin, Y. S. Lincoln and L. T. Smith (Eds.), *Handbook of Critical and Indigenous Methodologies*. Thousand Oaks: Sage.

Grande, Sandy. 2000. "American Indian Identity and Intellectualism: /The Quest for a New Red Pedagogy." *Qualitative Studies in Education*, 1,: 343–360.

Gregg, Melissa and Gregory J. Seigworth (Eds.). 2010. *The Affect Theory Reader*. Durham: Duke University Press.

Gruber, Ruth Ellen. 2004. "European Festivals Keep Wild West Alive and Kickin'." *New York Times*, 7 August. www.nytimes.com/2004/0807/style/07iht-trfest_ed3_.html

Gruber, Ruth Ellen. 2011. "Sauerkrautcowboys: Strum, Twang and Imaginary Wild West in Europe." http://saurkrautcowboys.blogspot.com/2011/05/germany-karl-may

Gubrium, Jaber F. and James A. Holstein. 1997. *The New Language of Qualitative Method*. New York: Oxford University Press.

Gubrium, Jaber F. and James A. Holstein. 1998. "Narrative Practice and the Coherence of Personal Stories." *Sociological Quarterly* 39, 163–187.

Gubrium, Jaber F. and James A. Holstein (Eds.). 2001. *Handbook of Interview Research*. *Interviewing*. Thousand Oaks: Sage.

Gubrium, Jaber F. and James A. Holstein (Eds.). 2003. *Postmodern Interviewing*. Thousand Oaks: Sage.

Guerrero, Ed. 1993. *Framing Blackness: The African American Image in Film*. Philadelphia: Temple University Press.

Gunsalus, C. K., E. M. Bruner, C. Nicholas, Dash L. Burbules, M. Finkin, J. P. Goldberg, W. T. Greenough, G. A. Miller, M. G. Pratt, I. Masumi and D. Aronson. 2007. "The Illinois White Paper: Improving the system for Protecting Human Subjects: Counteracting IRB 'Mission Creep'." *Qualitative Inquiry* 13(5), 617–649.

Haggerty, K. D. 2004. "Ethics Creep: Governing Social Science Research in the Name of Ethics." *Qualitative Sociology* 27(4), 391–414.

Halse, C. and A. Honey. 2007. "Rethinking Ethics Review as Institutional Discourse." *Qualitative Inquiry* 33(3), 336–352.

Hall, LeeAnn and G. Goehl. 2016. "Donald Trump's Victory is Not the Last Word." *Truthout*, 9 November. www.truth-out.org/opinion/item/38314-donald-trump-s-victory-is-not-the-last-word

Halley, Jean O'Malley. 2012. *The Parallel Lives of Women and Cows*. New York: Palgrave.

Hallie, Phillip. 1969. *The Paradox of Cruelty*. Middleton, Conn: Wesleyn University Press.

Hamera, Judith. 2007. *Dancing Communities*. New York: Palgrave.

Hamera, Judith. 2011. "Performance Ethnography." Pp. 317–330 in N. K. Denzin and Y. Lincoln (Eds.). *Handbook of Qualitative Research*, 4/e. Thousand Oaks: Sage. Hammersley, M. 2008. *Questioning Qualitative Inquiry: Critical Essays*. London: Sage.

Hammersley, M. and A. Traianou. 2012. *Ethics in Qualitative Research: Controversies and Contexts*. London: Sage.

Hanaur, David I. 2012. "Growing Up in the Unseen Shadow of the Kindertransport: A Poetic-Narrative Autoethnography." *Qualitative Inquiry* 18(10), 845–851.

Hayano, D. 1979. "Auto-ethnography: Paradigms, Problems and Prospects." *Human Organization*, 38(1), 99–104.

Healy, Patrick. 2008. "Matthew Shepard and Laramie: A Crime that Lingers." *New York Times*. 17 September. www.nytimes.com/2008/09/17/arts/17iht-llaramie.1.16232258

Hedgecoe, A. 2008. "Research Ethics Review and the Sociological Research Relationship." *Sociology* 42, 873–886.

Heidegger, Martin. 1962. *Being and Time*. New York: Harper and Row.

Heider, K. G. 1975. "What Do People Do: Dani-auto-ethnography." *Journal of Anthropological Research* 31(1), 3–17.

Hekman, Susan. 2010. *The Material of Knowledge: Feminist Disclosures*. Bloomington: Indiana University Press.

Heyl, Barbara Sherman. 2001. "Ethnographic Interviewing." Pp. 369–383 in *Handbook of Ethnography*, edited by Paul Atkinson, Amanda Coffey, Sara Delamont, John Lofland, and Lyn Lofland. London: Sage.

Hoffman-Davis, J. and S. Lawrence-Lightfoot. 2002. *The Art and Science of Portraiture*. NY: Jossey-Bass.

Holman-Jones, S. 2005. "Autoethnography: Making the Personal Political." Pp. 763–790 in N. K. Denzin and Y. Lincoln (Eds.). *Handbook of Qualitative Research*, 4/e. Thousand Oaks: Sage.

Holstein, James A. and Jaber F. Gubrium. 1995. *The Active Interview*. Thousand Oaks, CA: Sage.

Holstein, James A. and Jaber F. Gubrium. 2000. *The Self We Live By: Narrative Identity in a Postmodern World.* New York: Oxford University Press.

hooks, bell. 1990. *Yearning: Race, Gender and Cultural Politics.* Boston: South End Press.

hooks, bell. 1994. *Teaching to Transgress: Education as the Practice of Freedom.* New York: Routledge.

Howard, J. 2006. "Oral History under Review." *Chronicle of Higher Education*, 10 November. Available at http:///chronicle.com/free/v53/112/12a01401.htm.

Howe, K. R. 2004. "A Critique of Experimentalism." *Qualitative Inquiry* 10(1), 42–61.

Hudson, Jerome. 2015. "5 Devastating Facts About Black-On-Black Crime." www. breitbart.com/big-government/2015/11/28/5-devastating-facts-black-black-crime/

Hughes, E. C. 1952. *Men and Their Work.* Glencoe, Ill: Free Press.

Hutchinson, Louise Daniel. 1981. *Anna J. Cooper.* Washington, DC: Smithsonian Institution Press.

Indigenous Inquiry Circle. 2016. "Letter to Chancellor Robert J. Jones, University of Illinois." September 27.

Irish, Sharon. 2010. *Suzanne Lacy: Spaces Between.* Minneapolis: University of Minnesota Press.

Israel, M. 2015. *Research Ethics and Integrity for Social Scientists.* 2/edn. London: Sage.

Jackson, A. Y. and L. A. Mazzei. 2008. "Experience and 'I' in Autoethnography: A Deconstruction." *International Review of Qualitative Research* 1(3), 299–318.

Jackson, Alecia Y. and Lisa A. Mazzei. 2009. *Voice in Qualitative Inquiry: Challenging Conventional, Interpretive, and Critical Conceptions in Qualitative Research.* London: Routledge.

Jackson, Alecia Y. and Lisa A. Mazzei. 2012. *Thinking with Theory in Qualitative Research: Viewing Data Across Multiple Perspectives.* London: Routledge.

Jackson, Michael. 1998. *Minima Ethnographica: Intersubjectivity and the Anthropological Project.* Chicago: University of Chicago Press.

Jackson, Shannon. 2006. "Genealogies of Performance Studies." Pp. 73–86 in D. Soyini Madison and Judith Hamera (Eds.) *The Sage Handbook of Performance Studies.* Thousand Oaks: Sage.

James, William. 1912. *Essays in Radical Empiricism.* New York: Dossier.

Jameson, Fredric, 1981. *The Political Unconscious.* Ithaca: Cornell University Press.

Jameson, Fredric. 1990. *Signatures of the Visible.* New York: Routledge.

Janetski, J. C. 2002. *Indians in Yellowstone National Park.* Salt Lake City: University of Utah Press.

Jay, Paul. 2016. "Trump and the Fascistization of America (1/2): Interview with Henry Giroux." 19 July, *The Real New Network.* http://therealnews.com/t2/index.php?op tion=com_content&task=view&id=31&Itemid=74&jumival=16785

Johnson, Patrick. 1983. *Native Children and the Child Welfare System.* Toronto: Canadian Council on Social Development.

Johnson, E.Patrick. 2006. "Black Performance Etudies: Genealogies, Politics, Futures." Pp. 446–463 in D. Soyini Madison and Judith Hamera (Eds.) *The Sage Handbook of Performance Studies.* Thousand Oaks: Sage.

Johnson, E.Patrick. 2013. *Cultural Struggles: Performance, Ethnography, Praxis: Dwight Conquergood.* Edited and an introduction by E. Patrick Johnson. Ann Arbor: University of Michigan Press.

Johnson-Mardones, Daniel. 2014 "Crying a Thesis." *Qualitative Inquiry* 20(3), 248–252.

Johnson-Mardones, Daniel. 2015a. "Listening to Paulo Freire." *Cultural Studies-Critical Methodologies* 15(1), 61–63.

Johnson-Mardones, Daniel. 2015b. "Understanding Critical-Pedagogical Performative-Autoethnography." *Cultural Studies-Critical Methodologies*, 15(3), 190–191.

Johnson-Mardones, Daniel. 2016. Curriculum Studies as an International Conversation: Cosmopolitanism in a Latin American Key. Unpublished doctoral dissertation, University of Illinois at Urbana-Champaign.

Jones, A. 2007. Letter to Office for Human Research Protections. 20 December.

Jones, Alison and Kuni Jenkins. 2008. "Rethinking Collaboration: Working the Indigene-Colonizer Hyphen." Pp. 471–486 in N. K. Denzin, Y. S. Lincoln and L. T. Smith (Eds.) *Handbook of Critical and Indigenous Methodologies*. Thousand Oaks: Sage.

Jones, Joni L. 1997. "Performing Osun Without Bodies: Documenting the Osun Festival in Print." *Text and Performance Quarterly* 17, 69–93.

Jones, Joni L. and Omi Osun Olomo. 2007. "Review-Essay: D. Soyini Madison: Critical Ethnography: Method, Ethics, and Performance." *Text and Performance Quarterly* 27(5), 378–381.

Jones, Stacy Holman. 2013. "The Performance Space: Giving an Account of Performance Studies." *Text and Performance Quarterly* 33(1), 77–80

Jones, Stacy Holman. 2017. "Assembling a We in Critical Qualitative Inquiry." Pp. 130–135 in N. K. Denzin and M. D. Giardina (Eds.) *Qualitative Inquiry in Neoliberal Times*. Oxford: Taylor & Francis.

Jones, Stacy Holman, Tony E. Adams and Carolyn Ellis. 2013a. "Coming to Know Autoethnography as More than a Method." Pp. 17–48 in Stacy Holman Jones, Tony E. Adams and Carolyn Ellis (Eds.) *Handbook of Ethnography*. Walnut Creek: Left Coast Press.

Jones, Stacy Holman, Tony E. Adams and Carolyn Ellis (Eds.). 2013b. *Handbook of Autoethnography*. Walnut Creek: Left Coast Press.

Joyce, Joyce Ann. 1987. "The Black Canon: Reconstructing Black American Literary Criticism." *New Literary History* 18, 335–344.

Kamberelis, George and Greg Dimitriadis, 2011. "Focus Groups: Contingent Articulations of Pedagogy, Politics and Inquiry." Pp. 545–561 in N. K. Denzin and Y. S. Lincoln (Eds.) *Sage Handbook of Qualitative Research*, 4/e. Thousand Oaks: Sage.

Kaomea, Julie. 2004. "Dilemmas of an Indigenous Academic: A Native Hawaiian Story." Pp. 27–44 in Kagendo Mutua and Beth Blue Swadener (Eds.) *Decolonizing Research in Cross-Cultural Contexts: Critical Personal Narratives*. Albany: SUNY Press.

Kaplan, Esther. 2004. *With God on Their Side: How Christian Fundamentalists Trampled Science, Policy, and Democracy in the George Bush's White House*. New York: The New Press.

Kaufman, Moses. 2001. *The Laramie Project*. New York: Vintage.

Kaufman, Moses. 2014. *The Laramie Project 10 Years Later*. New York: Vintage.

Kelley, Robin D. G, 2014. "Why We Won't Wait." *CounterPunch*. 25 November. http://www.counterpunch.org/2014/11/25/75039/University of California Press.

Kemmis, Stephen, and Robin McTaggart. 2000. "Participatory Action Research." Pp. 567–606 in N. K. Denzin and Y. S. Lincoln (Eds.) *Handbook of Qualitative Research*, 2/e. Thousand Oaks: Sage

Kincheloe, Joe L. 2001. "Describing the Bricolage: Conceptualizing a New Rigor in Qualitative Research." *Qualitative Inquiry* 7, 679–692.

Kincheloe, Joe L. 2005. "Introduction." Pp. xli–xlix in Paulo Freire, *Teachers as Cultural Workers: Letters to Those Who Dare Teach*. Boulder: Westview Press.

Kincheloe, Joe L. 2007. "Critical Pedagogy in the Twenty-first Century: Evolution for Survival." Pp. 9–42 in Peter McLaren and Joe L. Kincheloe (Eds.) *Critical Pedagogy: Where Are We Now?* New York: Peter Lang.

Kincheloe, Joe L. and Peter McLaren. 2000. "Rethinking Critical Theory and Qualitative Research." Pp. 279–313 in Norman K. Denzin and Yvonna S. Lincoln (Eds.) *Handbook of Qualitative Research*, 2/e. Thousand Oaks, CA: Sage.

Kincheloe, Joe L. and Peter McLaren. 2005. "Rethinking Critical Theory and Qualitative Research." Pp. 303–342 in Norman K. Denzin and Yvonna S. Lincoln (Eds.) *Handbook of Qualitative Research*, 3/e. Thousand Oaks, CA: Sage.

Kittredge, William. 1987. *Owning It All*. San Francisco: Murray House.

Kittredge, William. 1992. *Hole in the Sky: A Memoir*. New York: Vintage.

Kittredge, William. 1996. *Who Owns the West?* San Francisco: Murray House.

Kittredge, William and Annick Smith (Eds.). 1988. *The Last Best Place: A Montana Anthology*. Seattle: University of Washington Press.

Klein, Naomi. 2017. *No is Not Enough: Resisting Trump's Shock Politics and Winning the World We Need*. Chicago: Hay Market Books.

Knowles, J. Gary and Ardra L. Cole. 2008. "Preface." Pp. xi–xiv in J. Gary Knowles and Ardra L. Cole (Eds.) *Handbook of the Arts in Qualitative Research*. Thousand Oaks: Sage.

Koro-Ljungberg, Mirka. 2010. "Validity, Responsibility and Apora." *Qualitative Inquiry* 16(8), 603–610.

Koro-Ljungberg, Mirka. 2016. *Reconceptualizing Qualitative Research: Methodologies without Methodology*. Thousand Oaks: Sage. Kovach, Margaret. 2009. *Indigenous Methodologies*. Toronto: University of Toronto Press.

Krieger, Susan. 1991. *Social Science & The Self: Personal Essays as an Art Form*. New Brunswick, NJ: Rutgers University Press.

Krieger, Susan. 1996. *The Family Silver: Essays on the Relationships Among Women*. Berkeley: University of California Press.

Krog, Antjie, Nosisi Mpolwent-Zantsi and Kopano Ratele. 2008. "The South African Truth and Reconciliation Commission (TRC): Ways of Knowing Mrs. Konile." Pp. 531–546 in N. K. Denzin, Y. S. Lincoln and L. T. Smith (Eds.) *Handbook of Critical and Indigenous Methodologies*. Thousand Oaks: Sage.

Kuhn, Manford H. 1962. "The Interview and the Professional Relationship." *Human Behavior and Social Processes: An Interactionist Approach*, 193–206.

Kuppers, Petra and Gwen Robertson. 2007. "General Introduction." Pp. 1–8 in Petra Kuppers and Gwen Robertson (Eds.) *The Community Performance Theatre*. New York: Routledge.

Kvale, Steiner. 1996. *InterViews: An Introduction to Qualitative Research Interviewing*. London: Sage.

Lacy, Suzanne. 1995. "Cultural Pilgrimages and Metaphoric Journeys." Pp. 1–20 in Suzanne Lacy (Ed.) *Mapping the Terrain: New Genre Public Art*. Seattle: Bay.

Lacy, Suzanne. 2006. "Art and Everyday Life: Activism in Feminist Performance Art." Pp. 91–102 in Jan Cohen-Cruz and Mady Schutzman (Eds.) *A Boal Companion: Dialogues on Theatre and Cultural Politics*. New York: Routledge.

Ladson-Billings, Gloria. 2000. "Racialized Discourses and Ethnic Epistemologies." Pp. 257–277 in Norman K. Denzin and Yvonna S. Lincoln (Eds.) *Handbook of Qualitative Research*, 2/e. Thousand Oaks, CA: Sage.

Langellier, Kristin M. 1998. "Voiceless Bodies, Bodiless Voices: The Future of Personal Narrative Performance." Pp. 207–213 in Sheron J. Dailey (Ed.) *The Future of*

Performance Studies: Visions and Revisions. Annadale, VA: National Communication Association.

Lather, Patti. 2007. *Getting Lost: Feminist Efforts Toward a Double (d) Science*. Albany: SUNY Press.

Lather, Patti. 2009. "Against Empathy, Voice and Authenticity." Pp. 17–26 in A. Y. Jackson and L. A. Mazzei (Eds.) *Voice in Qualitative Inquiry: Challenging Conventional, Interpretive and Critical Conceptions in Qualitative Research*. New York: Routledge.

Lather, Patti. 2016. "Top Tent + List: (Re) Thinking Ontologu in (Post) Qualitative Research." *Cultural Studies – Critical Methodologies* 16(2), 125–131.

Leavy, Patricia. 2013. *Fiction as Research Practice: Short Stories, Novellas, and Novels*. New York: Routledge.

Leavy, Patricia. 2015. *Method Meets Art: Arts-Based Research Practice*, 2/e. New York: Guiford Press.

Lee, Felicia R. 2013. "Festival of Short Plays Inspired by Trayvon Martin Case." *New York Times*, 5 August. http://artsbeat.blogs.nytimes.com/2013/08/05/festival-of-short-p lays-inspired-by-trayvon-martin-case/

Lee, Felicia R. 2014. "Michael Brown Case Inspires Readings." *New York Times*, 17 November, *The Arts*: C5; also http://artsbeat.blogs.nytimes.com/2014/11/14/new-bla ck-fest-to-present-short-works-responding-to-michael-brown-shooting/

Leibovich, Mark. 2016. "Her Way: Inside the Final Weeks of Hilary Clinton's High-Stakes Campaign." *The New York Times Magazine*, 16 October, 40–45, 65.

Leopold, Aldo. 1949. *A Sand County Almanac*. New York: Oxford University Press.

Levine, F. J. and P. R. Skedsvold. 2008. "Where the Rubber Meets The Road: Aligning IRBs and Research Practice." *PS: Political Science & Politics* 41(3), 501–505.

Lincoln, Yvonna S. 1995. "Emerging Criteria for Quality in Qualitative and Interpretive Inquiry." *Qualitative Inquiry* 1, 275–289.

Lincoln, Y. S. 2009. "Ethical Practices in Qualitative Research." Pp. 150–170 in D. M. Mertens and P. E. Ginsberg (Eds.) *The Handbook of Social Research Ethics*. Thousand Oaks: Sage.

Lincoln, Y. S. and Egpon G. Guba. 2013. *The Constructivist Credo*. Walnut Creek: Left Coast Press.

Lincoln, Y. S. and N. K. Denzin (Eds.). 2003. *9/11 in American Culture*. Lanham, MD: Rowman Altamira.

Lincoln, Yvonna S. and William G. Tierney. 2002. "'What We Have Here Is a Failure to Communicate...': Qualitative Research and Institutional Review Boards (IRBs)." Paper presented at the annual meeting of the American Education Research Association, New Orleans, April.

Lincoln, Yvonna S., Susan A. Lynham and Egon G. Guba. 2011. "Paradigmatic Controversies, Contradictions, and Emerging Confluences, Revisited." Pp. 97–128 in N. K. Denzin and Y. S. Lincoln (Eds.) *Handbook of Qualitative Research*, 4/e. Thousand Oaks: Sage.

Lockford, Lesa. 1998. "Emergent Issues in the Performance of a Border-Transgressive Narrative." Pp. 214–220 in Sheron J. Dailey (Ed.) *The Future of Performance Studies: Visions and Revisions*. Annadale, VA: National Communication Association.

Lopate, Philip. 1997. *The Art of the Personal Essay*. New York: Anchor Press.

Lopez, Ana M. 1991. "Are All Latins From Manhattan? Hollywood, Ethnography, and Cultural Colonialism." Pp. 404–424 in Lester D. Friedman (Ed.) Unspeakable Images: Ethnicity and the American Cinema. Urbana: University of Illinois Press.

Lopinto, Noemi. 2009. "Der Indianer: Why do, 40,000 Germans spend their weekends dressed as Native Americans?" *Utne Reader*, May–June, 1–2. Accessed online, 2 October 2011; www.utne.com/Spirituality/Germans-weekends-Native-Amer.

Love, Robert. 2015. "Bob Dylan Does the American Standards His Way." *AARP Magazine*, 22 January, 4–16.

Lowery, Wesley. 2017. *They Can't Kill Us All: Ferguson, Baltimore, and a New Era in America's Racial Justice Movement*. New York: Little, Brown.

Lyman, Stanford M. 1990. *Civilization: Contents, Discontents, Malcontents and Other Essays in Social Theory*. Fayetteville: University of Arkansas Press.

MacDonald, Susie and Daniel Rachel. 2000. "Augusto Boal's FORUM THEATRE for teachers" (notes from a workshop at Athens Conference); http://organizingforpower.org/wp-content/uploads/2009/03/games-theater-of-oppressed.pdf

MacLure, Maggie. 2003. *Discourse in Educational and Social Research*. Milton Keynes, UK: Open University.

MacLure, Maggie. 2006. "The Bone in the Throat: Some Uncertain Thoughts on Baroque Method." *International Journal of Qualitative Studies in Education* 19(6), 739–746.

MacLure, Maggie, 2011. "Qualitative Inquiry: Where Are the Ruins?" *Qualitative Inquiry* 17(10), 997–1005.

MacLure, Maggie. 2012. "The Death of Data?" ESRI Blog posted October 5, 2012; www.esriblog.info/the-death-of-data/

MacLure, Maggie. 2013. "Classification or Wonder? Coding as an Analytic Practice in Qualitative Research." Pp. 164–183 in Rebecca Coleman and Jessica Ringrose (Eds.) *Deleuze and Research Methodologies*. Edinburgh: University Press.

MacLure, Maggie. 2015. "The New Materialisms: A Thorn in the Flesh of Critical Qualitative Inquiry." Pp. 93–112 in Gaile S. Canella, Michelle Slazar Perez and Penny A. Pasque (Eds.) *Critical Qualitative Inquiry: Foundations and Futures*. Walnut Creek: Left Coast Press.

MacLure, Maggie. 2017. "Rethinking Reflexivity in the 'Ontological Turn.'" Keynote address, First European Congress of Qualitative Inquiry, City Centre of Leuven, Leuven, Belgium, 9 February. Congress Theme: Quality and Reflexivity in Qualitative Inquiry.

Madison, D. Soyini. 1998. "Performances, Personal Narratives, and the Politics of Possibility." Pp. 276–286 in Sheron J. Dailey (Ed.), *The Future of Performance Studies: Visions and Revisions*. Annadale, VA: National Communication Association.

Madison, D. Soyini. 1999. "Performing Theory/Embodied Writing." *Text and Performance Quarterly* 19(2), 107–124.

Madison, D. Soyini. 2005a. *Critical Ethnography*. Thousand Oaks: Sage. Cambridge: Cambridge University Press.

Madison, D. Soyini. 2005b. "My Desire is for the Poor to Speak Well of Me." Pp. 143–166 in Della Pollock (Ed.) *Remembering: Oral History Performance*. New York: Palgrave Macmillan.

Madison, D. Soyini. 2006. "Dwight Conquergood's 'Rethinking Eethnography." Pp. 347–350 in D. Soyini Madison and Judith Hamera (Eds.) *The Sage Handbook of Performance Studies*. Thousand Oaks: Sage.

Madison, D. Soyini. 2007. "Co-performing Witnessing." *Cultural Studies* 21(6), 826–831.

Madison, D. Soyini. 2009. "Crazy Patriotism and Angry (Post) Black Women." *Communications and Critical/Cultural Studies* 6(3), pp. 321–326.

Madison, D. Soyini. 2010. *Acts of Activism: Human Rights as Radical Performance*. Cambridge: Cambridge University Press.

Madison, D. Soyini. 2011. *Critical Ethnography: Method, Ethics, and Performance.* Thousand Oaks: Sage.

Madison, D. Soyini. 2012. *Critical Ethnography,* 2/e. Thousand Oaks: Sage. Cambridge: Cambridge University Press

Madison, D. Soyini. 2013. "That Was Then and This Is Now." *Text and Performance Quarterly* 33(3), 2017–2211.

Madison, D. Soyni. 2014. "Foreword." Pp. xi–xiv in E. Patrick Johnson and Ramon H. Rivera-Servera (Eds.) *solo/black/woman: scripts, interviews, and essays.* Evanston, Illinois: Northwestern University Press.

Madison, D. Soyini, and Judith Hamera. 2006. "Introduction: Performance Studies at the Intersections." Pp. xi–xxv in D. Soyini Madison and Judith Hamera (Eds.) *The Sage Handbook of Performance Studies.* Thousand Oaks: Sage.

Madley, B. 2016. *An American Genocide: The United States and the California Indian Catastrophe, 1846–1873.* New Haven, CO: Yale University Press.

Manning, Jimmie and Tony E. Adams. 2015. "Popular Culture Studies and Auto-ethnography: An Essay on Methods." The *Popular Culture Studies Journal* 3(1&2), 187–222.

Marcus, George E. 1998. *Ethnography Through Thick and Thin.* Princeton, NJ: University of Princeton Press.

Marble, Manning. 1986. *W. E. B. Du Bois: Black Radical Democrat.* Farmington Hills, MI: Twayne Publishing.

Marx, Karl. 1983. "From the Eighteenth Brumaire of Louis Bonaparte." Pp. 219–292 in E. Kamenka (Ed.) *The Karl Marx Reader.* New York: Penguin. Pp. (Originally published 1852).

Marx, Karl. [1888] 1983. "Theses on Feuerbach." Pp. 155–158 in Eugene Kamenka (Ed.) *The Portable Karl Marx.* New York: Penguin.

Maxwell, Joseph A. 2004. "Reemergent Scientism, Postmodernism, and Dialogue Across Differences". *Qualitative Inquiry* 10(1), 35–41.

Mazzei, Lisa A. and Alecia Youngblood Jackson. 2009. "Introduction The Limit of Voice." Pp. 1–13 in A. Y. Jackson and L. A. Mazzei (Eds.) *Voice in Qualitative Inquiry: Challenging Conventional, Interpretive and Critical Conceptions in Qualitative Research.* New York: Routledge.

McCall, Michal. 1985. "Life History and Social Change." *Studies in Symbolic Interaction* 6, 169–182.

McCall, Michal M. 2000. "Performance Ethnography: A Brief History and Some Advice." Pp. 421–433 in Norman K. Denzin and Yvonna S. Lincoln (Eds.) *Handbook of Qualitative Research,* 2/e. Thousand Oaks, CA: Sage.

McCall, Michal and Judith Wittner. 1988. "The Good News About Life History." Presented to the 1988 Annual Symposium of The Society for the Study of Symbolic Interaction, Chicago, Illinois, 29 April.

McCaslin, Wanda D. and Denise C. Breton. 2008. "Justice as Healing: Going Outside the Colonizer's Cage." Pp. 511–530 in N. K. Denzin, Y.S. Lincoln, and L. T. Smith (Eds.). Handbook of Critical and Indigenous Methodologies. Thousand Oaks: Sage.

McLaren, Peter. 1997. "The Ethnographer as Postmodern Flaneur: Critical Reflexivity and Posthybridity as Narrative Engagement." Pp. 143–177 in William G. Tierney and Yvonna S. Lincoln (Eds.) *Representation and the Text: Re-framing the Narrative Voice.* Albany: State University of New York Press.

McLaren, Peter. 2001. "Che Guevara, Paulo Freire, and the Politics of Hope: Reclaiming Critical Pedagog." *Cultural Studies–Critical Methodologies* 1, 108–131.

McLaren, Peter. 2002. "A Legacy of Hope and Struggle." Pp. 245–253 in Antonia Darder. *Reinventing Paulo Freire: A Pedagogy of Love.* Boulder: Westview Press.

McLaren, Peter. 2005. "Preface: A Pedagogy for Life." Pp. xxvii–xxxix in Paulo Freire, *Teachers as Cultural Workers: Letters to Those Who Dare Teach.* Boulder: Westview Press.

McLaren, Peter and Henry Giroux. 1994. "Foreword." Pp. xiii–xvii in Gadotti Moacir, *Reading Paulo Freire* (trans. John Milton Albany). Albany: SUNY Press.

McLaren, Peter and Joe L. Kincheloe (Eds.). 2007. *Critical Pedagogy: Where Are We Now?* New York: Peter Lang.

McKenzie, Jon. 2006. "Performance and Globalization," Pp. 33–45 in D. Soyini Madison and Judith Hamera (Eds.) *The Sage Handbook of Performance Studies.* Thousand Oaks: Sage.

McMahon, Christina S. 2005. "Globalizing Allegory: Augusto Boal's A Lua Pequena e a Caminghada Perigosa in Brazil and Cape Verde." *Latin American Theatre Review* 39 (1), 71–93.

McNulty, Charles. 2016. "Anna Deavere Smith takes on 'school-to-prison pipeline' in new show." *Los Angeles Times*; www.latimes.com/entertainment/arts/la-ca-cm-anna -deavere-smith-20150726-column.html

McRae, Chris, 2015. *Performative Listening: Hearing Others in Qualitative Research.* New York: Peter Lang.

Mead, George Herbert. 1934. *The Philosophy of the Act.* Chicago: University of Chicago Press.

Mele, Christopher. 2016. "Website Targeting 'Leftist' Professors Raises Fears of Threat to Academic Freedom." *New York Times*, 29 November, A14.

Mertens, D. M. and P. E. Ginsberg. 2009. *The Handbook of Social Research Ethics.* London: Sage.

Mienczakowski, Jim. 2001. "Ethnodrama: Performed Research – Limitations and Potential." Pp. 468–476 in Paul Atkinson, Sara Delamont and Amanda Coffey (Eds.) *Handbook of Ethnography.* London: Sage.

Mienczakowski, Jim and Teresa Moore. 2008. "Performing Data with Notions of Responsibility." Pp. 451–458 in J. Gary Knowles and Andra L. Cole (Eds.) *Handbook of The Arts in Qualitative Research.* Thousand Oaks: Sage.

Mienczakowski, Jim and S. Morgan. 2001. "Ethnodrama: Constructing Participatory, Experiential and Compelling Action Research Through Performance." Pp. 219–227 in P. Reason and H. Bradbury (Eds.) *Handbook of Action Research: Participatory Inquiry and Practice.* London: Sage.

Miles, Malcolm. 1997. *Art State and the City: Public Art and Urban Futures.* New York: Routledge.

Mills, C.Wright. 1959. *The Sociological Imagination.* New York: Oxford.

Milne, Drew. 1992. "Theatre as Communicative Action: Augusto Boal's Theatre of the Oppressed." *Comparative Criticism: An Annual* 14, 111–137.

Minge, Jeanine M. and Amber Lynn Zimmerman. 2013. *Concrete and Dust: Mapping the Sexual Terrains of Los Angeles.* New York: Routledge.

Mishler, Elliott, G. 1986. *Research Interviewing: Context and Narrative.* Cambridge, MA: Harvard University Press.

Monkman, K. 2007. *The Triumph of Mischief.* Acrylic on canvas.

Monkman, K. 2008a. *Mah-To-To-Pa (Four Bears) with Indian Dandy, No. 19, 233.* Acrylic on canvas.

Monkman, K. 2008b. *Dance to the Berdashe.* Video installation.

Monkman, K. 2009. *Dance of Two Spirits*. Video Installation, August 18. Montreal: Museum of Fine Arts.

Monkman, K. 2010. *Western Art, Colonial Portrayals of First Nations Peoples and the "European Male": The Triumph of Mischief and the Treason of Images*. March 9. Calgary, Canada: Glenbow Museum.

Montaigne, Michel de. 1572–1588/1958. *The Complete Essays of Montaigne* (trans. Donald M. Frame). Stanford, CA: Stanford University Press.

Moreira, Claudio. 2009. "Unspeakable Transgressions: Indigenous Epistemologies, Ethics, and Decolonizing Academy/Inquiry." *Cultural Studies – Critical Methodologies* 9(5), 647–660.

Moreira, Claudio. 2012. "I Hate Chicken Breast: A Tale of Resisting Stories and Disembodied Knowledge Construction." *International Journal of Qualitative Studies in Education* 25(2), 151–167

Moreira, Claudio and Marcelo Diversi. 2011. "Missing Bodies: Troubling the Colonial Landscape of American Academia." *Text and Performance Quarterly* 31(3), 229–248.

Moreira, Claudio, Tami Spry and Jonathan Wyatt. 2013. "Critical Beginnings: Reflections and Refractions Through Seven Years of ICQI." *International Review of Qualitative Research* 6(1), 149–164.

Morrison, Toni. 1994. "Rootedness: The Ancestor as Foundation." Pp. 490–497 in D. Soyini Madison (Ed.) *The Woman That I Am: The Literature and Culture of Contemporary Women of Color*. New York: St. Martin's Press.

Moses, Daniel David. 1992. *Almighty Voice and His Wife*. Stratford, On: Williams-Wallace.

Munoz, Jose Esteban. 2005. "Stages: Queers, Punks, and the Utopian Performative." Pp. 9–20 in D. Soyini Madison and Judith Hamera (Eds.) *The Sage Handbook of Performance Studies*. Thousand Oaks: Sage.

Mutua, Kagendo and Beth Blue Swadner. 2004. "Introduction." Pp. 1–23 in Kagendo Mutua and Beth Blue Swadner (Eds.) *Decolonizing Research in Cross-Cultural Contexts: Critical Personal Narratives*. Albany: SUNY Press.

National Research Council. 2014. *Proposed Revisions to the Common Rule for the Protection of Human Subjects in the Behavioral and Social Sciences*. Washington: National Academies Press.

Naylor, Gloria. 1998. "Excerpt from Mamma Day." Pp. 1838–1842 in Patricia Liggins Hill (Ed.) *Call and Response: The Riverside Anthology of the African American Literary Tradition*. Boston: Houghton Mifflin.

Nelson, Cary and Dilip Parameshwar Gaonkar. 1996. "Cultural Studies and the Politics of Disciplinarity." Pp. 1–22 in Cary Nelson and Dilip Parameshwar Gaonkar (Eds.) *Disciplinarity and Dissent in Cultural Studies*. New York: Routledge.

Neuman, M. 1996. "Collecting Ourselves at the End of the Century." Pp. 172–200 in C. Ellis and A. Bochner (Eds.) *Composing Ethnography: Alternative Forms of Qualitative Writing*. London, England: Alta Mira.

Nicholson, Helen. 2014. *Applied Drama: The Gift of Theatre*. New York: Palgrave Macmillan (first edition 2005).

Nordstrom, Susan Naomi and Alison Happel-Parkins. 2016. "Methodological Drag: Subversive Performances of Qualitative Methodologist and Pedagogical Practices." *Qualitative Inquiry* 22(8), 460–482.

Norris, Joe. 2009. *Playbuilding as Qualitative Research*. Walnut Creek: Left Coast Press.

Norris, Joe and Richard D. Sawyer. 2012. "Toward a Dialogic Methodology." Pp. 9–39 in Joe Norris, Richard D. Sawyer and Darren E. Lund (Eds.) *Duoethnography:*

Dialogic Methods for Social Health and Educational Research. Walnut Creek: Left Coast Press.

Oakley, Anne. 1981. "Interviewing Women: A Contradiction in Terms?" Pp. 30–61 in Helen Roberts (Ed.) *Doing Feminist Research.* London: Routledge & Kegan Paul.

Office for Human Research Protection (OHRP). 2009. *Belmont Report.* www.hhs.gov/orhp/BelmontArchive.html

Onwuegbuzie, Anthony I. 2012. "Introduction: Putting the MIXED back into quantitative and qualitative research in educational research and beyond: Moving toward the radical middle." *International Journal of Multiple Research Approaches* 6(3), 192–219.

Oudes, Bruce. 1989. *From the President: President Nixon's Secret Files.* New York: Harper & Row.

Panourgia, Neni and George E. Marcus. (Eds.) 2008. *Ethnographica Moralia: Experiments in Interpretive Anthropology.* New York: Fordham University Press.

Park, R. E. 1950. "An Autobiographical Note." Pp. v–ix in R. E. Park, *Race and Culture: Essays in the Sociology of Contemporary Man.* New York: Free Press.

Paterson, Doug. "A Brief Biography of Augusto Boal." *Pedagogy and Theatre of the Oppressed.* http://ptoweb.org/aboutpto/a-brief-biography-of-augusto-boal/

Pelias, Ronald J. 1992. *Performance Studies: The Interpretation of Aesthetic Texts.* New York: St. Martin's Press.

Pelias, Ronald J. 1998. "Meditations and Mediations." Pp. 14–22 in Sheron J. Dailey (Ed.) *The Future of Performance Studies: Visions and Revisions.* Washington, DC: National Communication Association.

Pelias, Ronald J. 1999. *Writing Performance: Poeticizing the Researcher's Body.* Carbondale: Southern Illinois University.

Pelias, Ronald J. 2004. *A Methodology of the Heart.* Walnut Creek: AltaMira Press.

Pelias, R. J. 2008. "Performative Inquiry." Pp. 185–193 in J. Gary Knowles and Ardra L. Cole (Eds.) *Handbook of the Arts in Qualitative Research.* London: Sage.

Pelias, Ronald J. 2011. *Leaning: A Poetics of Personal Relations.* Walnut Creek: Left Coast Press.

Pelias, Ronald J. 2013. "Writing Autoethnography: The Personal, Poetic, and Perrformative as Compositional Strategies." Pp. 384–405 in Stacy Holman Jones, Tony E. Adams and Carolyn Ellis (Eds.) *Handbook of Autoethnography.* Walnut Creek: Left Coast Press.

Pelias, Ronald J. 2014. *Performance: An Alphabet of Performative Writing.* Walnut Creek: Left Coast Press.

Phelan, Peggy. 1993. *Unmarked: The Politics of Performance.* London: Routledge.

Phelan, Peggy. 1997. *Mourning Sex.* London: Routledge.

Phelan, P. and J. Lane (Eds.) 1998. *The Ends of Performance.* New York: NYU Press.

Pillow, W. S. 2015. "Reflexivity as Interpretation and Genealogy in Research." *Cultural Studies? Critical Methodologies* 15(6), 419–434.

Pinar, William. 1975. "Currere: Toward Reconceptualization." Pp. 396–414 in W. Pinar (Ed.) *Curriculum Theorizing: The Reconceptualists.* Berkeley: McCutchan;New York: Peter Lang.

Pinar, William F. 1994. *Autobiography, Politics, and Sexuality: Essays in Curriculum Theory 1972–1992.* New York: Peter Lang.

Pineau, Elyse Lamm. 1998. "Performance Studies Across the Curriculum: Problems, Possibilities and Projections." Pp. 128–135 in Sheron J. Dailey (Ed.) *The Future of Performance Studies: Visions and Revisions.* Washington, DC: National Communication Association.

Pitt, William Rivers. 2016. "Electing the Fascist in November." *Truthout*, 09 November, www.truth-out.org/opinion/item/38315-the-fascist-in-november

Plath, David W. 1987, "Making Experience Come out Right: Culture as Biography." *Central Issues in Anthropology* 7, 1–8.

Plummer, Ken. 2015. *Cosmopolitan Sexualities: Hope and the Humanist Imagination.* London: Polity Press.

Pollock, Della. 1998a. "Performing Writing." Pp. 73–193 in P. Phelan and J. Lane (Eds.) *The Ends of Performance.* New York: New York University Press.

Pollock, Della. 1998b. "A Response to Dwight Conquergood's Essay 'Beyond the Text: Towards a Performative Cultural Politics.'" Pp. 25–36 in Sheron J. Dailey (Ed.) *The Future of Performance Studies: Visions and Revisions.* Annadale, VA: National Communication Association.

Pollock, Della. 1998c. "Introduction: Making History Go." Pp. 1–45 in Della Pollock (Ed.) *Exceptional Spaces: Essays in Performance and History.* Chapel Bill: University of North Carolina Press.

Pollock, Della. 1999. *Telling Bodies Performing Birth: Everyday Narratives of Childbirth.* New York: Columbia University Press,

Pollock, Della. 2005. "Introduction: Remembering." Pp. 1–18 in Della Pollock (Ed.) *Remembering: Oral History Performance.* New York: Palgrave Macmillan.

Pollock, Della. 2006. "Memory, Remembering, and Histories of Change." Pp. 87–105 in D. Soyini Madison and Judith Hamera (Eds.) *The Sage Handbook of Performance Studies.* Thousand Oaks: Sage.

Pollock, Della, 2007. "The Performative 'I'." *Cultural Studies – Critical Methodologies* 7 (3), 239–255.

Pollock, Della, 2009. "Beyond Experience." *Cultural Studies – Critical Methodologies* 9 (5), 636–646.

Porter, Eduardo. 2016. "After Vote, a Land Tinged With Racial Hostility." *New York Times*, 9 November, B1, B3.

Porter, Eileen J. 2000. "Setting Aside the Identity-Furor: Staying Her Story-Course of-Same-Ness." *Qualitative Inquiry* 6(2), 238–250.

Poulos, Christopher N. 2009. *Accidental Ethnography.* Walnut Creek, CA: Left Coast Press.

Poulos, C. N. 2016. *Accidental Ethnography: An /inquiry into Family Secrecy.* New York: Routledge.

Prendergast, Monica. 2001. "'Imaginative Complicity': Audience Education in Professional Theatre." Unpublished Master's Thesis. Victoria, British Columbia, Canada: University of Victoria.

Prendergast, Monica. 2003. "I, Me, mine: Soliloquizing as Reflective Practice." *International Journal of Education and the Arts* 4(1) [Online]. Available: http://ijea.asu.edu/v4n1.

Prendergast, M. 2003. "Found Poetry as Literature Review: Research Poems on Audience and Performance." *Qualitative Inquiry* 12(2), 369–388.

Prentki, Tim and Sheila Preston. 2009. "Applied Theatre: An Introduction." Pp. 9–15 in Tim Prentki and Sheila Preston (Eds.) *The Applied Theatre Reader.* New York: Routledge.

Raban, Jonathan. 1981. *Old Glory: A Voyage Down the Mississippi.* New York: Random House.

Rains, Frances V., Jo Ann Archibald and Donna Deyhle. 2000. "Introduction: Through Our Eyes and in Our Own Words – The Voices of Indigenous Scholars." *International Journal of Qualitative Studies in Education* 13, 337–342.

Reamer, F. G. 2006. *Ethical Standards in Social Work: A Review of the NASW Code of Ethics.* Washington, D.C.: NASW Press.

Reddin, Paul. 1999. *Wild West Shows.* Urbana: University of Illinois Press.

Reed-Danahay, D. E. 1997. "Introduction." Pp. 1–20 in D. E. Reed-Danahay (Ed.), *Auto/Ethnography: Rewriting the Self and the Social.* New York: Oxford.

Reinertsen, Anne Beate. 2013. "The Bike With Pink Tires: On Global Science Gateways, Safespaces and Benefiting from Confusions." *International Review of Qualitative Research* 6(4), 1–10.

Reinharz, Shulamit. 1992. *Feminist Methods in Social Research.* New York: Oxford University Press.

Republican Party. 2016. "Republican Platform, 2016, We Believe in America. Prepared by the Committee on Arrangements for the 2016 Republican National Convention." www.gop.com/platform/

Rice, Rebecca. 1990. "Losing Faith (or Gaining Perspective)." Pp. 205–213 in Mark O'Brien and Craig Little (Eds.) *Remaking America: The Art of Social Change.* Santa Cruz, CA: New Society.

Richardson, Laurel. 1992. "The Poetic Representation of Lives: Writing a Postmodernist Sociology." *Studies in Symbolic Interaction* 13, 19. 27. Greenwich, CT: JAI Press.

Richardson, Laurel. 1994. "Writing as a Method of Inquiry." Pp. 516–529 in Norman K. Denzin and Yvonna S. Lincoln (Eds.) *The Handbook of Qualitative Research.* Newbury Park: Sage.

Richardson, Laurel. 1996. "Educational Birds." *Journal of Contemporary Ethnography* 25, 6–15.

Richardson, Laurel. 1997. *Fields of Play: Constructing an Academic Life.* New Brunswick: Rutgers University Press.

Richardson, Laurel. 2000a. "Writing: A Method of Inquiry." Pp. 923–948 in Norman K. Denzin and Yvonna S. Lincoln (Eds.) *Handbook of Qualitative Research*, 2/e. Thousand Oaks: Sage Publications.

Richardson, Laurel. 2000b. "Evaluating Ethnography." *Qualitative Inquiry* 6, 253–255.

Richardson, Laurel. 2001. "Poetic Representation of Interviews." Pp. 877–892 in Jaber F. Gubrium and Jaes A. Holstein (Eds.) *Handbook of Interview Research.* Thousand Oaks, CA: Sage Publications.

Richardson, Laurel. 2007. *Last Writes: A Daybook for a Dying Friend.* Walnut Creek: Left Coast Press.

Richardson, Laurel. 2013. *After a Fall: A Sociomedical Sojourn.* Walnut Creek: Left Coast Press.

Richardson, Laurel. 2017. "Ethics and the Writing of *After the Fall: A Sociomedical Sojourn.*" Pp. 531–535 in Ivor Goodson, Ari Antokainen, Pat Sikes and Molly Andres (Eds.) *The Routledge International Handbook of Narrative and Life History.* London: Routledge.

Richardson, Laurel and Elizabeth Adams St. Pierre. 2005. "Writing: A Method of Inquiry." Pp. 959–978 in N. K. Denzin, and Y. S. Lincoln (Eds.) *Handbook of Qualitative Research*, 3/e. Thousand Oaks: Sage.

Richardson, Laurel and Ernest Lockridge. 2004. *Travels with Ernest: Crossing the Literary/Sociological Divide.* Walnut Creek: Left Coast Press.

Rinehart, Robert. 1998. "Fictional Methods in Ethnography: Believability, Specks of Glass and Chekhov." *Qualitative Inquiry* 4(2), 200–224.

Rinehart, Robert. 2016 "The New Zealand Case: Hope and Respect from the Antipodes." *International Review of Qualitative Research* 10(2), 147–151.

Rinehart, Robert. 2017. "Trump as Strumpet: Three Takes on the Performance Art of the Donald." *Qualitative Inquiry* 1(2), 171–172.

Rinehart, Robert E., Karen N. Barbour and Clive C. Pope. 2014. "Proem: Engaging Contemporary Ethnography Across the Disciplines." Pp. 1–11 in Robert E. Rinehart, Karen N. Barbour and Clive C. Pope (Eds.) *Ethnographic Worldviews: Transformations and Social Justice*. New York, London: Springer Dordrecht Heildelberg.

Ritchie, D. A. and L. Shopes. 2003. "Oral History Excluded from IRB Review." http:// web.archive.org/web/20080117043701/http://alpha.dickinson

Roediger, David. 2002. *Colored White: Transcending the Racial Past*. Berkeley: University of California Press.

Ronai, Carol Rambo. 1998. "Sketching With Derrida: An Ethnography of a Researcher/ Erotic Dancer." *Qualitative Inquiry* 4, 405–420.

Roos, J. P. 1987. "From Farm to Office: Family, Self-Confidence and the New Middle Class." *Life Stories/Récits de vie* 3, 7–20.

Rorty, Richard. 1980. *Philosophy and the Mirror of Nature*. Princeton: University of Princeton Press.

Rorty, Richard. 1998. *Achieving Our Country*. Cambridge: Harvard University Press.

Rorty, Richard. 2002. "Fighting Terrorism With Democracy." *The Nation*, October 21, 11–14.

Roy, A. 2009. *Fieldnotes on Democracy*. Chicago: Haymarket Books.

Rusted, Brian. 2006. "Performing Visual Discourse: Cowboy Art and Institutional Practice." *Text and Performance Quarterly* 26(2), 115–137.

Saldana, Johnny. 2002. "Finding my Place: The Brad Trilogy." Pp. 167–210 in Harry F. Wolcott, *Sneaky Kid and Its Aftermath: Ethics and Intimacy in Fieldwork*. Walnut Creek, CA: Alta Mira Press

Saldana, J. 2005. "An Introduction to Ethnodrama." Pp. 1–36 in J. Saldana (Ed.) *Ethnodrama: An Anthology of Reality Theatre*. Walnut Creek: Left Coast Press.

Saldana, J. 2011. *Ethnotheatre: Research from Page to Stage*. Walnut Creek: Left Coast

Salvo. James. 2019. *Reading Autoethnography: Homelessness, and Sharing Meaning and Time with the Intimate Other*. New York: Taylor and Francis.

Sandlin, Jennifer A., Brian D. Schultz and Jake Burdick (Eds). 2010. *Handbook of Public Pedagogy: Education and Learning Beyond Schooling*. New York: Routledge.

Sartre, Jean-Paul. 1963. *Search for a Method*. New York: Knopf.

Sartre, Jean-Paul. 1981. *The Family Idiot, Gustave Flaubert, Vol. 1: 1821–1857*. Chicago: University of Chicago Press. (Original work published in 1971)

Schechner, Richard 1985. *Between Theatre and Anthropology*. Philadelphia: University of Philadelphia Press.

Schechner, Richard 1986. "Magnitudes of Performance." Pp. 344–369 in Victor M. Turner and Edward M. Bruner (Eds.) *The Anthropology of Experience*. Urbana: University of Illinois Press.

Schechner, Richard 1988. *Performance Theory* (revised and expanded edition). New York: Routledge

Schechner, Richard 1993. *The Future of Ritual: Writings on Culture and Performance*. New York: Routledge.

Schechner, Richard. 1998. "What Is Performance Studies Anyway?" Pp. 357–362 in Peggy Phelan and Jill Lane (Eds.) *The Ends of Performance*. New York: New York University Press.

Schechner, R. 2002. *Performance Studies: An Introduction*. New York/London: Routledge.

Schechner, Richard. 2013. *Performance Studies: An Introduction*, 3/3. New York: Routledge.

Schechner, Richard. 2015. *Performed Imaginaries*. New York: Routledge.

Schechner, R. 2017. *Performance Studies: An Introduction*. New York: Routledge.

Scheurich, J. J. 1995. "A Postmodernist Critique of Research Interviewing." *International Journal of Qualitative Studies in Education* 8, 239–252.

Schugurensky, Daniel. 2014. *Paulo Freire*. London: Bloomsbury.

Schutzman, Mady and Jan Cohen-Cruz. 1994. "Introduction." Pp. 1–16 in Mady Schutzman and Jan Cohen-Cruz (Eds.). *Playing Boal: Theatre, Therapy, Activism*. New York: Routledge.

Schutzman, Mady and Jan Cohen-Cruz. 2006a. "Introduction." Pp. 1–9 in Jan Cohen-Cruz and Mady Schutzman (Eds.) *A Boal Companion: Dialogues on Theatre and Cultural Politics*. New York: Routledge.

Schutzman, Mady and Jan Cohen-Cruz. 2006b. "Glossary." Pp. 236–238 in Jan Cohen-Cruz and Mady Schutzman (Eds.) *A Boal Companion: Dialogues on Theatre and Cultural Politics*. New York: Routledge.

Schwandt, T. A. 1996. "Farewell to Criteriology." *Qualitative Inquiry* 2(1), 58–72.

Scott, Joan. 1991. "The Evidence of Experience." *Critical Inquiry* 17(4), 773–797.

Scott, Joan. 1992. "Experience." Pp. 22–40 in J. Butler and J. W. Scott (Eds.) *Feminists Theorize the Political*. New York: Routledge.

Scott, Joan. 1993. "The Evidence of Experience." Pp. 397–415 in Henry Ablelove, Michele Aina Barale and Jill Lane (Eds). *The Lesbian and Gay Studies Reader*. New York: Routledge.

Seale, C., G. Gobo, J. F. Gubrium and Silverman, D. (Eds.). 2004. *Qualitative Research Practice*. London: Sage.

Sedgwick, Eve Kosofsky. 1998. "Teaching 'Experimental Critical Writing.'" Pp. 104–115 in Peggy Phelan and Jill Lane (Eds.) *The Ends of Performance*. New York: New York University Press

Semaili, Ladislaus M. and Joe L. Kincheloe. 1999. "Introduction: What is Indigenous Knowledge and Why Should We Study It?" Pp. 3–57 in Ladislaus M. Semaili and Joe L. Kincheloe (Eds.) *What is Indigenous Knowledge? Voices from the Academy*. New York: Falmer Press. Senior, Jennifer. 2016. "Richard Rorty's 1998 Book Suggested Election 2016 Was Coming." *New York Times*: www.nytimes.com/2016/11/21/books/richard-rortys-1998-book-suggested-election-2016-was-coming.html?_r=0. A print version of this article appears in the *New York Times*, November 21, 2016: C1.

Shea, Christopher D. 2015. "It's a Strange World, After All." *New York Times, "The Arts"* (August 24), C1–C2.

Shildrick, M. 1997. *Leaky Bodies and Boundaries: Feminism, Postmodernism and (Bio) ethics*. London and New York: Routledge.

Shildrick, Margrit. 2005. "Beyond the Body of Bioethics: Challenging the Conventions." Pp. 1–26 in Margrit Shildrick and Roxanne Mykitiuk (Eds.) *Ethics of the Body: Postconventional Challenges*. Cambridge, Mass: MIT Press.

Shopes, L. 2011. "Oral History." Pp. 451–466 in Norman K. Denzin and Yvonna S. Lincoln (Eds.) *Handbook of Qualitative Research*, 4/e. Thousand Oaks: Sage.

Shopes, L. and D. Ritchie. 2004. "Exclusion of Oral History from IRB Review: An update." *Perspectives* online. Available from: www.historians.org/Perspectives/Issues'2004/0403new1.cfn

Shpigel, Ben. 2014. "Throwing His Voice Around." *New York Times*, 24 November (Sports Monday), D1, D3.

Sikes, P. and H. Piper. 2010. "Ethical Research, Academic Freedom, and the Role of Ethics Committees and Review Procedures in Educational Research." *International Journal of Research and Method in Education* 33(3), 205–213.

Smith, Anna Deavere. 1993. *Fires in the Mirror*. New York: Anchor Books.

Smith, Anna Deavere. 1994. *Twilight: Los Angeles, 1992*. New York: Anchor Books.

Smith, Anna Deavere. 2000. *Talk to Me: Listening between the Lines*. New York: Random House.

Smith, Anna Deavere. 2003. *House Arrest*. New York: Anchor.

Smith, Anna Deavere. 2004. *Piano*. New York: Anchor.

Smith, Dorothy E. 1989. "Sociological Theory: Methods of Writing Patriarchy." Pp. 34–64 in Ruth A. Wallace (Ed.) *Feminism and Sociological Theory*. Newbury Park, CA: Sage.

Smith, Dorothy E. 1990a. *The Conceptual Practices of Power: A Feminist Sociology of Knowledge*. Boston: Northeastern University Press.

Smith, Dorothy E. 1990b. *Texts, Facts, and Femininity: Exploring the Relations of Ruling*. New York: Routledge.

Smith, Graham. 2000. "Protecting and Respecting Indigenous Knowledge." Pp. 209–224 in Marie Battiste (Ed.) *Reclaiming Indigenous Voice and Vision*. Vancouver: UBC Press.

Smith, Linda Tuhiwai. 1999. *Decolonizing Methodologies: Research and Indigenous Peoples*. London: Zed Books.

Smith, Linda Tuhiwai. 2000. "Kupapa Maori Research." Pp. 225–247 in Marie Battiste (Ed.) *Reclaiming Indigenous Voice and Vision*. Vancouver: UBC Press.

Smith, Linda Tuhiwai. 2005. "On Tricky Ground: Researching the Native in the Age of Uncertainty." Pp. 85–108 in Norman K. Denzin and Yvonna S. Lincoln (Eds.) *Handbook of Qualitative Research*, 3/e. Thousand Oaks: Sage.

Smith, L. T. 2006. "Choosing the Margins: The Role of Research in Indigenous Struggles for Social Justice." In N. K. Denzin and M. D. Giardina (Eds.) *Qualitative Inquiry and the Conservative Challenge*. Walnut Creek: Left Coast Press.

Smith, Linda Tuhiwai. 2012. *Decolonizing Methodologies: Research and Indigenous Peoples*, 2/e. London: Zed Books.

Smith, Mark K. 2001. "Augusto Boal, Animation and Education." http://infed.org/mobi/augusto-boal-animation-and-education/

Smith, Mychal Denzel. 2015. "The Rebirth of Black Rage." *The Nation* 301(9&10), 28–33.

Speiglman, R. and Spear, P. 2009. "The Role of Institutional Review Boards: Ethics Now You See Them, Now You Don't." Pp. 121–134 in D. M. Mertens and P. E. Ginsberg (Eds.) *The Handbook of Social Research Ethics*. Thousand Oaks: Sage.

Spencer, Nancy E. et al. 2017. "Teach-ins as Performance Ethnography: Athletes' Social Activism in North American Sport." *International Review of Qualitative Research*, 10(1), 1–15.

Spender, Stephen. [1947] 1984. "Introduction." Pp. vii–xxiii in Malcolm Lowry, *Under the Volcano*. New York: New American Library.

Spooner, Marc. 2017. "Qualitative Research and Global Audit Culture: The Politics of Productivity, Accountability, & Possibility." Pp. 894–914 in N. K. Denzin and Y. S. Lincoln (Eds.). *Handbook of Qualitative Research*, 5/e. Thousand Oaks: Sage.

Spry, Tami. 2001. "Performing Autoethnography: An Embodied Methodological Praxis." *Qualitative Inquiry* 7, 706–732.

Spry, Tami. 2006. "A 'Performative-I' co-presence: Embodying the ethnographic turn in performance and the performative turn in ethnography." *Text and Performance Quarterly* 26, 339–346.

Spry, Tami. 2011. *Body, Paper, Stage: Writing and Performing Autoethnography.* Walnut Creek, CA: Left Coast Press.

Spry, Tami. 2013. "Unseating the Myth of a Girl and Her Horse, Now That's True Grit." *Cultural Studies – Critical Methodologies* 12(6), 482–484.

Spry, Tami. 2016. *Autoethnography and the Other: Unsettling Power Through Utopian Performatives.* New York: Routledge

Stake, Robert. 1994. "Case Studies." Pp. 236–247 in N. K. Denzin and Y. S. Lincoln (Eds.) *Handbook of Qualitative Research.* Thousand Oaks: Sage.

Stake, R. and B. Jegatheesan. 2008. "Access, a Zone of Comprehension, and Intrusion." Pp. 1–13 in *Access, a Zone of Comprehension, and Intrusion.* Bingley, UK: Emerald Group Publishing Limited.

Stake, R. and Fazal Rizvi. 2009. "Research Ethics in Transnational Spaces." Pp. 521–536 in D. M. Mertens and P. E. Ginsberg (Eds.) *The Handbook of Social Research Ethics.* Thousand Oaks: Sage.

Stegner, Wallace. 1980a. "Coda: Wilderness Letter." Pp. 145–153 in Wallace Stegner, *The Sound of Mountain Water: The Changing American West.* New York: Doubleday.

Stegner, Wallace. 1980b. *The Sound of Mountain Water: The Changing American West.* New York: Doubleday.

Stewart, K. 2013. "Cultural Poesis: The Generativity of Emergent Things." Pp. 1027–1043 in N. K. Denzin and Y. S. Lincoln (Eds.) *Handbook of Qualitative Research,* 3/e. Thousand Oaks: Sage.

Stewart, Kathleen. 2013. "An Autoethnography of What Happens." Pp. 659–668 in Stacy Holman Jones, Tony E. Adams and Carolyn Ellis (Eds.) *Handbook of Autoethnography.* Walnut Creek: Left Coast Press.

St. Pierre, Elizabeth Adams. 2009. "Afterword: Decentering Voice in Qualitative Inquiry." Pp. 221–236 in A. Y. Jackson and L. A. Mazzei (Eds.). *Voice in Qualitative Inquiry: Challenging Conventional, Interpretive and Critical Conceptions in Qualitative Research.* New York: Routledge.

St. Pierre, Elizabeth Adams. 2011. "Post Qualitative Research: The Critique and the Coming After." Pp. 611–626 in N. K. Denzin and Y. S. Lincoln (Eds.). *Handbook of Qualitative Research,* 4/e. Thousand Oaks: Sage.

St. Pierre, Elizabeth Adams and Wanda Pillow (Eds.). 2000. *Working the Ruins: Feminist Poststructural Methods in Education.* New York: Routledge.

Stoker, Bram. 1897. *Dracula.* London: Archibald Constable and company.

Stronach, Ian. 2017. "Can National Identity Ever Have 'Fundamental Values'?" Presented to the 13th International Congress of Qualitative Inquiry, May 19, 2017. Urbana, Illinois.

Stronach, Ian, Dean Garratt, Cathie Pearce and Heather Piper. 2007. "Reflexivity, the Picturing of Selves, the Forging of Method." *Qualitative Inquiry* 13(2), 179–203.

Striff, Erin. 2003. "Introduction: Locating Performance Studies." Pp. 1–13 in Erin Striff (Ed.). *Performance Studies.* New York: Palgrave Macmillian,

Sughrua, William M. 2016. *Heightened Performative Autoethnography: Resisting Oppressive Spaces within Paradigms.* New York: Peter Lang.

Tamas, Sophie. 2011. *Life After Leaving: The Remains if Spousal Abuse.* Walnut Creek: Left Coast Press.

Tashakkori, A. and C. Teddlie (Eds.) 2010. *Sage Handbook of Mixed Methods in Social & Behavioral Research.* Thousand Oaks, CA: Sage.

Taussig, Michael. 1993. *Mimesis and Alterity.* New York: Routledge.

Taussig, Michael and Richard Schecher. 1994. "Boal in Brazil, France, the USA: An Interview with Augusto Boal." Pp. 17–34 in Mady Schutzman and Jan Cohen-Cruz (Eds.) *Playing Boal: Theatre, Therapy, Activism*. London and New York: Routledge.

Taylor, Carl A. and Christina Hughes (Eds.). 2016. *Posthuman Research Practices in Education*. London: Palgrave Macmillian.

Tedlock, Barbara. 2000. "Ethnography and Ethnographic Representation." Pp. 455–486 in Norman K. Denzin and Yvonna S. Lincoln (Eds.) *Handbook of Qualitative Research*, 2/e. Thousand Oaks, CA: Sage.

Thompson, James and Richard Schechner. 2004. "Why 'Social Theatre'?" *The Drama Review* 48(3), 11–16.

Trinh, Minh-h T. 1989. *Woman, Native, Other: Writing Postcoloniality and Feminism*. Bloomington: Indiana University Press.

Trinh, Minh-h T. 1991. *When the Moon Waxes Red*. New York: Routledge.

Trinh, Minh-h T. 1992. *Framer Framed*. New York: Routledge.

Tuck, Eve and K. Wayne Yang. 2012. "Decolonization Is Not a Metaphor." *Decolonization: Indigeneity, Education and Society* 1(1), 1–40.

Turner, Victor. 1981. "Social Dramas and Stories About Them." Pp. 141–168 in W. Mitchell (Ed.) *On Narrative*. Chicago: University of Chicago Press.

Turner, Victor. 1982. *From Ritual to Theatre*. New York: Performing Arts Journal Publications.

Turner, Victor. 1985. *On the Edge of the Bush: Anthropology as Experience*. Tucson: University of Arizona Press.

Turner, Victor. 1986a. "Dewey, Dilthey, and Drama: An Essay in the Anthropology of Experience." Pp. 33–44 in Victor M. Turner and Edward M. Bruner (eds.) *The Anthropology of Experience*. Urbana: University of Illinois Press.

Turner, Victor. 1986b. *The Anthropology of Performance*. New York: Performing Arts Journal Publications.

Turner, Victor, and Edward Bruner. (Eds.) 1986. *The Anthropology of Experience*. Urbana: University of Illinois Press.

Turner, Victor (with Edie Turner). 1982. "Performing Ethnography." *The Drama Review* 26, 33–50.

Tyler, Stephen. 1986. "Post-modern Ethnography: From Document of the Occult to Occult Document." Pp. 122–140 in James Clifford and George E. Marcus (Eds.) *Writing Culture: The Poetics and Politics of Ethnography*. Berkeley: University of California Press.

Ulmer, G. 1989. *Teletheory*. New York: Routledge.

Ulmer, G. 1994. *Heuretics: The Logic of Invention*. Baltimore: Johns Hopkins University Press.

University of Illinois at Urbana-Champaign, Institutional Review Board. 2009. "Investigator Handbook Part II. Fundamental Guidelines." In *Investigator Handbook for the Protection of Human Subjects in Research*. Http://irb.illinois.edu/?q=investigator-handbook/part2.html#A

Van Maanen, John. 2011. *Tales of the Field: On Writing Ethnography*, 2/e. Chicago: University of Chicago Press.

Vecsey, G. 2000. "Kurt Warner Gives Hope to Others." *New York Times*, February 1, C29.

Vidal, Gore. 1989. "The Agreed-Upon Facts." Pp. 10–12 in William Zinser (Ed.), *Paths to Resistance: The Art and Craft of the Political Novel*. Boston: Houghton Mifflin.

Vidich, Arthur J. and Stanford M. Lyman. 1994. "Qualitative Methods: Their History in Sociology and Anthropology." Pp. 23–59 in Norman K. Denzin and Yvonna S. Lincoln (Eds.) *Handbook of Qualitative Research*. Thousand Oaks, CA: Sage.

Visweswaran, Kamala. 1994. *Fictions of Feminist Ethnography*. Minneapolis: University of Minnesota Press.

Vizenor, Gerald. 1999. *Manifest Manners: Narratives on Postinindian Survivance*. Lincoln: University of Nebraska Press.

Vizenor, Gerald. 2008. "Aesthetics of Survivance." Pp. 1–24 in Gerald Vizenor (Ed). *Survivance: Narratives of Native Presence*. Lincoln and London: University of Nebraska Press.

Warren, Louis S. 2005. *Buffalo Bill's America: William Cody and the Wild West Show*. New York: Alfred A. Knopf.

Weems, Mary. 2002. *I Speak from the Wound that is my Mouth*. New York: Peter Lang.

Weems, Mary E. 2013. "One Love: Empathy and the Imagination-Intellect." Pp. 1–22 in Mary E. Weems (Ed.) *Writings of Healing and Resistance: Empathy and the Imagination-Intellect*. New York: Peter Lang.

Weems, Mary E. 2015. *Blackeyed: Plays and Monologues*. London: Springer.

Weiss, P. 1988. "Party Time in Atlanta." *Columbia Journalism Review*, September/October, 27–34.

Wenner, Jann. S. 2013 (1969). "The New Dylan." *Rolling Stone: Special Collectors Edition: Bob Dylan: 40 Years of Rolling Stone Interviews*, 16 May, pp. 8–29 (from *Rolling Stone*, November 29, 1969).

West, Cornel. 1993. "Foreword." Pp. xvii–xxii in Anna Deavere Smith, *Fires in the Mirror: Crown Heights, Brooklyn, and Other Identities*. New York: Doubleday.

West, Cornel. 1994. *Race Matters*. New York: Vantage Books.

Wilder, Thorton. 1938. *Our Town: A Play in Three Acts*. New York: Coward McCann, Inc.

Willis, Paul. 2000. *The Ethnographic Imagination*. Cambridge: Polity.

Willis, Paul and Mat Trondman. 2000. "Manifesto for Ethnography." *Ethnography* 1, 5–16.

Wolcott, Harry F. 2002. *Sneaky Kid and Its Aftermath: Ethics and Intimacy in Fieldwork*. Walnut Creek, CA: Alta Mira Press.

Worley, David W. 1998. "Is Critical Performative Pedagogy Practical?" Pp. 136–140 in Sheron J. Dailey (Ed.) *The Future of Performance Studies: Visions and Revisions*. Washington, DC: National Communication Association.

Wyatt, Jonathan, Ken Gale, Susanne Gannon and Bronwyn Davies, 2011. *Deleuze & Collaborative Writing: An Immanent Plane of Comoposition*. New York: Peter Lang.

Yellow Bird, Michael. 2005. "Tribal Critical Thinking Centers." Pp. 9–30 in Waziyatawin Angela Wilson and Michael Yellow Bird (Eds.) *For Indigenous Eyes Only: A Decolonization Handbook*. Sante Fe: School of American Research Handbook.

Index